HALLE JØRN HANSSEN

LIVES AT STAKE

SOUTH-SUDAN DURING THE LIBERATION STRUGGLE

To the suffering people of South Sudan.

You and your freedom fighters struggled so hard and for so long for your freedom, for your human dignity, for your human rights. You had so many dreams for yourself and your children for a better future in peace and freedom and with social justice and development.

But you were let down by irresponsible leaders who forgot what the freedom struggle was about and made greed their creed and destroyed your beautiful land.

You did deserve something very different and much better.

HALLE JØRN HANSSEN

LIVES AT STAKE

With Norwegian Peoples Aid in South Sudan
during the Time of the Liberation Struggle

Translated from Norwegian by
Renee Hilda Waara

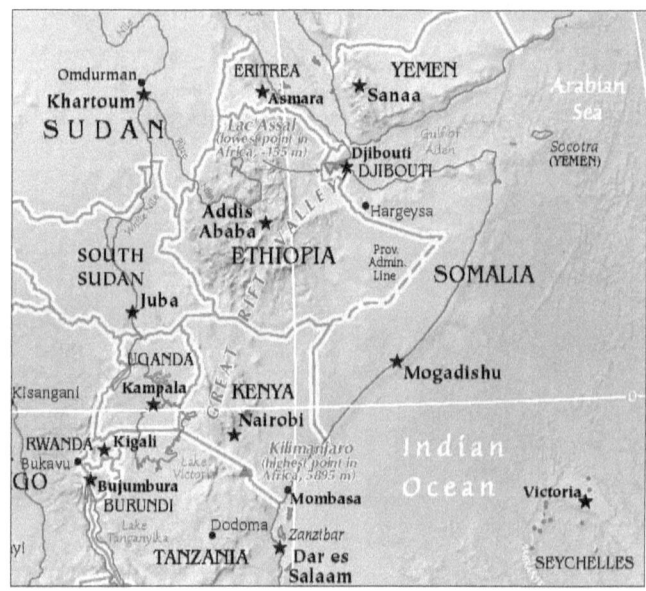

The Horn of Africa. The map also shows part of Congo, Rwanda and Tanzania.

CONTENTS

Abbrivations and words 6
Foreword by Pa'gan Amum 11
Foreword by Thorvald Stoltenberg 15

1 Introduction 23

2 Historical Background 35
    The British in Sudan 37
    SPLM/A 40

3 The Beginning of the NPA South Sudan Programme 45
    The covert Meeting in Addis Ababa in 1985 45
    A dangerous Mission 51
    Norwegian Peoples Aid takes a Stand 62

4 A Turning Point 67
    The Catholic Priest Dan Eiffe joins NPA 67

5 NPA at Work in the Field 79
    Some Glimpses from Areas of Priority 79
    The African Backbone in the NPA Programme 117
    "Women Can Do It" 123

6 Dramatic Challenges - creative Solutions 139
    The secret Project named "the Oslo Seminar" 139
    The Story about Garang's Satellite Telephone 143
    The River Boat, the International Red Cross and Jan Egeland 152
    The Famine Catastrophe in the Nuba Mountains and the Role of NPA 159
    The Battle at Aswa River in 1994 166
    The Meeting with President Museveni 169

7 Rumours of Gun Running 187
    NPA and the Conflict with UN 187
    How did SPLA get their Arms? 194
    The Role of USA 197

8 Administrative Challenges 201
A complex Programme 201
USA made NPA big in South Sudan 207
An unexpected Visit from the Kenya Revenue Authority 215
Acquitted 225

9 The Attack with poisonous Gas 229
Two Meetings with CIA 236

10 The Building of democratic Institutions sabotaged 237
The Concern of John Garang 238
The Establishment of the Consortium on Freedom of Speech 240
The political Will for Democratization of SPLM was destroyed 282

11 Dangerous Enimies 293
The Regime in Khartoum and its religious and ideological Nature 293
Crimes without Punishment 299
David Hoile - Omar Bashir's British Spin-Doctor who wanted to destroy NPA 314

12 Competitors, Networks and Relations 333
Norwegian Church Aid and Norwegian Peoples Aid, Competitors in South Sudan 333
NPA's Relations to Sweden 339
Kenya, Uganda, Ethiopia and Eritrea 344

13 Some of NPA's Key Supporters 351
"The lost Boys of Sudan," the long March to Ethiopia, the Tale of one Boy 351
Bethuel Kiplagat, the rock fast Friend of NPA in Kenya 356
Roger Winter, - a Pillar of rock Support in USA 358

14 Egil Hagen, the founding Father of NPA's Sudan Programme 371
Who was Egil Hagen? 375
Egil Hagen, a Legend in South Sudan 382

15 John Garang - the Liberator and the Legend 385
A very gifted, but poor Boy who rose to become the Liberator 385
The letter John Garang wrote to the Negotiators in Addis Ababa 391
Garang welcomed as the Victorious in Khartoum 419
The Helicopter Accident, John Garang dies 420

16 Dinner Guests at Home in Oslo 425
1992. Salva Kiir with a Delegation on their Way for Meetings in Bergen 425
Rebecca and John Garang for Dinner 433
Topics at the Dinner Table 444

17 A Freedom Fighter banned from his own Country 449
Suzanna and Pa'gan Amum at our Cottage in the Valdres Mountains 449
Salva Kiir and Pa'gan Amum, Pa'gan Amum's Life since the Summer of 2013 454
Rumour Mongers in Juba, Pa'gan Amum and Norwegian Peoples Aid 460

18 Riek Machar, a Freedom Fighter or a Wheeler Dealer? 465
A gifted and very ambitious Man 465
Hard-working Vice-President 469
The final Collapse of Trust. The Events in Juba on 8th July 2016 473

19 Threads in the Web between Norway, Sudan and South Sudan 477
The first Thread 477
Gro Harlem Brundtland and Mansour Khalid and their Threads in the Web 482
The Peace Negotiations, Norway, Hilde Frafjord Johnson and the Utstein Group 489
Norway's official Assistance to South Sudan 2005 – 2016 496

20 Decay, Breakdown and Destruction 499
October 2013, a Visit to Juba and what happened until July 2017 499
Friends of South Sudan trying to save the State and SPLM, but in vain 501
Large Scale Corruption 503
Some Key Facts from the following Sentry reports: 509
The Collapse of SPLM 528
The final Destruction of South Sudan 535
Omar Bashir and his Confidants in Khartoum are laughing 540
To sum it all up 544

21 Some Reflections 547
The Kenyan Artist Gado on South Sudan 557

Attachment 1: interview with Thorvald Stoltenberg 560
Attachment 2: NPA Policy Document on Sudan 568
Attachment 3: A letter to His Excellency Salva Kiir 590
Attachment 4: Bibliography, attachment 4, about the Author 594

ABBRIVATIONS AND WORDS

AMDISS. Association for Media development in South Sudan
AMREF. The African Medical and Research Foundation
ANC. African National Congress
ARCISS. Agreement on the Resolution of the Conflict in South Sudan, (August 2015)
Article 19. Article 19, defending Freedom of Expression and Information in the UN Declaration on Human Rights
AU. Africa Union
BBC World Service Trust. BBC's Trust for the Advancement of Information Technologies and Human Rights
Block Watne. Norwegian Company producing ready-made houses
CCM. Chama Cha Mapinduzi, (The Party of the Revolution), The governing party of Tanzania,
CNPC. China National Petroleum Company
CONCERN. Irish Charity (Civil Society Organization working in South Sudan)
COSATU. Congress of South African Trade Unions
CONTRAS. Extreme Rightwing Guerilla-Group operating in Nicaragua in the 1990ies
COT. Community Ox Trainer
CPA. The Comprehensive Peace Agreement for Sudan, signed on 9th January 2005
DFID. Department of International Development Cooperation, UK
Dolce Vita. Originally, the title of an Italian Film, that came to mean "Sweet Life".
ECHO. The Humanitarian Branch of the European Union
ECOS. The European Civil Society Coalition against the exploitation of Oil in Sudan
EDF. Ekvatoria Defence Forces
EPLRF. Eritrean People's Revolutionary Liberation Front
ESPAC. European Sudanese Public Affairs Council
EU. European Union

EUROSTEP. A European network of progressive NGOs in the field of Development Cooperation
FDP. SPLM Leaders, former Detainees, headed by Pa'gan Amum
FORD, Kenya. Forum for the Restauration of Democracy in Kenya
FRELIMO. The Mozambiquan Liberation Front
FSG. Front Service Group
GNOPOC. Greater Nile Petroleum Operating Company
GOAL. Irish Charity (Civil Society Organization working in South Sudan)
GOS. Government of Sudan
GOSS. Government of South Sudan
ICC. International Criminal Court
ICG. International Crisis Group
IFF. International Freedom Foundation
IFP. Inkatha Freedom Party
IGAD. Intergovernmental Authority on Development. Members, Ethiopia, Eritrea, Djibouti, Kenya, Somalia, Sudan, Sør Sudan and Uganda
IMF. International Monetary Fund
JEM. Justice and Equality Movement in Darfur/Sudan
IFF. International Freedom Foundation
JICA. Japan's International Development Agency
IDP. Internally Displaced Person
JMEC. Joint Monitoring and Evaluation Commission
KCHRED. Khartoum Centre for Human Rights and Environmental Development
KMFA. The Kenya Ministry of Foreign Affairs
LO. The Norwegian Confederation of free trade unions, the founding father of NPA,
LRA. Lord Resistence Army. A local terrorist organization in Uganda supported by the Khartoum regime
LTTE. Liberation Tigers of Tamil Eelam (in Sri Lanka)
MFA. Ministry of Foreign Affairs
MSF. Medecins sans Frontiers

NCA. Norwegian Church Aid
NCP. National Congress Party, Sudan
NDA. National Democratic Alliance of Sudan
NEAR. Network for East African Relief
NGO. Non-Governmental Organization
NIEO. New International Economic Order
NIF. National Islamic Front, Sudan
NLM. Norwegian Labour Movement
NMFA. Norwegian Ministry of Foreign Affairs
NOK. Norwegian Krones
NORAD/Norad. Norwegian Agency for International Development
NORFUND. Norwegian State Investment Fund
NORAGRIC. The Norwegian University for Life Sciences/ International Environment and Development Studies
NORLA. Norwegian Literature Abroad
NOREPS. Norwegian Emergency Preparedness System
NPA. Norwegian Peoples Aid
NRK/NBC. Norwegian Broadcasting Corporation
NRRDS: Nuba Rehabilitation, Relief and Development Society
NSGPSS. Norwegian Support Group for Peace in Sudan and South Sudan
NSU. Norwegian Seamen's Union
PRIO. The Peace Research Institute of Oslo
RENAMO. The National Resistance Movement of Mozambique, a right wing armed rebellion group that was established in Mozambique in 1976 with funding and other support from the Apartheid regime in South Africa and many rightwing institutions in many Western countries in order to fight FRELIMO and destabilize the country.
REST. Relief and Rehabilitation Society of Tigray
Reuters Trust. The News Agency Reuters Institute for the Promotion of Freedom of Expression

SIDA. Swedish International Development Agency
SOLIDAR. A network of European NGOs linked to the European Labour Movement and Trade Unions
SPLM: Sudan People' Liberation Movement
SPLA. Sudan People's Liberation Army
SPLM/A. Sudan People's Liberation Movement/Liberation Army
SPLM Mainstream. The name of the John Garang Faction of SPLM immediately after the split in Nasir in August 1991
SPLM United. The Name of the Riek Machar/Lam Akol Faction of SPLM immediately after the split in Nasir in August 1991
SPLM/DC. The Sudan People's Liberation Movement/Democratic Change, a minor opposition party in South Sudan headed by Lam Akol
SPLM IG, the fraction of the SPLM headed by Salva Kiir that took power and tried to govern South Sudan from December 2013 to April 2016,
SPLM inO, the fraction of SPLM that was chased away in December 2013 headed by Riek Machar.
SPLM-N. Sudan People's Liberation Movement in the North (Sudan)
SPLM/LFD. SPLM leaders, former detainees, led by Pa'gan Amum
SRRA. The Sudan Relief and Rehabilitation Agency (a Branch of SPLM)
SRF. Sudan Revolutionary Front
SSDF. Southern Sudan Defence Forces, a rebellious militsia group that operated and fought SPLA in the South with the support of the Khartoum Regime
TPRLF. Tigray Revolutionary Liberation Front (Ethiopia)
UDSF. United Democratic Salvation Front in South Sudan
UN. United Nations
UNDP. United Nations Development Programme

UNICEF. United Nations Children Fund
UNMISS. Un Mission in South Sudan
UoB. University of Bergen in Norway
UNITA. The National Union for the total Independence of Angola. Led by Jonas Savimbi, UNITA from 1975 onwards carried out a civil war against the MPLA government in Angola. UNITA had funding and other support from both the Apartheid regime in South Africa and many right-wing institutions in the West, for a period also from USA and Portugal.
UoK. University of Khartoum
USA. United States of America
WAN. World Association of Newspapers
WCDI. Women Can Do It. A training module developed by women members of the Norwegian Labour Party to raise the political awareness among women and make them join political and societal work. The WCDI module has become very popular and has been translated into English and other foreign languages and is now being used also by other political parties in their efforts to mobilize women for politics and society.
WCED. The World Commission on Environment and Development
WNPOC. White Nile Petroleum Operating Company
ZANU. Zimbabwe African Union
ZANLA. Zimbabwe African Liberation Army
I am using the names of different currencies in this English edition, but mainly NOK, Norwegian Krones and USD, An American Dollar.
The value of 1 NOK to 1 Dollar has varied in the period that is covered in this book, 193 – 2017.
The present rate is approximately 7.90 NOK for one dollar.

FOREWORD BY PA'GAN AMUM OKIECH

When I was approached by Halle Jørn Hanssen to write a foreword for his book; Lives at stake. *Norwegian People's Aid in South Sudan during the time of the liberation struggle,* I remembered a day in the autumn of 2013 in Juba, South Sudan. I received a surprise call from Halle, he was in town and would like to see me immediately. Although his voice sounded calm as usual, I could detect a slight tint of worry and trepidation. I knew that Halle was not escaping from the cold Norwegian autumn to the scorching heat of South Sudan for joy, but that something was deadly serious. It was an act of solidarity from the Labour Party and NPA, sending a long-time friend of SPLM, to try to prevent a split in the SPLM and a disaster for the peoples of South Sudan.

South Sudan gained independence from Sudan in July 2011 through a referendum where 98% voted for secession from Sudan, but only less than two years later things started unravelling. In the spring of 2013, the political tension within the leadership of the SPLM, had reached its peak. The party's highest organs could not meet, as SPLM's Chairman, Salva Kiir, continuously turned down all recommendations for such a meeting.

By summer, he, in his capacity as the President of the Republic, dismissed the Vice President and the entire cabinet. I, the Secretary General, was suspended and banned from travelling outside Juba, and from speaking to the media or any public gathering. The SPLM political organs were rendered ineffective and paralysed. The Chairman and his dubious presidential advisors, directed the "Party" and the SPLM government as if they were their own private institutions.

When the history of the struggle of the people of South Sudan for freedom, justice, equality and human dignity is recounted and recorded, the solidarity of the Norwegian people through Norwegian People's Aid (NPA), will shine. The resistance and struggle of our oppressed people, who were pitted against successive, oppressive regimes in Sudan, received a sympathetic ear from an unexpected far away land in the northernmost part of the world, Norway.

The brave man, Egil Hagen, travelled to Addis Ababa in 1985 and approached the SPLM representative, Deng Alor. Egil stated his solidarity with the oppressed people of Sudan and proclaimed that he would persuade NPA to bring humanitarian assistance to the people in the liberated areas under SPLM/A control.

Unlike all other humanitarian organizations that came to work in South Sudan during the liberation war in Sudan, NPA took a position of solidarity with the oppressed people and decided to support the struggle politically and with humanitarian means. By choosing SRRA, the relief wing of the SPLM, as its partner to provide relief to and development to the oppressed people, NPA incurred the wrath of the oppressive regime in Khartoum and its allies. NPA became a target, its hospitals were bombed, vehicles and staff were continuously attacked and its name and image came under diplomatic and media vilification by Khartoum and some of its hired international PR agencies like David Hoile of ESPAC. In many quarters in Khartoum the NPA was referred to as the Norwegian People's Army.

NPA did not bring humanitarian assistance as a demeaning charity delivered from top and down, but with respect and warm hearts as an act of solidarity with the people fighting for their freedom. The NPA way has been different from other organizations, in that it again and again took big risks whenever it provided assistance to people exposed to war, in desperate need and in inaccessible areas. Furthermore, it remained with the victims of war under fire and bombing, and other threatening situations when all other organizations evacuated. NPA focused its work on delivery of food, medicine, health care, education and training of people for health care, polytechnics, awareness raising and empowerment of women, agriculture and local food production.

Halle's book, Lives at Stake, rekindles the memory of the great solidarity brought by the people of Norway to the oppressed people of Sudan through NPA. Norwegians like Halle Jørn Hanssen, remind us of the great comradeship that once existed among revolutionaries as we were, and the forces of human progressive change in the global community.

The solidarity between the peoples of Norway and South Sudan remains strong This is of greatest importance at present when the dream of a better society has been destroyed by those in power in Juba. They have ruined the great vision that fuelled the struggle and gave birth to the solidarity of NPA. Soon after the SPLM leadership assumed power, it lost its vision and direction, and abandoned the SPLM Project of nation building within a progressive, democratic state. The failure of the SPLM leadership to deliver on its promises, during the struggle and at the last elections in 2011, has thrown the country into a deep existential crisis. We have since December 2013 had a devastating civil war, not against foreign enemies, but between two SPLM factions, one led by the Chairman, Salva Kiir, and the other by the first Deputy Chairman, Riek Machar.

The people of South Sudan both expected and deserved something very different after their hard-earned independence struggle, brought about through great suffering and sacrifice.

I have spent some 33 years of my life struggling for freedom and justice for the peoples of South Sudan and Sudan. But life sometimes takes unexpected turns. I wrote this foreword, for the Norwegian edition of the book, from a forced exile in Nairobi after months in detention accused for high treason by people who once were my comrades in the struggle. They wanted to get rid of me and many other comrades, to get an even stronger grip on power to continue their kleptocratic rule with an increasingly bloody dictatorship.

When a rewrote part of this foreword, I had had to flee further. I now live as a political refugee in USA, but I am still part of the struggle for freedom justice, a progressive democratic state, and human dignity in South Sudan.

I appreciate the effort of the people of Norway, through the Labour Party and the NPA, for dispatching Halle to Juba in 2013 to try and salvage a situation that unfortunately turned into a full-blown civil war. It has so far caused the loss of hundreds of thousands of innocent lives, the displacement of about two million people while another two million have fled to neighbouring countries. In addition, the state of South Sudan has collapsed and failed. It is bankrupt, and its institutions are ravaged.

Could anyone five years ago imagine that about five million South Sudanese today should be dependent on humanitarian aid from the UN and international NGOs? It was impossible to imagine, but it has happened. Now we must all raise to rescue the country and to rebuild South Sudan into a state and society that is human, democratic, and just, and that respect basic human rights and human dignity. It will be a monumental task, but it has to be done. We owe that to the innocent, but suffering and poor people of South Sudan.

We will, always treasure the solidarity of the Norwegian Labour Party and NPA, together with other likeminded organizations such as the African National Congress (ANC), EPRDF of Ethiopia and CCM of Tanzania.

Mr. Halle Jørn Hanssen, in his book, takes the reader through a long journey, related to humanitarian work in a war-torn land, carried out with hearts and minds of great humans. To the reader from South Sudan, the dedication of the committed staff of the NPA whether they come from Norway, Ireland, Scotland, Sweden, Denmark, USA, Kenya, Uganda, Ethiopia, Eritrea, South Sudan or other countries, will forever remain as a debt every one of us will strive to be able to repay someday.

Until that day comes, the presence of copies of this book in our homes and bookshelves, in Norway, South-Sudan and other countries, can be a fitting honour to the great women and men who worked for the people of South Sudan and the Nuba Mountains, in the hardest of times, through the NPA.

Pa'gan Amum Okiech
Nairobi, Kenya in April 2015,
and edited and updated in Denver,
USA in August 2016.

FOREWORD BY THORVALD STOLTENBERG

In his foreword, Pagan Amum is discussing both the present crises of South Sudan and the long lasting and important Norwegian engagement for independence and freedom for its people. Pagan Amum concludes his foreword by pointing to how a development of a new nation that in the beginning looked so promising, ended in a catastrophe.

Photo: Olav Saltbones, Red Cross

In my foreword, I want to stress some more general and principle political perspectives that at the same time relate to the experience of the people of South Sudan. This should be seen together with the interview I have given to the author, Halle Jørn Hanssen, and which the reader will find in attachment no. 1 in the back of this book.

When I, as a former minister of foreign affairs, meet younger journalists, they have a few questions that tend to be repetitive. What were the most important new foreign policy issues during your rein, and what issues do you think will be passed on to history?

I cannot be the final judge on these issues. Historians and others will have to do that. In addition it is my experience that it is wise to let some water flow into the ocean before such judgements are made. This is because issues that may seem to be very important at present, may fade and become less important as time passes, while other issues that seemed less important at the time of the present, gains more importance.

If I, in spite of what I just wrote, should dare to give some answers to the questions mentioned above, I have two overriding issues that I want to share with the reader.

Firstly, I consider the support that Norway, governments as well as civil society, rendered to the colonized peoples of Africa, as well as elsewhere in the world who struggled for independence and freedom, to be of utmost importance.

Secondly, the initiative I with the support from other government,s took around 1990 to establish fora and institutions for dialogue and cooperation with Russia about the Northern areas (Barents Sea and North Pol areas) have been and continue to be very important.

At present, both these very important issues are facing problems and opposition.

South-Sudan after more than 20 years of liberation war against the regime in Khartoum, with millions of death and more millions of displaced and refugees, finally gained independence and freedom for its many peoples in 2005. However, in the course of 2013, the elected leadership of the new nation let internal rivalry and conflict,s instead of nation building and development, dominate the political agenda. It ended with an unnecessary and very destructive civil war, and a humanitarian catastrophe that has not yet seen its end.

The cooperation in the North with Russia was developing very well when it was adversely hit by the Russian takeover of the peninsula of Crimea and the conflict in eastern Ukraine. Projects came to a standstill, and optimism disappeared.

I am by nature an optimist. I believe and hope that these setbacks of present mentioned above in a historical setting are unfortunate temporary political setbacks in a constructive long-term development that will be victorious.

I believe that history will judge the Norwegian support for the liberation of Afric,a that started in the early 1960ies, as our most important contribution to peace and stability globally.

I also believe that the change of policy, in the early 1990ies, from confrontation to cooperation with Russia in the North has been and will continue to be of great importance for both growth and stability in these neighbouring areas of ours in the North and for the wider East-West cooperation in Europe.

However, we shall not be naïve and overlook the seriousness of the conflicts, mentioned above. When things get difficult, it is important to learn from them, and in this context it is important that the actors themselves share their experience with others so that new generations may learn from the past.

In this book, Halle Jørn Hanssen shares with us developments in South-Sudan and Sudan with an emphasis on the role that Norwegian Peoples Aid (NPA) undertook during the time of the liberation struggle. Halle Jørn Hanssen has been an important observer and actor when it comes to the liberation of the colonies in Africa. He worked for 13 years as a foreign news reporter and correspondent for Norwegian Broadcasting Corporation. When he was its first Africa Correspondent based in Nairobi, from mid-1978 to mid-1982, he shared with his Norwegian audience conflicts and developments in a turbulent continent.

As Secretary General of Norwegian Peoples Aid (NPA), he was in charge of the many challenges that the organization was facing in Suda,n as well as in many other conflict-ridden countries.

In the summer of 198,7 Norwegian Peoples Aid made a solidarity decision, in political and humanitarian term,s to support the people of Sudan behind the frontline of SPLM/,A in their liberation struggle against the oppressive regime in Khartoum. Following that, NPA applied to the Ministry of Foreign Affairs for a grant of 20 Mill. NOK for its humanitarian work in Sudan. The decision by NPA to take a stand in support for the liberation struggle was a controversial one, and its application for the grant became controversial. I had to seek advice both internally and externally.

The final decision rested with me, and I decided to grant the amount applied for, 20 Mill. NOK.

My critics believed I was onesided and taking a stand in a civil war in an African country by granting this support for NPA. I did not see it that way. The African ethnic groups in Suda,n and in particular in South Sudan, had for many centuries been exposed to systematic oppression and barbaric acts from their oppressors, Turks, British and Egyptian, and finally, upon Sudan's independence in 1956, the Arab and African-Islamized elites holding power in Khartoum.

The African groups, particular in the South, had again and again throughout history risen against the tyrants and had been defeated. The exception to the rule was the Addis Ababa Peace Agreement in 1972. However, that agreement only came after the first long liberation war that started around 1960, and it gave peace and a form of confederation to South-Sudan that lasted for ten years. Then, the rulers in Khartoum broke many essential parts of the agreement, and a new war of liberation broke out in 1983.

When South-Sudan, after a transition period of 6 years, finally got full independence in July 2011, the political and humanitarian role of Norwegian Peoples Aid during the time of the liberation struggle was very much appreciated. President Salva Kiir in his independence speech, only stated words of gratitude to two organizations, the UN and NPA. Halle Jørn Hanssen as former Secretary General of NPA, was present as Guest of Honor at the celebration,s invited by the President himself. This made me feel happy. Norway with its government, government institutions and many civil society actors had since 2005 made big efforts to support the establishment and development of this new nation.

As I am writing this foreword, everyone knows that the first effort to make South-Sudan a democratic and viable state, failed miserably. An internal power struggle among the leaders of the liberation struggle about what policies to fellow, and who should be in charge of state and government in the future, set pace in the course of 2013. Halle Jørn Hanssen was, in October 2013, asked by the President to travel to South Sudan in order to mediate in the conflict. However, he like the Vice-President of South Africa, Cyril Ramaphosa, failed in their efforts. That he was invited as a mediator says something about what trust the staff of NPA and Halle Jørn Hanssen as former Secretary General had gained during the time of the liberation struggle.

However, all mediation efforts failed and a new and very destructive civil war broke out in December 2013. It has caused the death of as many as one hundred thousands people, more than 2 million people are displaced or refugees in neighbouring countries and very recently we have learnt that about 6 million of an overall population of 11 million, now are dependent on humanitarian aid. It is a political and humanitarian catastrophe of gigantic proportions. At the same tim,e whatever was established of state institutions and democratic structures are to a very large extent destroyed. It is a deeply tragic situation.

However, it is in this terrible situation important to remember that the peoples of South-Sudan carry a very tragic historic legacy of oppressive tyrants, slavery, violations of both human dignity and human rights, and a memory of past colonizers and their spilt and rule policies.

I have been politically active for more than 60 years, and I have held different important international positions. It is my experience that when people have been humiliated and terrorized for centuries, like the people of South-Sudan, it is often very difficult to build a degree of national unity that holds when internal political conflicts arise. In addition, leaders of war are seldom good leaders for peace, freedom and development. The South-Sudanese experience is a tragic case in point.

Now it is time to let Halle Jørn Hanssen tell the story of his staff and himself about NPA in the liberation war in South-Sudan. I have great expectations, and I shall read with great interest.

The Norwegian text was finalized in April 2015, and the English translation updated and slightly revised, in August 2016.

Thorvald Stoltenberg,
Oslo in August 2016

1 INTRODUCTION

I HAVE EVER SINCE MY STUDENT DAYS in the early 1960s been fascinated by and actively involved with Africa, African politics and the liberation struggles in different parts of the continent. From 1969 to 1982, I worked as a Foreign News reporter with Norwegian Broadcasting Corporation (NRK), frequently reporting from Africa. In 1978 I was appointed its first Africa Correspondent based in Kenya. I was, from late 1982 until 1992, Head of Information with the Norwegian Agency for International Development Cooperation (Norad) and travelled frequently in that capacity on missions in Africa. From the spring of 1992 until the spring of 2001 I held the positions as International Director, and later Secretary-General of Norwegian Peoples Aid (NPA), which had important programmes in several African states. Since then, I have worked as a free-lance journalist with frequent visits to many African countries, but first and foremost South Sudan.

Since 1972, I have been on missions to almost 40 African countries and spent almost nine years in one place or another on the African continent. I have in association with Norwegian People's Aid (NPA) engaged behind the front lines in South Sudan since the beginning of 1986. Between 1992 and 2001 while I held senior positions in NPA, first as International Director and later as Secretary General, I had the over-all responsibility for the NPA Programme in South Sudan.

After I left NPA in May 2001, I continued to follow the developments in South Sudan; through independent assignments, invitations from the Sudanese People's Liberation Movement (SPLM), and as an external advisor to NPA and the Norwegian Labour Party.

The accusations made against NPA about gun running has been a recurring theme since the very beginning of the first NPA operations in 1986. Only on rare occasions did people outside South Sudan ask the relevant questions: Why did you take a stand in support of the liberation struggle in South Sudan? What was it you did in the course of 20 difficult and dangerous years in South Sudan? What challenges and obstacles did you encounter?

This one-sided focus on the unsubstantiated claim of smuggling of arms has been a source both of frustration and inspiration while I prepared to write this book, because although it obscures the bigger picture of what NPA really did, it has been a driving force in conveying how comprehensive, complex, demanding and risky the NPA programmes at the time were.

It took a long time to get started on the Norwegian edition of this book, but finally in the fall of 2013, I sat down in a beautiful guest house in Lamu on the Northern Coast of Kenya, and began writing. Back in Norway I wrote something almost every day for 18 months, some days many pages, other days only a few sentences. I wrote the last sentences in the Norwegian edition in early July 2015 and the book launch was on 19th August.

There was a wealth and depth of material to choose from, and I had to make some difficult choices. I have primarily focused on an account of NPA's operations through to 2001, when I was most involved and had the overall responsibility. For the following period, I have written about two projects I continued to be part of. The first was the Freedom of Expression Project, on independent and free media in Sudan and the development of Democratic Media Laws in Sudan prior to the separation into two states, Sudan and South Sudan in July 2011. I represented NPA in this project and represented NPA from 2005 until 2010. The second one was the Party Building Project with Sudan People's Liberation Movement (SPLM), where I represented the Norwegian Labour Party until the fall of 2013.

In December 2013 the political power struggle within SPLM took a decisive turn for the worse when President Salva Kiir and his advisors made up a story about an attempted coup d'etat. In chapter 19 towards the end of this edition, I am adding an analysis of the political background for the power struggle that led to the devastating events and breakdown of state order in December 2013, and the terrible civil war that has destroyed South Sudan.

With all the tragic events that have occurred in South Sudan over the past few years, it has been a difficult task to finish, first the Norwegian edition in 2015, and the English one in the summer of 2017 even more. For the latter, I have both done some updates regarding the historical background and some additions for the period after 2012 that makes this edition somewhat more comprehensive.

Challenges and fundamental Questions

I hope the book may contribute to greater understanding of how complex and challenging international humanitarian work can be, whether you take a political stand or not. The same applies to the complex interaction between NPA, the Norwegian Ministry of Foreign Affairs/Norad and the major contributor in NPA's Sudan program, the United States Agency for International Development (USAID). The history of NPA in Sudan also includes an interesting interaction with the authorities first and foremost in Kenya and Uganda, but also in the other countries in the Horn of Africa.

With respect to the more fundamental aspects behind NPA's actions and the manner with which they were conducted, it is important to remember that they were based on a Norwegian solidarity traditio,n and the principles and values that underline the policies of the Labour Movement in Norway, Scandinavia and Europe.

During the civil war in Spain in the early 1930's, the Norwegian Labour Movement, supported the democratic forces and recruited volunteers to fight fascism in Spain. Various Norwegian governments have since the late 1960's provided humanitarian assistance to liberation movements first in Mozambique and Namibia then named South West Africa, Zimbabwe, then Rhodesia, Angola, Guinea Bissau and South Africa, and lately to Sudan People's Liberation Movement (SPLM) in Sudan.

I will never forget the guerrilla officer in Zimbabwe African National Liberation Army (ZANLA), the armed wing of Zimbabwe African National Union (ZANU), whom I interviewed on election day in February 1980 when I was reporting for Norwegian Broadcasting Corporation. He was queuing to vote. He stared at me with sceptic eyes and asked where I came from. I said, "*Norway*". He thought for a minute. His face lit up in a big smile, and he said, "*We like your sardines*".

At that time, Norwegian funds were used to provide food for the freedom fighters. It is worth noting that during the late 1970s and the 1980s The Royal Norwegian Consul-General to South Africa and a representative for the Norwegian Church, travelled with dollar notes hidden in their belts which they handed to those fighting the Apartheid system in South Africa. In the struggle against the dictatorial Milosêvic regime in Serbia during the late 1990s, both the Norwegian ambassador and the Resident Representative of NPA did the same. They handed out dollars to political parties and other groups and institutions that were using peaceful means to fight the regime.

When NPA began operations in South Sudan in 1986, there was then as there is now, a brutal and oppressive regime in Khartoum. The Arabic racist attitude towards black Africa was even more pervasive than it is today. Therefore, there was a liberation war in Sudan against racial and religious domination.

Willing to take a Risk

The impact NP'sA humanitarian assistance and solidarity work has had in Sudan has been closely related to the willingness to take risks. In many ways it appears that the willingness to take risks is steadily decreasing these days among donors both when it comes to humanitarian assistance and development co-operation. The bureaucratic requirements linked to control, risk assessment, result reports, and goal achievement have increased dramatically in the past few years.

I am convinced that more time and resources are used today than 30 years ago on checking and double checking what is done, than on discussing how a given programme can be planned, structured and developed to get the best results.

It is harder to get funds to work in unfamiliar territories and environments marked by conflict and war with the many inherent risks involved, today than some decades ago. Hesitance has become the key word.

Another issue that has been a concern of mine long before I joined NPA, is the donors' lack of patience. Repeatedly the message was, *"You must phase out this program. Enough time and money have been used on this now, and our priorities have changed."* In the language of development assistance, the three Ts are, things take time. But in practice, the wisdom of this statement has for the most, been systematically ignored.

In our world today, filled with conflict and complex situations, institutions such as the United Nations (UN) and the Norwegian Ministry of Foreign Affairs (NMFA) and non-governmental organizations are confronted with situations in which they face a moral obligation to try out possibilities instead of being overwhelmed by the problems. This, however, entails a degree of risk, and opens for harsh criticism if things fail.

A brief History of Norwegian People's Aid

To understand why NPA took a stand in favour of the liberation struggle in South Sudan and decided to provide emergency relief and development assistance to the people in the liberated areas behind the front lines, it might be useful for the reader to be familiar with some key aspects and principles of the history of NPA, the political values that guide its operations, and why it in many ways is different from other non-governmental organizations.

NPA is the humanitarian branch of the Norwegian Labour Movement. It was founded by the Norwegian Confederation of Free Trade Unions (LO) in December 1939, and the statutes clearly state that NPA can take a political position in favour of weak and oppressed groups both in Norway and abroad. Its precursor was the Norwegian Spain Committee which was rooted in the Norwegian Labour Movement and supported the democratic forces in Spain in the fight against fascism, and the Labour Solidarity Committee for Finland supporting the Finnish people when the Soviet Union attacked Finland in 1939.

Hitler and the Norwegian Nazi government banned NPA during World War II. Many of its leaders and members took part in the liberation struggle in Norway. Some were imprisoned and spent years in concentration camps either in Norway or Germany, others survived as active freedom fighters, hiding in towns, forests or mountain areas or fighting from exile in Sweden, United Kingdom and USA.

During the struggle against the Apartheid regime and for freedom and democracy in South Africa, NPA was from the mid 1970ies to the mid- 1980ies, the secret channel for the solidarity support from the Labour Movement to COSATU, and from 1986 the open channel for different Norwegian governments and their support to the African National Congress (ANC) in exile. In Latin America, NPA has a long history of solidarity support.

In the past few decades, NPA has with other International partners successfully worked toward establishing an international ban on use of landmines and cluster munitions. NPA is in other words; both a political and a humanitarian organization.

In South Sudan, NPA reversed China's Mao' thesis about guerrilla warfare. Mao said: "Drain all the water from the pond in order to kill all the fish". In other words, for Mao it was vital to destroy everything in the society, so that people died or fled, and the opposing forces were no longer able to fight.

NPA did its best to provide for the people behind the front lines so that they could survive and stay at home. That was a prerequisite for the success of the Sudanese People's Liberation Army's (SPLA). That is where NPA made a difference. A big difference in the light of the circumstances prevailing at the time.

About the Book and its Contributors

This book has two forewords, one by Pa'gan Amum, the other by Thorvald Stoltenberg. I thank them both very warmly for their contributions.

As Minister of Foreign Affairs, Mr. Stoltenberg made a principle decision in the summer of 1987 to support NPA's Sudan programme. Without this support from the Norwegian government at the time, and the continued support from succeeding governments, NPA would most likely not have been involved in Sudan in the first place, and certainly not in the manner and to the extent it did.

Mr. Pa'gan Amum was the leader of a revolutionary student group in the bush when the late Dr John Garang in 1983 contacted them and made them part of SPLM/A. In the years to follow he was one of SPLM/A's great leaders and commanders. After the signing of the Comprehensive Peace Agreement (CPA) in January 2005, P'agan Amum was elected Secretary General of SPLM. When John Garang died in July 2005, Salva Kiir his deputy, became the chairman of SPLM, and shortly thereafter efforts were undertaken to remove P'agan from his position, but they failed.

Since this book in many ways is a demanding project with numerous pitfalls, I have used a reference group for comments and advice on parts of the manuscript for the Norwegian edition. The group consisted of Gunnar M. Sørbø, professor at the University of Bergen, Oystein Rolandsen, Senior Researcher at the Peace Institute in Oslo (PRIO), Endre Stiansen, previous Minister-Counsellor at the Norwegian Embassy in Ethiopia, Kjell Hødnebøe, previous Senior Advisor in the Ministry of Foreign Affairs during the peace negotiations in Keny,a and Sharif Harrir, from Darfur and previous Senior Researcher at the University of Bergen.

While the negotiations for peace in Sudan was underway in 2002/3, Sharif Harrir, then at the University of Bergen, was called by one of the leaders of the freedom struggle in Darfur to return back to Sudan in to take part in the struggle. He honoured the call and went back home. He was almost immediately sent to Asmara in Eritrea (the site of National Democratic Alliance of Sudan in Exile) and appointed the Deputy Secretary -General of NDA with Pa´gan Amum as the Secretary General. During the time in Asmara, they also held military positions, Pagan being The Commander in Chief and Sharif Harrir a deputy commander in chief of the combined NDA/SPLA forces on the Eastern Front.

This book provides many insights from inside NPA from the time of the liberation struggle. It is not only my account, but an account that many people have contributed to, first and foremost the staff at NPA in Oslo, in Nairobi and in the field whom I worked with during my time at NPA. I have been communicating with almost all of them, Norwegian as well as African and other International staff. They have all been very helpful and supportive of this project. I have interviewed many of them face to face, others via telephone, skype, and mail. The same applies to old friends in the Sudanese Relief and Rehabilitation Agency (SRRA) and SPLM/A, other working partners and friends in the countries of the Horn of Africa, and senior staff members in the Ministry of Foreign Affairs in Oslo.

Former staff and colleagues in NPA have willingly contributed with other documentation. Without these very important contributions and support I had not been able to write this book. To all of those unnamed supporters and sources, you are not forgotten, I am eternally grateful. However, three former colleagues have to be mentioned, Helge Rohn, the NPA Resident representative during the period 1991-1996, Lars Johan Johnsen, NPA Resident Representative 1997-2000, and Sten Rino Bonsaksen, NPA Resident Representative 2000-2003. All three have read the draft of the Norwegian edition, commented and advised. I am particular grateful for their contributions.

Some important voices are not represented well enough. There is too little input from our many hardworking African project leaders and other African staff. I would have liked to discuss more with them, but finances were limited. Apart from the support from The Free Speech Foundation in Norway (Fritt Ord) and NORLA (Norwegian Literature Abroad), I have published both the Norwegian and the English edition out of my pocket: Consequently, there have been some limitations.

I also want to acknowledge Sebastiao Salgado, the great Brazilian photographer, who donated some of his best pictures to NPA after a reporting trip in Sudan in 1994, organized by NPA. Many of these pictures are in this book. Marit Hærnes, Henrik Stabell, Aage Vatnedalen, Ken Miller, Diress Mengistu, Bjørn Abelsen and Ivar Christiansen have all kindly allowed me to choose from their great picture collections from the fields of South Sudan.

Sebastian Bernard of Mapman UK has generously allowed me to use the maps you find in the book.

Three Norwegian larger publishing houses considered the story and the project, but concluded that there was no market interest. Oddbjørn Monsen at the small Skyline Publishers in Oslo had the courage to make the publication of the Norwegian edition possible while his partner Amund Nitter did an excellent design. Thank you!

The Swedish author and film maker Stig Holmqvist, and the writers Vegard Bye and Sverre Jervell, have provided important advice. So, has Jens Kristian Thune, NPA's lawyer during my time at NPA.

The translation of the text from Norwegian to English has been done by Renee Waara, an American, linguist and a university lecturer residing in Norway. I am very grateful to Renee for her work. The translation was only made possible with a grant from NORLA, Norwegian Literature Abroad, and my special gratitude goes to them as well.

My very old and close friend and colleague from my time in Kenya as the Africa Correspondent for Norwegian Broadcasting Corporation, the renowned Kenyan journalist and editor John Gachie, has read the English text before it was forwarded to the Publisher and provided valuable insights and important editorial advice.

It was my priority to find an East African publisher for the English edition, but I failed in my efforts. So, Skyline Publishers in Oslo with Oddbjørn Monsen in charge and with Ellen Renberg this time doing the lay-out work, came to my rescue and made the English edition possible. Again, thanks a lot.

Last but not least, I have a family who have stood by me during the long writing process, especially, my wife Marit. She has been critical, constructive, inspiring and encouraging. She has contributed profoundly to make the two editions of this book what they are. She gets the biggest hug.

Next but last, two Books in one in this English Edition

This book is a history of Norwegian Peoples Aid in South Sudan during the time of the liberation struggle, composed by contributions from many different sources, but edited and written by me.

The chapters 14 to 19 extend the NPA story.

Chapter 20, Decay, Break Down and Collapse, is my own political analysis and assessment of what has happened in South Sudan since the summer of 2013, and the forces at work that have made South Sudan a failed state. The final chapter 21, presents my reflections on what happened and what could have been done differently, in short what we can learn from this experience.

A final Point
An Advice from my Boss, the Director General of Norwegian Broadcasting Corporation

My journalism has been strongly influenced by a gem of an inspiring advice I was given as a young reporter with Norwegian Broadcasting Corporation (NRK), just three days after I started at the Foreign News desk in September 1969. I was sitting in my office when the Foreign News Editor Per Riste came and told me: "*Halle, the Director-General wants to see you!*"

I was terrified that I had done something wrong after only three days, and I asked very carefully: "*What is it?*" "*Nothing serious,*" said Riste. "*Ustvedt just likes to greet the new journalists.*"

When I walked into the Director-General's office, he sat knitting. By profession he was a Professor of Medicine and a surgeon. He was also a composer and piano player, very much involved in the making and shaping of policies for Norwegian Development Assistance, a humanist, extremely well read and a politician of the Labour Party. His name was Hans Jacob Ustvedt and he was smiling as he received me.

He gave me a friendly welcome, asked a little about what I had done earlier and offered a few kind words. I thanked him, bowed, and walked toward the door. Then I heard: "*By the way Halle Jørn Hanssen, there are a couple of more things.*" I turned and walked back to the desk. Then he said:

"*These days there is in Norwegian public life a lot of debate about the concept of objectivity. It is important for you to remember that this discussion is pure nonsense. But you must never forget that even the coin has two sides, and you must always be very knowledgeable and serious in your work. Good luck.*"

He smiled. I thanked him again, bowed and left.

Ustvedt's creed became my own and has ever since influenced the way I work, as a journalist and writer. This applies also for this book. I earnestly hope you will enjoy reading it.

Halle Jørn Hanssen, Oslo in July 2017

There are numberless paintings and drawings from centuries back about how the peoples of South Sudan were enslaved and mistreated.

FORCED LABOR

SLAVERY IN SUDAN

- Sudanese slaves are captured during military raids performed and supported by their own government
- The Sudanese government denies involvement
- It is thought that this may be a tactic by the ruling Northern Sudan to depopulate southern agitators who strive for independence or who oppose the construction of a lucrative oil pipeline, funded by foreign capital (Re, 2002)

"Courtesy of Googleimages"

2
HISTORICAL BACKGROUND

THE HORN OF AFRICA IS, by many scientists, believed to be the cradle of humankind. The first evidence of human activity is found in the Great Rift Valley, stretching from Ethiopia and Kenya through Tanzania and all the way south to Mozambique and South Africa. From here the first humans wandered out of Africa and eventually populated the world.

The history of the people in present day Sudan and South Sudan goes back tens of thousands of years. The river Nile, the world's longest river, found its way North some 15 000 years ago, from the African highlands through the tropical savannah lowlands and deserts in Sudan and Egypt to the Mediterranean Sea. In the aftermath of this development we find evidence of human activity from the last 10 000 years along the river banks of the Nile. In old Egypt, there is evidence of African groups once living there, and in Central Sudan in the Nile Valley numerous ancient African civilizations emerged.

In the twelfth century, Arab-Islamic forces expanded into Coptic Egypt, Christian Nubia, Christian/Amazigh and Barber Tunisia, Algiers and Morocco. These Arab-Islamic forces captured all these areas except for the Christian Nubia Kingdoms on the Nile that held on up to 1504 when the Alua and the Makuria Christian Kingdoms fell into the hands of the Black African Islamic Fung Kingdom. When North-Africa and Andalusia became part of the Islamic Empire, many African Islamic kingdoms emerged in what today is known as the Sahel region from the West to the East, such as Timbuktu, Kano, Chad, Waday, Fur and Funj.

Throughout history, the relationship between the new Arab-Islamic states of Northern Africa and the Black African states, situated in the Sub Saharan region with Sudan in many ways as the crossroad between North and South, were sometimes marked by peace, and at other times by conflict and war. The Islamic-Arabs brought with them another culture and a new religion, Islam. The Arabs gradually developed a religious and cultural dominance that sometimes turned into cultural arrogance towards the African peoples which created tension and conflict.

In the process, the Arabs gained control over the northern parts of Sudan while most black African groups were pushed to the South West and East.

When the Ottoman Empire expanded into Africa from 1821, taking control of Egypt and the northern areas of Sudan, the conflict intensified. The rulers in Istanbul and Cairo sent troops to the South to hunt for slaves, ivory and valuable minerals. These military expeditions with their superior weapons proceeded with great brutality, killing large numbers of local people and crushing local resistance. Every year for many decades, thereafter, every year they took tens of thousands of girls and young women to be sold as sex slaves and concubines in the Empire. Young African men were also taken prisoners by the thousands every year. The majority were trained to be soldiers while others were castrated and used as slaves.

The British in Sudan

Towards the end of the 19th Century, the British had occupied Egypt and Sudan as a colony. The British made an agreement with Egypt, called the Anglo-Egyptian Condominium, which secured full British control of Sudan. However, in Sudan there was a growing sense of resentment from the brutal oppression experienced by the rulers in Istanbul and Cairo (the Turko-Egyptian rule). The fact that Britain was now the ruler made little difference with respect to oppression, even though slavery was officially forbidden in British Colonial territories and spheres of influence.

The great religious and political leader, Muhammed Ahmed Ibin el-Sayyid Abdullah, forced the Egyptians and the British to retreat. Intense fighting over Khartoum ended with the beheading of General Gordon early in 1885. Muhammed Ahmed bin Allah declared himself the new leader with the title of al-Mahdi, the prophesied redeemer of Islam, and he is the founding father of the Mahdist state. He died from typhoid after only six months. His successors had a fundamentalist interpretation of Islam that negatively affected the relations with neighbouring states such as Egypt and Ethiopia.

In Great Britain, there was a growing demand to avenge General Gordon and reconquer Sudan. The task was given to General Kitchener, who recaptured Khartoum and Sudan in 1898. Great Britain then controlled Sudan as a Colony until its independence in 1956.

The British were faced with an unpredictable and strong local resistance led by the national religious Mahdist Forces, who were also against European modernization. The British chose as their counter strategy to modernize the society and improve living conditions for some selected groups of people in the northern part of Sudan. They built educational institutions, health and welfare services, not for everyone, but for those who could afford them. For the most, it meant the Arab tribes that some centuries before had invaded Sudan, and the Arabized African tribes in the areas surrounding Khartoum and in the Nile Valley.

The British and their partners first and foremost made the Eljazeera project their priority to have reliable supplies of cotton from Sudan for the British textile industries. All this mainly favoured the Elmahdi and Elmarghani families who were living around Khartoum. The two families, in partnership with the Britis,h built a capitalist base from which they increasingly also developed political power. These families still have a strong influence on politics in Sudan.

The British were quite successful with their political strategy and established themselves as the imperial power of Sudan.

Occasionally, there was tension and conflict between the colonial masters and their subjects, but the British had their own remedy for resolving such problems; the divide and rule policy.

The divide and rule policy was an effective method applied by the British in all their colonies. It left a very detrimental legacy amongst the peoples of Sudan and other former colonies in the British Empire. The British also applied this method on the oppressed people in South Sudan, and it was reinforced by the Arab and the African Islamized-Arabized elites when Sudan got independence in 1956.

When these elites inherited the political power in 1956, they continued the strategy of divide and rule in South Sudan. In my considered view, this historical legacy is an important part of the explanation as to why the leaders in South Sudan still today are unable to work together for the common good of their own people.

With respect to South Sudan, the British made a decision that had a very lasting impact that is prevalent even today. They perceived and viewed the people in South Sudan to be so primitive that there was no point in changing their way of life. The British wanted instead to keep the peoples of South Sudan as a kind of a veritable human zoo, which could be shown to visitors with particular interests. As such, a law was consequently passed in the early 1920s, called the Closed Districts Ordinance, which isolated the peoples and the land of Southern Sudan from the outside world. A special passport was needed to cross the border between the two parts of the country.

The British colonial authorities allowed primary education for boys, not for girls. Secondary education for boys was limited to acquiring skills like carpentry, handicrafts, simple book keeping and basic accounting. Academic pursuit of education was not allowed. For those who wanted further education, they had to go to the colonies of Kenya and Uganda. The responsibility for constructing and running schools was left to the missionary organizations, the first ones being Verona Fathers (Catholic), the Presbyterian Church (USA) and the Anglican Church (British).

When the British came to Sudan around 1898, the difference between North and South in terms of social, political and economic development was significant. When they left the country 60 years later, the wide gap between the North and the South was steadily growing. In the North, the British made substantial contributions to development, but left the South with nothing tangible, functional or appropriate after over fifty years of British rule.

Independence 1956

Sudan gained independence in 1956. The people in the South hoped for a federal state with self-rule, but remained part of the centralized state of Sudan with Khartoum as the capital. The Southern peoples and their leaders felt this to be a breach of promise both by the British and the Arab elites that inherited the state from the British.

From 1955 until 1960 there were sporadic uprisings in the South against the rule from Khartoum. The uprisings developed into a full-fledged liberation war, Anya Nya I. The government in Khartoum reacted violently. Hundreds of thousands of Southerners lost their live,s while whatever was left of a fragile infrastructure and social institutions, were destroyed.

In 1972, Sudan's president Gafar Nimeiri agreed to peace negotiations in Addis Ababa. After a few months of negotiations, an agreement was reached, called the Addis Ababa Agreement of 1972. The heart of the agreement was self-rule for South Sudan with their own president, government and parliament. Many South Sudanese leaders, including the late Dr John Garang, were sceptical to the agreement. They thought that it was too tenuous and wanted instead independence or a restructuring of the Sudanese state into a multicultural secular state united in diversity. However, and despite their misgivings, the peace lasted for close to 10 years, although there were periods of sporadic rebellion in several places in South Sudan.

Between 1980 and 1982, Nimeiri violated the central tenets of the peace agreement. He introduced Sharia Law in the South, Arabic was to be the language used in schools and Christian missions were expelled from South Sudan.

The peoples in the South were again exposed to many serious acts of humiliation, discrimination and oppression, and they were treated as second-class citizens by their Arabs superiors. The Arabic word "abeed" meaning slave, was revived and used by the Arab rulers. The people in the South called the people from the north "Arabs" or "jelabas" both words meant oppressors.

SPLM/A

Consequently, a new and stronger national uprising emerged. It started with soldiers in the Bor Garrison in the South in the spring of 1983. The late Dr John Garang, then a Colonel in the Sudanese National Army, was by his superior sent to Bor to pacify the rebels. But he had with great secrecy set up the rebellion, and as soon as he arrived in Bor, he joined it and took command. On May 16th, the government forces attacked the rebelling soldiers in Bor, and that day came to be the birthday of SPLA, the Sudan People's Liberations Army was founded. In August 1983, the supporting political organization, the Sudan People's Liberation Movement (SPLM), came into being.

Between May and August in 1983 the leaders of the rebellion in the South set-up their headquarters in Ethiopia while they held an intense debate among themselves about the goals of the rebellion. Some were in favour of fighting for the independence of South Sudan and were not convinced that Dr. John Garang shared their vision.

They were at the same time negotiating with Ethiopia for political and military support. Ethiopia's dictator, Colonel Mengistu Haile Miriam, before promising any support, demanded a political manifesto from the rebel leaders that stated the objectives and principles of the freedom struggle and what visions they had for the future.

The first social and economic political manifesto the South rebels wrote was a vague socialistic vision of an independent South Sudan. Colonel Mengistu rejected the entire manifesto and made it clear that Ethiopia would not support a war of independence. Furthermore, he made it clear that if the manifesto remained, they would be thrown out of Ethiopia.

The rebel leaders agreed to ask Dr John Garang who was the most scholarly and academically man among the rebels, to write a new manifesto. He agreed, and made socialism the ideological foundation, while stating a new and secular Sudan as the revolutionary vision for all of Sudan, thereby unifying all those groups in the state that had been marginalized by both the colonial power, Great Britai,n and the African-Islamized and Arab elites that had ruled Sudan since 1956.

Colonel Mengistu approved the manifesto and promised to support the liberation struggle. Dr. Garang's text was voted in as the SPLM manifesto and Dr. Garang was elected SPLM's Chairman and SPLA's Commander-In-Chief.

The long and bitter struggle for freedom of South Sudan began in the fall of 1983 and lasted until the Comprehensive Peace Agreement in 2005.

During this long and bitter war of 22 years, more than 2.5 million people lost their lives. The vast majority of those who died, came from the South with a population of 8-10 million people. Within the same time span about four million people were forced to flee from their homes and over one million people became refugees, mostly in neighbouring countries, but also in faraway countries of the world. Hundreds of thousands were mentally and physically damaged for life. The remaining, inadequate and fragile infrastructure in South Sudan consisting of roads, railways, telephones and ports along the Nile, were for the most part destroyed in the struggle.

The complexity of the conflict must be emphasized. Traditionally, the Pastoral-Agricultural Dinka and Nuer peoples of the South have lived peacefully side by side. However, in the 1980's there was a devastating incident. Between 1985 and 1988 the SPLM/A organized marches of primarily young Dinka boys to Ethiopia. The goal was to give them education and recruit them into the liberation struggle. Nobody really knows how many started the march, but the number is estimated at close to 40 000. According to SPLM about 28 000 boys reached Ethiopia, but other sources claim it was 20 000. The Dinka boys had to march across Nuer land, and were attacked by militia groups. The unarmed young boys, hungry and close to starvation, were killed by the thousands.

A coup attempt led by the Nuer leader Dr. Riek Machar and the Shilluk leader Dr. Lam Akol, against Dr John Garang who was a Dinka, divided the SPLM/A in August 1991. The massacre of the Dinka people in Bor in November 1991 led by Dr Riek Machar and his "White Army" followed. Between 1991 and 2005 as many as 30 militia groups came into being in South Sudan, mostly Nuer. The regime in Khartoum supported them with arms and money to fight the SPLA led by Dr John Garang.

These are some of the vivid and enduring memories of the Dinka people in the struggle for an independent South Sudan. It has to a large extent poisoned the relationship between the two peoples and it is still playing a significant role in the conflict in the current political military power struggle and dispensation.

When the peace agreement came in 2005, South Sudan was a militarized and mainly destroyed region, with a people hungry for peace, freedom with security and a better everyday life.

When you consider the population of South Sudan, the long war for freedom, lasting for 22 years, was more devastating for people, society and infrastructure than any other war since World War II, except for Vietnam.

2013, a new and devastating War

However, as I started writing the Norwegian edition of this book, political events in South Sudan in December 2013 took a dramatic turn for the worse. A simmering political conflict within SPLM exploded into a civil war. The President and Chairman of SPLM, Salva Kiir and his group of supporters mainly from the Dinka people, accused the opposing forces of an attempted coup d'etat and for this reason went to war against the opposition. This civil war has lasted since. More than one hundred thousand innocent people have lost their lives. The war has made more than 4 million homeless and forced most of them to seek refuge in neighbouring countries. At present, another 4 million, of a total number of some 10 – 11 million inhabitants are dependent on International humanitarian assistance for their survival. The economy is in ruin, inflation running close to 1000 percent, and the war has made the Dinka people the enemy of all the other 63 tribes in the country. This civil war has destroyed more in South Sudan than all the destructions that were done during the time of the liberation struggle. The capital Juba is again like it was during the time of the liberation struggle, an isolated island, in the midst of misery and death.

   I could not publish the English edition of the book without writing about this horrible experienc,e which has destroyed the future of the present generation of people in South Sudan. I could neither write about this horror without taking a stand on whom I hold as main responsible for the devastating war. I do not mince my words and I do this in chapter 20 of this edition.

Egil Hagen, the founding father of the NPA's Sudan Programme, had his first and secret meeting in the fall of 1985 in Addis Ababa with Deng Alor (below) one of the SPLM/A leaders at the time. They agreed that Egil Hagen should try and establish a humanitarian programme for the suffering peoples of South Sudan. Six months later Egil was in action in Nairobi.

3
THE BEGINNING OF THE NPA-SOUTH SUDAN PROGRAMME

The Covert Meeting in Addis Ababa in 1985

The history of Norwegian People's Aid's involvement in South Sudan is irrevocably connected to Egil Hagen.

In the fall of 1985, Egil Hagen was working on a six months' contract for UNICEF based in Khartoum. He was provoked by the indifference and arrogance shown by the Sudanese authorities concerning the people in the South, and how the UN system was indifferent in a way he saw as totally unacceptable.

Draught and war ravaged South Sudan at the time. Egil wanted to find better ways of supporting the starving people, and in the fall of 1985 he wrote to the Norwegian house-building company Block Watne to see if they had any work for him in East Africa. Erik Sunde was the sales director at Block Watne at that time and suggested that he could use Egil Hagen as a regional sales representative in East Africa in cooperation with UN and International NGOs, providing the market with low-cost housing for displaced persons and refugees. Erik Sunde met Egil Hagen in Khartoum, and together they travelled in secrecy to Addis Ababa in Ethiopia in the fall of 1985. They wanted to meet with the leaders of SPLM/A.

After some searching in the Ethiopian capital, in which everyday life was marked by the oppressive Mengistu dictatorship, they found the headquarters of SPLM/A, and a meeting was organized. It took place one evening in the restaurant at the Blue Nile Ras Hotel. Deng Alor, a member of the SPLM/A leadership, led the small delegation. Deng Alor was a Dinka and a close and trusted colleague of the Late Dr. John Garang. There were two more representatives from SPLM/A at the meeting, the late Dr. Justin Yaac Arop, the leader of SPLM's humanitarian division, Sudan Relief and Rehabilitation Agency (SRRA) and one more officer. On the other side of the table sat Egil Hagen and Erik Sunde.

Egil leaned over the table, towards Deng Alor and said: "*I know what is happening in your country. I have worked with the UN over the last few months, and I am frustrated and angry. Your people in the South are being horrendously assaulted and mistreated by the rulers in Khartoum. They are being denied food and are starving to death. I have given up working with the UN, but would like to help in your cause. I have worked previously with Norwegian People's Aid in Lebanon. What can I do to help?*"

Deng Alor listened to this man with a hoarse voice and an intense stare who sat on the other side of the table. Before he answered he took a minute to think, then he said: "*I know nothing about you or Norwegian People's Aid. We are fighting a just war for our people, but we are very alone. Our people in the South are faced with an enormous drought and hunger catastrophe, and we desperately need help.*"

Dr. Justin was also Dinka, very tall at two meters. He said: "*You can collaborate with the SRRA of which I am the Head, but you must have a humanitarian organization backing you. I don't know anything about Norwegian People's Aid either, but I know a little about Norway. It would helpful if Norwegian People's Aid were to be our partners."*

That was the gist of the conversation that evening in Addis Ababa. The next day Dr. Justin and Egil Hagen met again. Egil was given a letter from SRRA with an appeal for emergency relief and collaboration.

After the meetings in Addis Ababa, Egil Hagen travelled back to Norway for Christmas in 1985. We met at a café in Oslo during his holiday break, and he shared his experiences with the UN in Khartoum and the secret conversation in Addis Ababa with me.

He also mentioned that he had been employed by Block Watne as the Regional Manager for East Africa, and he added: *"This is my formal job. But my concern is the people in South Sudan. I want to help them with humanitarian assistance in all ways possible."*

Shortly after our encounter, Egil met with Erik Sunde and Vegard Bye who was the relief coordinator at NPA. Egil told them about his meeting with SPLM in Addis Ababa. The conversation turned to the situation in South Sudan and Egil asked whether Norwegian People's Aid would consider relief and humanitarian assistance to the peoples of South Sudan. Vegard responded that they would try to and suggested a meeting with the Head of the Advisory Committee of NPA on International Solidarity Work, Kaare Sandegren and Laila Nikolaisen, who at that time was Head of NPA's International Department.

Later, Erik Sunde told me he remembered that meeting very well. Kaare Sandegren took charge right away and was very positive towards both the involvement of NPA in Sudan and for the potential collaboration between NPA and Block Watne. They agreed that Egil Hagen would coordinate the efforts of Block Watne and NPA, with SRRA as the tentative partner, to ensure relief assistance for the peoples living in South Sudan.

The notion of NPA becoming a permanent partner with SRRA and thereby committing itself to a new and demanding project in South Sudan would have to be discussed later within the organization. But for now, as promised, Vegard Bye secured a small appropriation from the Ministry of Foreign Affairs for the first food relief consignment.

The first Food Relief
– the Problem-filled 1986 Consignment

Egil began working in Nairobi in the early months of 1986. After a short time, he took over the house and locations of Save the Children, Norway, that had left Kenya. His assignment was to procure contracts with the UN and International NGOs for services to be delivered by Block Watne. Erik Sunde was at that time on frequent assignments in East Africa during which he frequently met with Egil. On several occasions, they travelled to Addis Ababa and met with leaders of SPLM/A and SRRA.

Egil's heart lay with the people of South Sudan and to him that was his most important task.

There was drought, war, and hunger in South Sudan, and food relief was the priority. But the money granted by the Norwegian Ministry of Foreign Affairs through NPA covered only the cost of hiring a convoy of trucks. There was no money left for buying food. Egil had some frustrating conversations with people in the Emergency Sections of UN and ECHO, the humanitarian branch of EU, about getting food from their stores. Finally, one of EU's relief managers in Nairobi said that he would be away from the emergency store on an agreed day. Then Egil could drive up with his convoy and say that he had his permission to load the trucks.

The next problem to be solved was obtaining trucks. Transportation companies in Kenya were not willing to take the risk of driving into South Sudan. Both the drivers and trucks were targets, and the trucks risked being confiscated by the SPLA guerillas.

Finally, Egil met with a man from Eritrea. His name was Reedegayze. He had been a refugee in Norway, and he held a

Norwegian passport. He had previously worked with Norwegian Church Aid in South Sudan. Now he owned a transport company in Nairobi. He agreed to transport the food. A convoy of twelve trucks drove one day to the ECHO/EU store as agreed, and food was loaded on all the trucks. The next day the convoy headed towards South Sudan, led by Egil Hagen in a Landrover.

Two days later they crossed the border to Sudan and made a stop at the border town Narus. They were met by the SPLA guerillas under the command of Martin Manwiel. He was extremely skeptical of these white foreigners, and he knew nothing about any meetings in Addis Ababa nor the agreement between Egil and SPLM/A and SRRA. Egil used his skills of persuasion and showed Martin Manwiel the letter from Dr. Justin. Then, they were allowed to drive on.

But the truck drivers were Somalis and muslims. When they understood that they were bringing emergency food supplies to people who in their eyes were rebels in opposition to the Muslim regime in Khartoum, they refused to drive further.

Egil was faced with a difficult problem. Would the first relief transport he was responsible for end like this? He was angry, but his ability to find alternative solutions kicked in. He asked Manwiel if the SPLA could take the responsibility, provide for drivers and bring the food to the distribution centre. The commander who was not used to such suggestions from managers of international relief organizations, was taken by surprise, but agreed that the SPLA could do it.

In this way, Egil began a very important process of building trust with SRRA/SPLM/A. This proved to be essential to the spirit of cooperation between NPA and SRRA/SPLM/A, which developed in the following years.

The food was destined for the village Mogoth in Eastern Equatoria, but the road was mined. Therefore, SPLA had made tracks across the savanna landscape where there were no mines, and the NPA convoy, with drivers from SRRA, were ordered to stay in the tracks. Egil accompanied the convoy to Mogoth, and the food was delivered. This was how the first NPA Relief Convoy got its way into South Sudan.

What to do? Reluctance at the HQ of Norwegian People's Aid in Oslo

However, during the spring and summer of 1986, the cooperation between Egil Hagen and Norwegian People's Aid in Oslo became challenging. Egil pushed for more support, but in Oslo they were hesitant. NPA was still one of the smaller Norwegian humanitarian organizations even though they were entering a phase of growth. They had doubts as to if they had the capacity and the resources to commit themselves to prolonged support through SRRA for South Sudan. Therefore, the Secretary General Odd Wivegh, and the International Director, Laila Nikolaisen, decided late in the summer of 1986 to travel to Nairobi, to discuss with Egil the matter of future cooperation.

In Nairobi, Wivegh and Nikolaisen met with Egil who used his ability to persuade anyone who was not already convinced. In addition, Egil had set up an agenda with important meetings for the visitors, and they had an interesting and fulfilling political stay. They met with the powerful Permanent Secretary in the Ministry of Foreign Affairs of the Government of Kenya, Bethuel Kiplagat. Mr. Kiplagat was a strong personality and at the same time very charming with a strong ability to persuade, and he reassured the people from NPA that his government was very pleased to have NPA involved in humanitarian support for the peoples of South Sudan.

However, when the visitors from Oslo brought up the issue of obtaining legal status for NPA in Kenya, he responded that it was better for everybody that NPA kept its temporary status and had a low profile.

Wivegh and Nikolaisen did not approve of Egil's continued double role as a representative for Block Watne and at the same time doing practical relief work for NPA. He had to choose. After some consideration, Egil asked about the salary. Laila Nikolaisen immediately responded: "*Our salary is about 200 000 NOK less then what you get at Block Watne.*" Egil thought for a moment, and then he said: "*I choose NPA. The peoples of Sudan are closest to my heart.*"

In the following months, Egil managed to raise emergency aid support from an increasing number of international partners, and he intensified his efforts in South Sudan with food and medical supplies. He obtained some contributions from church organizations in Western Europe, first and foremost West Germany. At the same time, he used his network of American institutions and influential Americans from his time in Lebanon, to secure food and medicine from USA.

Even so, between 1986 and 1992 Egil operated with a small annual budget varying between five and ten million NOK, but more importantly, behind the budget was the personality and solidarity of the man, Egil Hagen. He worked long hours with the practical aspects of the relief operations, but from the very beginning, he developed a tradition of meetings and dialogs with leaders of SPLM/A and SRRA, where he left no doubt that he was politically on their side. But Egil Hagen was also a trained military officer from the National War College in Oslo. He had specialized on leading commando operations, and I take for granted that he, at times, might have discussed with the leadership of SPLA strategies and conducts of war.

A dangerous Mission in the Spring of 1987

In September of 1986, I was on leave from my position as Head of Information of Norad, and living in New Delhi with my wife Marit Berggrav, who was a staff member at the Norwegian Embassy in Charge of Development Cooperation. In India, I worked as a freelance journalist, while studying Indian history, politics and development.

One day in the winter of 1987, I received a call from Vegard Bye, the Relief and Emergency Coordinator at NPA. He briefed me about the relief cooperation in South Sudan that was developing between Egil Hagen and NPA. Vegard explained that Egil wanted a prolonged commitment from NPA. At Headquarters in Oslo they continued to be reluctant, and it was therefore necessary to conduct a field study to document the draught, the famine, and necessity for humanitarian assistance in South Sudan and the possibility of long term cooperation with SRRA.

"So, Halle, we need a politically minded person with experience from Africa to lead this work, and we want you." This was an exciting assignment, something I could not turn down.

Three weeks later I landed in Nairobi and met with Egil Hagen and Vegard Bye. During the next few days we discussed the mission with the three members of the team, the British nutrition/health specialist Jane MacAskill, Assistant Professor in Social Anthropology, University of Bergen, Erik Eriksen, and the Canadian water engineer Phillip Parry. SPLM's humanitarian organization, SRRA, would have two members joining us inside Sudan.

Meeting the Permanent Secretary in the Ministry of Foreign Affairs in Kenya

Egil arranged a meeting with the Permanent Secretary in the Ministry of Foreign Affairs, Bethuel Kiplagat. We met with a very friendly, accommodating man who had great political knowledge and insight and a particular interest for the conflict in Sudan.

Kiplagat praised Egil profusely and was especially pleased that NPA had begun providing emergency relief in Sudan. Kiplagat was open about the fact that Kenya de facto supported the liberation struggle in the South, but that the government officially maintained a neutral position. Then we talked about the upcoming mission, which he thought would be acceptable to Kenya and important for the future planning of the programme.

Towards the end of our conversation we discussed the future funding of the emergency operation. Kiplagat smiled and said:

"The government and I do not have money for these things, but I have a purse for myself. If you ever get into trouble, come to me."

Before we left, Vegard broached the subject about Norwegian People's Aid not being officially registered in Kenya, asking if that could be a problem. Kiplagat smiled again: "*No, it is in no way a problem. We welcome you, but for now let it be the way it is, your status is temporary. When you reach Lokichokio in Turkana, I want you to contact the local authorities, the District Commissioner and Chief.*"

With that, our visit was over, and we felt sure that we had the support of the Kenyan government.

A Mission with many Surprises and Obstacles

It was difficult to obtain cars, tents and other camping equipment for the trip. No company in Nairobi providing services for long safaris into the wilderness of Kenya, wanted to lend out anything for this kind of trip because the risk was too high. We were going into a war zone and could potentially end up in the middle of fighting. No insurance company was neither willing to take the risk.

We did not know what to do next, but then Egil's drivers found a rental agency in the industrial area in Nairobi. This agency lent out used cars, tents and camping equipment, and would do so with the Norwegian People's Aid's self-insurance. Four well-used Landrovers, tents and other necessary equipment were rented. Large amounts of food and water were purchased for the three-week long journey, for which we had to bring all our own supplies.

Early one morning, our journey began through Kenya. It is a beautiful landscape to drive through. Leaving the highlands of Nairobi moving north, we passed thousands of small farms with colorful vegetation and people at work. Beautiful flowering trees lined the road until the steep descent leading down to the Great Rift Valley, and then gradually climbing again to the highlands on the other side of the valley with vast grain fields, fields with thousands of cattle grazing, and large forested areas. Everywhere people were busy working their farms.

Eventually after another long drive through the semi-dessert area leading into Turkana we reached Lokichokio, at the time, a small village in Turkana not far from the border to Sudan. We located the residence of the Chief, and a very friendly man came forward. He said he had been told that we were coming and that we, of course, should stay with him in his compound for the night. He was a very hospitable man and ordered a goat to be slaughtered for dinner.

After a pleasant dinner, we crawled into bed under a beautiful starry sky, animal sounds were the only thing that could be heard in the tropical night. We were up early the next morning, ready for the next leg, when two Kenyan officers from the military camp nearby approached us.

They greeted us politely and asked what kind of mission we were on. I thought for a minute; what was all this about? Then I decided to explain about the NPA, the conversation with Kiplagat, the mission in Sudan, in short, to tell them everything. When I was finished, one of them said: "*We were notified in advance about this expedition, but still wanted to check on you. We appreciate your honesty and wish you well on your journey. You have a challenging task ahead of you.*"

Who were they? They were two friendly intelligence officers from the Kenyan Army, who were patrolling the border to Sudan, most likely trained by British or Israeli intelligence experts.

Inside Southern Sudan

We were now driving in a semi-arid area, and not long after we passed the border, a small group of SPLA soldiers approached us, wanting to know who we were. As soon as we said we were NPA, Norwegian People's Aid, everything was fine. They too had been informed about our arrival and mission and told us that we were to have four fully-armed SPLA soldiers as guards, as well as two local SRRA members to accompany us during our work in South Sudan.

Before we continued the journey, we were given strict orders to stay in the established tire tracks when we drove in open fields because large areas of the fields we were to travel through, were mined. Therefore, if we did not stay in the tracks, we risked driving on a landmine and in the worst of circumstances get killed. The mission took on a dangerous dimension that none of us had been told about in advance.

We drove with the SPLA guards in the cars until we reached the small village of Narus. At the edge of the village two unexploded bombs lay stuck in the dirt, one on each side of the road. We asked our SPLA/SRRA escorts what they were. They explained that these were barrel bombs dropped from a Russian Antonov plane that the Khartoum regime used to bomb civilian targets. Each bomb contained explosives, pieces of metal and nails, weighing between 200 and 500 kilograms.

When it exploded in a crowd, it had a devastating impact. Many would be killed immediately, while others would be wounded and some crippled, having to walk around for the rest of their lives with metal shrapnel in their bodies, as there were no or very few hospitals in the area. The SPLA officer explained that sometimes the bombs did not explode. These two bombs had landed in wet, swampy earth during the rainy season and did not explode for this reason. SPLA had sent for experts to come and disarm them.

WHO IS WHO?

The SPLA soldiers had another message for us that did not make the journey any easier. While the SPLA had their groups of guerilla soldiers in the area, Khartoum had paid local leaders to organize local militia groups to fight against them. We could be attacked by such a group, and it was not easy to tell the difference between the two groups. Both groups belonged to the Toposa people who were either naked or wore very little clothing on the savanna. There was, however, one difference. The SPLA always had Kalashnikov rifles, whereas the militia groups usually had old rifles with long barrels.

Consequently, every time we saw someone moving ahead on the track, we used the binoculars to see what kind of weapons they were carrying. We met several people with weapons, but luckily they all had Kalashnikovs rifles.

During our first night, inside South Sudan, we slept on folding cots, again under an open, starry sky with a family with cattle penned up next to us. We had flashlights and the glow from the campfire for light, so it was an early evening.

We used the next day to gather different information required for our study. The social anthropologist evaluated the way of living and local sustainability with respect to food production. The crops were small, and it was obvious that if the farmers had more knowledge and better technology and methods they could increase the crop yield. Jane examined their nutrition and health. There were many malnourished and hungry children, but also the women, their mothers were undernourished. The Canadian examined accessibility to clean water. Norwegian Church Aid had worked in the area before the war and had made several water holes, but the pumps no longer worked. There was a shortage of spare parts, and the pumps needed maintenance or repair, before they could function again. I discussed politics, the liberation struggle, supply lines and transportation with the people from SRRA, SPLM, and SPLA and tried to gain an overview of the situation.

Rich wild Life, but for how long?

When we finished with our work in the village, we headed for Boma town, the SPLA Headquarter on the border with Ethiopia. There was no road that way either, and we had to stay in the tire tracks. There was a constant danger of hitting landmines while we were inside Sudan.

As we travelled, we suddenly heard intense gunfire, both small and larger weapons. Were we about to be attacked? The SPLA guards gave the order to stop. They went ahead to assess the situation. When they returned, they told us that there was no danger, it was only SPLA soldiers hunting for food.

When we started driving again, we experienced something I have never seen in my life and probably never will again. A very large flock of wild animals, primarily antelopes and gazelles, but also bigger animals, zebra, wildebeest and giraffes crossed the road in front of us. It was like a vast flood passing in front, and it lasted for a couple of hours before we could continue driving.

After another couple of hours on the savanna, we saw something moving in the bush. Soon after, four or five tractors appeared loaded with dead animals that the SPLA soldiers had shot. Our SPLA guards quickly contacted them, and informed them about who we were. We got permission to continue and were soon on our way again. But it was impossible not to see that some of the soldiers were drunk. Another unpleasant observation we made was that they were using automatic weapons for hunting, and that they had killed several animals, between 50 and 70.

Just as the sun set, we drove into Boma. This was SPLA's main headquarters, and the town was heavily influenced by SPLA's military presence. There were soldiers with wives and children, and weapons and equipment everywhere, most of which had origins in Soviet Union or East Europe, but came via Ethiopia.

The leaders of SPLM/A present welcomed us with open arms, and for the rest of the evening we discussed politics. Later we were invited to a great barbeque dinner, with wild game on the menu.

(Before the liberation war started in 1983, there had always been large flocks of wild game in Sudan, particularly in South Sudan. Perhaps even the largest game population in Africa. In 1987 there were still many wild game left, and it was possible to experience what we had experienced. But after the Peace Agreement in 2005,

there were very few wild game remaining. Most had been shot and used as food for the soldiers.

However, in the peace period between 2005 and 2013 the number of wild game increased dramatically in the new, emerging state of South Sudan. It was about to regain the reputation of having very big herds of game which in some years with tourism developing might have become a potentially important source of income both for local people and public authorities.

But since the civil war broke out in December 2013, the soldiers have only had erratic food supplies and had to go back to the old practice of hunting game. Soldiers on both sides in the war have slaughtered enormous amounts of game for food.

Now in August 2016 all reports about the state of affairs carry one main message when it comes to South Sudan's vast herds of game. The game population is this time threatened with extinction because of the new war. Yet, even worse in the present state of lawlessness in South Sudan, foreigners have been paying large amounts of money to irresponsible warlords on both sides to hunt wild game. They have been flown in by helicopter to locate flocks of giraffes, elephants, and rhinoceros, and they have killed these animals in large numbers. The latest reports from South Sudan indicate that there are at best only a few hundred giraffes and elephants remaining.)

Shaft Trouble, one Landrover breaks down

After a few days in Boma, where we discussed the possibility of future cooperation about humanitarian assistance with the leader in SRRA/SPLM/A, we began our journey back. The goal for the day was to reach an area controlled by the SPLA just outside of the garrison town Kapoeta in Eastern Equatoria. The town itself was controlled by Khartoum's forces.

At first everything was fine, but suddenly one of the Landrovers came to a halt. The transfer axel from the motor to the drive shaft had loosened and fallen off.

We had only one choice, to tow the car and hope that we would arrive around darkness. We did better than expected, and reached our destination just at the time of darkness.

The next morning, we discussed our options and agreed that Phillip should drive back to Lodwar in Turkana and try to find spare parts there. Norad had, at that time, several large projects in Turkana and a workshop in Lodwar. Phillip set course for Turkana and was expected to be back late the next day.

The Antonov Bombers attacking?

Meanwhile, the next day we all started work on our individual assignments. We had just gotten started, when we heard the sound we feared most, Antonov planes. Two aircraft circled above us, and we knew that if they did not bomb right away, they were taking pictures so they could be more precise if they returned. The risk of an aerial bomb attack was very real, and the decision to move was made without hesitation. We packed and drove as fast as possible away from the nakedness of the savanna and into the woods. Luckily, the planes did not return.

The reason for the Antonov planes flying over us was most certainly that a spy from the Khartoum's regime somewhere along our travel route, maybe even while we were in Nairobi, had learnt about the mission and reported it. The Khartoum regime wanted to let us know that they knew about our whereabouts and were ready for action.

Later in the history of NPA in South Sudan the staff learned that there were spies, agents and informants in the most surprising of places throughout the long war, and terror bombing of civilian targets was an important part of Khartoum's war strategy.

While hiding in the woods, we waited for Phillip to return with the spare parts so that we could repair the Landrover, but Phillip never returned.

The evening came and with it a full moon. We decided not to wait any longer, but to start our journey back to Kenya that same night, with the broken Landrover in tow. We found the tire tracks and drove by the light of the moon without headlights. The drivers were skilled and the guards from SPLA knew the area. But anything could happen. The sound of the engines in the quiet of the night could be heard by people and animals from a long distance. Each time we had a short break, we listened in complete silence. Was anyone or anything out there? An enemy militia group or dangerous wild animals? But nothing happened.

In the middle of the night we had to cross a dry riverbed. It was no easy task. We found a part of the riverbank with a gradual slope and drove the first car over, then the next car with the damaged car in tow. Everything went well until we tried to get up on the other side of the river bank. There was not enough motor power in one car to pull the other. So, we had to level part of the riverbank, and then tie the damaged car to both the others to pull it up. It worked, but just barely. Having crossed the river, we felt that we were in safer terrain, only a few kilometers from the border of Kenya.

Return to Turkana, but where was Phillip?

We arrived in Lodwar in the early dawn, and found Norad's guest house. But my back had not managed the strenuousness of the ten-day journey off-road in old cars with poor shock absorbers. I had such serious back pain that I was barely able to move when we arrived in Turkana. Luckily I knew a Norwegian couple who worked for Save the Children, Svein Erik Odden and his wife Grete. They were very hospitable and took great care of me until my back recovered.

We agreed that Jane would take charge of the group until I recovered, and her first task was to find Phillip. At the mechanic workshop, they were told that Phillip had been there and gotten the parts. But he had told them that he wanted to let loose before returning. So, Jane and the others searched the bars in Lodwar, and finally found Phillip, in very bad shape, in the company of one of the barmaids.

The Report, - Observations and Recommendations

After a few days of rest, I recovered from my back pains. The Landrover was repaired, and we could head back to Nairobi, where we had a week to write the report.

The most important observations were the high level of conflict, drought, hunger and lack of food in parts of Eastern Equatoria, as was the case in most of South Sudan. The situation for women and children was extremely difficult because of the intense fighting, compounded with their weak status in traditional society. Nutrition for children in some areas was extraordinarily poor, with considerable undernutrition and malnutrition. Access to clean water near their homes would improve the situation greatly.

We recommended a substantial amount of food relief, but in such a way that it would reinforce the farmers' abilities to produce more local food, not undermine it. They could sell surplus from their produce to NPA that in return would distribute this food in areas with hunger and great need.

The cattle suffered from numerous diseases, and we recommended a vaccination project, which was something the farmers also supported.

SRRA was a new organization with a weak structure and lack of local leadership. In Eastern Equatoria, for example, none of the leaders of SRRA spoke the language of the Toposa, only Juba-Arabic and Dinka. We also noticed that some of the leaders and staff in general in the organization had problems with alcohol.

In the report, we pointed out these weaknesses, but we could not suggest any alternative to SRRA. We emphasized that SRRA was a new organization, and suggested that NPA should establish a project to develop SRRA as an organization. In this way SRRA could be an important contribution to what remained of civil society in South Sudan.

Based on what we learnt during our mission, we advised Norwegian People's Aid to establish a formalized agreement with SRRA. Our recommendation to politically support the liberation struggle was inherent in the proposed cooperation.

During our brief stay in Eastern Equatoria, we met with representatives of two other relief organizations, The International Red Cross and Doctors Without Borders. We worked well with these organizations, and were given access to material from studies they had done on the state of nutrition and living conditions in the area.

Norwegian People's Aid takes a Stand, and Foreign Minister Thorvald Stoltenberg approves

Upon return to Nairobi we had lengthy discussions with Egil Hagen about our findings and the written report. We agreed on the main issues, and then I travelled to Oslo to hand over the report to the NPA Headquarters.

Ivar Christiansen began his work as Head of Information of NPA in 1989, and his recollection from memory of the situation in the summer of 1987 was the following: "*It was not given that NPA would support the peoples of South Sudan. Rightly enough, Odd Wivegh and Laila Nikolaisen had been in Nairobi in the summer of 1986, but that resulted only in support for small projects. That was the situation when your report was tabled.*"

The report was first presented to the staff of the International Department and then to the Management Group with the Secretary General in charge. After some discussion, the Management Group and the Board of NPA accepted our recommendations and decided to support the liberation struggle. In the late summer of 1987, NPA sent an application with our report attached, to the Ministry of Foreign Affairs requesting 20 million NOK for its new solidarity programme in South Sudan in cooperation with SRRA.

The application went through the normal procedures at the Ministry of Foreign Affairs, but met with much resistance on its way. Norwegian Church Aid (NCA) had been the largest programme operator on behalf of the Norwegian Government in South Sudan since 1973, and they felt a kind of intrinsic right when it came to Norwegian NGOs operating in South Sudan. Leading members of NCA therefore lobbied key staff at the Ministry, and used as arguments against NPA both Egil Hagen's rather unconventional working methods in the field and the political fact that NPA had taken a stand in favour of the rebellion. Leading NCA staff members persuaded the Ministry to reject the application. The top officials of the Ministry in their final judgment referred to the NPA collaboration with SRRA being the humanitarian branch of SPLM, and the fact that NPA had taken a stand supporting the liberation struggle, and they concluded that for those reasons it was not possible for the Ministry and the Government to grant money to NPA. A letter from the Ministry then followed, stating that the application was rejected.

NO from the Ministry and NPA makes use of its Right to appeal

NPA used its right of appeal, changed some of the content in the application and sought a meeting with the new Foreign Minister, Thorvald Stoltenberg, from the Labour Party who recently had taken over after the death of his predecessor, Knut Frydenlund.

Stoltenberg had at the time more experience with and insight into African peoples' liberation struggles than any other Norwegian politician. Already at the end of the 1960s, he had as a young diplomat been used as a trouble shooter and had been sent on missions by Foreign Minister John Lyng, from the Conservative Party, to countries in Africa where people struggled for their freedom from their colonial masters. Whenever Stoltenberg returned from these missions, he had to make policy recommendations that sometimes went straight to the Minister himself.

His recommendations became sometimes the foundation for future government policies. In 1969, the Foreign Minister John Lyng, in a centre-right coalition government at the time approved the first Norwegian allocation for humanitarian aid to a liberation movement. It was given to FRELIMO in Mozambique.

Almost 20 years later, Stoltenberg himself was the Minister and the decision maker. He read the appeal and the renewed application from NPA, and he considered the reasons given by his own senior staff for rejecting the first application. He did not like the reasoning behind the rejection, and he called his political advisor in the Ministry, the clergyman and Labour politician Trond Bakkevig and said: *"Trond, look at this. NPA wants money for humanitarian relief in Sudan in collaboration with SRRA, the humanitarian wing of the SPLM. Our administration has rejected the application on grounds of principle. I want you to read through this. If you conclude that we shall accept the application and grant the money, I shall agree with you and override the administration's decision and approve the amount applied for to the project."*

The two talked about the case for a while, then Trond took the papers to read them. He concluded that NPA at times had a somewhat dogmatic political language in the text, and he had a couple of meetings with the NPA leadership about this. NPA agreed to modify the language a bit and a key point in the new text was that if a situation emerged in the field with a need for immediate support for both parties in the conflict, then such aid should be provided.

Bakkevig went back to Stoltenberg with the new text from NPA and recommended the application be accepted. Stoltenberg kept his word and NPA was given its first grant for humanitarian assistance behind the front lines in Sudan in cooperation with SRRA. The Foreign Minister at the same time approved of the principle that NPA and other Norwegian NGOs in a given situation could take a political solidarity stand in a given conflict in a foreign country.

Stoltenberg's decision had, in my opinion, ramifications that no one could imagine at the time. The decision created precedence for other governments, both Norwegian and foreign, and it also eased the decision of other international non-governmental organizations to support NPA's work in Sudan. Indeed, from the middle of the 1990s, UN-agencies, in limited ways, also became partners in the endeavour.

On the other hand, had Stoltenberg accepted the decision of his administration and said no, Norwegian People's Aid would not have been able to develop and maintain the humanitarian assistance and development cooperation behind the frontlines in South Sudan that continued up to the Peace Agreement in 2005 and after. It is also highly unlikely that any other international NGO would have been willing to support the same principles of solidarity as was the guiding principles in NPA's work.

What would have happened in Sudan without the role played by Norwegian People's Aid? No one will know for sure, but some reflections about the impact of this decision are allowed.

If the regime in Khartoum, sometime in the early 1990s when SPLM/A was at its weakest, had defeated SPLM/A and reestablished its political and physical control of the whole of Sudan, the southern areas of the country included, we would today, de facto have had the same Islamist dictatorial regime that in a coup d'état in 1989 took power, still governing the whole country.

That regime, which in political and military terms, would have been much stronger than the present one in Khartoum, would today have been bordering the neighboring countries of Ethiopia, Kenya, and Uganda. I do not believe that such a situation would have contributed to political stability, peace and development in the Horn of Africa.

On the other hand, the present misrule in the now, new and failed state of South Sudan was impossible to foresee at the time. It is important to keep in mind that during the hard years of the liberation struggle, the visionary and now legendary John Garang was in charge. But he was killed on 30th of July 2005 in what is still called a helicopter accident. If Garang in the period from 2005 and until now had continued to be in charge, South Sudan could today have been a very different and peaceful place where its citizens could have been enjoying the fruits of peace and development.

4
A TURNING POINT

The Catholic Priest Dan Eiffe joins NPA

Norwegian People's Aid decided in the summer of 1991 to employ Dan Eiffe from Ireland as a new member of the small staff in Nairobi. He was trained as a priest in the Catholic Church of Ireland, and his doctorate thesis was on liberation theology. During the 1980s he was a priest in the ghettoes in South Africa, where he had been very active in the fight against apartheid.

At some point in 1990, he came to Juba and worked for a volunteer organization. In that job, he was a consultant, in which he described five different scenarios for the future of South Sudan. As a consultant, he experienced firsthand SPLA's brutality towards its own people. So, when he started working for NPA's Sudan programme in the summer of 1991, he was quite critical of SPLM/A and its Chairman/Commander in Chief, the late Dr. John Garang.

Dan Eiffe has many qualities that I, over time, have come to appreciate a lot. His core values are rooted in the values of the International Labour Movement. He has vast knowledge and insightful understanding of African society, particularly about the peoples and communities of South Sudan. He is a remarkable speaker and has a unique ability to persuade an audience. These were traits NPA badly came to need in the fall of 1991.

When he in the summer of 1991 for the first time visited the NPA's headquarters in Oslo, he was briefed on NPA's Sudan Programme and the fact that NPA had taken a stand in solidarity support of the peoples' rebellion against the oppressors in Khartoum. The leaders in NPA also told Dan how difficult it was for them that both the Norwegian and International media carried so much criticism of SPLM/A and its Chairman, John Garang.

On August 27, 1991, shocking news came from the little town of Nasir in South Sudan. Two of the high ranking commanders of SPLM/A, Riek Machar and Lam Akol had rebelled against what was said to be the dictatorial leadership of John Garang from the Dinka people, and they had apparently taken over SPLM/A.

The news was highly exaggerated. Garang was on his way home from a visit abroad. As soon as he returned, he took command, but now of a divided liberation organization. SPLM/A was now to a large extent divided along ethnic lines. Riek Machar was a chief among the Nuer and Lam Akol was a high ranking member of the traditional Shilluk Kingdom. Many people from these two groups followed their leaders in the rebellion against Garang

The rebels, Riek Machar and Lam Akol, called their faction SPLM/A United while John Garang called what remained, SPLM/A Mainstream.

John Garang had no traditional social status. He was a poor boy from the countryside and belonged to the Dinka from Jonglei. Salva Kiir became his second in command and belonged to the Dinka from Bahr el Ghazal and Warrap.

A few days after the events in Nasir, Dan Eiffe started his new job in Nairobi and went immediately to Nasir to find out what had happened during the split. A few weeks later, in November 1991, he found himself in the middle of the massacre in Bor. He filmed and photographed the terrible scenes of violence and death only hours after the worst crimes were committed.

For the first time ever, he came in direct contact with John Garang and his closest colleagues. This changed Dan's opinion about the conflict, and he became one of NPA's most dedicated workers when it came to supporting SRRA/SPLM/A Mainstream.

In the Centre of the Conflict in Nasir and Bor

In a conversation, we had in the fall of 2013, Dan told me the following:

"*I was given permission from NPA in Oslo to go to Nasir and then Bor. This was only a few days after the rebellion. When I arrived in Nasir, I met with the Secretary General of Norwegian Church Aid, Jan P. Erichsen. He was with Bona Malwal, a traditional Dinka chief, a Christian, and one of the Dinka intellectuals, and they both supported the rebellion.*

I had a good relationship with Norwegian Church Aid's people in Torit and I pointed out to Erichsen that it was not entirely clear which side should be supported. He was not interested in discussing the matter. He was in favour of the rebellion against Garang and invited Lam Akol who was one of the two leaders of the rebellion to Oslo. Norwegian Church Aid paid for the travel and accommodations, Lam Akol stayed at the SAS Radisson Plaza for several days before travelling to other cities in Western Europe, sponsored by other European NGO's.

Norwegian media at the time based all of their reports and articles on Lam Akol's presentation of the conflict as well as other similar sources provided by Norwegian Church Aid. The media in Europe did the same. The founder of Doctors Without Borders, the French Undersecretary of State for Development Aid and Humanitarian Assistance at the time, Bernhard Kouchner, flew in his own plane to Nasir to give his public support and thereby the support of the French Government to the rebels. Local UN leaders and Ameri-

can politicians who were flown in from Washington, did the same. The rebels in Nasir were the heroes, John Garang and his co-leaders were the criminals, also because they were seen to be a kind of communists.

On November 15, 1991 as Lam Akol was travelling around Europe, forces from the rebel group SPLA/United, with the Nuer "White Army", attacked SPLA/Mainstream's forces and the civilian population in Bor and surrounding villages. The Nuer's "White Army" was formed earlier in the fall of 1991 by Riek Machar and other Nuer leaders. It consisted of adolescents trained to commit atrocious acts. What happened was terrible. They killed everyone they met from the Dinka, and in awful ways. Several thousand bodies of women and children, young and old were strewn everywhere. The scene was appalling. I took pictures and filmed.

Then I travelled as fast as I could back to Torit and hurried straight to the NCA compound and met with the NCA man in Charge, Jon Bjørndal. We were friends and on good terms, and Jon received me well. At this point in time, the news about the massacres had started to reach media outlets in Norway and Europe, and five Norwegian reporters had arrived in Torit. Bjørndal gathered the five journalists and representatives of International NGOs present in Torit in his house and said: "You should listen to Dan Eiffe. He is our consciousness when it comes to telling the truth about what has happened in Bor."

In the beginning the Norwegian journalists were very aggressive and critical, but then I showed my films and pictures. That changed their attitude, and one of the Norwegians reported back to his newspaper with the following headlines:
**THE POL POTS OF SOUTH SUDAN,
RIEK MACHAR AND LAM AKOL.**

Evening and night followed my briefing. I felt outraged, shaken and very tired by what I had experienced. I thought of my wife and the twins in Nairobi and cried as I fell asleep.

The next day I called NPA in Oslo and told them that I was about to travel to Nairobi and have a press conference about what

I had experienced in Bor. The NPA management in Oslo was for a while a little uncertain whether I should do this, but then they agreed.

In the morning hours a UN plane landed in Torit on its way to Nairobi, but the captain refused to take me as a passenger because I belonged to the very controversial NPA. We had frequently criticized UN for its indifference, and we were not part of OLS. This was their way of paying back.

However, the local management of the US World Vision in Torit reacted very sharply and demanded the captain to accept me as one of their staff members. So in this way I got to Nairobi.

As soon as I was in Nairobi, I travelled to Chester House, the hub of the Nairobi based foreign correspondents. I immediately approached the famous Kenyan filmmaker Mohammed Amin and the CNN Correspondent and gave my films and pictures to them for their free use. Mohammed Amin, who at the time was a world famous photographer, and the CNN guy composed a film documentary about the Bor massacre that was broadcast all over and choked the world.

The week after, I returned to Bor to follow up my documentary work, and I for the first time met with John Garang himself. He was updated about my former visit and the documentaries made, and he as very grateful indeed for my work and the NPA support. We had a very good conversation, and thereafter for as long as he lived, we frequently met and talked about the war and the dreams about peace and freedom for the peoples of all Sudan and in particular South Sudan.

Upon return to Nairobi from my second visit to Bor, I together with Peter Arnett, who was another of the famous TV reporters at the time, made another 30 minutes' documentary on the Bor massacre. The film was immediately used by BBC and NBC/USA, and we had 30 copies made, which were distributed free of charge to broadcasting companies having an interest. Furthermore, we selected about 100 still-pictures with some of the worst cases from the massacre which were sent to media outlets all over the world and used by for instance TIME and Newsweek.

PRESS BRIEFING

Southern Sudan Under Siege

Contact: Gabrielle Bushman
(202) 347-3507
gbushman@irsa-uscr.org

War, regular bombing, widespread famine and massive population displacement have shattered normal life in southern Sudan. Norwegian People's Aid (NPA) has operated one of the largest aid programs in southern Sudan for 11 years.

By providing assistance to southern Sudan outside the framework of the UN's Operation Lifeline Sudan (OLS), NPA has avoided many of the restrictions imposed on OLS relief efforts by the Sudanese government. NPA has a close working relationship with the main Sudanese rebel group and has long engaged in open advocacy on Sudanese issues. NPA describes itself as a non-neutral agency working in solidarity with the people of southern Sudan.

Mr. Eiffe will discuss humanitarian conditions in south Sudan, the political roots of the current famine, and will offer his political analysis based on his 11 years of personal experience living and working in the Sudan region. Mr. Eiffe will express the views of NPA, as well as his personal views.

Political lobby work in Washington.

It was in this way in an interplay with the big international media networks that NPA and I won the big media battle internationally about what had actually happened in Bor. In the aftermath of that we, the staff in Nairobi and in the field, had a lot of praise from NPA in Oslo.

However, at the same time NPA and myself had to face severe criticism from the UN Heads in Charge of the operations in Sudan. The Head of OLS at the time was a Swede, Thomas Ekvall. He had immediately sided with Riek Machar and Lam Akol when they rebelled in August, and in December 1991 he ordered for food to be flown from the UN emergency stores in Lokichokio to the rebels in Nasir.

Ekvall once came to our office in Nairobi and demanded that the film documentaries that I had made together with Peter Arnett, should not be distributed. But I contacted NPA Oslo on the matter, they flatly refused Ekvall's demand and encouraged us to continue distributing the material. The conflict between Ekvall and the SPLM/A/Mainstream eventually became so bitter that Ekvall was made persona non-grata in SPLM/A controlled areas.

Media and political Influence

Dan Eiffe continues:

We in NPA's Sudan Programme were always short of money, but despite this we almost always managed to put some money away earmarked for action with reporters on short notice.

We did that in 1998. Early in that year our people in the field as well as SRRA and SPLM/A reported that the rains had failed in large areas in the northern parts of South Sudan and that a drought and hunger catastrophe was in the making. The situation was also worsened by intense war activities in the same areas.

In addition, the Khartoum regime had banned all OLS airdrops of food in the areas struck by the catastrophe. We sent out to UN and all other agencies our first early warning messages in February 1998, but the response from UN and others was that we were exaggerating, there was no substance in what we said. We repeated our warnings in April, but again no response.

Then in May 1998 we invited 12 foreign and local correspondents to travel with us into the field to see for themselves. Many more showed an active interest to travel. We had a plane that could seat 12 journalists, and we had to cooperate with the Foreign Correspondents' Club in Nairobi about the selection of the 12. In the end BBC, CNN, Reuters, AFP, AP and seven others travelled. The visit was very well planned in cooperation with SRRA and SPLM/A. The security for the journalists was a top priority."

From a journalist's perspective, it was a successful trip. They returned convinced that there was a famine. It was exacerbated by the military actions in the area, and by the fact that Khartoum was banning airdrops of food. A few days later, headlines all over the world read:

"**New drought and famine in the war-devastated Sudan, hundreds of thousands might die.**"

This time the UN got awakened and sent a strong appeal for international emergency assistance. A new and very large emergency effort began. But it was too late. The famine in Sudan in late summer and the fall of 1998 took the lives of more than 200 000 people. Had the NPA appeal from February 1998 been listened to, and the relief had come sooner, fewer people would have died.

Once again, NPA's mobilization of international media played an important role in the mobilization of world support to combat the 1998 famine.

Dan Eiffe was invited several times to Washington to brief congressional committees regarding the developments in Sudan. During his visits, he would meet with the press and non-governmental organizations. One of his visits took place in August 1998, and Dan told me the following story from that visit:

"As a representative of NPA I was in August 1998 invited to meetings and hearings in committees of the USA Congress. The main theme was the famine and the hunger catastrophe in South Sudan. But I also had the opportunity at many occasions to speak about the peoples' rebellion against the dictatorial regime in Khartoum, its historical background and context, the liberation struggle and how the freedom war evolved. I also frequently criticized the international oil companies for supporting for the regime in Khartoum and their exploitation of natural resources, which we considered illegal.

My visit to Washington came in the aftermath of the Al Quaida's terrorist attacks with the bombings of the US embassies in Nairobi and Dar es Salaam. In Nairobi 213 people were killed and about 4000 wounded. There were less casualties in Dar es Salaam.

I was well informed about Osama bin Laden, his longtime stay in Khartoum and his close cooperation with the Khartoum regime at the time. Of course, I had some comments and reflections on this in my briefings and lectures in Washington. No doubt, I and NPA at the time experienced a lot of good will and support in Washington."

Sten Rino Bonsaksen who was the NPA Resident Representative from 1999, said the following about NPA and the media:
"*During my time, as Resident Representative the media were losing interest in the profound tragedy that was evolving in Sudan. There was a kind of apathetic fatigue in response to Sudan conflict. Therefore, it was important for us to mobilize interest at every opportunity possible. I often had a Kenyan journalist or international correspondent with me when I travelled into to South Sudan.*

When there were problems or dramatic events in South Sudan, we rented a plane and invited groups of journalists to see for themselves. It was always successful. At other times, we were asked to take American politicians into South Sudan who wanted to see firsthand the situation in the field."

As Secretary General of NPA I had many encounters with journalists and the media.

From 1986, when Egil Hagen started in Nairobi, to 1993, the Norwegian media showed a considerable interest in the war, famine and the general situation in Sudan and East Africa. Reporters such as Gunnar Kopperud, who wrote for *Dagbladet*, *Arbeiderbladet* and some other papers and weeklies, were central in covering NPA's work and the developments in the field of Sudan.

TV-reporter Rune Larsen from NRK, Norwegian Broadcasting Corporation, also took a great interest. The same goes for the German-Norwegian priest and freelance reporter Jochen Schilde, who made many documentaries out of Sudan.

But from the mid-1990s a kind of media-fatigue struck the Norwegian media when it came to developments in Sudan and Africa in general.

From the middle of the 1990s and for a long period, most pieces written about NPA's involvement in Sudan were quite critical and connected to the rumours about gun-running.

Many things happened in the Sudan programme during the fall of 1998. At that time, there was a freelance journalist in Nairobi who also wrote for the prominent Norwegian newspaper, *Aftenposten* (Evening Post). She was invited to join some of NPA's staff on a mission inside South Sudan, and agreed immediately. But first she had to check with her foreign news editor. Unfortunately, she was told she could not go because the security was insufficient. At this point NRK's Africa correspondent had just returned from a tour with NPA inside South Sudan.

Our situation was different with the international media. We had a consistently good relationship with positive interest for NPA's activities, especially after 1992. There was always a security risk when going into the areas of conflict in South Sudan. But with respect to the international media and NGO community, NPA was known for being a safe partner to travel with. Over time, we had developed an excellent system of communication and security. This was made in close cooperation with SRRA, who worked very closely with SPLA intelligence network. They made it a high priority to ensure that nothing happened to airplanes chartered by NPA, and to NPA vehicles in the field, especially when there were journalists travelling with them. Therefore, *CNN*, *Reuter*, the *Washington Post*, The *Guardian*, The *Daily Nation*, the *Associated Press*, *Agence France-Presse* and many others again and again travelled safely with NPA into South Sudan.

When it came to foreign politicians and diplomats, many travelled with us for the same reason. During the entire period 1986 - 2001, there were about 20 American Congress representatives and many American diplomats travelling with us. The Nederland's Minister of Development, Jan Pronk, travelled with us, the world-famous photographer Sebastiao Salgado and many others. The goal for these trips was to see NPA's projects and to gain an understanding about the conflict and its complexity.

With all this great international interest, it was strange to take note of the fact that with two exceptions, as far as I can recall, no Norwegian Minister, State Secretary, Member of Parliament, or Senior Official officially ever travelled into South Sudan with NPA in the 13 years between 1986 and 1999.

One of the exceptions was in 1999 when the Chairman of the Board for NPA, Harald Øveraas, invited the Labour Party member of Parliament Kjell Engebretsen and the Chair of the Labour Youth Movement (AUF), Anniken Huitfeldt, to travel with him and leading staff members into South Sudan.

Kjell Engebretsen was the first and last Member of Parliament who travelled there before the Comprehensive Peace Agreement in 2005. Anniken was the first AUF member, but many more followed her example.

The second exception to this de facto rule for Norwegian officials, was the Minister for Development Cooperation and Human Rights, Hilde Frafjord Johnson, who at the start of the peace negotiations sometime in 1998 travelled into South Sudan to see John Garang. NPA, then in close cooperation with SRRA/SPLA, was responsible for the transportation and the security.

Helge Rohn, NPA's Resident Representative 1992 – 1996, and Dan Eiffe a key staff member and the Director of Communications until 2002, visiting one of the hospitals in the liberated areas in 1994.

The traditional Ethiopian Maresha plough was introduced into South Sudan I 1995. It caused a quiet agricultural revolution. The production of cereals doubled.

5
NPA AT WORK IN THE FIELD

SOME GLIMPSES FROM AREAS OF PRIORITY

Food for Millions, USA becomes a partner to NPA

Wheat, corn and rye grown on the American prairie normally yield plentiful crops. For many decades, this grain surplus has been the most important part of American emergency food aid. In the summer of 1993, the Head of USAID's Nairobi Office invited NPA's Resident Representative, Helge Rohn, to discuss the idea of using NPA's network for channeling American aid and emergency relief into South Sudan. They agreed that Rohn and his staff would draft an application to USAID for a combined food relief- and agricultural development programme.

In 1993, at the NPA annual meeting in Oslo, Helge Rohn, as the Resident Representative reported to us in the management-group about his discussions with the USAID people in Nairobi. Many objections of an ideological and political nature were raised. It was not easy to agree to USAID, and thereby USA, becoming a partner with NPA.

In several countries in which NPA was active, the groups we worked with were in political opposition to various regimes supported by the USA. However, more importantly was the fact that if we agreed, we would gain access to large amounts of food relief and substantial economic support for other projects, and we could combine these efforts to develop agriculture in South Sudan.

Last, but not least, it would give us a political edge, with respect to both Norway and other Western countries who were involved in development cooperation in African countries, because we could say that USAID, and thereby the US Government, had chosen NPA as its main partner in South Sudan. For these reasons, we said yes to the American invitation, and gave Helge Rohn the authority to make an agreement.

NPA's proposal was accepted by USAID, which included support for food relief and local food development in areas not directly affected by war. As far as I know, this agreement with USAID was one of the few, at that time, made with a non-American humanitarian organization.

In December 1993, everything was in place, and NPA's Sudan programme that in the beginning of 1993 had a budget of about 25 million NOK, experienced almost a four-time increase toward the end of that year, and a further increase to more than 125 million NOK in 1994. The USAID entry into the NPA Sudan Programme, made NPA a major humanitarian actor behind the front lines with the political consequences that followed.

Sometime early in 1994, the first ships loaded with grain left US ports and sailed for the Mombasa port in Kenya with the load addressed for NPA's Sudan Programme.

A few weeks later, the ships arrived in Mombasa. The Kenyan authorities had given advance clearance for the unloading and the transportation of grain and related food items to South Sudan. NPA had their own people in Mombasa who cooperated with the Kenyan port authorities to move the grain quickly on land.

Whenever new shipments arrived, sometimes carrying loads of more than 5000 tons of grain, several hundred trucks with drivers and assistants had to be hired to transport the grain to the NPA transit stores in Turkana, Kenya, and in Koboko in North-West Uganda. One truck could carry at most 20 tons. This was a rather lucrative business, which many transport companies wanted to be part of.

There were many problems and challenges associated with food transportation. It was 1500 kilometers from Mombasa to the transit base in Lokichokio in Turkana, which had to be transported with Kenyan trucks. But when the grain was to go from Mombasa to the transit base in Koboko in North-west Uganda, approximately 1800 kilometers away, we had to use Ugandan transport companies to avoid a conflict of interest between Kenyan and Uganda companies.

The roads between Mombasa through Kenya in the early and mid-1990s were in a terrible condition. Time and time again trucks broke down and were delayed for a day, sometimes longer, to repair damaged shock absorbers, broken drive shafts, or broken wheel axels.

In Uganda, during president Museveni's first years of office, the road standards in Uganda were drastically improved, making transportation in Uganda much easier.

When it came to transportation and distribution of food and other items inside South Sudan, there were many challenges. NPA provided agricultural equipment, seeds, and large amounts of grain as well as other food supplies that had to be transported from Lokichokio in Turkana and Koboko in North-West Uganda with small trucks to destinations in South Sudan. Only a small amount of food relief and other supplies were flown in, and only from Lokichokio.

From Lokichokio and Koboko to the border of Sudan our drivers were driving on roads, albeit they were in terrible condition, but they were roads. The road came to an end at the border to South Sudan. In South Sudan, the few roads that had once existed were destroyed by lack of maintenance and war.

The risk associated with local conflicts along transportation routes, mines, and dirt roads that dissolved during the rainy season, limited the number of transportation companies willing to do the job. NPA had to use smaller companies, who often had small, worn-out trucks that could take 10 tons at the most on dry roads, and half that during the rainy season.

NPA worked hard to increase the transportation capacity inside South Sudan, trying to get more companies with stronger trucks involved. There were not many to choose from, so at one point we decided to buy a small number of very big 8 wheel trucks from a Kenyan/British company who had been operating in Yemen.

These trucks could move in all kinds of terrain and were used for transport from Lokichokio onwards to destinations inside Sudan. However, these heavy trucks created new problems because they damaged the surface of the dirt and gravel roads during the rainy season to the extent that the roads could not be used at all. So, these new heavy trucks could only be used during the dry season. Furthermore, it became increasingly difficult to find drivers willing to take the risk to drive into areas with no roads and unpredictable war zones.

For all these reasons, NPA needed to find a new and better solution to the very difficult problems of logistics and transportation inside Sudan. The issue was thoroughly discussed by the staff in Nairobi and in the field, and after recommendation from our people in the field, we decided to let SPLA organize their own company for the transportation of food and other related items. We consulted with our major donors, first and foremost USAID, and they gave their consent. Then, all this was put into operation. The agreement was signed with SPLA, and the new SPLA companies started buying new trucks with four-wheel drive that could be used in the areas with no roads. A few Ugandan and Kenyan companies continued at the same time to provide for transport inside Sudan.

It was of course a difficult and controversial matter to let SPLA establish its own companies for our food transport, but NPA had the choice between having a very unreliable transportation situation with unpredictable Ugandan and Kenyan company owners and drivers, and the alternative, a stable, and reliable solution to the transportation problem with the SPLA companies in charge. Our primary task was to secure stable routes for food transportation for those starving in South Sudan.

It goes without saying that the SPLA companies did not work for free. They had contracts with reasonable commercial rates. Exactly how much money it was, is hard to say in hindsight, but former colleagues who were responsible for transportation, estimate it to be about 100 million NOK over the course of ten years between 1995 and 2005. That amounts to about ten million NOK per year.

What did the companies use the money for? I do not know, but I would guess that SPLA would reinvest in their transportation capacity.

A Visit from the Office of the USA Auditor General

NPA always had inspectors present during loading of grain on trucks in Mombasa to ensure that nothing irregular was loaded. But we were not always able to control and inspect what happened on the road between Lokichokio or Koboko and further on regarding transport to the final destinations inside South Sudan. The transport distances were 200 to 700 kilometers in terrain mostly without roads. Transportation was slow and moved for the most in low gear. During the rainy season, trucks would often get stuck on mud roads that had turned into swamps. Sometimes during the rainy season, these trucks could spend several weeks on the road and in the mud before they arrived at their destinations. The amount of food and other items that arrived at the delivery points, was always inspected. This was part of the reporting requirements for transportation and food distribution set by USAID.

It happened from time to time that our partners in Washington were not satisfied with our reports, and voiced criticism. We had on one occasion in 1995, some serious discrepancies in our audit, and the USAID recommended to the Office of the American Auditor General to send a representative to inspect our operations.

The man who came was a big black American named Rosevelt Holt. Before he arrived in Nairobi he made it clear that he would not settle for a regular audit of the books. He wanted to go through the entire operation, which meant that he would join the shipment from it was loaded in Mombasa to it being distributed to those in need in South Sudan.

This was a demanding task for both us and the auditor. Rosevelt Holt came, went to Mombasa and did what he had planned to do. He then followed a shipment consisting of a couple of thousand tons of mostly grain, but also some other items, all the way from Mombasa to the villages in South Sudan.

This operation took several weeks, but when Rosevelt Holt came back to Nairobi, he was not only satisfied to have completed his mission. Our people were praised for their skills and sense of responsibility, almost to the point of being embarrassing. Rosevelt Holt returned to Washington with his reports, and after that we rarely had any problems with our accounting and reports to USAID.

Agricultural Development, Seed, Grain, new Knowledge and improved Cattle Care

The amount of food that was transported each year varied from 5000 to 15 000 tons, depending on the demand in South Sudan. When the combination of drought, war and famine was at its peak, a couple of million people needed food assistance. The families, who received assistance, never got all of what they needed. They always had to provide for some food themselves. During the most difficult periods, this could mean 75 percent food aid coverage, during other periods 25 percent.

In addition to food assistance from the USA, food was produced by local farmers in areas where the conflict had subsided. NPA made sure that seed, grain, mineral fertilizer, agricultural equipment, education, and counseling were made available.

A quiet agricultural Revolution

In the aftermath of an extensive drought and famine catastrophe in 1993-94, NPA in collaboration with SRRA conducted a comprehensive study of living standards in the liberated areas. Among the things the study documented, was that grain and other food production were low. A family could produce enough food for six to eight months of the year. The rest of the year, they were dependent on buying food from local merchants, who were almost always Arabs from the north. But the war had made all the Arab merchants flee to the north, causing the local food markets to collapse.

At this time, the Ethiopian, Diress Mengistu, became the head of the Agricultural Programme, and quietly he and his African colleagues revolutionized agricultural production in Southern Sudan over the course of a few years.

Diress Mengistu in the following in his own words explains how the programme evolved:

The NPA agriculture program started in the context of a complex emergency in 1993/94 in Chukudum area (Eastern Equatoria) and from 1995 it expanded to Yirol and Rumbek areas (Lakes States Counties). In 1998, following the liberation of Yei, Kajo Keji, Morobo, and Lanya areas (Central Equatoria), the programme further expanded and covered large areas and populations living in those counties. After the signing of CPA in 2005; NPA agriculture pro-

gramme expanded and covered areas in Jonglei, Upper Nile, Unity States.

Background: *In 1995, NPA conducted a comprehensive agriculture and food security situation analysis. The analysis revealed that there were three major causes for the recurrent and severe hunger: insecurity, draught, and very low agricultural output. These factors could potentially lead to severe food crisis or famine (unless some interventions such as farmer training with provision of farm tools and seeds were made available). One of the main causes, in which NPA could intervene, was the very low agricultural production that was far too low to feed a family for the entire year.*

Before the war, this was not an alarming situation because families could purchase food grain such as sorghum, peanuts and sesame from Arab traders who purchased these items from big markets in neighbouring countries and in the north of Sudan. However, due to the civil war markets had collapsed. There were no more any traders and transporters, they had fled. Farmers had very little or no seeds for planting; the fields that they cultivated with traditional hoe were simply too small. There was also shortage of labour as young men were serving with the SPLA as freedom fighters while the remaining ones took care of the animals belonging to the family.

There were no extension services to help farmers to improve on crop production and animal health. All these had resulted in widespread food insecurity and frequent hunger. In the end people came to suffer from lack of food, and those most affected were children and women. A typical family was only able to produce grain, which at most would last for 4-6 months every year. The rest of the year, they had to look for indigenous food plants (fruits and vegetables) to supplement the food and some milk from their cows.

The situation analysis also suggested that it would be possible for the farming families to produce more of their own food grains and save seeds for the next season since the soil was good and the annual rainfall enough for the production of traditional crops. But in order to succeed, they needed to be trained to cultivate more land using

The natural resources of the land of Sudan are in the main in the South. The map shows both the dryland areas and the areas best suited for food production.

better methods such as ox ploughs rather than the small hoe; and to be able to obtain skills in improved crop production and management techniques.

NPA agricultural interventions: NPA initiated a cost-effective approach to address the root causes of some of the problems. We organized training courses for farmers in order to improve their knowledge of farming in grass-thatched Tukuls (see image). They learnt how to improve crop production by using the oxen-plough, so they could produce sufficient grains to feed the whole family throughout the year. NPA also combined the training activity with food assistance programmes to provide relief food for the most vulnerable families during the cultivation season so they could concentrate on farming and have more energy for ploughing. The food aid was provided by USAID, while agricultural training was covered by NORAD/NMFA funds.

NPA *started a small demonstration of the traditional Ethiopian Maresha ox-plough at Mabuy Farmer Training Center, Yirol West Payam (Lakes State), in June 1995. However, the response of farmers was in the beginning very slow, mainly due to the traditional cultural values related to oxen/bulls, which are held by the Dinka and other peoples in South Sudan who are cattle holders. However, NPA's agricultural staff, together with the staff from SRRA and the local administration, continued their joint efforts to bringing in some willing farmers to the NPA demonstration farm. In the demonstration farm, farmers could easily observe and be taught about the advantage of using the ox-plough in cultivating land. The tilling of the land went much faster, and the plough penetrated deeper into the soil than the hoe. The result was larger and better crops for the farmers which increased their total annual crop production up to 100 percent.*

The use of ox-plough, combined with skills training and provision of seeds for planting, helped farmers to produce more than enough food. In addition to feeding themselves throughout the year, they could sell grains to the local markets.

Lessons from Yirol and Rumbek areas in the use of ox-ploughs for increasing food crop production, increasing farmers' income and contributing to food security is now widely acknowledged by government authorities and donors. Donors such as the EU, in cooperation with NPA, are investing more than ever in the demonstration and use of the ox-plough in Lakes States for the period 2015-2017. The Comprehensive Agriculture Master Plan (CAMP; 2015), which is a government agriculture master plan supported by the Japanese International Agency for Development Cooperation, JICA, also acknowledges the importance of an extensive use of ox-ploughs by farmers in Lakes State.

NPA's success ("one of the victories") in introducing and expanding the use of ox-plough has been achieved through its own field staff's creative approach, known as the Community-ox trainer

(COT), a sustainable community-based extension service approach [1]. COTs are paid by the local community, or an individual family pays for the services from a trainer who demonstrates the use of the ox-ploughs. This training takes place even in areas where NPA no longer operates. In 1996, in Yirol West Payam, there were only six farmers using ox plough. In May 2000, the number of farmers who were using the technology had reached more than 110 in Yirol West alone; while by 2005, there were more than 1,000 farmers using ox ploughs in Yirol and Rumbek Counties alone, and more than 500 farmers were reported to do the same in Kajo Keji County.

Local production of ox-ploughs

Following the extensive training in the use of ox ploughs, the demand from farmers for ox ploughs could not be met by NGO support alone. The plough was not availible in the local market. The NPA agriculture programme was then able to identify talented and interested rural artisans (blacksmiths) who were trained to produce both the plough itself and spare parts for the plough. Interested artisans from Yirol, Rumbek, Kajo Keji and Yei were identified in year 2001 and trained for 1 month in Uganda, paid for by NPA with Norad funding. The artisans learnt fast and were able to manufacture the most needed spare parts and the complete ploughs to sell to farmers through NGOs or directly at local markets. These ploughs are still being manufactured in two rural blacksmith workshops located in Kajo Keji and Yirol West Counties.

These two blacksmith-workshops (another victory) are still the only workshops manufacturing ploughs in the history of South Sudan. This is perhaps one of the most important contributions until today that NPA has left for the agricultural sector.

An unforeseen result of the NPA Agricultural Development Programme with increased cultivated areas was that a new line of interest conflict emerged, the competition over land for grazing versus crop production. This led, in 2003, to a collaborative study between

---

[1] A term developed by NPA agriculture staff in Yirol and Rumbek Counties

NPA and NORAGRIC to design and implement a pilot project known as community-based resource management project (CO-REMAP) with the aim of addressing the causes of conflict through natural resource management techniques. Another study known as "South Sudan Land Tenure Study, funded by NORAD, was initiated and implemented between 2004-2007. This study aimed at understanding the different land tenure systems related to agricultural development to advise the government of South Sudan to develop policies and laws that balanced the interests of different stakeholders.

Other important outcomes (victories) of the NPA agricultural development Programme, included the establishment of two blacksmith workshops by local artisans to produce and sell ox-ploughs to farmers; the establishment of Yei Agricultural Training Center in Central Equatoria State (in 1998) which is still providing training of extension workers to be employed by public authorities (free of charge) and NGOs (on cost bases).

Challenges: During the early phase of the liberation war and the famine and emergency situations that frequently occurred at the time, donors and NGOs were reluctant to provide funds for farmers' training. They would rather provide food aid.

It was, however, at that time possible to do otherwise as we have seen from NPA's approach. It is possible, also in times of war, to provide training of people in local communities, to provide for them agricultural implements, to help them construct communal grain warehouses so that farmers can go beyond production of food only for the family, to be able to sell surplus production and earn some income to purchase non-food items.

NPA, as an independent NGO outside of the OLS Consortium had the freedom to work in a flexible manner and remain behind in relatively insecure areas without the instruction of "evacuation". This helped restore hope among the populations NPA worked with, particularly in areas along the front lines. In all project areas, NPA worked closely with civil authorities explaining the rationale of its operations. This helped prevent "abuses" of relief food reported by other agencies.

That concludes Diress Mengistu.

Despite the civil war that has been raging since December 2013 ,and still is destroying South Sudan, the farmers use of the ox-plough is still increasing. Many thousand farmers are now using it, and it is now a permanent part of almost all development programmes for agriculture in South Sudan.

When it came to cereals for seeds, there were about 2000 family farms each year from the end of the 1990s, that were given the task of producing local varieties. The surplus harvest was sold to local cooperatives that NPA had helped establish, primarily located in Central Equatoria. Each growing season the cooperatives sold the cereals as seeds to between 25 000 and 30 000 family farms, for the most part in the states of Lakes, Jonglei, and Upper Nile.

During good years, with rain at the right time and good growing conditions, these farmers could produce so much grain that the surplus yielded many thousand tons. NPA bought this and, through the cooperatives, redistributed the grain to approximately 38 000 new families in drought and war stricken areas, primarily in Bahr el Ghazal, Unity, and the eastern part of Equatoria.

Support for Cattle Owners

Most southern Sudanese live in villages, and depend on agriculture and cattle. About half of the cattle owners are nomadic and move around with their herds. In the tropics, cattle are often exposed to contagious and sometimes epidemic diseases, especially during periods of deadly insect plagues. That is why, from the beginning of 1987, the SRRA wanted NPA to have projects for cattle owners. Consequently, NPA very early started a vaccination programme for cattle that yielded good results and became very popular.

The Iimpact of the Food Aid provided by NPA

How many people received food? On an annual basis, this was partly dependent on climatic conditions, which affected food production, and partly on how the war developed. The number of people to receive food aid was estimated at between 50 000 and 150 000 families per year, with a family size from 6 to 10 persons. The American food aid distributed via NPA saved between 500 000 and 1 million people from starvation each year. The added value of the assistance to local food production and cattle husbandry was also substantial. It is estimated that up to 50 000 families had significant benefits from local food production projects needed for survival each year.

A high number of people survived each year due to NPA's efforts, and the number increases when one considers the long period from 1993 to 2005, during which about eight to ten million people benefited from food aid. In addition, during the period between 1993 and 2002, NPA procured 60 percent of all the imported cereals for seed that was used in the liberated areas, and about 80 percent of all the agricultural equipment and implements.

Did any of the relief food feed the liberation fighters in SPLA? Yes, it did and the reason is simple: There was hardly a family in NPA's large geographical work area that at some time during the year did not have one or more family members in SPLA; father, mother, son or daughter.

The same applied for UN's Operation Lifeline Sudan (OLS). They released thousands of tons of food by airplane on both sides of the frontlines. I was on one such operation, watching as hundreds of people waited for food on the ground. There was no way of knowing whether there were SPLA soldiers in the group, or government soldiers from Khartoum.

It was pointless to try and control who would get food by asking the question: 'Are you with SPLA?'

Two Transit Camps

Two years after NPA and Egil Hagen started their emergency relief operations in South Sudan, the UN in 1989 established Operation Lifeline Sudan (OLS), with its base in Lokichokio (Kenya). The UN had built a new and bigger airport, warehouses, living quarters, guest houses, and a large restaurant for their personnel and travelers. Soon, there were several thousand people living in the UN base. But access to all facilities except the airport, which was owned by the Kenyan government, was restricted to UN personell and NGO-members of the OLS.

NPA did not join OLS, and Egil Hagen had since 1986 been criticizing the UN for its unwieldy bureaucracy and its indifference to the starvation of the peoples of South Sudan. UN leaders and staff, and many NGO members of the OLS, disliked NPA. In addition, the UN and most members of the OLS, NGO network were critical of the fact that NPA had taken a political position in support of the liberation struggle. The UN and OLS wanted to remain neutral. The message was very clear: NPA was not welcome at the UN facilities in Lokichokio.

Therefore, NPA had no choice but to establish and develop its own camp in Lokichokio with our own warehouses, housing for personnel and guest houses for travelers, in part financed by USAID and in part by the Norwegian Ministry of Foreign Affairs (NMFA). The task was given to Aage Vatnedalen, who began working as one of our Norwegian staff members in 1993, and he has shared the following story with me:

"At the time, I was directing the steadily expanding programme in Chukudum, but a few years into the programme, I received a new message from Helge Rohn. Can you go to Turkana and take over the camp in Loki, and make it run with a profit? Well, that was a new kind of challenge. I went to Turkana and immediately

saw that to attract others to the camp, we had to make it both bigger and better. I did not have much money in the budget, so I went to the Somali merchants in Loki and negotiated a good deal for cement and other building materials.

We started improving the old huts and building new ones, and we built a proper restaurant with a bar. At the same time, we dramatically increased our storage capacity for emergency relief. When everything was in place, we approached other NGOs that operated outside of OLS. NPA now had a viable alternative. The first group to join us was Doctors Without Borders. GOAL and CONCERN from Ireland followed, and soon thereafter all the extra capacity in the camp was rented out to other NGOs. The economy of the camp improved drastically."

NPA was now equipped with halls of storage capacity for several thousand tons of food and other equipment, its own fuel tanks, mechanic workshop, 15 well-built African huts, good toilets and washing facilities, not to mention a large, pleasant restaurant with a bar. We hired a good Kenyan chef from one of the better hotels in Nairobi and paid him well. Therefore, he stayed with us for a long time, and he, with his excellent cooking ability, was an important part of a development that made our camp and its facilities very popular. Rosemary, a Kenyan woman, was hired as the daily manager for the entire camp. This proved to be a good choice. She was an able, hardworking, friendly and strict manager, and ran the camp with a firm, but friendly hand.

The restaurant and bar became the meeting place in the evening. The guest houses were almost always full. The camp became quite a cosmopolitan place. Aid workers, journalists, diplomats and politicians, and more than likely spies of various kinds came to the NPA camp to drink, eat, talk and catch up on the latest news from the neighbouring UN camp, from inside Sudan or from Nairobi.

I spent a few nights there, and each time it was like living in a fairy tale. There were all sorts of people, young, old, women and men, all with different shades of skin colour.

In a corner of the bar you could find local Turkana men in traditional clothes who only spoke a few English words. They spoke to each other in a local language while observing everyone else. In another corner, you could find a group of pilots from countries such as the USA, Kenya, South Africa, Ukraine, or White Russia, gossiping about everything.

At that time, working in South Sudan was very demanding, both physically and mentally. One was constantly exposed to the impact of war, famine and poverty, disease, all kinds of danger and death. It was good to be able to have a break from life in the field of South Sudan, and to take a few days of rest at the NPA camp in Loki.

The NPA camp in Loki was a success. NPA had many travelers. Everybody used the airport, but then Kenya introduced an airport tax of 250 NOK per departure. The airport tax for NPA personnel alone would be a considerable expense. NPA had just received a contract with UNHCR for transporting 2600 South Sudanese refugees from the big camp in Kakuma in Turkana to their homes in South Sudan. With an airport tax of 250 NOK per refugee the expense or NPA would be enormous. In addition, there were more trips in and out of South Sudan in connection with the peace negotiations. So NPA, with Aage Vatnedalen in charge in Turkana, looked for other options, and Aage told me the following:

"We agreed rather quickly that there were better ways to use NPA's money, and we decided to build our own airstrip in South Sudan. We crossed the border, and in collaboration with SRRA we found an area that looked good. We started building the airstrip.

I didn't have much cash for the project, but did have food and other supplies that people needed. That is how we made the Food for Work Project with local South Sudanese workers. However, after a few days, they went on strike and demanded cash payment, no more food. I didn't have a choice and had to pay with money instead. The workers were happy and everything was fine. After three weeks, we had a fully functional airstrip, 1500 meters long and 50 meters wide. The total cost was about 50 000 NOK.

At that time, we had a contract for food transportation by air with a Kenyan company that used Russian pilots. The day the airstrip was finished, I got a call from the Russian captain. He wanted to test the new airstrip. There was a lot of wind as he approached, and he miscalculated both the wind direction and speed. The big cargo plane landed with a bang and a boom in a cloud of dust. For a moment, I thought there had been an accident. The landing was rough, but with no damage to the plane and out came the pilots who apologized for the miscalculation of the wind."

The airstrip was next to a new village, New Site, which John Garang and his wife Rebecca had built as their home during the war. Garang and his colleagues used the airstrip often, as did the foreign diplomats and SPLM partners who wanted to talk to Garang. NPA used it for shipping food and for repatriating South Sudanese refugees who were on their way home after the peace agreement was made. The project was a big success.

A few years after the peace agreement was made, the necessity for the transit base at Loki was minimal, and the base became a burden for NPA. It had to be dismantled, but how? In the end, it was sold for one NOK to a group of local workers under the direction of the able Kenyan female manager, Rosemary. They were given the task of adapting the camp to the changing times.

In 2005, the CPA and the peace that came in Sudan led to an increase in normal transportation between Kenya and South Sudan. Loki was once again a good place to stop on the way into South Sudan.

After the tragic collapse in December 2013, and the civil war that followed, Lokichokio is again a base for emergency relief. At the same time, several hundred thousand South Sudanese refugees have come to the big refugee camp in Kakuma, not far from Loki.

In the middle of all this turmoil, Kenya has struck oil in Turkana. At present, there is extensive searching and testing. In a few years there will be oil production, and that means that many people will be travelling through Loki. Rosemary and her staff are busier than they have been for a long while.

NPA's transit camp in Koboko, in the north-western part of Uganda, is a considerable distance from the border to South Sudan. A better alternative would have been Gulu in the central part of Northern-Uganda. But that was impossible because that area was controlled by the brutal terrorist organization, the Lord's Resistance Army (LRA). The regime in Khartoum supplied them with weapons and other supplies. Transport planes from Khartoum would often drop weapons and equipment in Uganda for LRA at night. If LRA was given the opportunity, they would most likely have attacked our convoys carrying food and emergency supplies. Therefore, we had to go far west in Uganda to find a safe place for the transit camp.

With respect to warehouse capacity for food and supplies, the Koboko camp was larger than Loki, but with fewer guest houses. It was managed well by the local employees, and served our needs and our partners'. Today, the Koboko base is run by local owners.

Comprehensive Health Care for Civilians and Soldiers

Aage Vatnedalen is the son of a Norwegian missionary, born and bred in Ethiopia. He was trained as a pilot, but had other talents as well. As already mentioned, NPA in 1993 hired him to head the construction of a hospital in the liberated zones of Southern Sudan. He has both good and bad memories from that time:

"I landed on the airstrip in Nimule one day in May 1993, and was picked up by NPA's driver. The jeep was old and falling apart. The steering wheel was loose, and the driver held it in his lap as we bumped along, ascending the steep pass over Aswa River. The roads

were narrow, the left side dropped straight down 100 meters to the bottom of the valley. A couple dozen smashed SPLA trucks were at the bottom, I thought to myself that either their brakes or front steering must have given out.

After a couple of hours, we reached the NPA camp. It was beautifully located on the hill by the Loa Mission. The view was magnificent. Most medical doctors and nurses were Norwegian and lived in simple huts made of brick with straw roofs.

A bamboo fence divided the camp, it was known as the Berlin Wall. NPA was on one side, and the adventurer Arne Clausen with drivers on the other. He had been in the former East Germany, DDR. He bought a couple of dozen IFA trucks at a low price from NPA on the condition that NPA would have priority to use the trucks. But Clausen thought that he did not earn enough from NPA. He wanted to earn money on the trucks and thereby terminated the agreement with NPA. Now, both groups lived in the camp separated by the Bamboo Berlin Wall.

The hospital in Aswa had been built by the authorities in South Sudan during the peace between 1973 and 1983 and had 400 beds. By the early 1990s it had deteriorated and been vandalized. We worked for almost six months restoring the building. Just as we were finishing, rumours came that government forces from Khartoum were on their way to occupy the area and chase SPLA out of South Sudan. The attack could come at any time.

We packed our trucks and trailers with all the beds, x-ray machine, generator, and cords, absolutely everything we could use at another location. As we were preparing to leave, we heard the most dreaded sound that struck fear in everyone. An Antonov plane came straight at us with bombs. We threw ourselves on the ground, hoping that the shrapnel would miss us. After a few minutes the attack was over, and miraculously nobody was hurt and all the trucks were still intact. The convoy started moving, and we drove slowly east towards Nimule.

There we found an area with large mango trees that would be suitable for a new camp. The local mission owned the area, and we bought the right to use it with 40 bales of wool blankets. We started building immediately, sleeping under the stars for the first weeks. After a short time, the new field hospital was finished, and we also repaired the old mission hospital, so we could use that as well. In connection with this we were given prefabricated modules by the Catholic father Leo.

One day I had to go to Gulu to buy some building materials. On the road, I passed 15 burning buses that the LRA had just set on fire. LRA always attacked with incessant brutality. First, they stopped the buses. Then they took all the valuables from the passengers. Then they took young girls and boys as prisoners and killed everybody else. At the end, they set whatever was left on fire. As I was driving past the buses, I started thinking; what if they are hiding in the bushes waiting to take me too!

We decided to never use that road again, and built a new road with rocks and sand with a bridge over the Aswa River. By doing this, we made a new route into Uganda, and could avoid the areas that the LRA controlled.

I was out on a reconnaissance mission for the new road with two of the commanders in SPLA, Kuol Manyang and Abdul Aziz, when our truck broke down. We sat and talked in the bush far into the night as the truck was being repaired. At four in the morning we reached the ferry over the Aswa River. It was camouflaged with palm branches so it could not be seen from the air. On the other side, there was a small fire, so we in the dark could navigate across the river. There were constantly rumours about new attacks by the Government forces in Khartoum, people were very scared about what was to come. NPA had the responsibility for three refugee camps in the area. We called them the three As, which stood for Ame with 55 000, Atepi with 35 000 and Aswa with 35 000 refugees.

One day, one of the doctors at the hospital, Dr. Temesken from Ethiopia, and I decided to drive to the Aswa camp, not far from the hospital, to check out the conditions there. It was raining, the fog hung along the mountain sides. The road was muddy. Then we experienced something that was burned into my memory.

An endless black procession of people moved towards us. There were mothers with children in their arms and holding others by their hands, many pregnant. Parents had children on their shoulders, a child in each hand and bags on their heads. The bigger children carried the smaller ones, or bags containing everything the family still owned. Some children were leading a goat, or carrying a chicken that constituted all of the family's food. Old men and women using sticks with a cross on the end crawled more than they walked.

Everyone was starving and emaciated, many were obviously sick. There were thousands and thousands of them, almost everyone was Dinka, and their homeland was many hundreds of kilometers farther north. They had been chased from their homes many years ago, and chased from camp to camp as the war-zone moved. Now, the fear of a new attack was pushing them on.

We continued driving and came to the abandoned camp. It was quiet, deadly quiet, but then one person crawled out of a hut, then one more, then many more. Many were too sick or too old to walk. There were many, and they were left there to die. We put them in the trucks and brought them back to the hospital where they received food and care. They cried and cheered and were so grateful for being rescued from a certain death."

The war was always brutal. Sometimes there were a dozen dead or dying, other times the number was much higher, and it included both civilians and soldiers. That is why it was of utmost importance to increase the medical services in the field. But the front lines were in constant flux, and therefore flexibility and speed were necessary means in our daily operations.

The health centre, with the hospital and the polyclinic, was placed in the old hospital building by the Aswa River, about 20 kilometers north of Nimule, and was established in November 1992. NPA was given a new field hospital with 60 beds by the new NOREPS program. Halvor Lauritzen from the Norwegian Red Cross came to assemble them. This new hospital was placed in Nimule, next to the old hospital building, which was also repaired so that it could be used for polyclinic services that were in great demand by the civil population.

There was a constant and increasing need for health-care services and hospitals, and NPA received more money, in 1993, for the health-care program. Aage Vatnedalen explains:

"*After we had completed everything in Nimule, we received word from Helge Rohn that a new hospital in Labone was to be built, a little farther east along the Uganda border. I was assigned to do this. It was in the middle of the rainy season, and it was not very tempting, but we had no choice.*

When I arrived in Labone, the workers had already put up the shelters for us to live in. The walls had just been coated with a mixture of clay and cow dung, which would not dry during the rainy season. It smelled bad inside the huts. Plastic covered the ceiling and grass was put on top of that. The grass did not dry either with all the rain, but rather rotted slowly and transformed into a yellow, sticky liquid that dripped everywhere. There were insects and bugs everywhere in the hut and these were particularly bothersome at night. I woke up one night with a rat giving birth in the middle of my hair.

There were dangerous snakes everywhere; constrictors, mambas, spitting cobras and many more. The toilet was a latrine with a low thatched roof. Every time we went there in the dark, we brought a stick and a flashlight. First, we beat the roof, in case there were snakes there waiting to strike. Next it was important to check around and in the latrine. It was not a pleasant thought to get bit on your buttocks while you sat there in the middle of your business.

We repaired the hospital and built the airstrip and the access road. The African workers did a fantastic job. They were very motivated. After four months, everything was in place in Labone."

A new message came over the radio from Helge Rohn. He wanted Aage to go to Chukudum to set up a third hospital. 1993 was the year USAID made a large contribution, and NPA's budget had more than tripled in 10 months.

Aage had to return to Nairobi before he took on the project in Chukudum:

"The missions in Aswa, Nimule, and Labone had been demanding in every possible way. I needed a break with my wife in Nairobi. The day before Christmas Eve we had a small gathering with some friends, but early the next morning I was on the plane with headache and all, heading for Chukudum. David Evans and William Watkins met me at the airstrip, and we drove to an abandoned camp once run by Norwegian Church Aid.

Only ruins remained. People had lived there with an open fire. The walls were dirty, covered in soot. In some places, there were drawings of SPLA soldiers executing Arabs. The elephant grass was over two meters tall. There were insects and bugs everywhere, and some got inside my shirt. It itched terribly. We took stock of all the problems and challenges ahead.

Then it was Christmas Eve. David, William and I celebrated in all simplicity with a small grilled hen, while we drank water purified with chlorine tablets. David and William reproached me mildly for not having managed to bring some wine or whisky from Nairobi.

Soon Christmas was over, and we started building the hospital, living quarters for personnel and a larger house for vocational training. Once again, the motivation and work moral were high. In the course of a few months, Chukudum was in operation.

But we were in constant danger of being bombed by Antonov planes. One day I was sitting inside, writing my monthly report to the office in Nairobi. In the yard, some guys who had substantial war injuries, one had lost a leg, a second an arm, and a third a hand, were making crutches out of wood. They had learned carpentry.

One of them shouted: "Look, there is a UN plane" I looked out and confirmed that it was a plane painted white with UN markings. But suddenly it turned towards the hospital and released a bomb. Once again, their aim was poor. The bomb detonated about 150 meters away. Nobody was hurt this time, *but it was a shock to find out that Khartoum would paint their bombers with UN colors and UN insignia."*

A tragic Plane Crash

As the work in Nimule progressed, NPA staff in Nairobi started to rent small planes to transport people and medicine to Nimule. Just before Christmas in 1993, while Helge Rohn was still in Washington negotiating for more US assistance, one such small plane loaded up its cargo at Wilson Airport. The plane belonged to an Ethiopian, Meskin Marcos, who was a trained pilot, having worked with Ethiopian Airlines. He was an experienced pilot and had flown Twin Otters with Aage Vatnedalen. In addition to the cargo of food and medicine, there were five passengers on board. Two of them were Norwegian, Dr. Olav Petter Niels Grüner, who was a medical doctor in charge at Bærum Hospital, and the medical nurse Audhild Hennie Lund, from Nesodden. The two others were officers in SPLA; Salva Kiir, who is currently president in South Sudan and his adjutant at the time, Bol wek Agoth, who in the fall of 2014 became South Sudan's first ambassador to Norway. He is now the Director of Protocol at the President's office in South Sudan. The fifth passenger was David Evans, a bright competent deputy director at the NPA office in Nairobi.

The plane took off and after 45 minutes had engine trouble near Nakuru, about 150 kilometers west of Nairobi. The pilot looked for the airport, but lost altitude and had to aim for a large field in an otherwise rugged terrain. The pilot managed a controlled emergency landing, but only seconds after landing, the wheel hit a wet hole on the ground.

As the plane was thrown to the side, some of the cargo came loose and hit the passengers from behind. Dr. Grüner died instantly. Audhild Hennie Lund was also hit and sustained severe chronic injuries. Salva Kiir broke some ribs. Bol wek Agoth injured his back resulting in severe, chronic pain. Meskin Marcos sustained massive head injuries that ruined the rest of his life. David Evans also sustained severe injuries.

As head of the International Department in NPA, I was informed directly from Nairobi. The news rattled me. I felt the responsibility. I had as Head of the International Department. One member of our staff from NPA had died in an airplane crash, while the other passengers were injured. At that time, we did not know how severely. Five families in Norway, South Sudan, Ethiopia and Great Britain were affected.

Helge Rohn, who was in Washington negotiating with USAID when it happened, flew immediately to Nairobi and took over the difficult task of following up the airplane crash. The Kenyan Civil Air Aviation Authorities found that the airplane was carrying too much cargo, something that was the pilot's responsibility.

The emergency landing could have been successful, if the wheel had not hit the mud puddle. The Commission noted also that the landing would have been more successful without wheels. The reason the pilot attempted to put the plane down with wheels was assumed to be that he was trying to save the plane, and that the terrain at the landing sight looked suitable.

Of all possible days, the coffin with Dr. Grüner remains arrived at the Oslo Airport on Christmas Day in 1993. I was with the grief-stricken family, and was so shaken by the whole situation that I experienced a kind of black out.

The nurse came home a few days later in a wheelchair. She was distraught over the future prospects in her life, and blamed NPA for the accident. A painful and difficult lawsuit followed, which she lost. In NPA it was decided only to follow the judicial principles with respect to our renunciation of her claim of restitution. The court concurred, but whether this was the right way to solve this case, has always bothered me.

Salva Kiir and Bol wek Agoth were both guerilla leaders and just happy to get a ride back to Nimule. Salva Kiir's broken ribs healed. Bol wek Agoth, who had just recently come back from training in guerilla warfare and intelligence gathering in Cuba, had such massive injuries that he was no longer able to go into combat.

He received some support from NPA for medical and physical therapy in Nairobi. After that he became the project leader for NPA's new vocational training project in Chukudum. He was there for a few years, but his back pain grew worse. He ended up going to a university in Great Britain, arranged and paid for through the cooperation between SPLM and a solidarity institution in Great Britain.

Glimpses from Everyday Life at our Hospitals

NPA took in several medical personnel from Norway in 1993 on short term contracts to the hospitals in Aswa and Nimule. We once had a doctor there from the southern part of Norway who had moral objections to treat soldiers from the war-zone, both SPLA and government soldiers. He was there to treat civilians, not contribute to anything war related, he said. Helge Rohn pointed out what was expected of health care personnel during wars in the Red Cross Charter, and this solved the problem.

During this period, NPA also established a mobile medical unit that was led by the South Sudanese medical doctor Kaneri Gribani. It operated in areas behind the front lines. This unit was important for both the medical and moral support it gave to the SPLA-freedom fighters because the soldiers knew that if they were injured, there was medical support available.

Inside South Sudan there was an enormous need for health care services of all kinds. NPA's three employees at the office in Nairobi worked hard, but they had a large and complex job to do. The need for medicine was close to insatiable.

At one point in 1993, a partner from the Netherlands sent a message that a container with several hundred kilos of medicine was on its way to NPA in South Sudan. When it arrived in Nimule, the hospital personnel were gathered and had great expectations. They were however, disappointed to say the least;

the container was full of outdated suntan lotion. How could this happen? In Netherland, at that time, businesses could get a tax benefit by giving away material gifts such as food or medicine. The factory in Netherlands had registered medicine and had got its tax benefits, but had sent outdated suntan lotion instead.

In the beginning, NPA prioritized using Norwegian health personnel at the hospitals. But daily life was difficult. It was not possible to maintain anything near the standards found in Norway.

The living quarters were poor, with not much room for privacy or relaxation. Some days there was water, other days not. The food was dull. The war sounds of bombing and canon fire were always close. Cultural differences and language problems were challenging. The patients were often illiterate and spoke a language the Norwegians could not understand. Out in the villages, there were drought, war, hunger and destitution. This combination made recruiting Norwegian health personnel difficult.

An Italian offered his services to the hospital and it turned out that he was a good cook. Consequently, he became the chef. But there was not much money for food supplies. One time large amounts of pasta were bought in Nairobi, and the personnel had pasta with beans as their main meal week after week, even though the Italian did his best to vary the menu.

One day the Norwegian personnel rebelled. They demonstrated with posters, written in Norwegian: "WE WANT BETTER FOOD NOW". The case resolved itself with the understanding that those who wanted to go home to Norway could. A few left.

A young Norwegian medical Doctor, Ling Merete Kituyi becomes Director General of the Hospital

One of the first Norwegian doctors to work in the field for NPA was Ling Merete Kituyi. She had just finished her medical studies at the University of Bergen. During her studies, she met a young Kenyan student named Mukhisa Kituyi, who was working on his doctorate in Social Anthropology. Ling Merete and Mukhisa were married and moved to Nairobi. (Mukhisa Kituyi became in the 1990s a renowned Kenyan opposition politician, was Minister of Trade and Industries in Mwai Kibaki's first government and is now the Secretary General of UNCTAD)

In the fall of 1993, NPA was looking for a new doctor for the hospital in Nimule. Ling Merete applied and got the job. Barely 30 years old and pregnant in her third month, she came to the hospital in Nimule and became the director. She was immediately confronted with a special type of problem. The man who had previously been the acting director was an old revered South Sudanese veterinary doctor and a Dinka. When he was told that his new chief was a young, blonde Norwegian woman, it was too much for him. He made it very clear that it was an insult to any man's dignity. During one of the first meetings with Ling Merete, there was a disagreement regarding whether a certain medicine was to be used or not.

Ling Merete was very clear about how the medicine should be applied. The tall Dinka, standing over two meters, protested loudly and asked her when she was born. She replied 1962. The old man retorted by saying that in 1962 he had just finished his degree at the Agricultural University in Alexandria Egypt. Therefore, his recommendations about medicine use should be followed. But Ling Merete did not relent, and the old man had to give in. However, despite this episode, their relationship improved after some time.

While Ling Merete was in charge, a serious epidemic of measles broke out in the villages around the hospital.

Ling Merete shared her memories with me:

"The epidemic spread even though the children had been vaccinated in a programme the Irish volunteer organization GOAL had initiated. Mothers carried their sick children to the hospital, but our treatments had no effect. The children only became sicker.

We had a few horrendous days shortly after I started. I came to work early in the morning, and was shown to the children's ward. There were 70 children who had died during the night. Mothers were crying in desperation. The personnel were in despair. I was stunned. What had happened? Was there something wrong with the vaccination?

I went with some colleagues to meet with the people in GOAL who had administered the vaccination. No, they were certain that the vaccination was good. What could it be then? I read myself up on the consequences of starvation, malnourishment and measles. There I found the answer. When children who are malnourished and starving, get the vaccination, there is not enough protein in their blood to convert the vaccine to antibodies and they die. That explained what had happened.

We had many problems. Being able to understand what the patients said was a problem. Very few of them spoke English, only the local tribal language. I needed a translator, and the chief of administration who was South Sudanese said he could help me. But when I went on hospital rounds and asked him what the mother or child said, he replied for example: "She said that the child became ill yesterday". It was an impossible situation because I never knew what the patient said and that made it difficult to treat them.

But then I noticed a small, apparently bright boy, who was 10-12 years old, following us on hospital rounds. His name was John. I asked him if he spoke English, and he responded in reasonably good English. Maybe you can be my translator, I asked him. Yes, he would like to do that, and so it was. Every day for the next three months John followed me around in all contexts related to patients and sickness, and he became quite skilled at translating between me and the patients.

Another problem was related to the use of medicine. The local health personnel had little or no medical training and they had a rule of the thumb when it came to using medicine, the more tablets the better. It was difficult for them and the patients to understand that over medication could be dangerous. To make them understand how multi-resistant bacteria could be devastating for an entire population was not easy either.

SPLA commanders who came in as patients could be difficult in many ways. They disliked sharing a room with 50 other patients, and they disliked even more being examined in the same room. One day a commander came in who obviously had tuberculosis, and we did not have the right medicine. The Nairobi office promised to send it, but something went wrong. We only received 60 tablets of one kind, while we needed three kinds of medicine to be applied as a package to treat the tuberculosis.

The commander demanded that he should be given the 60 tablets as his treatment. I said that it would not help, in the worst of circumstances only make his illness worse, and I refused him medication. I was then summoned by the regional SPLA-leader. Surrounded by his heavily armed soldiers he stood there, almost yelling at me: "Are you going to let our comrade Deng die?" Then he demanded the treatment of 60 tablets to be started. I refused and tried to explain. Luckily, Dan Eiffe was there, and the difficult show of power ended with the beginning of an understanding about how difficult and complex the treatment of tuberculosis was.

In short, being a young female doctor at a hospital in a male-dominated, ethnic diverse and traditional African society in Nimule in 1993 was no easy task. However, for the most part, things worked, and the NPA health program steadily expanded and improved."

In Nimule, it could be difficult to find something to do, when you did get some occasional free time.

Ling Merete and the others discovered that about two kilometers from the hospital there was a large, old church ruin, where a service was held every Sunday. They started to go there, and it became an experience also for Ling Merete:

"It was a large church that had been bombed by Khartoum some years earlier, and the roof had fallen in. The ruins were painted blue, and there was a large picture of Maria painted in yellow with light hair on one of the walls. The church ruins were packed with people at all the church services, and many had to stand outside. The congregation sang as only Africans can sing, and the old Irish priest preached and went around talking to people inbetween the psalms. Over us was the clear blue sky.

I often spoke with the old priest. He had been there for over 40 years. He had been offered a place at the Vatican's nursing home, but had declined. "I am old and I want to die and be buried where I belong, among the people of my parish here in South Sudan", he said. He also appreciated the visits by Dan Eiffe, when he brought a little tobacco and a bottle of Irish whisky for the old priest."

Challenging daily Experiences

The resources for health care increased, making it possible to extend activity behind the front lines. However, the challenges of the daily work were extremely difficult.

In 1996-97 NPA set up a hospital in Yei in the south-west part of the country. The South Sudanese Doctor Kaneri Gribani became the hospital's director. I had, both throughout my time with NPA and after, many meetings with him, and in an interview in the winter of 2013 he shared a few glimpses of what daily life at the hospital was like:

"*Thanks to the support from Norway, not only money, but also hospital equipment and medicine, we managed to get this hospital started. The famous Sophie's Minde Hospital in Oslo was closing at the time, and through NPA we got most of their equipment. This made the hospital well-equipped by South Sudanese standards. We had a surgery ward and several other important medical wards.*

The staff and patients at the hospital had a spirit of their own. The atmosphere was marked by the values of solidarity which NPA and their staff had shared with us, and by African values related to togetherness and human dignity. We treated all who needed medical care. First and foremost, civilians, children, women, young and old. We, of course, also treated soldiers, SPLA freedom fighters as well as soldiers from the Khartoum regime. As a surgeon, I did all kinds of surgery, also brain surgery.

However, again and again, the horror of war struck. We painted the Red Cross sign on the roof in an attempt to escape from the Antonov bombers. But when those in the planes saw the Red Cross sign, they aimed as directly as possible at the hospital buildings. They succeeded hitting us on several occasions. Once a bomb landed in the hall of the surgery, another time a bomb hit the waiting hall of the Polyclinic Centre, which was full of patients. Lives were lost every time.

One day, several bombs hit an air-raid shelter we had dug into a hillside, and one bomb hit the entrance area. A flood of soil and stone came down over the entrance and blocked it completely. Staff and others tried with their spades and other hand tools to move away the soil and stones covering the entrance. But it took too long. When they finally were able to open the entrance, 12 people had died from suffocation. We had many horrible days at the hospital and in its immediate surroundings. so many killed and so many wounded, both patients and staff. In addition, many people in Yei town were killed and wounded.

One day, we learned that the attacking planes were on their way, and we managed to move the patients in the surgery hall into the neighbouring forest. When the bombers came, they could not see us, but we were carrying out surgery on many patients during that bomb attack. On that day, those in charge of dropping the bombs had a poor day because they failed utterly in hitting any of their targets.

It says something that during my time as medical director of the hospital, the hospital was bombed more than 50 times."

Sten Rino Bonsaksen, the NPA RS, was often involved in rescue operations after military assaults.

"Sometimes the pressure on our health care personnel was extreme. One time we received word that government forces had attacked some villages in Bahr el Ghazal, and there were large numbers of dead and wounded. We immediately chartered a plane. There were two pilots and four of us on the plane, with space for 18 more. We landed on the nearby airstrip, and our local workers met us with cars. The sight that met us was unbearable. There were dead, dying and wounded everywhere. They called out and cried in pain and fear. About 100 of them were severely wounded, but alive. We could only take 18 on the plane.

Using our best judgement, we had to choose the 18 of the severely wounded that we believed would survive after medical treatment, and got them on the plane. That meant that we had to leave behind about 80 severely wounded who would suffer a painful death. We did not have the capacity to take any more. No other organization could or would help. The choices we had to make were dreadful and heart breaking.

The psychological scars and strain are something we must live with. Somebody who has not experienced, this cannot understand how horrible it was."

NPA had, at the most, five hospitals in South Sudan: Chukudum, Nimule, Labone, Yei and Akak in Bahr el Ghazal. In addition, we had a mobile medical unit. Over the course of a year we could treat between 60 000 and 80 000 patients. Between 1993 and 2005 NPA treated about 800 000 patients.

Cooperation with Red Cross

We always had excellent cooperation with the large and well-equipped hospital run by the International Red Cross Committee in Lokichokio. They accepted patients with complicated war injuries and diseases that we were not able to treat at our hospitals. In addition to receiving patients they would often send us life-saving medicine.

Dan Eiffe put it like this:

"The Red Cross was always available and supportive. They provided medicine for our hospitals, and their basic argument for doing that was that the more NPA could provide at its hospitals, the less pressure would be on their hospital in Loki which was always full of patients."

With these health-care programmes, NPA, from 1986 to 2005, saved more than a million people. Both the civilian population and the freedom fighters knew that if they got sick or injured, then NPA would be there to help. All this added to the people's moral and fighting spirits. They stayed in their villages behind the front lines instead of fleeing.

Vocational Training in Health Care, Agriculture and Trades

Southern Sudan was a British colony for almost 60 years, and during most of that time everyday life was marked by the Closed Districts Ordinence, which de facto kept South Sudan as a kind of human zoo. When independence came in 1956, with South Sudan as part of the whole of Sudan, people in the South rebelled and an armed liberation struggle broke out. In 1956 South Sudan was one of the most undeveloped parts anywhere in Africa. The vast majority were illiterate, because it was British policy not to educate the people in the South.

When the second civil war started in 1983, approximately 90 percent of the women in South Sudan and about 70-80 percent of the men were illiterate. When the peace agreement came in 2005, the situation was even worse because the war had made access to education almost impossible. No other people and state in Africa had such a poor education status as the peoples of South Sudan in 2005.

NPAs Contributions in the field of education and vocational training

Just after Helge Rohn took over as the NPA Resident Representative in 1992, planning started for the NPA Vocational Education Programme in the liberated areas, with a sewing workshop and carpentry training in the village of Choye. These activities were moved to Nimule in 1994, and supplemented with training of car mechanics, using NPA's cars and motorcycles for their training exercise. In 1995-96 a bigger centre for vocational training was set up in Chukudum.

Several years prior, NPA had started up hospitals, but there were hardly any nurses or laboratory assistants. Therefore, a two-year course for nursing and laboratory education was prioritized. But all types of skilled labour was needed. So shortly after, shorter courses were given in woodwork, metal work, brick making, bricklaying, housing construction and textile production.

The man behind the first vocational training courses was a dedicated South Sudanese man who very early every morning went to his field to till the land. Then he went to the vocational centre to teach his pupils until late in the evening. One of his mottos was "no sweat, no sweets". Unfortunately, he died all too soon after a brief illness.

Trude Falck at the NPA HQ in Oslo was responsible for the Sudan programme in the middle of the 1990s. She paid her first visit to the programme area in 1996 and afterwards shared the following stories with me:

"I visited the training centres both in Chukudum and Akot, and it struck me right away that this was a particularly important initiative for a community with few alternatives. I spoke with one of the pupils and asked where he came from. He said he came from a town on the border to the Central African Republic. But how did you get here? He answered quickly: "I walked." "But how long did it take you?" "Six months" was the reply. This meeting made me see how important the programme was.

I was also in Akot, where they were training agricultural instructors. We trained about 12 instructors in courses, each lasting for six-months. I remember very well these very tall, young men, for there were only male instructors, who rode their bicycles over the vast savanna, where the grass was more than two meters high and the bicycle path barely a meter wide. I could only see their black heads over the grass for a little while before they slowly disappeared in the savanna. I didn't understand how they new where they were going, but they did.

They biked from village to village, living with poor families several weeks at a time. They taught farmers, both men and women, young and old, more efficient ways of tilling the land and provide better care for their animals. They were in the field many weeks at a time and worked very hard.

It was very impressive that they managed to do the job even with all the difficult challenges they faced in their everyday work. They were extremely motivated, and they rarely gave up. Not only were there South Sudanese, but young men from Ethiopia, Eritrea, Uganda and Kenya came to take the courses and then work in the field as instructors. They sacrificed much, and they were the everyday heroes for the people in South Sudan, during a painful and difficult war."

The Ethiopian, Diress Mengistu, was responsible for the agricultural programme and led the development of the agricultural school in Yei, which is still the best in the country. With his colleagues, they developed a training programme for farmers with several training centres in the liberated areas.

Around 1997 there were some problems in the Chukudum area. The conflict between SPLM/A on the one side and a local tribe on the other side became increasingly difficult. It was fueled by the regime in Khartoum, who armed the local militia with weapons and money. Their goal was not only to fight the SPLA, but to also intimidate NPA's workers. Consequently, NPA shut down the vocational training center in Chukudum because the risk of losing lives became too great.

But in 1997 Yei and the surrounding area was liberated by the SPLA. All the vocational training was relocated to Yei. At the same time the health worker education was expanded and improved.

Marit Hernæs who was the NPA Programme Director in the field in 1999, and had the responsibility for all the vocational programmes, said the following about the education of the health workers:

"It is very good. The Ethiopian G.K. Wolde Tsadik who was the principle of the school for health workers was extremely competent in his profession and also a very creative person. He grew old, and then his son, Ezana took over. He also had a solid medical education from Ethiopia and was like his father. The father was eager to build a proper library, and he did. The library has become better and better and is in use today. At the time, about 40 health workers were educated each year, most of them nurses or midwifes, and some laboratory assistants.

Doctors and nurses who worked at the Yei hospital also taught at the school for health workers. They were competent in their fields and highly motivated for the job. It was impressive. They worked long days and sometimes nights, and more than one time risked their lives for the sake of the cause.

I respected these people, and can still see them in front of me. Every time I left, I didn't know whether they would be there next time I came to visit.

The remaining vocational training in Chukudum was in the late 1990s moved to Yei, and it has since been steadily expanding. Today, the centre has acquired national importance.

In my time, when the pupils received their course diplomas, they were given the tool set they had used during their training. When they returned home, they newly educated tailor had everything he or she needed to start a business. The same applied to carpenters and metal workers and all the others.

Many of the pupils had been through tough times before they took the courses. Many had been wounded in the war. I remember one young man. His leg was so damaged from the war that he could not walk. He had to use a homemade wheelchair. At the graduation ceremony following the tailor course, his mother who was a widow, attended the graduation because it was a big event in their lives.

The boy was called forward to get his diploma and he moved with his wheelchair to the podium. He accepted the diploma with thanks. And then he turned to his mother, bowed deeply and thanked her as well. She was so beautiful while she at the same time conveyed her gratitude and pride. Then she smiled and the tears started to roll down her cheeks. A mother and son without words expressing pride and joy over having accomplished something that only a few months earlier did not seem possible."

There is a sad story to add about NPAs important contributions in establishing vocational training centres in Yei. In the summer of 2016 the civil war escalated into the states of Equatoria, and all NPA training centres had to be closed. They remain closed, and it is very uncertain when or if they ever can reopen again.

THE AFRICAN BACKBONE IN THE NPA PROGRAMMES

NPA's Sudan programmes have always had people with strong personalities and perseverance, not willing to give up. The hard work from the African colleagues has been the invaluable mainstay. Between 1994 and 2001 there were 1100 to 1300 African workers in the programme. They worked at all levels, and many of them worked for long periods. Some held leading positions in the health care programmes and in our hospitals. Some were surgeons, working night and day. Others headed the development of the agricultural and vocational training centres. Many held important jobs within the administration in Nairobi. Last but not least, Africans always had the responsibility for security both at our Nairobi Office and at all programme centres in the field. Most of them were men, but there were also many women.

Sometimes NPA's bank accounts in Nairobi were empty because the money transfers from the NPA HQ in Oslo got delayed, or the funds were delayed from our donors. When these delays occurred, our African staff would not get paid until the money arrived in the accounts. I remember one situation in particular. SIDA, the Swedish Agency for International Development, had without beforehand notice cut all grants for our health programmes in South Sudan, and one of many consequences was that the African staff at Yei hospital did not get paid for almost two months. The hospital Director, Dr. Gribani did not like it, but he said:

"*But we cannot just stop working and go on strike. It is our own people we work for and together and in different ways we are fighting our liberation war.*"

It is not possible to name all our great, competent and devoted African managers and staff by name, even though they deserve it. But I would like to point out a few people, beginning with the women.

When we employed the manager for the NPA camp in Loki, we chose the Kenyan woman Rosemary. I do not think anyone who has been in Loki and experienced Rosemary, would have anything but praise for her work. She had control, was always cheerful and pleasant and kept the order, but was strict when necessary.

Margarethe Lugo was the daughter of a bishop in Juba. She fled and came to Nairobi and started to work with NPA during the 1990s. She had several important jobs, one of which was the agricultural programme. When NPA set up a new office in Juba in 2006, Margarethe was given the task to establish it. She had to find housing and offices, while running the programmes from Juba. She did a fantastic job, and it was no surprise when she was called to be part of the staff in the Office of the President.

Lona Lowilla Eila from South Sudan was in charge of the NPA local community development programme and did a great job. On the momentous National Day of July 9, 2011 when

South Sudan was celebrating its independence, Lona was responsible for the female part of the big parade. Today she works with UNDP, in South Sudan.

Abeny Nataneal was a commander like her husband in SPLA. Her husband was killed in battle. Abeny was in charge of organizing security for the staff at the NPA camps for displaced people. Abeny was so revered for her leadership qualities that she was given leave to do special assignments for SPLM/A. She became SPLM's first female representative in the interim National Assembly for South Sudan after the Comprehensive Peace Agreement in 2005.

Patriciah from Kenya was at NPAs Nairobi office for over 20 years, an exceptionally skilled, polite and devoted staff member.

Halima Mutonga from Kenya was the deputy Chief Administrator for some years at the Nairobi NPA Office. She was very devoted, very much in support of the liberation struggle in South Sudan, while she did a very solid job in the office

Working with the security issues for the NPA staff at the many project sites in the field such as hospitals, camps for displaced people was a constantly pressing and utterly important issue. This work was always carried out by African managers. Here I want to name the South Sudanese Peter Dut, Kuir Dau Atem, Chaat Paul, Mac Mika and the Kenyan Charles Aloo. During my time with NPA, we never had serious security break downs or breaches, which says everything about the quality of their work.

I would also like to say a few extra words about a couple of these people.

First, Mac Mika. He was a policeman in Juba, and Juba in the 1990s despite many SPLA attacks, remained a very important garrison town for the Government forces in Khartoum.

Mac Mika had a dangerous, double role. He was not only a policeman in the service of Khartoum, but at the same time also an agent for SPLM/A. He reported on the situation in the town, movements of troops and other military issues. One day in the middle of the 1990s he was captured, interrogated and exposed to the most severe torture. Finally, they threw him into a dark cellar to die. However, some good people found him and smuggled him out of Juba across the lines of the enemy and got him to a hospital in Nairobi. For nine days, he drifted between life and death, until the doctors in Nairobi brought him back to life. He survived the torture and regained his mental health, but his back had taken too much beating and would never be the same again. As he recovered in Nairobi, he was employed by NPA as a security officer and he served with NPA for many years.

In 2009 the government of South Sudan appointed him Head of the National Election Commission. Mac Mika was the chief responsible for the administration of the national referendum on independence in South Sudan in 2010 and the National elections the following year. The last time I saw him was in October 2013. He walked with a stick, but was just as friendly and gentle as ever. Mac was one of several of my old colleagues and contacts in South Sudan who were tortured by Khartoum's regime.

Chaat Paul was seconded to NPA by John Garang himself to work as a security officer because he was seen to have a special talent for that kind of work. I came to work very closely with Chaat Paul, and he was the middleman for most of my many meetings with John Garang. He was always very friendly and polite, and at the same time very reliable and efficient. I cannot remember that one agreement between him and me failed.

When CPA was a fact in January 2005, Chaat Paul was called back to be part of John Garang's security team. When Garang died in the helicopter crash in July 2005, Chaat Paul was assigned to Khartoum as part of the security team for the first Vice-President, Salva Kiir. He was later employed as a Director for Press and Communication in the Office of the President in Juba. I met Chaat last when I in October 2013, as a guest of the President, was invited as a mediator in the internal conflict of

SPLM. We had as usual a couple of very friendly and interesting informal gettogethers, talking about everything.

In the early winter of 2016 Chaat together with 12 other staff at the Office of the President were accused of corruption and arrested. In the spring of 2016 the 13 were tried, found guilty and a sentence for life was passed an bloc for all. It seems to be a common view that the accusation of corruption was at least in part baseless, and for Chaat Paul unjustified, but used as an accuse to get rid of staff members whom President Salva Kiir no longer liked and trusted, and who may have known about the many big corrupt deals, that had taken place in the Office of the President. The Ethiopian, Diress Mengistu was, as noted earlier, a great manager of NPA's agricultural programme. His work among the Dinka is well known. He introduced the traditional Maresha plough from Ethiopia that is pulled by the ox. He then managed to convince the Dinka to use the ox, which is considered almost a holy animal, to pull it. Diress was primarily responsible for training advisers in agriculture, and many were trained, having Diress as their teacher.

Large herds of cattle are important for both the Dinka and the Nuer, but in the tropics the danger for disease is greater than any other place. NPA's vaccination programme was headed by the dynamic Kenyan veterinary doctor, Dr. Maina.

NPA's constantly growing vocational training programme that began in Chukudum in 1993, continued in Yei in 1998 and after that was expanded into other places in the country, always led by competent African managers.

The Ethiopian nationals made themselves invaluable to NPA's health programmes. Doctor Temesken was an important person, first as hospital doctor then as the Director of the Health Programme.

Another Ethiopian, Dr. Elias Mitsale was first employed by NPA in Tanzania in the middle of the 1990s as a medical Head of the NPA camps for refugees from Rwanda. In 2003 he was asked by the NPA Resident Representative to take over as the new Director of the South Sudan Health programme. In 2006 he became NPA's first Residential Representative stationed in Juba. He was also the first African to hold this position. Regarding NPA's Health Programme in South Sudan, I have already mentioned the South Sudanese Dr. Gribani. He was for many years a legendary Director of the Hospital in Yei. In 2006 he became the deputy director of NPA's South Sudan Programme.

The administrative work in the Sudan Programme was for the most part done by African managers and staff. One of them who did an outstanding job for many years, was the Kenyan, David Lisamula.

The list is almost endless, but I will end it here and let a Kenyan professor of social science and development studies have the final word when it comes to the NPA Sudan Programme and the role Africans played.

Dinner with a Kenyan Professor

One day in 1999 I was at a working dinner in Oslo in connection with the evaluation of international non-governmental organizations' ability and willingness to use local staff and local resources in emergency relief operations in African countries. NPA was not part of the evaluation.

I was seated next to the Kenyan professor Monica Kathina Juma. She was an exciting conversation partner. When she heard whom I was, she said: "Oh, you come from NPA." I nodded and she continued.

"We are a little group of East African researchers who are closely following what is happening in South Sudan, and we have noticed how NPA works. We are convinced that you are more successful than any other international NGOs in the area.

We see three reasons why you are so successful.

Firstly, it was of great political importance that you from the very beginning took a solidarity stand in support of the liberation struggle.

Secondly, you have demonstrated a confidence and trust in Africans being able to run programmes and projects that is unique among International NGOs, none of them can compare.

Thirdly, you have demonstrated solidarity and trust in practice by never withdrawing from the field in periods of heavy war action with the risk of lives for your own staff. In that you are clearly unique.

For these reasons, we hold the view that NPA has succeeded better in South Sudan than any other international NGO."

I was both happy and flattered by the praise NPA received, and I shall never forget this very pleasant dinner talk with the Kenyan professor.

Professor Monica Kathina Juma has since done well both in her academic and diplomatic career in Kenya and internationally. Among other things she has been Kenya's ambassador to Ethiopia and was a Principle Secretary in the Kenyan Ministry of Defence and currently the Principle Secretary in Kenyas Foreign Ministry.

"WOMEN CAN DO IT"
Mobilizing the Women of Southern Sudan

NPA had already at the very beginning of its work in South Sudan in 1987 strong calls from women about how weak and undignifying their situation was, and that there was a strong need for assistance. However, in the beginning we had neither the money nor the resources to do anything about it. The situation improved gradually.

In the middle of the 1990s Marit Hernæs was with UN and worked for a year at the big refugee camp in Kakuma in Turkana. There were refugees from Sudan, Rwanda, Burundi, Zaire, and the Central African Republic. She and her UN colleagues started different activities for women using the UN's Universal Declaration of Human Rights as a basic document in all their work. They got women to come together, and in short courses the UN staff told them about their basic human rights in addition to other literature about women working for peace and conflict resolution.

In 1999 Marit Hernæs became the NPA Program Director for the Sudan Programme, stationed in Nairobi/South Sudan with a special responsibility for the NPA education and vocational training programmes in South Sudan. Being an advocate for equality between sexes, she threw herself enthusiastically into the work of organizing and increasing political awareness among women.

There were many challenges to address. In South Sudan women have been oppressed and discriminated against for hundreds of years. In addition, the war had created a situation in which local communities were often comprised of as much as 65 percent women because so many men had been killed in the war. Many women had had important tasks during the war for liberation as soldiers or nurses at the front lines. They gained an experience that made it difficult to go back to the traditional roles they had in the old society.

Marit, in an interview told me the following:

"For me it was important to find the African women, preferably the South Sudanese, but also Kenyan, Ugandan and Ethiopian who could take local leadership responsibility, and whom I could cooperate with.

During the first meetings, we in NPA explained about the Universal Declaration of Human Rights, and that women were equal to men and therefore had equal rights. Then, we asked what their priority was when they were planning of their local communities. They all answered; "Education." They wanted to learn to read, write and calculate numbers. And they wanted schools for their children. Secondly, they wanted the right to have a say in politics.

I remember one course particularly well. We were in a village, and several dozen women had come for the course. They were so poor, and many did not have any cloths at all. I thought maybe it was a little out of place to talk about human rights given the circumstances, but ran the course as planned with a local translator.

I remember one of these women particular well. She thanked us profusely for the course and then she said: "I have always thought that it must be that way, that I and all the other women were equal to all men. But after listening to you today, now I know it. Still, I am afraid that I will not experience equality in my lifetime. Maybe my children will."

During the war and in the first years after CPA, NPA chose to work with the mobilization and political awareness raising of women within the framework of SRRA and SPLM. This undoubtedly, during the period up to 2012 contributed in a big way to the growth of SPLM's Women's League, but in 2012/13 with the internal conflicts in SPLM, the decline of also the women's league began, as I shall write more about in chapter 16.

From the Norwegian side, women from the Labour Party without any pay, travelled to South Sudan and held tens and tens of basic courses with the curriculum from the Labour Party training module: "Women Can Do It (WCDI)." It started with courses in all the states including the Nuba Mountains and Abyei, 12 courses in all with about 500 participants, but it did not stop there. Women who participated, got strongly motivated for the women's cause. They took their course material together with what they themselves had learnt, back to their local communities and started their own training courses.

WCDI courses got extremely popular and became a force that just kept growing. In 2009 NPA tried to find out how many women had participated, and according to Marit Hernæs it was estimated to be at about 150 000 women.

The experience that the young women from the Labour Party gained from South Sudanese daily life and the fate of women, left strong impressions. Many of them were active in the Labour Youth Movement's (AUF) project that aimed at assisting the SPLM Youth League develop into a democratic and progressive political youth organization. The Labour Party in cooperation with NPA also had a cooperation project with SPLM, assisting in developing SPLM into a democratic political party having social democratic values and principles as their core and with a membership stemming from the whole of South Sudan.

Between 30 and 40, for the most part, young, active members of the Norwegian Labour Party have participated in these projects in South Sudan. What they experienced, developed their interest in international political solidarity work. This in turn during critical times for South Sudan in the period between 2009-2013 contributed to the development of a political support base within the Labour Party and the Labour Youth Movement that in appositive way also influenced Norwegian policies towards South Sudan.

I shall write more about the tragic fate of these projects in a chapter later in the book.

Other Initiatives, - Support for SPLM's Nordic Resident Representatives

SPLM began from the mid- 1980s establishing its political-diplomatic offices in an increasing number of countries, first and foremost in Africa, but also in Western Europe and USA. In 1992 they started an office for the Nordic countries in Copenhagen. SPLM's first and only representative was John Duku Andruaga. He had to escape with his family from the famines and war ravaging Sudan in the 1980s and ended up in Denmark. John Duku came from one of the smaller ethnic groups in Central Equatoria. He was politically a very committed person and very hardworking and a good representative for SPLM. He reported quickly to NPA as well as NMFA in Oslo. He had almost continuing communication and many meetings with staff members of NPA in charge of our Sudan programme and because of my strong interest in African politics and in Sudan, John Duku and I have had many meetings and frequent telephone talks. We became friends, and we have kept this friendship since.

Every time John came to Norway, NPA set up meetings for him with the Ministry of Foreign Affairs and with Members of Parliament and relevant Norwegian NGOs like NCA.

John Duku also made sure that I had continual access to most of the documents and briefs from SPLM/A's intelligence service. Therefore, I was well informed about what was happening in Khartoum, SPLM's interaction with other countries in Africa and other political and military strategic questions that were relevant and important at any given time.

But SPLM did not have much money, so John Duku had his office in his apartment in Copenhagen. He did not always have money for rent, so he sometimes had to ask for an advance, from private people and sometimes from NPA.

The constant lack of funds became a problem after a while. I decided to discuss it with my colleague Bjørn Førde, Secretary General for the Danish Association for International Co-operation (MS), now Action Aid Denmark. We agreed to split John Duku's expenses between NPA and MS.

Sometimes MS paid the telephone bills, travel expenses and other times NPA did. Over the nine years I was with NPA, I would estimate that NPA and MS paid a total of about 800 000 NOK to cover the expenses of John Duku, the SPLM Representatives in the Nordic countries.

This support made it possible for John Duku to travel in the Nordic countries and Germany and pay visits to Brussels, the EU Headquarter. John was very knowledgeable. He had a strong commitment to the cause, and was an extremely eloquent speaker. Sometimes he was as stubborn as a donkey, while in other situations, he could turn around and be the most pragmatic diplomat. In other words, he was a good and effective representative for SPLM.

His abilities were noticed by John Garang and other leaders in SPLM. In the summer of 2002 John Duku was called home as an adviser during the peace negotiations in Kenya. He worked closely with John Garang. Every time I visited Kenya between 2002 and 2005, we met, and he often arranged meetings with

Garang. As soon as the Comprehensive Peace Agreement was in place in 2005, John Duku was sent to South Africa to be trained as a diplomat.

In January 2014 John Duku was appointed a member of the South Sudan Government's delegation to the peace negotiations in Addis Ababa. He was there for a while, but then resigned and went back to his farm in Central Equatoria. When we spoke in the spring of 2015, he said he was satisfied with his life as a farmer. The crops were doing well, and there was a big need for food. He, however, also said that he would gladly return to the Ministry of Foreign Affairs in Juba as soon as things returned to normal in the country.

John Duku obviously believed in normality coming back when he in the summer of 2016 reported back in Juba and by President Salva Kiir was reappointed an ambassador.

John Garang at the NPA's National Convention in August 1999 and his visits at the time to the other Nordic Countries and the European Union HQ in Brussels

In the winter of 1999, SPLM's chairman, John Garang, with a delegation was invited as guests of honour to NPA's National Convention to be held in August the same year. The National Convention was an important part of the celebration of NPA's 60th Anniversary.

However, this invitation had some difficult political aspects. Therefore, Harald Øveraas, NPA's Chairman of the National Board of Directors, made it clear to me that before an invitation would be sent, he wanted to go to South Sudan to familiarize himself with the conflict as well as paying a visit to the field to see for himself NPA at work.

One day in January 1999, Øveraas and his delegation arrived in Nairobi, and they were met by John Garang and some of his closest advisors. During meetings held at John Garang's residence in Nairobi, NPA was praised for its work. The next day, the delegation flew to the NPA camp in Loki and then on to Yei in South Sudan. While the delegation was at NPA's hospital in Yei, both the hospital and the town were bombed. There was no doubt that the target of the bombing was the NPA Chairman and his delegation.

Harald Øveraas who was an old and very experienced trade union leader, was enraged by the fact that the Khartoum regime wanted to kill him and his delegation. Therefore, the first thing he did when he was back in Norway was to give me the following instructions:

"*The regime in Khartoum is a regime from hell. They bombed us while we were in Yei. Halle, you can invite John Garang and whoever you want from SPLM to the National Convention.*"

John Garang came with his wife Rebecca and a couple of his closest advisers. We also invited NPA's most important partner in the USA, the Director for the American Refugee Committee, Roger Winter.

Garang gave a speech to the delegates at the Convention in which he praised NPA's work in South Sudan. Roger Winter, who is another very gifted speaker, also praised NPA's work.

In addition to being a guest at the National Convention, Garang had several important meetings with the Ministry of Foreign Affairs and with members of the Norwegian Parliament. The most important conversation was with the Minister of International Development, Hilde Frafjord Johnson. It mainly dealt with the peace negotiations for Sudan that had just begun.

In addition to these meetings in Norway, John Duku and I, as Secretary General, arranged for important meetings with high level staff in the Ministries of Foreign Affairs in Helsinki, Stockholm and Copenhagen. In the ministries that had a Social Democratic Minister of Foreign Affairs, I used my social democratic network to arrange for the meetings with the minister concerned. Garang's Nordic tour was a huge success.

NPA also assisted in having meetings with leading staff of the EU Commission and members of the European Parliament Our main partner in this endeavour in Brussels was SOLIDAR's Secretary General, the British Giampi Alhadev.

In the European parliament Garang and his delegation met with the German Christian Democratic Chair and other members of the Foreign Affairs Committee. When the meeting was over, the German Christian Democrat put his hand on Garang's shoulder and said:

"*Doctor Garang, you have given me a political understanding of the conflict in Sudan that I have never had before. Thank you very much.*"

The Foreign Affairs Committee of the Parliament of Kenya in Southern Sudan

When Sten Rino Bonsaksen in the fall of 1999 was appointed NPA's Residential Representative for the Sudan programme, he already had considerable experience from Africa. He was a student at the University of Bergen in the 1980s, and he did the field work for his master's degree in Social Anthropology in the Red Sea Mountains of Sudan. During his studies in Bergen he became acquainted with Mukhisa Kituyi from Kenya who as well was studying social anthropology. Having finished his PHD in Social Anthropology, Mukhisa returned to Kenya and became an active opposition politician. In the first election with several parties in Kenya in 1992, Mukhisa Kituyi was elected member of parliament, representing the opposition party, Forum for Restoration of Democracy (FORD), Kenya.

Sten Rino and Mukhisa kept in touch, and were central in starting a youth exchange programme between the pupils at a high school in Mukhisa' s home region and the pupils at Mosjoen High School, Mosjoen, a town in the middle of Norway.

When Sten Rino came to Kenya in the fall of 1999, Mukhisa Kituyi had become the leader for the Foreign Affairs Committee in Parliament. A central issue for the committee was the conflicts and wars in neighbouring Sudan, and NPA was asked whether they could cooperate with SPLM to arrange a trip for the Foreign Affairs Committee to the liberated areas. It was done, and one week early in 2001 six members of the Foreign Affairs Committee of the Kenyan Parliament with Sten Rino in charge of the journey, travelled to South Sudan. They visited the towns of Rumbek and Yei and a village in Bahr el Ghazal and held meetings with top leaders in SPLM/A. The committee members also visited NPA's projects. In this way, they were given an introduction as to how daily life in the fight for liberation was for ordinary people of South Sudan. The visit was a huge success. It contributed to a consensus in the Kenyan Parliament about what kind of policies should be pursued in relation to Sudan. All this contributed to the Kenyan government's strong support in the peace negotiations that were just getting started in Kenya.

Warlords and the NPA secret Channel

A significant and at the same time very difficult problem in the peace negotiations in Kenya was how to create security and military stability in South Sudan when the CPA was concluded and agreed upon by the partners.

SPLA and the army of the Khartoum regime were not the only military actors in the war in South Sudan. There were also about 30 militia groups inside South Sudan which were nothing more than bandit gangs ravaging in the areas they controlled. The commanders of these gangs were called warlords and had almost dictatorial control of their groups.

The largest one was the South Sudan Defense Force under the infamous warlord Paulino Matiep. Peter Gadet was another and just as infamous, commanding his own group. Riek Machar had his own militia group, Lam Akol had his, and so on. Together they made up an army the size almost comparable to SPLA's own forces.

As a rule, these forces were paid for and equipped by the regime in Khartoum, that used them as it best suited their political and military strategy against SPLA. However, sometimes these bandit gangs would change sides. At times, they could fight on the same side as SPLA, until Khartoum made a new and more lucrative offer. Money, arms and other favours decided where their loyalties stood.

The warlords who led these militia groups were skilled in military combat but were completely without morals. They were ruthless in battle and vicious in their treatment of civilians. They raped, killed and murdered for fun, and they stole food and supplies from an impoverished civilian population.

Towards the end of the peace negotiations around 2002-2003, it was obvious to the negotiators and their international support partners that there would never be peace in South Sudan if a new government was not able to gain control of these militia groups. Some way had to be found to bring the warlords into a dialog that might convince them that their own future and the future of their bandit soldiers were better served by joining the new government army, SPLA.

But it was not possible for the negotiators themselves or their closest associates to begin a negotiation process directly with the warlords and their militia groups. They needed a middle man who could operate in all secrecy.

John Garang discussed the problem with the American delegation at the negotiations. The Americans understood the problem and promised money. But they could not do more than that. Then the question was raised: Could Norway contribute towards a solution? The Americans met with the leader for SPLM Peace Desk, James Kok, and Kjell Hødnebø, one of the Norwegian advisors at the negotiations and asked if they could help in getting the militia groups to join SPLA. If this was achieved, it would be an important step towards reconciliation between the Dinka and Nuer people.

Kok explained during these conversations that Riek Machar was willing to come back to SPLM, but it was contingent on reconciliation measures. The reconciliation measures had to include both military leaders and soldiers in the militia groups, and people-to-people dialog meetings, where people talked about what had happened during the war and how peace could be built.

Hødnebø presented the case to the Minister of International Development, Hilde Frafjord Johnson, and other superiors in the Ministry of Foreign Affairs. The problem was discussed, and then, they gave the green light. The next step for Hødnebø was as discreetly as possible to contact the two top-managers of NPA's Sudan programme in Nairobi, Sten Rino Bonsaksen and Ken Miller. They were positive to the request, but asked for some time to reflect on what challenges that were to come if they said yes.

The first thing they did, was to ask for a secret meeting with John Garang and James Kok. Garang and Kok made it very clear that NPA's assistance in this matter would be highly appreciated.

Then, the local NPA management secretly accepted the challenge. But I had at the time left NPA, and Sten Rino could not discuss the matter with the NPA management in Oslo.

The reasons were the following ones: The Chairman of the National Board of Directors of NPA, Reiulf Steen, and the new Secretary, General Eva Bjøreng, stated shortly after my departure from NPA in May 2001 that they wanted to get rid of the whole Sudan programme. They wanted to divide it and give the pieces to other Norwegian organizations that worked in South Sudan. Given that situation, it was impossible for Sten Rino to discuss this highly risky and at the same time secret task with his superiors at the Oslo HQ.

So, without the knowledge and consent of NPA, Oslo, Sten Rino reported in secret back to Hødnebø that they were ready for the task, as long as the extra expenses it entailed for NPA, could be reimbursed.

When the agreement was in place, the Head of the Team for the peace negotiations, General Lazaro Sumbeiywo from Kenya, and the Head of American delegation to the negotiations were informed about the role to be played by NPA.

It was now imperative that the agreement could remain an absolute secrecy. No other partner being part of the peace negotiations should know. But most importantly: The regime in Khartoum had to be kept in the dark about what was to take place. Because, if they did, they would do anything to destroy the effort and keep the loyalty of the warlords.

Sten Rino and Ken Miller began to negotiate. NPA received money for the project, primarily from the USA. At the same time Garang made it clear that if the warlords did not cooperate, the alternative was an all-out war until the militias were finished.

The project was successful. Riek Machar, Peter Gadet and heads of several other militia groups accepted the offer of integration into SPLA.

But Sten Rino and Ken who were the NPA operators, met with some big surprises.

One day a secret message came to the NPA office from the field: *"Warlord and rebel leader Peter Gadet is on his deathbed in an isolated region of South Sudan, most likely with a ruptured appendix."*

It was easy to imagine what would happen if he died. His army of many thousands of men would be without a commander. They could go loose and rampage the civilian population, and not only that they could threaten the entire peace process. There was not much time to act.

NPA sent in an airplane and rescued Peter Gadet. A last minute and very risky surgery was carried at a Nairobi hospital. Peter Gadet survived and regained his health. Then he continued the negotiations to have his militia group transferred and integrated into the SPLA forces. But Peter Gadet was a difficult negotiator and used unconventional methods.

One day in the winter of 2003, Ken Miller was in the office in Nairobi. Suddenly the door was kicked open and in came Peter Gadet in his field uniform and fully armed, accompanied by two body guards each armed with a Kalashnikov. He sat down on the chair across the table from Ken, looked him in the eyes and said:

"*I see that you are visiting my local community in Nuerland. I do not like that. Neither do I like your friends, the people who are sending you on visit. If you one more time visit my community, I will have you arrested and brought to me. And I will kill you.*"

But Ken Miller was not an easy man to scare. He explained why he had been travelling and urged Peter Gadet to continue the negotiations regarding the conditions for joining SPLA. Peter Gadet calmed down, and after a while he and his gunmen left the NPA office. It took a few weeks, and then Peter Gadet put his thumbprint on the contract. It was the way it had to be done because Peter Gadet could not read or write.

Sten Rino Bonsaksen had during this project for the most, the secret contacts and meetings with Riek Machar, and the main impression of Riek left with Sten Rino after it was all over, Sten Rino summed up in the following:

"*Riek Machar is a completely unreliable person. I would not even buy a new car from him.*"

At the time in 2002/2003, I knew nothing about the project. Kjell Hødnebø told me about it in a conversation we had in the fall 2014. Then, Sten Rino and Ken Miller in separate meetings confirmed. A little later I asked Hilde Frafjord Johnson whether she knew about it, and she answered:

"*I was informed that such a channel would be attempted with NPA behind the scenes and I agreed to it. The details were left to Kjell Hødnebø and his colleagues. They made the deal with NPA who did a fantastic job together with others. They played an important role in the peace process, and that I want to emphasize.*"

A comparable reconciliation process was carried out in Equatoria, where Hødnebø and NPA maintained contact with central SPLM leaders from the region. These reconciliation meetings resulted in that most of the rebel groups from 1997 rejoined SPLM and could participate in the celebration of the peace agreement in January 2005. This is an example of what the UN later called

Peace Building, and has now become an important part of the peace operation concept.

Community Building

The young Canadian social science researcher Matthew LeRiche came to South Sudan in 2004 to do field work for his doctoral (PHD) study: "How Humanitarianism Affected the Conduct and Outcome of War in South Sudan".

The thesis was how member organizations in OLS (Operation Lifeline Sudan) and NGOs outside of OLS influenced the discussion within SPLM on future politics and state building in South-Sudan. In practice, there were only two organizations which were outside of OLS, namely NPA and the Red Cross.

Matthew LeRiche documents in his doctoral study that International actors had an influence on the SPLM development of policies. In the time after 1991 this meant, first and foremost, the Red Cross with the Geneva Conventions mandates about warfare and NPA's values of solidarity and social security as the basis for the development of societies in which people lived in freedom.

Sten Rino Bonsaksen described it this way:

"*There is no doubt that our continuous dialogue with SPLM's leaders was anchored in a set of values. We always had a humanitarian message in which solidarity was the core value, and we also emphasized human dignity and human rights in general.*

SPLM for their part, listened to us because of the position NPA had, and because they wanted to learn about these concepts related to ethics and politics. During these conversations, we also talked about the regime in Khartoum and what they stood for in terms of politics, community building and warfare. Here we had a critical view that was also noted by the leaders in SPLM."

Helge Rohn left his position as the NPA Representative for the Sudan programme in the spring of 1996. He and Dr. Peter Adwok Nyaba, one of SPLM's leaders and one of its well-known intellectuals, were given the assignment to sketch a model for the rebuilding of the local political and administration systems in South Sudan. The study included among other things, workshops with local leaders in West Equatoria. It also included an evaluation of the systems for public administration and local government in Kenya, Uganda, Rwanda, Eritrea and Tanzania.

Rohn and Nyaba wrote a comprehensive report that was given to SPLM's leadership. In this report, Uganda was selected as the best example to follow in terms of building a new political system and a new public administration in the liberated areas. Uganda was chosen because the authors of the report thought that Uganda had succeeded better in getting the participation from people. It was seen as a bottom up approach.

John Garang had long working hours, from around 5 o'clock in the morning until late night. In this picture, he is at work on the first version of the satellite telephone he received from the Norwegian Ministry of Foreign Affairs.

From around 1990 until 2005 NPA had some 12000 emergency flights into and inside South Sudan, providing food and medicine and bringing visitors. In two flights, we had serious accidents that caused death.

6
DRAMATIC CHALLENGES – CREATIVE SOLUTIONS

THE SECRET PROJECT, NAMED THE "OSLO SEMINAR", AND THE STORY BEHIND JOHN GARANG'S SATELLITE TELEPHONE

Late in the fall of 1993, Sudan's ambassador to the Nordic countries, knocked on the door at the Ministry of Foreign Affairs in Oslo. He had an important errand and wanted to speak with the State Secretary Jan Egeland. He explained that he was impressed by the secret Oslo-Channel that had resulted in the agreement between Israel and Palestine, called the Oslo Accords. He wanted to see peace negotiations between the regime in Khartoum and SPLM/, being initiated, and he wanted Norway to establish a secret channel like the secret Israel-Palestine Channel.

Maybe the ambassador had an ulterior motive. In 1993, the Intergovernmental Authority on Development (IGAD) had started peace negotiations out of Kenya and Ethiopia. But Khartoum did not like countries from Black Africa taking initiatives like this. It was better with a country far North and far from Sudan.

Jan Egeland shared from the meeting the following with me and Mr. Egeland's first question was:

"Are you authorized by your government to present this proposal, we asked. No, replied the ambassador, and added that this was such an outlandish conflict that he had decided to take things into his own hands. We talked for a while, and got the impression that the ambassador was serious, and maybe, in reality, he had support from his government for the proposal he made.

The ambassador was very concerned that the proposal was kept secret, and he made it clear from the very beginning that no one from NPA must ever get to know about it. NPA was in his mind allied to SPLM/A.

After this first meeting I discussed the matter with one of our most experienced diplomats, Tom Vraalsen. He then contacted Gunnar Sørbø, at the time the Director for the Center for Development Studies at the University of Bergen and a leading academic member of the Christian Michelsens Institute, CMI. We agreed that we would try a new channel à la FAFO (another name of the Oslo-Channel for the secret talks between Israel and PLO), and this new initiative was given the preliminary name, the CMI-Channel.

Gunnar Sørbø and the Sudan group at the Christian Michelsens Institute (CMI) and other academics at the University of Bergen had a long-standing cooperation with the University at Khartoum. Therefore, the people in Bergen knew Sudan politics and society, and they had contacts in high political circles in Khartoum.

We at the Ministry of Foreign Affairs did not have such contacts in Khartoum, but we had excellent contacts with the leadership of SPLM through NPA and Norwegian Church Aid.

We started in all secrecy, making preparations for the project. In the beginning of 1994 Gunnar Sørbø, Tom Vraalsen and myself tra-

velled to Khartoum. We met with President Omar Bashir and the Speaker of Parliament, Hassan al Tourabi. Al Tourabi was at that time also the religious and ideological leader in Khartoum. We had very constructive meetings. When we left Khartoum, we had in all secrecy been given the green light from the National Islamic Front to make contact with the SPLM Chairman, John Garang."

Thus Egeland and his colleagues had come so far in the preparations that they felt they could start the secret talks. But it was more important than ever that as few people as possible knew about the project. The project was classified top secret and given the code name "The Oslo Seminar".

After the successful visit in Khartoum, Tom Vraalsen went to South Sudan and met with Garang and others leaders in SPLM. Garang agreed to a secret round of peace negotiations.

Gunnar Sørbø was now responsible for the contact with the regime in Khartoum, while Tom Vraalsen was responsible for the contact with SPLM. The two parties appointed their delegations and travelled secretly to Oslo.

The delegation from Khartoum consisted of important leaders from the Government and the Parliamentary Group of the National Islamic Front with Nafie Ali Nafie as the Head of Delegation, and the group from Khartoum was almost the same from meeting to meeting. Nafie was at that time, also the leader of the National Internal Security and Intelligence Service in Sudan (NISS). NISS under Nafie' s leadership was known for its extensive and brutal use of torture methods, something the Norwegians were not aware of at the time. The Ministry of Foreign Affairs was pleased that Khartoum brought so many high ranking people to the negotiation table, unaware of NISS's role. However, after the first meeting, another top man from Khartoum took over as Head of Delegation, Ghazi el Attabani.

Pa'gan Amum, one of John Garang's younger and closest confidants, was the Head of the SPLM Delegation, which in addition consisted of a few of the other central leaders from

SPLM. Pa'gan remained for the whole time Head of Delegation while the other members of the delegation changed frequently.

In the interview I had with Jan Egeland, he told me:

"*The first secret meeting was at Staur Guest House in Stange in the Eastern part of the Norway. The second was at Sem Guest House in Asker, close to Oslo, and the third and final meeting was held at Holmenkollen Park Hotel in Oslo.*

Our starting point for the discussions was that we had a very bloody and destructive war going on for the 11th year, and that it should be in the best interest of both sides to help put an end to the war. But we soon realized that the two sides had very different principle starting points for the negotiations.

The delegation from Khartoum was interested in negotiating some kind of partial independence for South Sudan, but nothing more. SPLM had a fundamentally different agenda. They viewed themselves as a revolutionary liberation movement, and they wanted to change the whole political system in all of Sudan. The new Sudan should be secular and democratic with respect for human rights.

The Khartoum delegation represented a Fundamentalist Islamic State System with Sharia Law, and this was the system SPLM/A fought against and wanted to remove.

In addition, we had the impression that both sides liked to travel to secret meeting places and stay at nice hotels, but putting an end to the war was something else. The Norwegian delegation concluded that there was no real political will with neither party to resolve the conflict with peaceful means. At the same time, other countries were offering forums for peace negotiations. Both Egypt and Gaddafi in Libya made such offers.

After the third negotiation round, the representatives for the Government of Norway concluded that our attempts to provide a secret Oslo-channel for peace negotiations in Sudan had not been successful. We informed the parties, and that was the end of our attempts to make peace in Sudan.

At the same time in the Horn of Africa, IGAD entered the political scene as a forum for continuing peace talks. At the Ministry of

Foreign Affairs, we appreciated the IGAD initiative, and we were the first to allocate financial support so that they could begin negotiations."

The Story about Garang's Satellite Telephone

While writing this book, I have spoken with many people who have shared their experience and insight with me. This also applies to this chapter on the secret peace negotiations and the secret satellite telephone which John Garang received during the negotiations in Norway.

One of the many I have talked with, is Tomm Kristiansen a senior reporter and a former Africa Correspondent with Norwegian Broadcasting Corporation (NRK). Tomm also served as a UN seconded communication advisor to President Salva Kiir in the period between 2007 and 2009.

Tomm met Garang several times as the NRK correspondent. After an interview in 1993, Garang brought up a rather delicate issue. He needed a satellite telephone. Tomm could not help him, but promised to pass on his request to the right person in the Norwegian Ministry of Foreign Affairs (NMFA).

Jan Egeland explained:

"Already at the first meeting of the two delegations, the question about a satellite phone was raised. Regarding this matter, we had some very important experience from the talks between Israel and Palestine. We knew it was of the utmost importance to always to have lines of communication that we controlled, and that were accessible to us at all times.

Pa'gan Amum said during one of our first conversations that for SPLM to be able to have continuing contact with us in the Norwegian delegation, they needed a satellite telephone as there was no other telecommunication available in the battlefields of South Sudan. I knew that satellite telephones were part of the Norwegian Emergency Preparedness System (NOREPS) concept which the Ministry had set up. It was therefore rather easy to hand over such a telephone to John Garang and his confidants within SPLM. But I made it perfectly clear that the telephone could only be used in connection with the peace negotiations, and that we retained the right to turn it on and off. They agreed to these terms."

It should be noted that being able to communicate was very, very important to John Garang. There were no telephone lines or mobile networks that worked inside South Sudan or between South Sudan and the outside world. The only other means of communication was radio and satellite telephone.

But NMFA could not pay the telephone bills via its own accounts because that was politically too risky. Therefore, they had to find a way of keeping Garang's telephone bills a secret. Hence, in the winter of 1994 a clandestine agreement was made between the Ministry and CMI in Bergen that CMI would pay the bills. The expenses would be refunded by the Ministry. CMI was not enthusiastic about this, but accepted.

But CMI needed a telephone company that would play along with the whole clandestine operation, and they were given permission to open a secret account with the state owned Norwegian Telenor Company through which the invoice would be paid. Only then could CMI forward the invoice to NMFA for reimbursement. The NMFA negotiation team was supposed to be the only one who had access to the on and off button on the phone. Garang and his men were not supposed to be able to call just anywhere. They in theory needed consent from Oslo to do that.

This satellite phone was at the time produced by the Norwegian Telecommunication Company "Nera" in Bergen, weighing about 40 kilos and was packed as a luggage bag. Tom Vraalsen travelled to Nairobi and South Sudan to hand over the phone. In Nairobi, he met with the NPA Resident Representative Helge Rohn, who agreed on behalf of NMFA to hire a plane and accompany Tom Vraalsen into South Sudan to hand over the new equipment to John Garang.

As telephone technology improved, and the equipment became lighter, Garang was given newer models. Garang had complete trust in Helge Rohn, and he was therefore one of the few in Nairobi who could make an appointment to meet Garang anywhere in the field, so he agreed in secret to help NMFA when there was a need for transportation and meetings inside South Sudan.

At the NPA Headquarters in Oslo we still did not know anything about the peace negotiations or the satellite telephone.

In 1996 Telenor joined a new Kenyan partner, Telemedia Communication, the co-owner and director for this company was Magne Albrigtsen from Vesteraalen in Northern Norway. He had a military background from Norway, and he had worked as a telecommunications specialist for the UN in the Middle East for 16 years. Early in the 1990s he left Beirut and moved to Nairobi. There, he established Telemedia Communications together with a Kenyan partner, and Telenor had the billing for Garang's satellite telephone transferred to this company.

1994-96 and most of 1997 passed. NMFA kept their part of the agreement with CMI and Garang. Tom Vraalsen had the responsibility for the contact with SPLM, and he was using the phone frequently. The same applied to the leaders in SPLM/A, but allegedly within the conditions set by NMFA. CMI paid the Telenor bills in the beginning using the secret Telenor account in Oslo, then later the account with Telemedia Communications in Nairobi. Whenever payments were made, NMFA was asked to reimburse the sum. I am not sure of the exact amount paid annually by NMFA, but I have indications that in 1996 the telephone bills were a little more than 300 000 NOK, and during the first half of 1997 the amount was about the same.

Time passed. The Norwegian Parliamentary Election in 1997 resulted in a change of government, and the leader of the Christian People's Party, Mr. Kjell Magne Bondevik, became the Prime Minister and formed a minority coalition government with the Liberal Party and the Center Party. The young woman politician Mrs. Hilde Frafjord Johnson from the Christian People's Party was appointed as the new Minister for International Development Cooperation and Human Rights. A little later, probably in the fall of 1997, a pile of bills from CMI, including telephone bills and other expenses connected to the project "The Oslo Seminar" landed on the desk of the NMFA.

The amount was so large that the Director in NMFA in charge of finances refused to sign for it. The case had to go up to the new Minister for International Development Cooperation, Hilde Frafjord Johnson. However, she was not at all pleased about cleaning up after her political predecessor, but after some persuasion, she agreed. This happened before Hilde Frafjord Johnson had decided to involve herself in the peace negotiations for Sudan. While dealing with these payments, she also made it very clear that the payment of Garang's telephone bills had to stop with immediate effect, and that no future bills would be paid.

However, the NMFA people who had access to Garang's phone were not in practice able to decide when to turn it on and off. Garang developed an ability to use the telephone for any purpose, and he needed the satellite phone around the clock.

The arrangement that NMFA had for payment for the telephone bills, came to an end in the fall of 1997. But the telephone continued to be used, and used intensively by Garang and his confidants. Therefore, an ever increasing load of unpaid telephone bills piled up at Telemedia Communications in Nairobi. They had a straight forward policy about unpaid bills, after a short while, they simply disconnected the telephone.

Lars Johan Johnsen took over as the new Resident Representative of NPA's Sudan Programme in early fall of 1997. Previously, he had done an exceptionally good job as the regional Director for NPA's humanitarian assistance to war struck areas in the Balkans in the 1990s.

One morning in the late winter of 1998 Lars Johan called me from Nairobi. He was usually a man of quiet talk, but this morning he was not his normal self, but very agitated.

"Halle, I just got a bill for Garang's satellite telephone. It is about 600 000 NOK and since it has not been paid, the phone has been disconnected. I just got a message from Garang in the field over the radio.

He is furious. He and SPLA are in the middle of a large military battle, and Garang has lost his most important source of communication and line of command, the satellite telephone. He says that NMFA has broken its promise about paying the bill, and he is demanding that NPA takes responsibility and make sure the bill is paid immediately. What am I supposed to do? I know nothing about this!"

I replied: "Lars Johan, I don't know anything about this either, but when Garang says NMFA is responsible then I would assume this to be true. So, my message is: Pay the bill as fast as possible, and I will deal with NMFA."

"Alright," said Lars Johan, and the conversation was over.

I immediately contacted my closest staff members at NPA, informing them in confidence about Lars Johan's telephone call, and what I had decided. I then carefully inquired with relevant staff both at the International and Administrative departments whether they knew anything about Garang's satellite telephone, and the way telephone bills were being paid.

Nobody knew anything. Many were quite amazed at the question.

I then contacted the relevant level in NMFA, but nobody there seemed to know anything either; or they pretended not to know anything. We tried several times and in different ways to raise a discussion with responsible people in NMFA on the matter, but we failed. At the same time, we soon found out, now having established contact with Telemedia Communications in Nairobi that a satellite telephone invoice had been paid by them with money from NMFA.

1998 passed. Once during 1999 I asked Lars Johan what had happened with the invoice for Garang's satellite telephone. He answered that he had quickly understood both how important the telephone was for SPLM and Garang, and how delicate the matter was in political terms. So he had decided to incorporate the bills in the administrative expenses for the Sudan Programme. Since USAID at that time was NPA's biggest donor, most of the invoice was absorbed by USA's contributions to the administration of the programme., while the remaining sum was paid with funds from Norway.

I thanked Lars Johan and complimented him for the way he handled the case.

This conversation took place just before Lars Johan's contract was coming to an end and his successor, Sten Rino Bonsaksen was to begin in the job as the NPA Resident Representative. Unfortunately, Sten Rino Bonsaksen was not informed about the satellite telephone, the history behind it and how the bills were being paid.

So one day in the spring of 2000, while I was participating in an internal NPA leadership seminar, Sten Rino called me from Nairobi:

"*Halle, I have to talk to you right now!*" I went out in the hallway and Sten Rino continued: "*Halle, I have just received an invoice for a satellite telephone for Garang running at more than 800 000 NOK. It is not paid, and the telephone is disconnected. Garang is in the middle of an important military battle. He has just given word via radio that he is furious that he is once again betrayed by NPA and NMFA, not paying the telephone bill again. What do I do?*"

This happened at a time with significant criticism both internally and externally about NPA's Sudan Programme and my role in it. Therefore, I did not want to make any decision alone and asked for a break in the seminar. Then I called the management group and other relevant staff and informed them for the first time about the secret story about Garang's satellite telephone, what NPA had inherited from NMFA, and how I and our Resident Representative, Lars Johan Johnsen had handled the situation.

Then I said: "*This time it is important that all of you are informed and take part in the decision making. What do we do? If we say no, it will have immediate military and political consequences for SPLM/A, and will probably have great consequences for our Sudan programme as well.*"

My colleagues looked at each other. This was quite unexpected news, and the decision could not wait. After a brief discussion, they said simultaneously: "*We shall pay!*"

I was relieved and called Sten Rino: "*I have just discussed the matter with the management group and other relevant staff, and we have agreed that NPA shall pay the invoice. You just need to find a practical way to put it in the accounts as administrative expenses.*"

At this time however, there was a new political situation for Sudan. The peace negotiations were under way in Kenya, in part due to the political initiatives taken by the Minister for International Development Cooperation, Hilde Frafjord Johnson. She took the first initiatives in the spring of 1998. When the Government of Bondevik I was replaced in March 2000 by Stoltenberg I, Thorbjørn Jagland as Minister for Foreign Affairs and Raymond Johansen as State Secretary took over the responsibility for the Norwegian participation in the peace negotiations on Sudan.

In the summer of 2000 Raymond Johansen needed to contact Garang quickly. He wanted to discuss an important, difficult issue in the negotiations, but he and NMFA no longer had his satellite telephone number. Therefore, he called me to ask for help:

"*Halle, can you get me in touch with Garang? It is urgent.*"

I called Sten Rino in Nairobi, who had both Garang's number and the responsibility for paying the telephone invoice. It took five minutes before Garang called Raymond Johansen. Whether Garang at the time gave his new satellite phone number to Raymond Johansen or not, I do not know.

My contract with NPA came to an end in May 2001, and I decided to leave and continue working as an independent advisor and writer on African and other International issues. The satellite telephone issue was no longer my responsibility.

But after I left, the new combined leadership of NPA, the President of the Board of Directors, Reiulf Steen, and my successor, the new Secretary General, Eva Bjøreng, raised the matter of terminating the NPA Sudan Programme because it was costly, difficult and controversial. What stopped this process within NPA to bring an end to the Sudan Programme, I do not know for certain. But the idea caused great worries with the political leadership and the high level staff in the NFMA who were involved in the peace negotiations for Sudan in Kenya. Senator John Danforth, President George Bush's Special Envoy on Sudan, paid a working visit to Oslo in the summer of 2002. During his time in Oslo, he also paid a visit to NPA and discussed the Sudan Programme with them. Representatives from NPA who met with Mr. Danforth were the President of the Board of Directors, Reiulf Steen, and the Resident Representative for the Sudan Programme, Sten Rino Bonsaksen who was called from Nairobi for the meeting. Mr. Danforth as well most likely shared a word about the importance of the NPA programme, seen from the viewpoint of the US Government.

In the summer of 2002 the problem with the satellite telephone invoice surfaced again. Sten Rino was informed about the discussion at NPA in Oslo regarding the termination of the Sudan Programme. Therefore, he did not risk paying the invoice, because Mrs. Bjøreng had already vetoed any payment. The story about the satellite telephone had to come to an end. In her view the telephone was the responsibility of the NMFA. Øystein Botillen who was responsible for the Sudan programme in Oslo, once again had taken the issue to NMFA. In the Ministry, there were varying opinions. Some thought that it was politically risky to disconnect the phone while the peace negotiations were in progress, while others in more powerful positions, thought it should be done. The final decision was that NMFA would not pay.

But taking the satellite telephone away from Garang now, could have very serious consequences. There were no telecommunications in South Sudan. Garang needed the phone more than ever before, not just for military and political purposes inside South Sudan, but also as a means of communication in the ongoing peace negotiations. Sten Rino called me immediately after he had been told by the new Secretary General to stop all payments. He saw the serious implications of cutting the telephone service for John Garang. I had been out of NPA for over a year, but Sten wanted to discuss with me whether or not there was any possibility to avoid disconnecting Garang's satellite telephone.

I advised him to ignore Bjøreng's decision and look elsewhere for the money. Sten then told me that he knew Magne Albrigtsen who was the Co-owner and Director of Telemedia Communications that had the franchise for satellite communication for most of the Horn of Africa We agreed that Sten would ask Magne Albrigtsen for a substantial discount. If he succeeded in doing that, he could without the knowledge of the NPA HQ and the Secretary General in Oslo cover the remaining amount as administrative expenses in the NPA accounts. This was in my opinion a practical solution to the problem.

Sten Rino went to his Northern Norwegian friend Magne, and negotiated a discount. He also convinced his friend that if he could ensure that Garang's satellite telephone would remain operational, there might be business opportunities with the SPLM Government in South Sudan in the future. During the summer of 2002 the peace negotiations were going well. The likelihood of peace in Sudan was real, and with peace, many new opportunities would ensue. Not only that, Sten Rino added that he could help arrange a meeting with Garang.

NPA was given a 40 percent rebate. The remaining amount was absorbed by NPA's Sudan Programme as an operating expense for 2002.

Magne Albrigtsen never met Garang, but Garang's politically smart and loyal wife, Rebecca Garang, and other top leaders in SPLM met with him, and they discussed many possible projects together.

This was the way the story of NPA and Garang's satellite phone came to an end in the summer of 2002. The new agreement between Telemedia Communications and SPLM contained much more than the satellite phone. Telemedia Communication in Nairobi became in short the main supplier of Information and Communication Technology to SPLM, and the cooperation between the two partners went well for many years.

But then other interests, for the most part Chinese, took over the responsibility for developing communication in South Sudan. Corruption in the battle of obtaining contracts has flourished in the aftermath, and to this day there is anarchy and non-functioning telecommunications in Juba and South Sudan.

Magne Albrigtsen was given the contract by SPLM to build the first container hotel in the liberated South Sudan in Rumbek. Today he has a hotel with 100 beds and a long-term contract with UN for the hire of the hotel.

So, how big was the financial burden that NPA carried, paying the bills for the satellite phone? All together NPA paid somewhere between three and five million NOK during a five-year period. But in relation to the overall budget for the Sudan Programme it was a very small part of the whole, between 5 and 7 permille.

The telephone was originally a secret gift from NMFA, given by the State Secretary, Jan Egeland. For four years, the information was kept away from us, the leaders of NPA. Nevertheless, in 1998 NPA inherited the cost of the telephone from NMFA while the Ministry and the new Norwegian government, refused to acknowledge any responsibility for their actions. SPLM did not have any other international partner willing to cover the expenses. I and my colleagues in NPA did not see any alternative to paying the bills. NPA had taken a stand in support of the liberation struggle in Sudan, and we stood in solidarity with the millions struggling for independence and freedom. We could not refuse payment in the winter of 1998 or later, because the military and political stakes were too high.

The River Boat, the International Red Cross and Jan Egeland

In 1988 Jan Egeland took up his first leadership position as Director of Information with the Norwegian Red Cross. A year later he was Secretary General in the same organization. Two years after that, he was appointed the political adviser and shortly after State Secretary with Foreign Minister Thorvald Stoltenberg at NMFA.

At that time, another of many droughts and famine catastrophes was ravaging Sudan, while at the same time, the conflict between SPLM/A and the regime in Khartoum was escalating. There was a constant need for emergency relief, first and foremost food, but also medicine.

On one of his first trips to Sudan, Jan Egeland asked UN and the other organizations a simple question: Why do you not use the Nile and boats to transport emergency aid?

There was no reasonable answer.

Jan Egeland and others from the Norwegian Red Cross went to Genève in 1988 to talk to colleagues at the International Red Cross Committee about using a river boat.

Egeland told me the following in an interview in March 2014:

"Genève said they would gladly have a boat on the Nile, but did not think the Red Cross in Norway could help with that. Then somebody in the Red Cross office in Oslo suggested that we ourselves should build the river boat with light metal and transport it to South Sudan.

Red Cross contacted a shipyard in the county of Vestfold, west of Oslo. They agreed to construct the boat, and NMFA agreed to finance the project. The boat was built in two pieces, at a cost of about five million NOK.

The Red Cross rented the biggest Antonov transport plane from Russia. At the time, it was the biggest airplane ever to land in Norway. The two parts of the boat were loaded and flown to Nairobi.

There we rented two of the biggest trucks that could be found in Kenya and transported the boat via Lokichokio to Bor in South Sudan, a distance of about 2000 kilometers. In Bor the two parts were welded together, and the boat was launched on the Nile.

It was used for a few trips under the auspices of the International Red Cross Committee before the tension of the military conflict increased so much that it was no longer possible to use it. The Red Cross experienced several times that both sides would fire at the boat to prevent food being transported to those in need. It was an impossible situation, and the boat was put on shore.

That was when I experienced the best and worst of Egil Hagen at NPA. He was extremely good with the media; he spoke in a very convincing manner. He was also exceptionally operational.

> Egil started an enormous campaign in the media in Norway and USA claiming that the NMFA had financed the building and transportation of the river boat so that it could transport food, but that it was now on land because the International Red Cross Committee did not have the imagination to use it in the conflict situation that was prevailing in South Sudan. At the same time, he claimed that he had SPLA's guarantee that they would not misuse the boat if NPA took it over for food transport on the Nile.
>
> I was under terrible pressure. The boat was de facto seen as the property of the Ministry as we had paid for both the construction and the transport. But the Red Cross Committee thought it was insane to give the boat to NPA. They claimed that NPA was a political partner in the struggle and not reliable. The Committee further argued the boat could not be used without an absolute guarantee from both warring parties, and Khartoum would never give any guarantee to NPA.
>
> I had to make a decision. The worst alternative was not using the boat. After a long internal debate, NMFA decided to hand over the boat to NPA.
>
> This was a very significant decision. I was involved from the beginning, first as Secretary General of the Norwegian Red Cross, then as the Political Adviser and later as State Secretary in NMFA. In the cause of this process I had the experience of sitting at all sides of the table."

That concludes Jan Egeland.

The river boat was no doubt a difficult issue both for Jan Egeland and the Red Cross Committee. After the boat was grounded, Egil Hagen bombarded Red Cross with criticism. In the spring of 1991 Egil became ill and had to go to Norway for further medical treatment. The diagnosis from the doctors at the National Hospital was bad news, there was a stomach cancer that had spread. Egil underwent a major surgery, but it was too late. Egil's health deteriorated fast and he died on Boxing Day in 1991.

During the winter of 1992 the river boat was handed over to NPA. Helge Rohn was now the new NPA Resident Representative. He recalled the following about his first encounter with the river boat:

"In March 1992, a few weeks after my arrival, we had a new challenge. A few years earlier the Red Cross had constructed a river boat in Vestfold in order to transport food on the Nile. It had made several trips under the auspices of the Red Cross, but now NPA had taken over responsibility for the boat.

During the time of the SPLA internal conflict and split in 1991-92, government forces advanced southwards. They were currently so close to Bor that we when visiting our people in the field, could hear heavy artillery fire just north of Bor.

The river boat was hidden in one of the Nile's many side streams near Bor. I decided to go and see the boat and see to it that some maintenance was done. In Nairobi we hired a mechanic and his assistant for the purpose, and we had an American pilot who flew us to Bor. I remember that we brought a fishnet to camouflage the boat. In Bor we hired a little boat with an outboard engine, and a local guide who took us to where the boat was anchored.

We found the river boat in surprisingly good shape and with a Sudanese crew permanently on board. They made detailed lists of what belonged to NPA. We helped put the fishnets over the boat, and after a day of work we started our return to Bor. About half way back, far away from people and in the middle of the Nile, the outboard engine stopped. I did not at the time have much experience with that kind of journey, and thought the whole situation was rather frightening. There were signs of crocodile and hippopotamuses all along the river bank, and there were very many mosquitos.

Fortunately, our two mechanics immediately started repairing the engine. They located the problem and carried out some temporary repair that they feared could not last because of lack of spare parts. But by some miracle, it held until in the middle of the night we got back to Bor. Back on land, SPLA's commander, William Nyon, invited us to a late night dinner with fresh fish from the Nile.

Shortly after our visit Bor was taken by government forces, and we were not able to use the river boat as planned. Both sides of the war saw the military value of the boat. Both SPLA and the govern-

ment forces wanted to control the boat in order to transport soldiers and equipment. Khartoum made it a priority target to bomb it."

NPA as well had to admit that they were not able to use the boat as planned, and therefore had to hand it over to its next owner, SPLA. They established their own river boat transport company, to use the boat both for civilian and military purposes.

But now, Khartoum wanted more than ever to destroy the boat. SPLA also had to admit that it was dangerous for them to use it for transportation. The captain of the boat, a very able South Sudanese, convinced the SPLA commanders to take the boat out of service and move it to a hiding place either on the Nile or on one of its many tributaries. SPLA agreed, and the decision to take the boat out of operation was taken sometime in 1993. The NPA staff in Nairobi was informed about the matter.

The captain steered the boat to a place on the Nile where the trees were tall with big branches that stretched out over the river bank. The crew camouflaged the boat so well that it became almost invisible. The captain and most of the crew remained on board. Then they started an important routine. The machinist started and ran the two engines 15-20 minutes a day. The crew polished and cared for the boat every week, as if it were their most valued possession. This maintenance routine started in 1993 and continued until 2000.

Dan Eiffe was in Jonglei and Bor in 1999. He thought the river boat had been destroyed in the war. To his amazement, a SPLA commander asked if he wanted to see it. He was even more amazed to see that is was in extremely good condition.

Around 2000 there were many both political and military challenges in Sudan. SPLA had reconquered most of the territories it had controlled until 1991, and they had taken physical control of most of South Sudan. Garang and SPLM had wide popular support, and SPLM had broken the ice diplomatically and politically with key countries in Europe. The peace negotiations were under way. Many refugees dreaming about peace, began returning to their homes. Many thousands of them were in Uganda, and they were starting the long march back home. NPA in cooperation with SRRA informed its own drivers in the field to pick up refugees when they had space in their trucks. Sten Rino also made an agreement with SPLA that the river boat should be taken from its hiding place and used to transport refugees.

During the entire war, Khartoum held Juba as a garrison town. Refugees coming from the South by the thousands therefore had to first pass west of Juba, and then north-east towards the Nile. At agreed places along the banks of the Nile, the river boat picked up refugees and transported them the last 50 to 70 kilometers to their homes near Bor.

This transportation lasted for a few weeks, until Khartoum became aware of what the boat was used for. The fear of it being bombed became so great that the boat was once again hidden away. However, during periods of political and military peace, the river boat was brought back into service on several occasions between 2002 and 2005, transporting refugees who were returning to their homes.

When the CPA became a reality in January 2005, the crew immediately brought the boat back into service and established a commercial route between Juba and Malakal. The same SPLA company owned it, and the same captain and crew were on board.

In May 2008 when I was in Juba attending the SPLM Congress as a guest of honour, I had an afternoon off, Marit Hernæs from NPA mentioned that the crew as well had a day off in the harbor. Did I want to see them? Of course I did! We went down to the harbor, and found the boat with the captain and the crew. It was a pleasant meeting. The captain and the crew shared many stories with us from the war, bomb attacks, failed sabotage episodes and risky refugee transport, as well as stories from the long silent periods the boat was in hiding.

NPA's Chair of the Board of Directors, Finn-Erik Thoresen, was also in South Sudan on business, and he also visited the river boat and talked with the crew. They told Finn-Erik among other things about the problems with one of the defunct engines, and the damage to the rudder.

Finn-Erik always worked diligently on securing NPA more political and financial support from the Norwegian Confederation of Free Trade Unions (LO) and its member organizations. Before he left for South Sudan, he contacted the Norwegian Seamen' Union (NSU) and tried to reach an agreement, but they rejected the idea. NPA did not have any programme abroad that was directly related to the well-being of seamen.

But then there was a new possibility. Finn-Erik spoke with the captain and the crew about was necessary for the maintenance and repair of the boat. He assessed their needs and took pictures of the boat. Then, he went home and asked for a new meeting with the leaders of NSU, and he told them that he now had a very relevant international solidarity project for them. He then suggested that the union should take responsibility for buying two new engines, a new rudder and other equipment. The leaders in NSU agreed to everything. The new engines were ordered and a few months later it was all in place in Juba.

There was excitement both with the crew and the passengers. The boat now went faster than at any time before, and it continued to serve both passengers and commercial transport on the Nile until December 2013 when the disastrous civilian war broke out. At that time, 26 years had passed since the boat was built in Vestfold. No one, in her or his wildest imagination would ever have been able to predict anything close, to what is now the exciting history of the river boat. But it has in the main served the interests and needs of ordinary war-ravaged and poor people in South Sudan which was the original plan when the Norwegian Red Cross had the boat built in Vestfold, flown to Nairobi and trucked to Bor in South Sudan, melded together and put on the Nile.

It is difficult to say what has become of the boat after the outbreak of war in 2013. Maybe it is still used to transport food to the hundreds of thousands of civilians who are starving because of the war? Maybe Kiir's forces have taken the boat and have been using it in his destructive war in violation of all kind of agreements? I don't know.

The Famine Catastrophe in the Nuba Mountains and the Role of NPA

Helge Rohn and others in Nairobi were in 1993 informed about an accelerating humanitarian catastrophe, developing in the Nuba Mountains. The British activist and researcher Alex de Waal was particularly active in mobilizing the attention and the concern of the world to the severity of the crisis.

Alex de Waal developed as a very young man, a strong interest in Africa, especially Sudan. In 1989, he received his doctorate in Social Anthropology for his work on the famine in Darfur in 1984-85. The dissertation formed the basis for his book *Famine That Kills, Darfur, Sudan*. In 1993, he founded a human rights organization called African Rights, in order to document human rights abuses in African countries. He used this organization to get the world's attention on the famine and the systematic mass killing of the peoples in the Nuba Mountains that the regime in Khartoum was responsible for then, and still is today.

Alex de Waal wanted to establish reliable ways of documenting the crimes committed in the Nuba Mountains, so he contacted Helge Rohn and asked for support from NPA. There were two critical problems that had to be solved in order to get an emergency operation working.

Firstly, reliable radio communication had to be established. To achieve this, local people from the Nuba Mountains needed to be trained as radio operators. Secondly, more airstrips needed to be built, to secure safe landing places for planes bringing in food, medicine and clothes.

Helge Rohn explained in an interview in the winter of 2014 how the Nuba Mountains operation came into being:

"In 1993, Khartoum banned all kinds of emergency relief aid to the peoples in the Nuba Mountains. The outside world had very little knowledge of the very serious humanitarian crisis in the area. The security situation was bad for anyone trying to bring in relief. Alex de Waal and African Rights had made several attempts to establish radio networks in the Nuba Mountains, but had failed, and now they wan-

ted NPA to assist in the efforts. We agreed and started by strengthening our own radio station in Lokichokio. Doctors Without Borders, Belgium and Nederland provided radio equipment and a couple of highly competent radio technicians from Nederland. Firstly, they made strong improvements on our station in Loki, and then they took a big risk. They agreed to go into the Nuba Mountains. NPA hired a plane and had them flown in to set up the necessary local radio stations while at the same time train local people how to operate the stations. Everything went well. They set up the stations, tested them and taught a few local people how to operate them, and they indeed became very skilled.

At the same time, those of us working with humanitarian aid were getting many messages about extensive fighting, increasing famine, more and more death, and more and more documented cases of ethnic cleansing in the Nuba Mountains. The lives of tens of thousands of people were at stake. We were all concerned with this, but did not have the ability to do anything on our own. The Nuba Mountains were so far away from our base in Lokichokio.

Mel Middleton, who worked for the Canadian International Development Agency (CIDA) at the Canadian embassy in Nairobi, was getting particularly concerned with the situation in the Nuba Mountains, and he took an initiative and called a meeting with some of the International NGOs in Nairobi to try and organize help.

I was together with five-six other NGO representatives at this first meeting, some of the others worked in NGOs that were associated with OLS. Mel suggested that we should establish a consortium, with a general and vague name; Network for East African Relief (NEAR), with the aim to get emergency aid and relief into the Nuba Mountains. The suggestion was supported by all of us present, but a few requested that their participation ha to be kept secret as their own NGOs were part of OLS. They were participating in the meeting without permission from Headquarters in Western Europe.

We agreed that everyone would contribute money, medicine and food. But it was more difficult to find an organization that would take the lead responsibility, so I suggested that NPA could take the role as Lead Agency. Since the nature of the group was politically controversial and quite sensitive for some of the organizations, we agreed to use a cover name at all the meetings and only have secret minutes from our meetings. The operation had to be kept secret, and we managed this. We had as our partner, the Nuba Relief, Rehabilitation and Development Society (NRRDS), which also had a representation in Nairobi.

The other partners in the consortium transferred money from their budgets to NPA, and they acquired food, medicines and other supplies from their warehouses. NPA was given money from NMFA for the project. We did most of the purchasing, hired planes, kept financial records and ran the radio communication from Lokichokio. NPA's base in Lokichokio was the base for the Nuba operations.

But we did not have any experience from field visits in the Nuba Mountains. In South Sudan, we were mostly in the low lands. In the Nuba Mountains we were faced with a very different terrain, high mountains and deep valleys. We did not have reliable information about topography, weather or landing conditions, or even where the fighting was. Therefore, it was essential that we established radio communications and built two new airstrips in advance.

This improved the security situation. We had continuous contact with the radio operators in the Nuba Mountains, who were in contact with the leaders in SPLM/A, commander Yousef Kuwa was in charge. He was an exceptional personality, very gifted, very knowledgeable, and very human and caring for others. He had a team of people who really loved him, and on top of all this he was an outstanding guerilla commander. When communication was working the way it should, and it usually did, we had updated information on the weather, locations of fighting, and which airstrips that were relatively safe to use.

An important American partner for us in this work was the Director of the US Committee for Refugees, Roger Winter. He had considerable influence in political circles in Washington. We brought him at an early stage in our relief operation to the Nuba Mountains, and it was a very successful visit."

The Norwegian Pilot Bjørn Abelsen and his Nuba Experience

Bjørn Abelsen was one of the pilots in the Kenyan Company SKYWAYS, which the consortium used for the flights into the Nuba Mountains from 1994 to 1997. He is from the island of Kjerringøy, in Northern Norway. He shared with me some very important stories from his many missions to the Nuba Mountains:

"In my flat in Nairobi the alarm clock rang just before 03 a.m. whenever we had a flight to Nuba. I had a light meal and went to the international airport in Nairobi, Jomo Kenyatta Airport. There the plane had been loaded the night before with 2,5 tons of food, medicine and clothes, and it was ready for take-off. I almost always flew with the American pilot Dale Roark. There were never any papers with the cargo because in the worst case scenario that Khartoum shot us down, they should not be able to find out who we were and what kind of mission we were on. In order to cross the border to Sudan while it was still dark, we took off from Nairobi at 0430 in the morning and climbed to 7000 meters above sea level.

A fictitious flight plan was always filed, so that for the air traffic control tower in Nairobi, it looked like we were flying to Lokichokio. When we were close to Loki, we asked for permission to land which always was granted. But the crew at the airport knew of course that our call for landing was part of our cover up operation. We continued our flights into Sudanese airspace, but now we turned the transponder off, so that we would disappear from the radar screens. Next we cut all radio contact and turned off our lights. Everything possible had to be done so that Khartoum could not detect us. When we crossed the border to Sudan, it was still dark. We listened to the frequency of Khartoum's air traffic control and the international emergency frequency, and then climbed to 8000 meters. Then, Khartoum's land-to-air artillery could not reach us. As we got closer to the Nuba Mountains, the day began to dawn. We did not risk any radio contact with our people on the ground, but we had spoken with them through SPLAs HF-radio from Nairobi the night before. They knew about our arrival. The descent was every time done in sharp spirals in order to reduce chances of being hit by fire from the ground.

The first times we landed with food, the people were in very bad shape. Everyone was thin and showed signs of malnourishment and starvation. Everyone was naked. It was an awful sight, but at the same time it made us feel that the mission was meaningful. We flew in food twice a week, and after a few months we could see a change. People began looking healthier. Everyone, especially the children, looked healthier. They were also wearing clothes.

One morning when we landed, there was a thick fog and difficult landing conditions. But we succeeded to land and started unloading the cargo. Then all hell broke loose. The government forces had been informed in advance about our flight, and they had been hiding in the cover of the fog and had managed to move close to the airstrip without SPLA discovering them. There was heavy shooting from mortars and smaller weapons. People ran in all directions looking for shelter, and many were killed or wounded.

Dale had walked down the airstrip to fill a dangerous mud hole so we could avoid it during departure, and disappeared in the fog. I spotted a fallen tree just outside the airstrip, ran there and threw myself behind it. Not long after, I saw Dale running towards the plane. He jumped into the cockpit, and I knew what he was going to do. He wanted for us to try and get the plane out of there before it got shot. I ran back and jumped in through the back cargo door, pulled it up and yelled that it was clear for take-off. He gave full throttle and while the gunfire hit around us, we took off, reached once again an altitude where we were safe, and we had a safe journey back to Nairobi.

On the way to Nairobi we talked about what had just happened, our narrow escape, and the big difference in fire power between SPLA on one side and the government forces on the other.

A week later we landed again on another airstrip in the Nuba Mountains. This time our arrival was not compromised and everything went smoothly. But there were more SPLA soldiers at the landing strip and in the surrounding area than usually. Dale and I went over and asked them about their weapons and ammunition.

They showed us their old Kalashnikovs and rifles and told us that they had been given six shots each. That was all they had to defend themselves with when the enemy attacked.

We went back to the plane and Dale looked at me and said: "This is ridiculous. We fly in emergency aid and save thousands of people, but they have nothing to defend themselves with. As soon as the forces from Khartoum attack, they are helpless and are murdered by the thousands. Are you ready to do what's necessary?" I nodded and said: "Dale, I agree with you and am very ready."

We flew back to Nairobi. On the way home we agreed to see the Director for SKYWAYS, Patrick Ikenya. Our message was simple. "We know that SPLA has asked you for transport of arms to the Nuba Mountains. Here we are. You have two pilots willing to fly for you." Patrick who was interested in making money and sympathized with the people in the Nuba Mountains, said that was fine.

Dale and I then had several flights with arms supply to the SPLA in the Nuba Mountains. The weapons and ammunition came from other black African countries, and we increased SPLA's defense ability substantially.

When the missions for SPLA were finished, we continued flying aid relief for the NPA Consortium. They were two separate missions."

Nothing ever really went terribly wrong during the many hundred flights of aid relief that Bjørn Abelsen and Dale Roark made for NPA and the consortium to the Nuba Mountains. But there were some close calls. One time they were behind schedule and it turned daylight while they were still in Sudanese airspace. Just after they crossed the border, air traffic control at the airport in Khartoum started calling them by their plane's call sign. Next, they tried to call them on the emergency frequency. Dale and Bjørn took it for granted that they would be attacked in the air. The Mig-23-plane was what they feared the most.

They prepared for what they had practiced many times, to maneuver the plane so they could avoid fire from the Mig-23. But everything was quiet. No more call signs came from Khartoum. They continued to Nuba, landed, unloaded and flew out again. When they approached the area where they had expected the jet fighter to attack, they saw smoke. They could not resist flying low to take a closer look, and then they saw the wreck of a Mig-23, still burning.

What had happened? SPLA in the area had seen the jet fighter taking off from the airport of Juba and fired with everything they had, and hit it. The pilot had ejected and survived. He was now a prisoner of war with SPLA.

There were many other narrow escapes. Another time the nose wheel broke right after landing in Nuba. The plane dived and was damaged but Dale and Bjørn crawled out unhurt. What now? Getting a message back to Loki was not easy, and could be detected, but they managed to send it.

Two days later a plane came to pick them up. It had two pilots and an assistant. When they took off, the nose wheel collapsed on this plane too. But it did not dive, and they stopped and could repair it. They tried again, but the same thing happened, but the plane did not dive this time either. The pilot then turned and said:

"*We have too many people. One has to get out.*"

One was an American Dale Roark, the other Bjørn, a young Norwegian. He quickly understood that he had to get out. Before he left, Dale shouted: "*I'll be back for you.*"

So Bjørn stayed a couple more days with the people they had saved and supplied with guns so that they were not defenseless when the enemy attacked. Bjørn remembers his stay as if it were today. He was taken well care of. The people there showed him, the young man from the island of Kjerringøy in Northern Norway, exceptional great kindness and warmth.

When Bjørn had told me about all of this and more, he was quiet for a while and then he said:

"*I have never met such friendly people as those in the Nuba Mountains. I have a dream, to be able to fly there again and greet them.*"

The Battle at Aswa River in 1994

After six years of fighting for freedom SPLM/A were in 1989 in a very strong position both militarily and politically. SPLA had driven the government forces and their allies on the defensive all over South Sudan and controlled most of the land. The government forces were pushed into a small number of garrison towns. *See map on the adjacent page.*

But the collapse of the communist regimes in Eastern Europe and thereby also Ethiopia, weakened SPLM/A substantially both militarily and politically, and the new rulers in Ethiopia expelled thousands of young boys in camps for military training for SPLM/A, from the country. The disruption and split of SPLM/A in Nasir in August 1991, led by Riek Machar and Lam Akol, weakened SPLM/A further. The latter two were encouraged and supported by the regime in Khartoum, and praised by many other international actors. Garang's fraction was called SPLA/Mainstream, but is in this account referred to as SPLA, while Riek Machar called his fraction SPLA/United.

1992, -93 and -94 were damaging years for SPLM/A. There was constant and extensive fighting, and SPLA was defeated time and time again, and finally cornered on the south side of Aswa River, a tributary to the Nile along the border to Uganda. The government forces and their allies, the break-away group of Riek Machar and Lam Akol, SPLM/A/United, were superior in number and much better armed and equipped, and they were organizing for the attack on the Northern side of the river bank while SPLA was digging in on the other side. Many observers expected that SPLA would face its final defeat in the coming battle, an excruciating defeat that would force whatever was left of SPLA into Ugandan territory.

NPA had a hospital in the area. In addition, we had three refugee camps, Ame, Atepi and Aswa. These people had been chased from camps in Ethiopia in the summer of 1991 by the new rulers in Ethiopia, and they had become homeless in South Sudan in part because of the fighting between SPLA/Main-

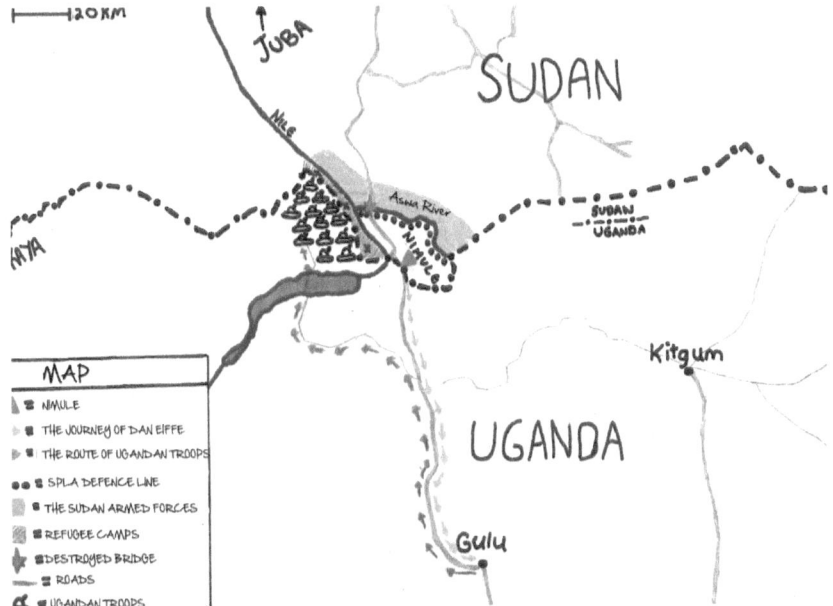

The battle at the Aswa River in 1993: *While I did the interview with Dan Eiffe, he made a simple sketch of the battlefield on a napkin on the table. My grandchild, Markus Almendral Berggrav, read the interview and then redrew the sketch more in detail.*

stream and SPLA/United. There were about 130 000 refugees in the camps, mostly Dinka people.

Dan Eiffe at the Aswa River

Dan Eiffe was currently in charge of NPA's humanitarian activities in the region. He was working closely with the leaders both of SRRA and SPLA, just prior to the impending attack.

In an interview in November 2013 Dan told me the following story:

We experienced some very dramatic days and nights. On the Southern side of the river bank were the SPLA units, heavily marked by weeks and months of fighting and defeat, while lacking proper medical care and food. They were digging trenches in the hillsides above the river bank, but they were short of arms and ammunition. There was limited water, food supplies, diesel and petrol. Moral was low; the fighting spirit was at breaking point.

On the other side of the river were the units of Machar's and Lam Akol's SPLA/United allied with the government forces of the Khartoum regime, numbered some 18 000 soldiers. They were very well equipped, and their fighting spirit was high. They felt sure that they finally would crush Garang and his forces. Their Commander in Chief was Dr. Riek Machar.

One of the leading commanders of SPLA/Mainstream, Kuol Manyang came to me and said: "Dan, can you in NPA take the full responsibility for the people in the three refugee camps? Neither SPLA nor SRRA are able to do anything for them now". I replied with a yes, but NPA had very little humanitarian supplies in the area. We could not make much of a difference. The only thing we had, were packs of dry biscuits. The refugees were starving, many were ill, and all were very afraid of what would happen when the attack came. The young ones, in fear and desperation, left the old and sick ones behind, while they fled for their lives into Uganda. Misery and death was everywhere.

NPA had sent from Norway hundreds of meters of very strong fishing lines with hundreds of big hooks. The idea was to teach the local people to catch some of the big fish that were in plenty both in the Nile, its tributaries and the lakes in South Sudan.

I figured out that these fishing lines also could have a military purpose, and we put them into the river at spots where it was likely that the attacking forces would cross. The lines and the hooks were hidden by water, and when the soldiers jumped into the river in order to cross, they hopefully would be caught by some of the big hooks that easily would penetrate the skin and go into the flesh of the body. In the best scenario, maybe dozens or more soldiers would be victims to NPA's fishing lines.

While I was busy with the fishing lines, SPLA blew up the only bridge over the river so that the attacking forces only had one option, and that was to jump into the river and cross it.

NPA had at this time just received 12 big trucks from USAID for transport of food and medicine to the refugee camps. But our drivers had run away because of fear of being victims of war, so we could not use the trucks.

Then Garang came to see me. He was in despair, almost broken. When I saw his face, I said: "Garang, you have drivers, take the trucks and use them to save the lives of as many refugees as you can when the attack comes. We have no drivers, and cannot use the trucks. The enemy would no doubt direct its artillery towards the camps to create as much havoc as possible, when the attack begins. We all have a duty to do what we can, to try and avoid a major massacre".

In this desperate situation there was again internal conflict within the group of the chief commanders of SPLA/Mainstream. Salva Kiir who was deputy in Command, was very critical of Garang's planning and prioritizing when it came to organizing the defence. One night we were talking, Salva said: "I cannot stand Garang anymore, and I shall now go against him". I replied: "My dear Salva, don't do that, there is more than enough of split and divide as it is. If you act against Garang, another fraction will occur, and only the enemy will benefit. I shall give everything I do not have, if you stay away from such a conflict". Salva listened and stayed away.

The meeting with President Museveni

That same night I received a radio message from a Ugandan friend, the officer Charles Angina, who held an important position within the Ugandan National Intelligence Service. He was stationed in the big military garrison of Gulu town in Northern Uganda. He was updated on the critical situation for SPLA at the Aswa River, and he had informed the President, Yoweri Museveni.

The message to me was: You have to come to Gulu as soon as possible! I was tired and worn out and could not even think of driving to Gulu in the middle of the night. The road was a very dangerous one. The notorious Lord's Resistance Army, LRA, that was supported by Khartoum, had some of its strongholds in the area and could ambush anywhere along the road. I replied back to Charles that I would travel in a couple of days.

Charles immediately replied back over the radio. "No, this meeting cannot wait. You will have to come now. There is a very important person in the camp waiting to see you". I replied: I will travel tomorrow at day time. I need to rest and prepare myself". Immediately, there was a new message over the radio. "No, this cannot wait. You must travel tonight. The man waiting for you is a very important person. That is all I can say"!

I responded: "I understand. I will travel tonight". Then I went down to the SPLA Headquarters to talk with Salva Kiir and Kuol Manyong and I told them: "I have got a message that I have to go Gulu tonight because a very important person is waiting there to see me. I do not know, but I think it might be President Museveni".

Salva looked at me and said: "It has no purpose neither to see President Museveni nor any other in the political and military leadership of Uganda. We have done everything possible in order to make them listen to us, but they do not listen. We have told them that we are in desperate need of arms, ammunition, petrol, diesel, but we have got nothing".

I said: "OK, but make a list of what you need which I may hand over in case they ask. I now have to make the car ready for the drive, as I shall obey their insistence and drive tonight".

I got the car ready and went back to Salva and Kuol who had made a list. I got it, did not look at it, but put it straight into the pocket of my shirt.

I started driving, praying to my God to protect me from all evils. Because to drive through Northern Uganda at night at that time was seen as absolute madness. LRA was everywhere, having ambush in the oddest places and always attacking to kill. I was very afraid, and I was driving at very high speed.

It was a strange night. It was full moon and the beautiful landscape was bathed in moonlight. No traffic, it was quiet all along the road. It was as if an almighty power was holding his hand over me.

I am a Christian, I thought of my beautiful wife and our twins, and I prayed and thanked my God.

I arrived in Gulu just before dawn and headed for the UNICEF Camp in order to have a little rest before I called Charles Angina and told him that I had arrived.

He came to pick me up and said: "The President will see you. He is in the camp. Dan, be mentally prepared, because this is going to be a very, very important meeting".

I gathered all my strength as I arrived at the military camp, and was shown to the room where President Museveni was waiting. He was together with the Chief of Staff, Brigadier Moses Ali. I gave my visiting card to the President that showed that I was a staff member of NPA, and I told him a little about myself.

Museveni had quite a few questions regarding my past anti-Apartheid work in South Africa, and also how I looked at developments in Zimbabwe.

I could not wait, so I stopped the president and said:" I came to see you Mr. President first and foremost because I am a humanitarian worker, a solidarity worker, concerned with the survival of people whose lives are at stake and who desperately need help".

Then I started talking about the situation along the frontlines at Aswa River and the hopeless situation for the approximately 130 000 refugees in the three camps. The words gushed out of me. I was so engaged and committed, and at the same time so afraid of failing. I among other things said: The battle in the making, may most likely be the last one SPLA will be able to fight, as they do not have the strength and the firepower to withstand the attack when it comes. Riek Machar's and Lam Akol's forces together with the government forces from whatever angle you see it, are very superior with regard to number of soldiers and firepower. They will easily cross the river, assault the SPLA positions and defeat SPLA. Then, they will chase the surviving SPLA soldiers into Ugandan territory. On the way, they will take control of the bordertown of Nimule and establish direct contact with your worst enemy, the LRA, that you know is being supported by Khartoum. These Sudanese forces will most likely gang up with LRA, and you will have the worst of bandit gangs ravaging the Southern border areas of Sudan and the Northern parts of your country. If this was to happen, it is my reading that your own government might be at stake. It will take these bandits only hours to reach this town of Gulu.

I continued and said that Machar and Lam Akol were Sudan's Butulezi, the black South African politician who in the 1970s and 1980s betrayed the course of the freedom struggle and sided with the Apartheid regime.

I talked and talked, may be more than an hour without a break. I took a piece of paper and made a drawing of the area on both sides of the Aswa River for a stretch of 25 km and with the military positons of the two armies. I showed the drawing to Museveni.

Then I said: "Mr. President, I am a catholic priest from Ireland and an International solidarity worker, trying to persuade you Mr. President to intervene militarily in this conflict. Why do I do this? It is because I am as a priest and a human being, scared to death by the thought of what shall happen with the 130 000 refugees in the three camps when the attack and the onslaught comes. SPLA will most likely be defeated. The refugees have very little water and food, so they are all thirsty and hungry. Many are ill, and many of them are dying. What is in the making is a terrible massacre."

The President raised his hand, stopped me and said: "Dan, you are fighting my war."

I replied: "Do you know what kind of arms I am using? I have put strong Norwegian fishing lines with big hooks into the Aswa River in order to hinder or delay the soldiers when they attack. SPLA/Mainstream has blown up the only bridge over the river in order to stop the enemy from bringing over tanks and other heavy arms when they cross the river. The sides of the valley down to the river are pretty steep. When the enemy attacks and crosses the river, I do hope many of them will be hanging in my fishing hooks."

Museveni asked: "What do they need"? I replied: "SPLA needs large quantities of diesel in order to bring their motorized artillery into position. What more they need, I do not know, but they have *given me this list."* I pulled the list from my pocket and gave it to Museveni.

Museveni looked at the list. Then he turned to his Chief of Staff, Brigadier Moses Ali, gave him the list and said: *"How much do we have of all this in the camp?"* The Chief of Staff looked at the list and replied: *"Most".* Museveni then asked: How fast can you organize for this to be ready for use?" The Chief of Staff answered:" We can start the work to make it ready tomorrow morning". Then Museveni said: "I order you to start already this afternoon, and your people must be ready by tomorrow morning".

Dan Eiffe was invited to stay and rest for the night in the military camp. He woke up the next morning to a lot of noisy military activity. He looked through the window and saw a large military convoy of trucks with 12 tanks, some artillery and many other trucks with soldiers, and trucks with diesel and gasoline and ammunition. There was no doubt in Dan's mind; they were going to the front line. Dan Eiffe was overwhelmed by what he saw. He had not dreamed that this would be the result of his conversation with President Museveni the night before. The convoy left the camp, and Dan followed in his own car. They reached Uganda's border to the front lines in the evening. SPLA got a lot of new ammunition, new weapons and diesel to move the artillery.

During that night the Ugandan intelligence units and SPLA's intelligence together mapped out the artillery positions and troop positions on the other side of the river. There, the soldiers were preparing their onslaught, certain of being victorious.

Under the cover of darkness, based on the intelligence reports, the Ugandan forces positioned themselves in the hills called Gordon Hills, on the Ugandan side of the border and behind the SPLA frontline.

The day dawned. The red morning sun was just visible on the eastern horizon. Then the SPLA side of the front exploded in an unexpectedly fierce and heavy counter attack. From their hidden positions in the Gordon Hills, the Ugandan tanks and other artillery fired on the concentrations of troops and artillery on the other side, hitting again and again while SPLA soldiers with a revived moral stormed over the river where the fishing lines had been removed.

The combined fire of the SPLA and Ugandan forces was massive and intense. Khartoum's forces never managed to organize and return the fire against this totally unexpected and very aggressive counter attack. In the course of a few hours the situation changed from a belief of certain victory on the side of Khartoum, Lam Akol and Riek Machar, to chaos and death. The losses were massive. The retreat was messy and painful. SPLA forces crossed the Aswa River and collected large amounts of weapons, ammunition and other military supplies that remained after the retreat.

For many, this story may seem unbelievable. But for those of us who know Dan Eiffe, we know it is true. Dan is a remarkable and resourceful person. He has a strong sense of justice and a strong moral commitment to people in need. His ability to convince others is one I have rarely seen in another person, neither before or after I met Dan.

The battle at Aswa River turned the war around. In the years that followed SPLA won most of their military battles. By 2002 most of the land that SPLA had lost during the 1991-94 period was recovered. Peace negotiations were underway, and SPLM under the powerful and experienced leadership of John Garang was able to negotiate for peace from a strong political and military position.

A crazy Commander, threatening to kill four Nuns and three Priests

It was early morning in Oslo, late in the fall of 1997. I was in the office and the telephone rang. Our Resident Representative, Lars Johan Johnsen, was calling from Nairobi with this dramatic message:

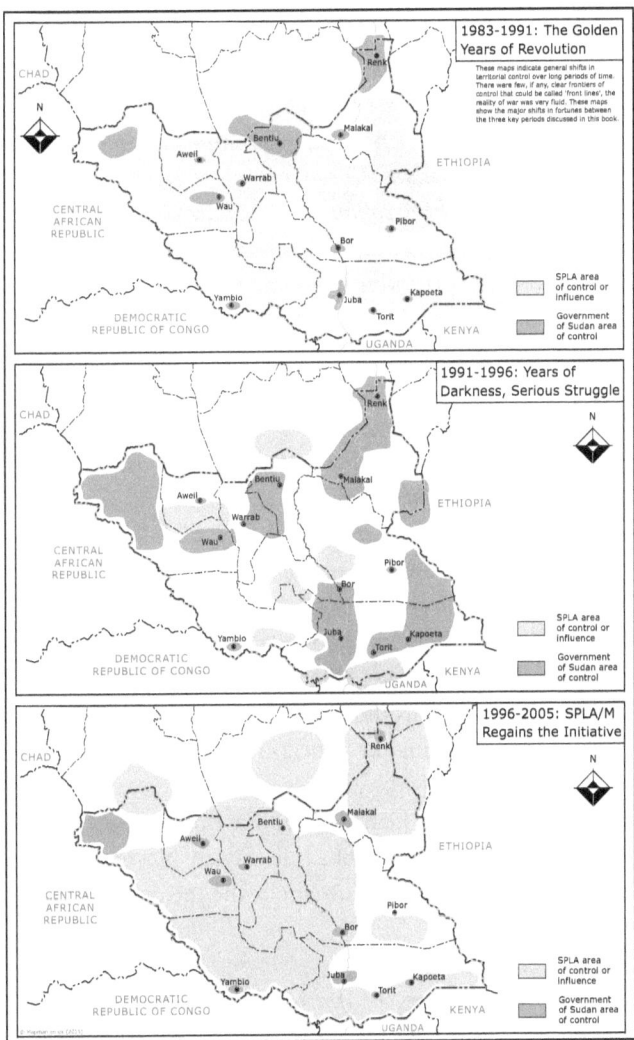

A CHALLENGING LIBERATION STRUGGLE: *The first map above, named The Golden Years of Revolution, covers the period from 1983 to 1991 and shows the big military advances that SPLA made during that period. The second with the name, 1991-1996. Years of Darkness. Serious Struggle, with the split in Nasir in 1991, shows the big defeats that SPLA suffered during that period. Then, from 1996 SPLM/A regained both the political and military initiative and had decisive progress.*

"*Halle, something terrible has happened. Our people in the Bahr el-Ghazal-province cooperate with the people at the vocational training center that is run by two American and one Australian Catholic Church organizations. They have just received word over the radio that a crazy SPLA commander has arrested four nuns and three priests from the center. The commander is accusing them of espionage, and says he is going to execute them.*"

Lars Johan continued: "*We have sent Dan Eiffe who was already in the area. He will try and negotiate with the commander for their release. But if he fails, this will be a human tragedy as well as a political catastrophe, not only for SPLM, but also for us in NPA.*

And he added: *Not to mention the fact that these days Garang is in Washington negotiating for more American aid in the war for liberation. If he gets seven murders to defend, all is lost. In addition, the Catholic churches are some of our most important partners in the field. This can be a catastrophe.*"

Lars Johan was right, in the worst-case scenario; this would be a disaster for everyone. I told Lars Johan who like me, was deeply worried, that I would get in touch with the NMFA immediately, while keeping our fingers crossed that Dan could perform another miracle.

I have spoken with Dan Eiffe about this incident many times. When we met in Nairobi one day in November 2013, I asked him to tell me once again about the incident and his role in it:

The Dan story:

"*It happened towards the end of 1997. Garang and his advisors planned for new and big military offensives. The SPLA top-command therefore needed new recruits and had told its commanders in the field to increase recruitment all over South Sudan. Based on this order, some of the commanders turned their eyes on schools and similar centres for education in the liberated areas. All these schools and educational centres were financed and managed by Christian Mission organizations.*

One of these centres was close to the village of Akot in Bahr el-Ghazal and had approximately 3000 pupils and students. The SPLA Commander in the area was Marial Nuor Jok. He saw the possibility of recruiting new soldiers both among teachers and students, and he had therefore approached the management of the School on the matter, but had had a negative response.

At the same time, the commander had picked up some rumours that the nuns at the school in their letters to the Church Order at home had written some critical remarks about SPLM/A. On this ground he placed a spy in the secretariat of the school who copied all letters sent by the nuns and the priests. It did not take long for him to be able to confirm that such criticism was being voiced in letters sent. Commander Marial considered this to be acts of subversion and sabotage, and he decided for this reason to arrest the leaders of the centre. Four Australian nuns, one American priest, one Australian and one South Sudanese priest, they were arrested accused of subversion and sabotage.

Commander Marial made it clear that all seven would be executed. While the accused were waiting for their final verdict, commander Marial had them beaten up. Then he had seven fox holes dug, into which he had them thrown. Then the fox holes were covered with sticks and stones.

The political emergency alarm went all over the place, and the first to react was the South Sudanese Council of Churches led by the Catholic Bishop of Rumbek. He was furious, scolded the SPLA in public and condemned what commander Marial had done. At the same time people in the company of the bishop were asking: "Is there anything that can be done to save the lives of the nine people?" Somebody said: "Call up NPA in Nairobi and ask them to send in Dan Eiffe. He has a good hand with SPLA Commanders."

The situation was without doubt very dangerous. I was at work at an agricultural project a few hundred kilometers away, and Lars Johan at NPA Nairobi told me to do whatever I could to save the lives of those threatened with execution. I was able to hire a small plane and landed at an airstrip close to the village and the centre.

The first thing I did was to get in contact with the regional SPLA Commander, Daniel Deng, whom I knew very well. We quickly agreed that the situation easily could end as a political catastrophe for SPLM/A.

I had full authority to negotiate with commander Marial while the regional commander Daniel Deng accompanied me to the centre. It was dusk. We went straight to commander Marial who immediately saluted a military welcome greeting as if I was his military superior.

I said: "Commander Marial, you have without any discussion with and without any approval from your military superior officer arrested four nuns and three priests. I order you to release them immediately."

Commander Marial reacted instantly to my order and asked some soldiers to remove the cover of the foxholes and assist the arrested in getting up from the holes.

Then, commander Marial turned to me and said: "Dan, it is very good to see you here."

The seven arrested were freed, and they were all, and in particular the nuns who were in their seventies, strongly marked by their ordeal. I had some tea and biscuits that I gave them.

Then, the American priest started to scold at commander Marial, and he abused him heavily. Commander Marial then got extremely angry, lost his temper and raised his pistol to shoot the priest.

I shouted:" Marial, don't shoot. Come with me around the corner of the house so that we can talk freely about this. Marial obeyed, and we walked around the corner. Then I said: "Garang is in Washington, negotiating with the Americans for more assistance in the liberation struggle. If you do the least more of harm to any of the seven arrested, you will definitely destroy all what Garang is trying to obtain.

Then of a sudden, I lost control of my temper, got completely furious and screamed: "Marial, what the hell, do you not understand what you are doing. You can destroy everything we are trying to do. We need the nuns and the priests here. They are among our strongest religious and humanitarian supporters. They are our friends!"

Then Marial became afraid. I lowered my voice and said in a friendly-like voice: "My friend Marial, please set the seven free". He replied: "I shall think it over". A minute passed, and then he said: "OK, I set them free".

Then I said: «Thanks a lot. Now you will take full responsibility for their well-being this evening and the coming night. This is an order; you shall treat them well. They shall have food, and rest and they shall sleep in their own rooms. Tomorrow morning, you shall bring them to the airstrip. I shall be waiting there to have them flown to Lokichokio in Turkana".

As I prepared for departure in order to go back to my own resting place, the American priest started screaming again. I got angry and told him to shut up, and I added: "Do you know what sometimes is the most important to do for a Catholic priest? It is to be able to use his brain, demonstrate humbleness and keep tight. This is now your task! Because the way you behave now, you are not only putting your own life at stake, but the lives of all seven. As a priest, you shall now demonstrate humbleness. I ask you again: "Shut up! The crisis is now solved!"

But the priest did not stop. He was so marked by the ordeal that he was totally out of balance mentally and continued screaming and abusing the commander and others. I turned to Marial and said:" Overlook this crazy guy; if not, he can destroy everything we are trying to save. Now, you and I have an agreement for tomorrow morning. You shall keep this agreement. I will take the seven out from here for a couple of weeks so that they may have some rest and recreation after this ordeal. You must not forget that this educational centre is one of the very best in South Sudan, 3000 pupils and a poli-clinic where hundreds of sick and wounded people are treated every day. We cannot do any damage here. We have to encourage the staff and support their work".

Marial replied: "We are in agreement".

The next day, Marial as promised, came to the airstrip with the seven people, he originally had planned to execute. We boarded the plane, took off and landed safely at the Loki airstrip. I could see that several international reporters were waiting at the terminal. I did not want them to see the American priest who was still out of balance, have another outburst against Marial and SPLA. I therefore asked the pilot to stop at the other side of the airstrip. We left the plane, and we were picked up by NPA drivers who took us to the NPA Camp".

Marial Nour Jok

(HJH: That makes the end of this story with Dan. But there is an addition with commander Marial Nour Jok which is not very pleasant, and needs to be told. He had before this incident as a commander, behaved in ways that had caused him military imprisonment, but he had been taken back to SPLA as a local commander. However, after this incident he was sacked, and all military distinctions that he had gained, were taken from him. He was tried before a military court, found guilty and was in prison for some years. When he was released, he went back to his village and became a farmer until 2009.

Then, he was brought back for military service by President Salva Kiir who promoted him to Major General in Charge of Internal Security in the Ministry of Interior. But he behaved in a very vulgar and dangerous manner frequently abusing his powers to have people he did not like, arrested and tortured. He also became known during this period as one of those responsible for sexual torture of women, and he even had people murdered.

The criticism against him became so serious that the President in 2011 had to have him sacked. But in the fall of 2013 President Salva Kiir had him again brought back, now to be one of those Dinka leaders and commanders who in secret were training young Dinka boys for what was called The New Presidential Guard. These units were the ones that were brought into the immediate surroundings of

Juba in the fall of 2013. This was part of the political and military build-up that was carried out by some traditional Dinka leaders under the leadership of Paul Malong (the Chief of Staff of SPLA from May 2014 until May 2017) with the blessing of the President himself, Salva Kiir. They were palnning a confrontation with the internal opposition in SPLM in the meeting of the National Liberation Council on 13th and 14th December 2013. There were many fall outs from that meeting. The most important one was the de facto coup d'etat by the President and his Dinka advisors on the 15th of December. It was followed by the attack on the opposition within SPLM in the morning hours of Monday 15th December with the attempted assassination of Riek Machar and the arrest of most of the most outstanding and experienced leaders of SPLM from the days of the liberation struggle.

Marial Nour Jok is believed to be one of the commanding officers who with the approval of the President, ordered and took part in the massacre of the nuers in Juba in the days following 15th December. Indications are that around 20 000 people were murdered. They also arrested and tortured whoever else of opposition his subordinates could get hold of.

In April 2014 Marial Nour Jok was awarded for his loyalty to the President when Salva Kiir appointed him Director of the National Military Intelligence. This position with the authority provided for in the new and fundamentally undemocratic security laws approved by Parliament in the summer of 2014, has given Marial Nour Jok a free hand to continue his murderous business in Juba and South Sudan. The president has let him and his likeminded loose for the most dangerous spiral of death that has destroyed the state of South Sudan. Marial Nour Jok and his likeminded and equals are obvious candidates for the International Criminal Court in Hague when the day of reckoning comes, and it will.)

A dangerous Mission

It was in 2003. I was no longer with NPA, but in Nairobi on another assignment. NPA had an airlift going to an airstrip in Akot in Bahr el Ghazal. Ken Miller invited me to join him and his colleagues for the trip.

This time the plan was to depart from the international airport in Nairobi. I understood the reason when I boarded the plane. The plane had a large cargo space and was loaded with an airplane engine and some food and medicine, and there was an extra 1000-liter tank of gasoline welded to the body of the plane. I was told that the main purpose of the mission was to replace the engine on an airplane stranded in Akot.

It was 11 o'clock in the morning, and we were ready for departure. Then, a message came from the tower that the airport authorities had rescinded our permission to take off. Khartoum did not want this flight to succeed, and someone had coerced some staff high up in the airport authority to stop the flight.

Ken Miller was both angry and desperate. He tried to get a more senior official at the airport to overturn the decision, but without success. Then, he called high ranking public officials in the Ministry of Transportation, but again without success. Finally, he was able to speak with the State Secretary who instructed the head of the airport authority to let us take off. But it was already 4 p.m. in the afternoon, and we could not reach Akot in daylight. Yet, we had to fly while we still had the permission, but we had to make a stop-over somewhere on the route.

NPA had a programme in Rwanda. Ken called Geir Ommundsen, NPA's Resident Representative in Kigali and explained our precarious situation. He asked Geir to talk with the authorities in Rwanda about a landing permit. In less than ten minutes, Geir called back and had good news: The landing permit had been granted.

We took off and flew towards Kigali, less than an hour later while the sun slowly dipped towards Rwanda's green horizon, we landed. I have never experienced a friendlier and more expeditious reception. NPA's good reputation in the country was obvious. We passed very quickly through the migration check point, and outside, Geir Ommundsen was waiting for us. After a pleasant evening at a nice restaurant, we got an early start the next morning from the hotel, and once more, we experienced exceptionally friendly and efficient passport and security checks at the airport.

We had a heavy load and the pilot needed a long runway before we could take off. The plane rose slowly over Rwanda's beautiful green landscape and headed for Uganda. As I looked down on the equally beautiful Ugandan landscape, I thought about what this area looked like early in the year of 1980, right after the Tanzanian forces had repulsed the invasion of Tanzania and chased Idi Amin and his gang out both of Tanzania and Uganda. I was at the time the Africa Correspondent for Norwegian Broadcasting Corporation, based in Nairobi, and I made a reporting trip through the area. Towns and villages were destroyed by the withdrawing forces of the dictator, and the people had left. It was all marked by the tyranny of ten years of dictatorship and societal decline. Now, 30 years later, the towns and villages were rebuilt, the scares in the landscape healed, and people at large were enjoying some progress and peace.

Mike, the pilot, did not say much. But some distance inside Uganda he said that he had to climb as high as possible, to about 8000 meters to avoid artillery fire both from the LRA and the Khartoum forces. He added that he would fly some distance inside the Central African Republic, before he set course for Sudan's airspace. Then he turned off the radio and all the other instruments that would allow Khartoum to discover us. He had to use all means available to avoid the Khartoum regime's anti-aircraft fire.

I looked out at a sunny blue sky, not a cloud in sight and below us was an ocean of green rainforest, stretching hundreds of kilometers in all directions. I thought about the fact that the weather conditions were perfect for anti-aircraft fire, and that the LRA had relocated from Uganda to the Central African Republic. They were Khartoum's lackeys and had orders to shoot us down.

Then we crossed into Sudanese airspace, and the pilot signaled that we were going to land. From an altitude of 8000 meters, the landing process started towards the little airstrip in Akot. I eyed the reserve tank with 1000 liters of gasoline that was welded in the middle of the cargo room. It struck me that if Khartoum's forces on the ground shot through the body of the aircraft and the tank, then with all the cigarette smoking passengers on board, we were finished.

But nothing happened, the landing was perfect. We met NPA's local workers who were busy from early morning until late evening with emergency food and medicine flights into the Upper Nile, where a famine rampaged.

There were barracks with a cafeteria and some small huts to sleep in. Shortly after we landed, we heard another plane landing. I heard Ken Miller whisper a comment, obviously relieved: "*He made it again.*"

A few minutes later a man climbed out of the plane, a man whose name is often found in books and stories on South Sudan, the American Dale Roark. He was an old war pilot, spy and much more. He had had more than his fair share of the global American military activity. I would guess that Dale weighed about 120 kilos. He was starting to get old, but he was still as strong as an ox. What more was Dale Roark? I do not really know, but I think he is a man of many talents with both a soft heart and a hard heart.

He once told me:

"*I am a big and strong man. One of my grandfathers was Indian, the other was black, the third was white and the fourth was from India. I have the best genes from all races.*"

I walked around the airstrip where a group of SPLA soldiers were standing guard. The officer in charge nodded at me. He was a young man who spoke English well. I watched as he gave his soldiers orders for the night watch. He had a long stick and made a drawing of the airstrip in the sand. Then he marked points on the edges of the drawing while he spoke with the soldiers in their different local languages. I understood that he asked if the orders were understood. Everyone nodded. Then the officer erased the drawing with his foot, and it was gone forever.

A little later that evening I joined the others in the canteen. It was quite an experience. Pilots from different parts of the world were there. I spoke for a while with a Kenyan who was an academic, interested in literature, politically radical and very critical of both the Khartoum regime and the government at home in Kenya. He had ended up as an emergency aid pilot, now working for NPA.

A little further down two white South African professional pilots sat talking. They strongly disliked that there was a black majority in political control in their homeland. Therefore they wanted to stay away from South Africa. They made a living of flying emergency and catastrophe aid missions. That was why they were in South Sudan. On the other side were two men from The Ukraine. They had been in the air force when the Soviet Union and the Warsaw Pact existed, but in the political thaw that followed the break-down of the Communist regime, they had been made redundant. Therefore, they had become freelance pilots who took whatever mission they could get, and now they were in South Sudan, flying emergency flights with NPA.

Ken and I went over to sit with Dale, whom we knew from before. He had flown many emergency missions for NPA, some of them very dangerous ones like the airlift to the Nuba Mountains in the 1990s. Dale is fun to talk with, and as we sat there we talked about everything. Then I asked him what he had been up on that particular day, and who his employer was this time. He answered without hesitation SPLA and Darfur. Then I asked him what he did in Darfur. Dale smiled and said: *"No comment Halle, no comment."*

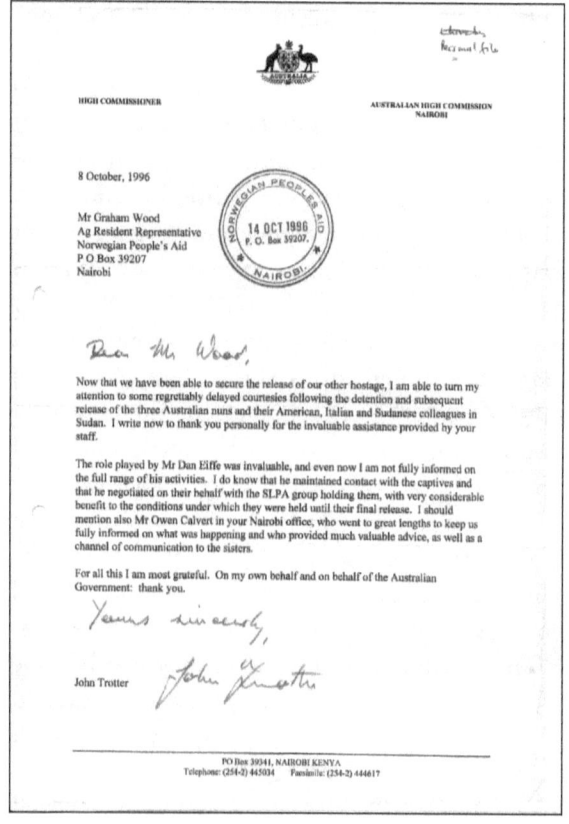

The Australian Government through its Ambassador to Kenya extended its gratitude both to NPA and Dan Eiffe for the successful rescue operation.

7
RUMOURS OF GUN RUNNING

THE NPA CONFLICT WITH UN.
HOW DID SPLA GET THEIR ARMS?

Egil Hagen was the kind of man who viewed one's actions as either good or bad; you were either a friend or an enemy, there was no middle ground.

He was not interested in Nairobi's night life and long nights of bar hopping. Egil was a puritan-like idealist, and being a soldier by training, he was like one of the ancients from Sparta in old Greece. He often criticized, sometimes severely, both UN and non-governmental organizations for inefficiency and indifference.

If one invited him for a meal at a nice restaurant in Nairobi, he would usually select a minor dish with water accompanying. He did not fit into the international circles of aid workers in Nairobi in the 1980s and 90s. Maybe for this reason, there was much gossip and rumours about Egil. The first allegations about gun running surfaced in a report from the American Embassy in Nairobi to the State Department in Washington sometime in 1986, even before Egil started the small relief operations in South

Sudan. That report was baseless, but later, rumours about NPA and gun running flourished and remained highly visible until 2005. It was always a popular topic among aid workers, journalists and UN workers spending time in Nairobi's nightly bars.

But the most difficult part for NPA was that the relationship between Egil Hagen and the UN from the very beginning was strained, and it developed into a political conflict that for years, kept the relationship to UN chilly.

Dan Eiffe who was employed by NPA in the summer of 1991, still has vivid memories of those days in Nairobi:

"*Halle, sometimes it was really bad. I could walk into a café or bar in Nairobi and if anyone from the International aid community or the UN was there, they would point and laugh, saying 'here comes the gun-runner from NPA' or 'here comes one of Garang's lackeys'.*

Sometimes I was out in the field and did not have a place to stay for the night. If I tried to get a place at a UN camp, I was turned away. If I asked to get a ride on a UN plane, I was turned down. One time, late at night, I had an accident with my car near the UN camp in Loki in Turkana in Kenya. But the people in charge at the UN camp would not let me in because I was NPA staff. I managed however to drive the car to the house of a priest of the Catholic Church in Turkana. He was very helpful. We managed to fix the car, and I was invited to spend the night at his house. Halle, when the conflict was at its worst between the UN and us, the harassment and witch-hunt was extreme."

During my own numerous stays in Nairobi, I frequently met people who had no interest in what NPA was actually doing in South Sudan. They had a hang up, and they always started their conversations with the rumours of arms smuggling. To some, these rumours became an obsession.

Between 1987 and 2005 the Norwegian journalist Gunnar Kopperud made many trips to Sudan for the Norwegian daily *Dagbladet* and other Norwegian and Nordic newspapers. One time he was invited to dinner by one of the leaders of Norwegian Church Aid in Nairobi:

"I accepted the invitation. There were many people from the international aid community there, and everyone was talking about the gun runners, NPA. Everybody said the same thing, and they were absolutely certain about what they talked about. So I asked: Are you sure that this is true? Have you ever seen any evidence of this happening? No, nobody had seen anything, but everybody had heard something."

But the rumours persisted. For example, the Swedish writer, Bengt G. Nilson, published his book, *Sveriges afrikanska krig* (Sweden's African War) in 2008 with the right-wing publishing house Timbro. In a chapter he once more, and without even one factual reference, repeats the rumours about NPA.

A title covering an entire newspaper page in *Dagbladet* on July 3, 1990, heading an article by Gunnar Kopperud, reveals the mindset:

"THE UN DELEGATION BACKSTABS NPA, ACCUSING IT OF GUN RUNNING"

The gist of the article was that UN's special envoy to Sudan, Michael Priestley, had contacted the Dutch Government Agency in Charge of Development Assistance and asked them to discontinue support to NPA through Doctors Without Borders (MSF/Holland) in the Netherlands. The reason given was that NPA was a gun runner.

NPA's leaders promptly responded. The Head of International Department of NPA at the time, Mr. Jan Erik Lindstad accused the UN Director of using slander in his attempts to stop Dutch co-financing of NPA in Sudan. The Dutch Government Agency listened to the advice from UN, and it decided to put pressure on Doctors Without Borders so they would discontinue their cooperation with NPA, but Doctors without Borders resisted the pressure and continued its cooperation.

Three days later, on July 6th, 1990, Gunnar Kopperud published a new article with a title covering the entire page of Dagbladet:

"DIRTY TRICKS BY UN"

"*UN's staff in Sudan is controlled by the Sudanese military regime. UN's allegations against NPA regarding smuggling weapons to the liberation movement in South Sudan, are fabricated by Khartoum.*"

Egil Hagen was quoted as saying this in a long interview. Egil went on to attack the UN and the newly established Operation Lifeline Sudan (OLS):

"*In 1989 the UN entered the conflict with a massive emergency operation that was later criticized for mismanagement of funds, inefficiency and pure bluff.*"

"NEW UN-SCANDAL"

"*The UN is trying to start a new emergency operation called Operation Life Line Sudan (OLS) and this time all the voluntary organizations are being told to sign an 'association agreement' with the UN. The agreement is drafted by the military regime in Khartoum and will result in two things: the UN gets a monopoly on emergency aid to South Sudan, and it will also have access to the money that is distributed today by International NGOs because UN desperately needs more funding. Until now the UN has only been able to finance a third of what the new emergency operation is estimated to cost*", says Egil Hagen.

This was in *Dagbladet*, a Norwegian newspaper. But Kopperud was a freelancer, and he also wrote for other newspapers such as *Arbeiderbladet* and *Vårt Land* in Oslo, *Stavanger Aftenblad* on the Southwestern coast of Norway and *Politiken*, a major newspaper in Copenhagen, as well as for weekly magazines and newsletters in Norway and other Nordic countries. Kopperud had a rather strong influence on public opinion and set the tone in Norway and other Nordic countries.

At the same time, Egil Hagen worked closely with Roger Winter, the Director for the U.S. Committee on Refugees in Washington, who also communicated a similar and very critical opinion of UN's work in South Sudan to members of the US Congress as well as staff at State Department.

But in the battle fields of South Sudan the conflict with UN had other fall outs. On August 27th, 1991 Riek Machar, one of leaders of the Nuer people, and Lam Akol, a leader of the Shilluk people in South Sudan, both top leaders of SPLM and commanders of SPLA, rebelled and split from John Garang and SPLM/A. As already described in chapter 4, the rebellion took place in the town of Nasir, and the reasons were stated for leaving, were Garang's dictatorial leadership style and the Marxist ideology of SPLM. The news was received with enthusiasm by UN leaders and UN-staff in Sudan and elsewhere in East Africa, by governments and politicians in many Western capitals and by most International NGO-members of OLS.

The Head of OLS, the Swedish UN-diplomat Thomas Ekwall, flew to Nasir and profusely proclaimed the support of UN and OLS for the new faction of SPLM/A. The Minister for Humanitarian Assistance and Development Cooperation in the French Ministry of Foreign Affairs, Bernhard Kouchner, arrived in a government plane with a similar message even though Mr. Kouchner also visited SPLM/A/Mainstream in Kapoeta at the same time.

The American ambassador in Nairobi with some members of Congress visiting Kenya, chartered a plane and flew into Nasir to express their praise and support for the dissidents. Many others, including the Secretary General of the Norwegian Church Aid, Jan P. Erichsen, did the same, and Mr. Erichsen also invited Lam Akol to Oslo in order for him to address media and the public at large about the reasons for the rebellion and the split.

NPA had Dan Eiffe in the field. He went against the rebellion and its leaders and declared that NPA's allegiance was still with Garang and his SPLM Mainstream.

A year later Gunnar Kopperud was again in South Sudan, this time on assignment for *Arbeiderbladet*.

On Monday, August 31, 1992 the newspaper ran a whole page with a large picture of a smiling woman receiving food from NPA. But the headline read:

"NPA TRANSPORTS WEAPONS TO SUDAN"

In the article Kopperud once again referred to allegations by UN staff claiming that the SPLA offensive, at the time against the Government garrison town of Juba, had been planned from the NPA's headquarters in the village of Pagari in South Sudan.

This happened six months after Egil Hagen had died and only a few months after Helge Rohn had taken over as the new Resident Representative in Nairobi of NPA's Sudan Programme.

Rohn was a fellow student of Egil Hagen at the Norwegian Military College in Oslo, and Egil and he were friends from that time. Rohn had a different hand with the media. He calmly and firmly renounced the allegations from UN and characterized them as malevolent rumours with the sole intention of destroying NPA's reputation in order to stop its financing of emergency aid and humanitarian assistance.

In the same article in Dagbladet Kopperud reported that according to SPLA, six UN planes were used to transport weapons and soldiers for the regime in Khartoum to the garrison town Juba which at that time was controlled by the Khartoum regime.

The conflict between the UN and NPA escalated until 1993, when it was reinforced by a similar conflict that developed between UN/OLS and SPLM/A.

The Late Eliah Malok who was a central leader in SPLM at the time, a close advisor to John Garang, and also a former leader of SRRA, described the conflict in this way in his book:

THE SOUTH SUDAN STRUGGLE FOR LIBERTY

As OLS increasingly grew and got power, it started meddling into the internal affairs of the Liberation Movement and became a tool for CIA and other Western Intelligence organizations. OLS had a particular and big responsibility for the split within SPLM/A in Nasir in 1991. Not only that, the day after the attempted coup, a senior diplomat with the American Embassy in Nairobi used an OLS plane in order to bring into Nasir a group of American members of Congress who wanted to have first-hand news about the fact that Garang and his people were out.

This meddling into the affairs of SPLM/A and the propaganda against SPLM and its leaders continued until 1994. OLS provided the breakaway group with supplies of food and equipment. OLS further stated that it could not work in the liberated areas of the South without permission from Khartoum. From 1991 until 1994 OLS was an enemy of SPLM. They considered Garang to be a Communist and a kind of lackey of the old regime in Ethiopia.

Fortunately, in 1994 the leadership of SPLM put its foot firmly down and forced a change of attitude and will with UN and OLS. The criticism of SPLM came to an end, and they started working together with us. SPLM could now decide when and where humanitarian assistance and emergency relief could be supplied in the liberated areas.

It is self-evident that this conflict, going back almost to the beginning of the liberation war, also heavily influenced the relationship between UN /OLS and NPA.

I began working as Head of the International Department of NPA in May 1992, and I often participated in international meetings where UN representatives also were present. Almost without fail, one of them would in the course of the meeting come over to me and start talking about the conflict with NPA in Nairobi. Many were critical of Egil Hagen and his ruthless criticism. Others would mumble something about weapon smuggling. And yet others thought we should put it all behind us and start cooperating.

Luckily, we started to cooperate. Many factors contributed to this positive development.

The most important factor was the ideological shift within SPLM that took place between the fall 1991 and 1994. After the fall of the Soviet Union, SPLM went through a process of change. All of the communist and Marxist revolutionary rhetoric was discarded.

After Nasir in 1991, SPLM's political language changed; human rights, democracy and similar concepts became the new mantra.

Helge Rohn was more diplomatic than his predecessor Egil Hagen, and he contributed greatly to improve relations between NPA and the UN.

In 1993 the American Government changed its political relationship with Sudan, and USAID chose NPA as an important bilateral channel for aid and emergency relief into the liberated areas. The Minister of Development Co-operation, Jan Pronk, in the Dutch Government followed, suit shortly after.

Different governments in Norway supported NPA's work in Sudan, even though there occasionally was substantial friction between the administration in the Ministry of Foreign Affairs and NPA.

Hence, the conflict with the UN slowly dissolved by the end of the 1990s. NPA's workers could eventually use the UN facilities in Loki, enjoy food at the restaurant and have a beer at the UN bar, after a joint mission on a UN plane.

HOW DID SPLA GET ITS ARMS?

Even now in 2017, NPA is beeing accused of having been gun running in the past. The primary source of these rumours was the regime in Khartoum and their paid allies, which included first and foremost, David Hoile and The European Sudanese Public Affairs Council (ESCAP). But there were others as well, such as local UN workers, staff members of non-governmental organizations, diplomats and journalists. None of them had any evidence, while they all fished in the murky water of rumours and slander. Furthermore, I never met any of them who asked or tried to answer the question as to how and where SPLA got their arms.

This is the answer:

More than half of all the arms and ammunition that SPLA had at any one time, were taken from the enemy in the battlefield, the government forces in Khartoum and their South Sudan lackeys, Riek Machar, Lam Akol and the numerous militia groups that were supplied by Khartoum.

Some examples:

In 1999, SPLM and the democratic opposition in the north of Sudan established a new front organization called The National Democratic Alliance (NDA). Its main headquarters was in Asmara, the capital of Eritrea. Pa'gan Amum from SPLM/A was appointed Secretary -General of NDA, and Sharif Harrir from Darfur, who had worked as a senior researcher at the University of Bergen and had become a Norwegian citizen, became the Assistant Secretary- General.

NDA had its military organization, as did SPLM, and Pa'gan Amum was the overall Commander in – Chief for the joint military forces of NDA/SPLA, while Sharif Harir from Darfur and from Bergen in Norway was one of the deputy commanders. For a couple of years, starting in the late 1990s, the guerilla units of NDA, under the command of Pa'gan Amum, conducted several attacks against military targets on what was known as the eastern front, such as several successful sabotage actions against the oil pipeline to Port Sudan, military convoys, weapon depots and garrison towns.

The Attack on Kassala

One of the most famous and spectacular attacks was in November 2000 against the garrison town Kassala which at the time had some 300 000 inhabitants, and it is located not far from the borders to Eritrea and Ethiopia. Both Sharif and Pa'gan have described this attack to me, where the goal was to seize as many arms, ammunition and other military equipment as possible.

The guerilla forces struck as they always did when Pa'gan was in command in the middle of the night, with intense speed and fire power. After heavy fighting, the SPLA/NDA forces conquered all the 6 government military camps with many thousand soldiers in the Kassala area. The loss of lives among the sleeping government soldiers was enormous. The NDA/SPLA combined forces held Kassala for one day. During that time, they emptied the weapon and ammunition depots. They took several dozen large trucks, a dozen tanks, several hundred machine guns, about 3000 Kalashnikov automatic rifles and lots of thousands of rounds with rifle ammunition.

The other Arms Suppliers, among them, many African States

Where did the rest of arms come from? Ethiopia and Libya were the most important partners for SPLM/A from the beginning of the liberation struggle in 1983 until 1990 when the Mengistu/Dergen dictatorship fell. Ethiopia received military equipment and arms from the Communist East Bloc countries which she was allowed to share part of with SPLA. Libya was another important supplier of arms for SPLA because Gadhafi was against Nimeiri in Sudan.

With the power shift in Ethiopia in the summer of 1991, things changed. The new government with the Tigray People's Liberation Front (TPLF), under the leadership of Prime Minister Meles Zenawi, ceased all support to SPLA and chased SPLM/A, as well as all South Sudanese refugees, out of the country. It was in short, a major setback and a tragedy for SPLM/A.

After a couple of years in power the new government in Addis Ababa changed its policy towards SPLM and the liberation struggle in Sudan, and they and SPLM/A began to cooperate. Meles Zenawi and John Garang liked each other and developed a friendship.

Israel, who had provided arms for the Anyanya I rebellion in the 1960s, did probably not provide any arms for SPLM/A.

Uganda's support to SPLA in the battle at Aswa River in 1994 led to a renewed and close political cooperation between President Museveni and the SPLM Chairman John Garang. The cooperation developed into friendship, and Garang was often a welcome political guest in Kampala. He made Museveni agree to host secret political meetings in Uganda with high ranking government representatives from black African countries. At these meetings they discussed how black Africa could contribute politically and militarily to the liberation struggle. Countries that were represented, included South Africa, Zimbabwe, Namibia, Nigeria, Eritrea and Ethiopia, and sometimes also Tanzania and Kenya.

At these secret meetings Garang would provide an update on the political and military situation in Sudan, what SPLA was up to in the battlefield and what were their military needs. I was told by an SPLM participant that Nelson Mandela, the President of South Africa, once attended such a meeting. In his update, Garang mentioned the humanitarian assistance forthcoming through NPA to the people behind the front lines. Then Mandela said: "*Ah, NPA, it is a house-hold name with ANC.*"

From 1994 until the Comprehensive Peace Agreement (CPA) in the summer of 2004, considerable amounts of weapons were sent from these countries, via Uganda and Ethiopia, to SPLA at the front. In addition, Nigeria contributed financially.

The Role of USA

When Bill Clinton became the new American President in 1993, USA began reshaping its African policies. USA needed strategic allies on the continent. In the diplomatic process that followed, two of Sudan's neighbouring countries were chosen, Ethiopia and Uganda.

Consequently, the relationship between Ethiopia and the USA fundamentally changed, and they began developing a cooperation that eventually has become quite extensive. Ethiopia was chosen as a strategic ally for the USA on the Horn of Africa, and the USA began to supply Ethiopia with weapons and other military equipment. USA made it clear that the American Government also supported SPLM/A's liberation struggle, and

Ethiopia was encouraged to forward some of the military aid it received from USA to SPLA. Hence Ethiopia was once again a close political and military ally of SPLM/A.

With respect to Uganda, the relationship between Museveni's government and SPLM/A had after 1994 developed and become very strong. When the USA decided to have Uganda as a strategic partner, it became even easier for the Ugandan government to support SPLA with weapons.

Eritrea was also an important supporter for SPLM/A both politically and militarily. The Liberation Movement in Tigray and in Eritrea had worked closely to bring down the Mengistu dictatorship. After Eritrea's independence the situation between the government leaders in Eritrea and the regime in Khartoum became increasingly tense, and the Eritrean leaders were determined to do everything possible to weaken Khartoum. For this reason, as well, SPLM and NDA was allowed to establish their headquarter in Asmara.

Eritrea was also a transit country for large weapon convoys to guerilla units of the NDA/SPLA who operated in the Red Sea Mountains, the Nuba Mountains and the eastern part of Sudan. It was known as the Eastern Front.

SPLA and Weapon Transport inside Sudan

How were the weapons and ammunition transported to areas of fighting, the land area of South Sudan being three times the size of Norway, mostly without roads?

In the middle of the 1990s SPLA formed a transport company. It had two primary functions. It transported food for NPA and other aid organizations, and it collected weapons and ammunition from secret depots in Ethiopia and Uganda. In addition, some weapons and ammunition were airlifted between military depots in the liberated areas. The private air companies providing planes for these transports, were often the same as

NPA and other humanitarian organizations used for transporting food, medicine, and other emergency relief.

SPLM/A had a secret agreement with these companies that when they flew empty and in transit between assignments for humanitarian organizations, then they could transport soldiers, weapons and ammunition at SPLA's expense inside South Sudan.

In light of these facts, the allegation that NPA smuggled weapons is without foundation. Why should NPA smuggle weapons when SPLA received their weapons through the channels described above?

Even so, it is not inconceivable that there might have been military equipment on rare occasions hidden in the NPA convoys when the transport companies were delivering food and supplies to the reception points behind the front lines. The distance between Mombasa to reception points in Sudan was more than 2000 kilometers, and the cargo was reloaded several times. NPA could never have 100 percent control over what happened inside the road less South Sudan. It was also the case that when SPLA was in desperate need, NPA would assist SPLM/A with gasoline and diesel.

Norwegian Peoples Aid is a gun runner in Sudan.

- Norsk Folkehjelp frakter våpen i Sudan

«SKITTENT AV FN»

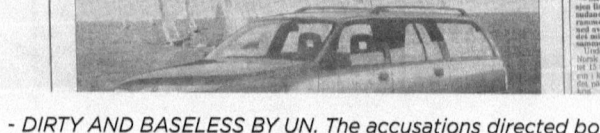

- DIRTY AND BASELESS BY UN. The accusations directed both by UN and NPA against each other were hard hitting.

ADMINISTRATIVE CHALLENGES
IN A DEMANDING POLITICAL ENVIRONMENT

A complex Programme

Egil Hagen was the powerful founding father and the first Head of the NPA Sudan programme, but administration and accounting were not his strongest suit. During the first years, he had a couple of local staff, and that was it. When Helge Rohn took over as the Resident Representative of NPA in March 1992, he described the administrative side of the programme like this:

"*It was a very non-bureaucratic programme, almost hard to believe that any of the major donors were willing to give money to someone who was single-mindedly focused on effect and not on administration and reporting. There were some papers in a drawer, a kind of budget and the accounting was done by a local Kenyan staff member. In an independent report on overhead costs in the programme, I discovered that the NPA South Sudan programme used only one percent of the total cost of any project on administration. This was partially explained by that the fact that Egil Hagen did some field work for World Vision International in exchange for their accounting and administration services for NPA."*

A year later Helge Rohn had straightened things out and had managed to continue building on the very important trust Egil Hagen had established with the people and leaders of the liberation struggle in South Sudan. He had also strengthened the credibility with the donors. But Helge Rohn was faced with new administrative challenges, and he described the situation in this way:

"*I decided that we should employ local people for the accounting and administrative work of the programme. The Kenyan authorities expected us to provide new jobs. I understood the importance of this, but I underestimated the challenges and problems connected to accounting and documenting such a rapidly expanding programme. It turned out that our new and rather inexperienced local staff could not handle everything.*

I therefore hired a Kenyan accountant who had been working with Norwegian Hydro in Africa. I thought it was a good choice, but it was not. The man was used to well-established routines and standard book-keeping, and was unable to adjust to the complex and fast changing situations that is part of any emergency assistance in war-like surroundings. So, he resigned and left us. Then, we hired KPMG, a well-known international auditing and accounting company with a good reputation, to the accounting work. This improved the situation, but did not solve all the problems related to a combination of weak accounting skills with our local staff, and the incredible growth of the programme and the strict documentation requirements, especially from USAID.

Because of the increased support from USAID, the programme from 1993 onwards grew very fast. In a timespan of a couple of years the programme expanded vastly both in volume and activity, the number of project managers and other staff steadily increased both at the HQ in Nairobi and in the field. But getting the right people for the right positions was very difficult. My experience from construction projects in Norway was that even under the best of circumstances, this can be difficult. In the Sudan programme it was extremely difficult. I did my best to impress upon the project managers in the field and those in administration that it was important that the accounting reports reflected what was in fact purchased and done, even in a very demanding work environment."

At one point, Helge Rohn started going through and correcting the worst posting errors himself. He told me later that he had to do this work at night, and that it almost completely exhausted him.

A growing Programme with growing Challenges

The challenges that Helge Rohn was confronted with, continued in the years to follow.

After a while, as the programme continued to grow, new managers were mostly recruited from Anglo-American aid circles, or among well-qualified Africans. There were several reasons for this. Firstly, the salary for local workers was lower than for Norwegians taking up positions in the field. They expected an international salary level. But NPA always had small budgets for administration, and we could save money that way. Secondly, the Kenyan authorities wanted us to hire Kenyans and other Africans. Thirdly, and not least important, local workers usually had a better understanding of African culture and the working environment than a newcomer from Norway.

Those who were hired on local contracts were usually competent and they developed a strong commitment both to their work and to the liberation struggle in Sudan. Many of them had close relations to the leadership group both of SRRA and SPLM/A. But they had hardly been to Norway, and they did not know NPA's history and its strong links to the Labour Movement, and they knew barely nothing about Norwegian development policies. Therefore, understandably enough, they did not have their first loyalty to Norway or NPA's HQ in Oslo which could have been the case if there had been more Norwegian managers and staff in Nairobi and in the field in Sudan.

We tried to remedy this somewhat by searching for qualified Norwegians for management positions within our Sudan programme, but we often had difficulties finding people who were qualified. At the same time, NPA's international donors did not share our worries on this point, they were satisfied with our staff.

Whoever was in charge of our regional HQ in Nairobi or in the field in South Sudan had a challenging and complex political landscape to navigate. They had always to have good a relationship, firstly with the governments in Kenya and Uganda, but also to the governments in Ethiopia and Eritrea.

Kenya came for a long period to represent a special challenge.

Kenya breaking the diplomatic Relations with Norway

President Moi broke off the diplomatic relations with Norway in the fall of 1990. The story behind is a long and complex one. Here are just some of the main points. The Kenyan opposition politician Koigi wa Wamwere had for several years been living as a political refugee in Norway writing books and articles and giving lectures in which he in the most uncompromising manner criticized President Moi and his government. In the late 1980s, Koigi, ignoring our advice, decided to go back to Kenya to fight the government politically from inside. He was arrested by Kenyan Security in Uganda and brought to Nairobi for trial and imprisonment. The Norwegian government at the time, decided to grant financial support through a Norwegian Solidarity Group for Koigi's defence lawyers in Kenya. When the trial started and the Norwegian Ambassador decided to demonstrate his government's sympathy with the accused by being present in the court room, it became too much for the very authoritarian Kenyan Head of State. In a public speech in Nairobi, he broke off diplomatic relations to Norway. The Norwegian Government complied with the order, but answered back in its own way by instantly cutting off all kind of development assistance to Kenya.

So, in a couple of days, dozens of Norwegian diplomats and more than a hundred NORAD experts with their families left the country. There were many attempts to try and repair the break and normalize relations again, but nothing worked. This unnecessary and unjustified diplomatic break lasted for eight years before any improvements could be made. For NPA and other Norwegian civil society organizations like Norwegian Church Aid operating in Kenya or having their main regional offices in Kenya for field activity in neighbouring Sudan, it was eight years with sometimes difficult problems arising in our frequent communications with Kenyan government institutions. NPA in these situations often missed the presence of the Norwegian Embassy in Nairobi.

NPA and Wangari Maathai

Second, during this same period, NPA was the intermediary for Norwegian government support to The Green Belt Movement and its great and renowned leader, the Late Wangari Maathai. Around 1990 she became a very important national leader of a steadily increasing political rebellion against Daniel arap Moi's authoritarian rule. The relationship between the two became extremely difficult. In short, President Moi developed a personal hatred for Wangari Maathai. I was the Secretary-General of NPA and I had since my days as a correspondent in Nairobi developed a close friendship with Wangari. This did not help the situation much for NPA.

Helge Rohn was put in difficult situations with the authorities because of the support that went through NPA to The Green Belt Movement. It became so problematic towards the end that Helge Rohn told us at NPA HQ in Oslo that we had to choose between the Sudan programme and Wangari Maathai. We had no choice because the Sudan programme was getting so important both from a humanitarian assistance point of view and politically, that the Green Belt Movement and Wangari Maathai had to go. But, before this happened, I was very active and successful in finding other ways of channeling continued Norwegian Government support to the Green Belt Movement. In that and other ways, Arman Aardal, the Norwegian Ambassador to UNEP based in Nairobi (which was a way of having a kind of Norwegian diplomatic presence in Kenya) also provided very important support for Wangari Maathai and the Green Belt Movement.

So, there were many ups and downs in our relationship with the Kenyan authorities, but whenever a crisis developed, we ultimately managed to find an amicable solution with the authorities.

I should add, to make the story about NPA and Kenya more complete, that NPA from the very beginning in 1986 until 2005, had a Kenyan personality, Bethuel Kiplagat, a leading diplomat, church leader, NGO leader, peace negotiator for Somalia and more, as a strong supporter. He was the Secretary General of the Kenyan Ministry of Foreign Affairs in 1986 when Egil Hagen set up his first office in Nairobi, and Kiplagat gave full support to this initiative, and later he was an invaluable supporter and advisor whenever the NPA management needed to talk to a Kenyan voice of reason. In 1998 we had a particularly difficult period with the Kenyan governmental NGO- Office. They demanded that NPA had appointed a local Kenyan Board of Directors for its Sudan programme. We thwarted a plan for the NGO-Office to have access to our budget, and thereby preempted corrupt activities. Kiplagat agreed to become the Chairman of the local Kenyan Board of Directors. Not only that, in co-operation with our Resident Representative, Lars Johan Johnson, composed the whole board. When the proposal was presented to the governmental NGO-Office, they had to accept it in full because Kiplagat' s name was on it.

We also had to develop our co-operation with SRRA/SPLM. Building reciprocal trust was most important. Without which we could not work together in South Sudan.

The war-hungry regime in Khartoum was always our most dangerous enemy. They succeeded sometimes in placing their agents within our staff, and the regime in Khartoum was always trying to influence Kenyan authorities and institutions to impede our work. Last, but not least, they would bomb and shoot at us and our staff in order to kill, in the field in South Sudan.

USA made NPA big in South Sudan

In 1993, a change of decisive importance took place regarding NPA'S Sudan programme. We started the year with a budget of about 20 million NOK, and ended the year with a budget of about 80 million NOK, a four-time increase. The reason was that the USA in the middle of the year decided to ask NPA to be their implementing partner for American humanitarian assistance to the peoples in the liberated areas of South Sudan. As a result, in the fall of 1993 NPA received food and other forms of aid for about 60 million kroner from the USA.

In the years following, the American assistance increased substantially, and NPA had overall annual budgets of more than 150 million kroner for South Sudan. Between 1993 and 2005 the USA share of the whole constituted between 60 and 80 per cent of the total budget. The fact that such a large part of the funding came from the USA, probably made several of the staff in Nairobi and South Sudan feel more obligation towards Washington than NPA and NMFA in Oslo.

From 1993-94 and in the years following, NPA employed between 1000 and 1300 workers behind the front lines in South Sudan each year. Almost all of them were Africans, primarily South Sudanese. Many of them had a limited understanding of accounting and administration, and many South Sudanese could not read or write.

Between 1994 and 2005, NPA was the largest employer in South Sudan. Even though local workers on the main kept their jobs for longer periods, there is no doubt that several thousand South Sudanese worked on NPA projects during this period. I would guess that NPA in this way contributed to the local communities in South Sudan somewhere between 1 and 1.5 million NOK per month in salaries that were used for food, improvements of family houses, health and education for the family. My estimate of the size of the total amount of salaries paid to South Sudanese for the whole period is between 100 and 150 million kroner.

Despite the problems and challenges that NPA faced both in Nairobi and in the field, most of our programmes were successful. Feedback from politicians in different donor countries, journalists and people from other aid administrations who often came to visit, was almost always positive. The reputation that NPA has been enjoying among those who experienced the liberation struggle in South Sudan, confirms this.

However, the situation for NPA has in the period from early January 2014 until the summer of 2016 gradually changed from being a NGO-favourite with the government to be seen as an enemy of the government, as have been the case also with other international NGOs operating in South Sudan at present. Security forces have raided the offices of NPA, hunting for local staff they wanted to eliminate. They have taken cars and other equipment from NPA, and they even made the situation for the present Resident Representative so difficult that he at times had seek refuge and protection with the Norwegian Embassy in Juba. For a period in 2016, he was heading the programme from the NPA Office in Nairobi.

A Crisis of Trust

Hans Havik began as the new director of administration at the NPA HQ in Oslo in 1994. He had a reputable academic education as well as an interesting and relevant work experience. He gradually developed a special interest for the book-keeping at our field offices. In the spring of 1996 he went to Nairobi to look more closely at the situation. During his stay, he did not express any critical viewpoints to the NPA management in Nairobi, but when he returned to Oslo he was angry and irate. He asked for a secret meeting with me and claimed that there were clear signs of corruption in the Sudan programme, and that the main responsible was Helge Rohn.

I was in general very worried about allegations about corruption and had a long, confidential conversation with the Chairman of the Board, Harald Øveraas. He gave me the necessary authorization, and we both felt that it was vital to move quickly. Then I made a fatal misjudgment, and I fired Helge Rohn. He was dismayed, but chose to leave. He told his staff that under the circumstances, given the lack of trust in him from the main office, he had no choice. He accepted the resignation to prevent possible damage to the entire Sudan programme that could be caused by internal NPA conflict.

The criticism regarding my decision came instantly from the staff both in Nairobi and at HQ. The Chairman of SPLM, John Garang, got very angry and asked me to reverse my decision. USAID in Nairobi and many others protested as well. But since I was very worried about the economic situation in the Sudan programme being out of control, I overlooked the criticism and named Havik as Rohn's successor.

The change of Resident Representative did not go well. Havik did neither manage to cooperate with the staff in Nairobi nor with the staff at HQ in Oslo. The relationship with SRRA/SPLM suffered terribly. Finally, the criticism became so intense, that in the late winter of 1997 I sent Irene Wenaas Holte who was the deputy head of NPA's International Department, to

Nairobi to assess the situation. She returned with a very critical report. Havik had been unable to handle his role as Resident Representative, there was a lot of mistrust and internal conflict. The programme could collapse. I decided to have an external evaluation and choose the experienced and renowned Norwegian consultant Kjeld Rimberg to do the work. Meanwhile I had in writing and in public apologized to Helge Rohn for my misjudgment.

The Clean Up

Rimberg returned with another critical report. While I was writing this book, he sent me a letter, remembering what he experienced:

"I had a had a short meeting with the NPA top management in Oslo one day in the spring of 1997 before I travelled to Nairobi. When I arrived in Nairobi I was going to have a meeting with Havik to get his perspective, but to my surprise I was told that he had left his job and was missing without a trace. Second in command, Vidar Anzjoen had taken over and was willing to assist me. He was an excellent man, a missionary son and married to a Kenyan woman. He was wise and helpful. We agreed in our first meeting that I should try and chart the situation through interviews.

The background was that a large number of trucks were impounded by the Kenya Tax and Revenue Authority, reportedly because a custom's charge was not paid. NPA's staff explained that something like this had never happened before, and it was highly surprising that the Kenya Authorities completely had changed their requirements regarding NPA. The plan this time as always before had been to drive the trucks to South Sudan, and the rule from the authorities had always been that this was done free of charge.

Now it was claimed that NPA owed a lot of money to the government. Fees and taxes had to be paid before the trucks would be allowed to move. The demand was large, I don't remember exactly but it was a two-digit million NOK amount, which was way beyond NPA's budget and liquidity. Halle had mentioned before the trip that there was an increasing uneasiness because of the signals from several workers in Nairobi that something was wrong with the finances and accounting department in Nairobi. My mission was to chart the situation and suggest changes that would improve management and leadership. And the whole thing started with the Resident Representative running away the day before I arrived.

I interviewed heads of departments and projects as well as other staff. On the surface, everything was calm and apparently in order. NPA practiced extensive delegation of authority in its international programmes, and it made the organization very dependent on the loyalty and trust of local managers and staff who took responsibility and had sufficient routines.

I concluded that this delegation should be more limited, and that the overall programme activity should be managed much more closely from HQ. It was necessary with stricter economic management and control from Oslo. Stronger management in Nairobi that had closer links to HQ was also necessary.

Several of the people I spoke with, hinted at economic disorder, but they were unable to be specific in their comments. At the same time, NPA in Nairobi had become involved in a couple of legal battles that required legal expertise both from Norway and Kenya.

In my report, after my return, I stated that future Norwegian support to the Sudan Programme should be linked to a demand both for stronger Norwegian management presence in Nairobi and more senior staff on the programme at HQ. Furthermore, it was necessary with legal expertise to solve the legal cases that NPA was now involved in. I had myself, signaled to the staff in Nairobi that NPA in Oslo would see it as a top priority to bring the Sudan programme back on track.

After some rounds of discussion with NPA's management in Oslo, I was asked to make another trip to Nairobi, this time together with NPA's legal advisor, Supreme Court Lawyer Jens Kristian Thune. We also needed local legal assistance and hired a local Kenyan lawyer who worked for an English/Kenyan company. He was *skilled and competent, and he quickly understood the complexity of the problem: Trucks detained by custom, internal unrest in the local administration and uncertainty with respect to the authorities.*

One afternoon while we were working with the Kenyan lawyer at his office, a telephone message came from NPA's main office in Nairobi: Police with trucks were taking everything from the office, papers and inventory. We rushed back to the NPA office. The Kenyan lawyer parked a couple of blocks away. He did not want to risk that his car should be seen to be part of the NPA inventory. At the office, we met two muscle bound Kenyans in leather jackets. They were policemen who were given the task to seize all property because NPA had not paid their debts which included the custom charge on the detained trucks. In other words: They wanted to take everything that was moveable inventory. Our Kenyan lawyer was diplomatic and proved to be a good negotiator, despite his young age.

He managed to create a calm atmosphere. After a couple of hours of private conversation, he asked the two men who had claimed to be on a police assignment, if they worked for a police station nearby. It took a while before they answered: No, they worked for a private firm. They did this kind of jobs in their spare time. The police station they belonged to, was in a completely different part of the city.

NPAs young lawyer handled the new information masterfully. Ok, he said, so you are working for somebody else? Interesting, yes, he understood very well that this was an important case, but maybe they together with him should use a little extra time discussing such an important case before further action was taken? What about a meeting tomorrow? Our friends hesitated a bit; the mood in the room was completely transformed from open hostility only a few minutes earlier to a relaxed almost friendly mood.

They had planned to use the day for this, but they could change their plans....

The conversation ended amicably, and NPA was off the hook. But this episode confirmed that there were powers in the country who wanted to put pressure on NPA, and it was not easy to figure out what to do next.

At the office, the local staff was uneasy because of the uncertainty created regarding how the programme would be managed in the future. One elderly worker who had been there forever, contacted us, informing us that he and several others would be presenting a pension claim that would total about 10 million NOK that they held was their right. He was not the least concerned with NPA's financial situation, but his and his fellow workers' future.

We travelled home and informed Halle and others in the NPA's management group about our findings and recommendations. Jens Kristian went to Nairobi a short time later and worked for a couple of years as NPA's volunteer and unpaid legal advisor, to assist in the necessary cleaning up operations in the administration of the Sudan programme.

A couple of months later Vidar Anzjoen surprised me with a local call from Oslo. He and his wife were staying in an apartment hotel in Oslo. He explained that he had been contacted by the Norwegian police attaché at the Embassy in Nairobi, who had connection to the Kenyan Government Intelligence Agency. Kenyan police had evidence to the fact that Vidar was on a list of people to be liquidated, and he was asked by the Embassy soonest to travel to Norway with his family. A few days before they left Nairobi, a car without ordinary registration plates had tried to force him off the road, but he had been able to control his car and had escaped unscathed from the incident.

It was obvious that local groups in Nairobi that had criminal connections, were trying to sabotage NPA's efforts to improve on their administration and programme work for South Sudan. Vidar became anxious from this experience, and he and his family stayed in Norway for several months before he went back to work on the Sudan programme."

That concludes Kjeld Romberg's note.

While Rimberg and Thune were doing their work in Nairobi, Hans Havik turned up in Oslo. I asked him to come to my office to discuss the critical situation in the NPA Sudan Programme. I told him, based on the reports I had received from Nairobi that I had no other choice but to terminate his position as Resident Representative of the Sudan Programme with immediate effect. Havik exploded in fury and stormed out of my office. He went directly to the Ministry of Foreign Affairs (NMFA), with his version of how incompetent everyone was in NPA, and how unjustly he had been treated.

The damage done during the Havik period was not easy to repair. I had to recreate trust within my own organization towards me. Together, we had to find a new Resident Representative for the Sudan programme quickly. The Resident Representative of the NPA programme in Bosnia-Herzegovina, was Lars Johan Johnsen. He had gained a reputation as an able and even-handed manager. I travelled to Sarajevo and persuaded him to move to Nairobi. Shortly after when I gathered the local staff in Sarajevo for a meeting and told them that Lars Johan soon was to leave them, all were shocked and many had tears in their eyes. He was a loved and a very respected manager. In addition to all this, there was another difficult task ahead; we had to regain the trust we had had with SRRA/ SPLM/A. I had been part of the process that had led to mistrust, and I decided that I had to use a lot of my time as Secretary-General on recreating the lost trust.

In the months that followed, Lars Johan, the Head of NPA's International Development and the desk officers for Sudan in Oslo, and I worked closely together. Lars Johan soon developed a good working relationship with his staff, and with his friendly disposition and even-handedness he soon earned the trust with the leaders of SRRA and SPLM/A. During the fall of 1997 and winter 1998, several internal seminars were conducted in Nairobi to strengthen the internal cooperation and develop a sense of purpose and unity among the staff. We also had two large seminars with the leadership group from SRRA and people from the leadership of SPLM, where we discussed our common challenges and how to improve our ability to work together.

An unexpected Visit from the Kenyan Revenue Authority

One day in the spring of 1998 a few representatives from the Kenyan Revenue Authority presented themselves unannounced at NPA's Nairobi office. They were brusque and arrogant and claimed that NPA had not paid income tax to Kenya for their local staff on the Sudan programme. They therefore demanded full access to all accounting records which we gave them. A short time after this visit, a letter arrived on Lars Johan's desk from the Kenyan Tax Authority demanding immediate payment of 30 million NOK for taxes not paid. This was quite an unexpected shock. NPA could not afford to pay this amount because it would have meant bankruptcy. We suspected that this action against NPA, and the amount demanded, was another part of the dirty tricks of the Khartoum regime against NPA. They always had agents in Nairobi, trying to buy and corrupt politicians, bureaucrats in Kenyan government institutions and others to work against us, SRRA and SPLM.

We decided to be polite and correct in our dealings with the Tax Authority. The first thing we did was ask for the details of the tax demand, and the way it had been calculated. It turned out to be that we were not the only international non-governmental organization in Kenya that had not paid taxes for our local employees. The case also applied to many other NGOs with offices in Kenya.

NPA is a respectable, law-abiding organization. Therefore, we apologized to the Tax Authority for having failed to pay tax for our Kenyan local staff, and we informed them that we would pay all outstanding taxes for our Kenyan staff. Then, we asked how much it was. We had many Kenyan employees. The lack of payment went back several years and amounted to 2.5 million NOK. We paid this without further discussion, but it negatively affected the financial balance of the Sudan programme, and reduced that year's anticipated small surplus.

However, the tax authorities wanted another 27.5 million NOK. Their argument was that since the salaries to the local employees from South Sudan, Ethiopia, Eritrea and Uganda were paid from a Kenyan bank account, the income for these groups of employees were to be considered taxable income for Kenya. It did not help that these nationals both resided and had their entire work day in South Sudan.

We refused to accept this line of reasoning and referred to the situation on the ground in war-torn Sudan.

In South Sudan, there were no banks or post office services in the areas where we were working. We sought advice from Kenyan staff members who knew lawyers in Kenya, about who to hire. However, our first try ended as a small catastrophe. The lawyer we hired was thoroughly corrupt and sent us invoices with an hourly wage that was horrendous, higher than the lawyer fees in the Norwegian oil industry. We were in trouble.

At that point, NPA's lawyer Jens Kristian Thune asked to see me in my Oslo office. He told me that he during his recent visits to Kenya had fallen in love with its people and beautiful nature. He had therefore come to to tell me that he and his wife wanted to move to Kenya for a couple years, and that he wanted to work as a legal advisor for the NPA Sudan Programme free of charge. This was just short of a miracle. I did not hesitate and agreed.

A short time later, Jens Kristian and his wife were stationed in Nairobi. The first thing he did was to propose a new Kenyan lawyer as our local lawyer. He was a very serious young man, and during our first meeting he confided with us that he was very religious, a "Born again Christian". However, it turned out that he was perfect for the job. He was very skilled, honest and hard-working, and he sent us reasonable invoices.

Even though the tax authorities were now facing professional opposition from NPA, they upheld their claim of 27,5 million NOK. We hired another Kenyan consultant who knew both different political networks and the political environment in Kenya, and after a short time he said there was no way around it. We had to ask for a meeting with President Daniel arap Moi and appeal to him for help.

At the same time, we were given a tip that it might be enough to meet with the Director General for the National Civil Service, the famous scientist and writer Richard Leakey. After heavy pressure from the World Bank and the International Monetary Fund, the Kenyan Government had recently agreed to ask Leakey to take this position in order to combat corruption in Kenya.

It was easy to get an appointment with Leakey. He was friendly, and he listened to our plight, but said that the case was outside his jurisdiction.

The Meeting with President Daniel arap Moi

Now, it was more pressing than ever to get a meeting with the president. At that time, Moi was considered a de facto dictator in Kenya, even if he was re-elected in 1997 in an election with several other parties participating. He was also known for being very difficult to meet, but we had to try. We decided to keep the Norwegian Embassy and Norwegian Ministry of Foreign Affairs in Oslo out of the case, because they would probably advise us not to meet with the president.

In the meantime, I tried to find out a little about Moi's health, and what we could expect if we had a meeting. It was an interesting experience.

The Kenyans I spoke with said, that Moi was sick and had throat cancer, and that he was getting old, uninterested and a little out of date; in short, a weak old man.

We worked intensely to get a meeting, and we got appointments, but both the first and second appointments were cancelled. The third time was lucky. We were told to be available at the State House at eight o'clock, one morning, in November 1998.

I arrived in Nairobi a few days in advance. A message was waiting for me from the State House: NPA was asked to prepare a 15-minute presentation about our work in Sudan and the tax problems that had arisen. I was to give the presentation when the president's man signaled for it. While we were waiting for this very important date to come, we spent many hours preparing the statement, making countless revisions. I read the draft again and again while staff members listened with an order to be critical of my performance. Finally, we agreed, both the text and my performance were deemed to be good enough.

The State House also informed us that according to protocol, we were to have monetary gifts in the form of two checks for two of Moi's foundations, one to support the education of girls, and the other to support orphaned children. 100 000 NOK for each foundation was expected. We were allowed to have four members in our delegation.

We travelled early morning on the agreed date to be on time at the State House and reported to the reception. They received us graciously. At precisely eight o'clock we heard: "*The NPA delegation, please present yourself.*" We were led into a large hall where at least 100 people were waiting to see the President. I thought, my goodness, we will have to wait for a long time. It will be late afternoon before it is our turn. But after a few minutes we heard: "*The NPA delegation!*" We stood up, walking quickly towards the open door. We were very nervous. This was it. If this did not work, we were finished.

We entered a beautiful reception room and there he, the President, stood, tall, dark and stiff as a statue. At his side, was a man I knew from my time as the Africa Correspondent of the Norwegian Broadcasting Corporation. He was now the senior presidential advisor, Charles Njonjo, the very conservative, pro-British, authoritarian and very controversial former Minister of Justice.

We bowed deeply, and Moi and Njonjo nodded briefly in return. Then there was one nod from the advisor on the side; I could begin my speech. I spoke from a manuscript as well as I could for 15 minutes. When I was finished, I nodded.

Moi looked at me for a moment. Then he responded very precisely with five points, and he spoke no longer than five minutes.

Firstly, he said that he was quite familiar with NPA's good work for the people of South Sudan who were suffering in a terrible way while fighting for their liberation, and he stated very clearly that he was very appreciative of what we did.

Then he said a few words about his and Kenya's relationship to the conflict, and that they sympathized with and supported the people in their liberation struggle.

Thereafter he turned to our special tax problem and emphasized that we had presented him, as Head of State and Government, with a very difficult matter. Tax related matters belonged to the Ministry of Finance and the Tax Court, and it was therefore not an issue the President could resolve alone. Then he explained to us how tax cases were handled in his government.

He paused for a little, and then finally, came the words that we were desperately hoping for.

"However, *I shall make sure that you will be able to continue your good work for the suffering peoples of South Sudan.*"

He nodded briefly, and a person from the protocol nodded at Njonjo. The two checks could be delivered.

The visit had come to an end. We again bowed deeply and left.

We were overwhelmed. We had succeeded, and the most important part was that the President had assured us that he knew about NPA's Sudan programme, and that he praised us for our work.

But I also had to take note of another very important observation I made during our meeting with President Moi.

What we had been told prior to the meeting about Moi, his aging and his poor health had proven to be wishful thinking by those Kenyans as well as those in the international circles in Nairobi, with whom we had discussed the matter.

Moi was at that time 74 years old, and he had a workday that was both long and strenuous, but he lived a simple life. He stood upright throughout the entire meeting, and he demonstrated that he was in good mental and physical health. We had met a Head of State who with his presence and the way he held himself, sent out a message of being in full control.

We got what we wanted. We did not hear from the tax authorities for a very long time.

Corrupt Accountants fired

But we still had a feeling that something was wrong with the accounting office. We had employed a Swede as our new Director of Administration and Accounting. In conversations in closed chambers he expressed a repeated concern that we were being exposed to some kind of corruption.

After thorough discussions with him, the Resident Representative, Lars Johan Johnsen, the legal advisor, Jens Kristian Thune and myself, we made a drastic decision. We decided to fire the local Kenyan workers in accounting and finance. But this had to be done in a way that was in accordance with the Labour Laws of Kenya.

At the beginning of the workday on November 30, 1998, the people in question were asked to come into the meeting room. Lar Johan Johnsen gave a short orientation explaining that they were fired because of suspicion of corruption. Then, they were given two envelopes with letters. In one there was the salary for November and December. In the other one there was a legal explanation of their termination, where all the requirements specified in the Labour Laws were fulfilled. The employees concerned, were of course shocked and tried to protest, but to no avail. They were not allowed to go back to their workplace, but were handed their personal belongings. Then, they were escorted out by a guard and told to never come back to NPA.

NPA followed a hard line as an employer in this case. In the worst-case scenario, it could lead to more and difficult problems with Kenyan authorities, but we heard nothing.

Immediately after the sacked staff members had left the office ground, Lars Johan and the Director of Administration and Accounting had a thorough investigation of their laptops and desks, looking for substantive proof, and they found more than we believed was possible.

In the drawers, there was a double set of NPA letterheads and other various application forms with NPA's name printed. One set was used for NPA's communication with the Kenyan authorities; for example, application forms for permission to move goods from Mombasa through Kenya and into South Sudan.

The other set was used in secret collaboration with Kenyan business companies. These companies were given pre-filled forms in NPA's name that could be used to avoid import duties and taxes of different kinds; because the papers from 'NPA' said that the goods in question, mostly cars, spare parts and tires were in transit for South Sudan. Instead they were sold at full price on the Kenyan market without the company concerned, paying the import tax required by law. We also found names of some of the companies.

A large foreign brewery was in the process of building a subsidiary in Kenya. In the falsified papers, we found that most of the technology for the brewery was imported in NPA's name as goods in transit to South Sudan. Another and well-known national company had imported large quantities of cars and tires that in the falsified papers had South Sudan as the destination, but they were sold in the Kenyan market without import tax being paid.

The staff members who had been fired, had thus been part of an extensive swindle league of Kenyan businessmen. Over several years, they had most likely swindled the Kenyan Government for large amounts of shillings. I do not believe that the staff members who were fired, made large amounts of money from this corrupt practice, but rather that they had become tangled into a mafia network that would stop at nothing to make a profit. The poor former employees of ours had been caught in that corrupt mafia network, and they were unable to get out of it.

A couple of weeks later, two of our staff were having lunch at a restaurant near the office. One very well-known and influential politician and businessman at the time, was having his luncheon as well. He was drunk and ill-behaved. When he discovered our two staff members, he rose from his table and walked over to them and said: "*I hear that you at NPA are firing Kenyan staff and accusing them of corruption. You better watch out or…*" Then, he put his finger to his throat. It was not possible to misunderstand his message. He was one of the businessmen behind the corruption that we had recently uncovered, and now he told us that he might be prepared for revenge. The signal could not be misunderstood. He was ready to have members of our staff assassinated.

Terminating so many employees only a month before the end of 1998, created severe difficulties for the administration at our office in Nairobi. We hired new accountants as fast as we could, but they had to be taught how our accounting system worked. In short, we had almost insurmountable problems in finishing the annual report for the Sudan programme 1998. But the staff did a fantastic job and finished just in time.

The Meeting with Vice-President George Saitoiti

In the fall of 1999 the Kenyan Revenue Authoritie once again renewed its demand for the outstanding income tax of 27.5 million NOK. We were as unable as ever before to pay the amount. It would not only destroy NPA's Sudan programme. It was a deadly threat to the survival of NPA as a humanitarian organization.

We repeated in our reply to the Tax Authorities that we considered the claim to be illegal and invalid.

We felt sure that President Moi in his own way had communicated with the tax authorities about leaving us alone. But nine months had passed since we had our meeting with him, and now the tax authorities felt they could try again. This time we could not go back to the president.

What now?

I was again in Nairobi, discussing the case with our staff when one of them, Halima, suggested that we should ask for a meeting with Vice-President George Saitoiti. Yes, a very good idea, but how could we do that, was the next question. "*I live in his constituency, and there is an election meeting with him on Sunday. I can go there and try to talk with him*", answered Halima. She was a beautiful Kenyan woman, and it was common knowledge that Saitoiti had a weakness for beautiful women.

Sunday found Halima in the front row, very visible to the Vice-President.

When the meeting was over, he walked over to her and asked: "*Why are you staring at me in this way?*" Halima answered that she worked with NPA on the Sudan programme, and that the Secretary General had an urgent need to see him. Saitoiti looked at Halima for a moment, and then he said: "*Ok, Tuesday morning, nine o'clock at my office.*"

Tuesday came, and Halima and I went as agreed to the Vice-President's office. We were expected, and were shown in. Saitoiti was at first in a lousy mood and would barely speak with us. But after a little while he loosened up and became very friendly. I explained about the tax problem, the difficult relationship we had with the tax authorities, and I told him about our meeting with president Moi in the fall of 1998. Saitoiti was a professor in mathematics and had been the finance minister for several years. Therefore, he had very good insight into finances and management, and he explained in detail how we could take the case through the system to resolve it. He also said that he would assist me in obtaining a meeting with the Minister of Finance.

As the conversation ended, I had one very political question I wanted to ask, and I said: "*It is a problem for you, Mr. Vice-President and your Government, that NPA takes such a clear position in support of the liberation struggle in South Sudan?*"

Saitoiti looked at me for a moment, his gaze intensified. Then he stood up and pounded his fist into the table: "*No, Mr. Hanssen! On this point, we are in total agreement.*" Then he smiled and wished us well both on the tax issue and regarding our work in South Sudan. We left the office relieved and invigorated about what the Vice-President had just said. As we passed through the reception area, on our way out, there was a man standing, but I did not notice who he was.

An unexpected Meeting with Raila Odinga

But as we were walking down the hallway, the Vice-President came running after us, yelling: "Mr. Hanssen, there is a friend here who would like to say hello!" I walked back and there in the reception was my old friend Raila Odinga standing. We hugged, and Raila whispered to me: "*Don't say anything about me being a political refugee in Norway.*" Then we had a pleasant talk. In hindsight, I know that the meeting with the Vice-President was one of several attempts by Raila Odinga to get back into politics with the hope that Moi would nominate him as his successor as president of Kenya. But Raila failed in his efforts. Therefore, in the summer of 2002 Raila chose to join the Rainbow Coalition with Mwai Kibaki. The coalition won the Kenyan presidential and parliamentary elections in 2002 by a landslide.

The Tax Case goes to Court

A few weeks after our meeting with the Vice-President, I was invited to meet with the Minister of Finance, Mr. Chris Okemo.

Lars Johan had in the summer of 1999 notified me that he wanted to leave as Resident Representative. He had been working as a manager for NPA in countries with conflict and war since the early 1990s, first Bosnia Herzegovina and then South Sudan. He had had enough and wanted to go back to peaceful Norway for a while. At the time, I was to meet with the Minister of Finance, Lars Johan's successor on the Sudan programme, Sten Rino Bonsaksen had just arrived in Nairobi, and he joined me for the meeting. Okemo was both very friendly and professional. He listened to what I had to say, and then he said: "*Mr. Hanssen, I suggest that NPA takes the case to our Tax Court. If you win, I promise to uphold the ruling without hesitation.*"

Jens Kristian Thune was still NPA's legal advisor, and he and Sten Rino worked closely with our skilled Kenyan lawyer to get the case to court. Early in 2000, the case came up, but Jens Kristian had then as planned returned to Norway. Consequently, Sten Rino and our Kenyan lawyer had to present the case in court without him.

The court decided to give the case a thorough treatment. They wanted to see all NPA's records for payment of taxes and fees of all kinds from past years, prolonging the court case for close to two years.

Acquitted

One day in 2002 Sten called me from Nairobi elated, and said: "*Halle, the ruling is in, and we are acquitted on all counts. But we did get two minor fines for not submitting transit forms for goods to South Sudan in a timely manner.*" I had at the time left NPA, the responsibility was no longer mine, but I was also elated. I had had so many worries and had put in so many hours on the case. If NPA had been found guilty, it might have destroyed NPA.

The tax case was over, and NPA, as far as I know, has not heard anything more from the tax authorities in Kenya.

This experience gives me an opportunity to reflect on a few things. Kenya is well known as a society with corruption at all levels, both in the public and private sectors. Under Moi the political system was strongly influenced by nepotism, by favoring family and friends.

NPA used contacts that were available to get meetings with political top leaders in Kenya, but we played above board.

In regards to the tax case, we had highly skilled and loyal lawyers, and it was the interpretation of Kenyan laws and our arguments that convinced the judges, and nothing else.

I have since 1972 had assignments in about forty African countries, and I have experienced many kinds of problems. Some of these could have been resolved with bribes, but I have only done so once.

It was in Angola in 2007. I handed over my vaccination card at the airport to the health worker, who said: "*Your yellow fever vaccination has expired. You need a shot.*" I checked the card and to my dismay, the man was right. My card was no longer valid. Stories of dirty vaccination needles and contagious diseases such as HIV and others, raced through my head.

After a short time, I was called into a waiting room. It was my turn, and I was shown into a booth. The man who had checked the card was sitting there. He looked at me, and he said: "*The vaccination costs 25 USD. You are probably scared to get the shot, and I will not force it on you. If you pay me 25 USD, I will stamp your card and everything is OK.*"

"*Yes, let's do that,*" I replied.

My dominant experience is simple. Most people are decent and honest and should be treated fairly and with respect whether in Africa or anywhere else.

Raila Odinga holding a press conference after the 2007 elections. The elections in Kenya in August 2017 were followed by a complain by Raila Odinga and his political alliance, NASA, to the Court of Justice. The Court ruled on 2nd September that the presidential elections had not been conducted in accordance with the Constitution of Kenya. New elections will therefore be held before the end of October 2017. Picture: Bård Anders Andreassen

An Antonov bomber in action in South Sudan.

People in a village in South Sudan seeks protection during a bombing raid.

9
THE ATTACK WITH POISONOUS GAS

IT WAS A BEAUTIFUL AFTERNOON in Oslo in July 1999. I was in my car, on my way home from work when my mobile phone rang. I stopped at a bus stop shelter. The call was from the News Room of the Norwegian Broadcasting Corporation. The reporter told me that they just had gotten news from Nairobi that warplanes from Khartoum had bombed NPA's project areas in the villages of Lainya, Kaaya and Loka, near Yei in South Sudan, suggesting that gas seemed to have been used in the attack.

I was shocked to hear the news. Use of gas in warfare is strictly forbidden, not only that; it is a war crime. On the other hand, we knew that the regime in Khartoum was capable of anything. I answered without hesitation to the reporter's question:

"*If the dictatorship in Khartoum believes that they can bomb NPA out of Sudan by using gas, they are mistaken. We will not be intimidated. We are staying, and we will take the matter of using gas to the Norwegian Government, UN and other relevant authorities.*"

The South Sudanese doctor Kaneri Gribani was at that time the Director of NPA's hospital in Yei. People came to him in the afternoon of July 23, afraid and confused and told that something terrible that had happened. In an interview Gribani said this:

"*We understood that something new and dangerous had happened. Terrified people said that several Antonov planes flew over the villages and dropped bombs from high altitude. But this time the bombs exploded in a different way. There was a muffled explosion, and then a strange smell.*

After a few hours, people and animals started getting sick. Some became nauseous; some had pain in their eyes and chest. An old man died of sharp pains in his chest. A couple of women miscarried. Birds died and fell out of trees, shortly after, smaller animals died on the ground. The day after, the grass withered and died.

I understood immediately that this must be a gas attack and instructed a selected group of qualified personnel to go out straight away and take samples of the dead animals, blood, urine, grass and soil."

Lars Johan Johnsen was at the time the NPA Resident Representative in Nairobi. Doctor Gribani contacted him by radio about what had happened. Lars Johan told me the following about what actions had been taken.

"*We agreed that NPA's two security directors, a former Kenyan military officer, Charles Aloo, and the South Sudanese security director Chat Paul, should immediately hire a plane and go to Yei, investigate the crime scene together with Gribani and his people and bring back samples. They left in a hurry, and came back the next day with samples. They also had verified that 22 bombs had been dropped in the area.*

We were all aware of the possibility that a war crime had been committed, but we had to get the samples examined to prove it. Therefore, we contacted the Netherland's Embassy in Nairobi because Netherland was the Custodian of the UN Convention banning dangerous chemical weapons such as gas. Initially they were interested, but the next day they had changed their positon and said they were not able to follow up the case. What a cowardly and irresponsible response, I thought.

At the same time, we contacted the American and British embassies. Both were very interested in the case and our samples. The British came first and got some of the best samples. They also signed an agreement with us that they would, as soon as they had examined the samples, report back to us about their findings. However, we never heard a word from the British. Then the Americans came and got what was left of our samples. They also promised to report back to us."

That concludes Lars Johan Johnsen.

NPA's management group in Oslo viewed the case as extremely serious and decided to bring it to the attention of our Ministry of Foreign Affairs.

International Interest

NPA's Director of Information, Ivar Christiansen, had most of the contact with media about the case both in Norway and internationally. He informed them about what NPA had done to secure evidence, and that the samples had been given to relevant embassies. There was no independent professional institution in Kenya that could conduct the necessary laboratory tests. Christiansen also communicated NPA's unequivocal condemnation of the poisonous gas attacks.

Samson Kwaje, at that time SPLM's official spokesperson, held a press conference in Nairobi where he told about the women who had miscarried, the animals that had died, and the withering grass and plants. Samson also explained about the lack of large craters characteristic from bomb attacks, but that instead there were deep dents in the ground surrounded by a green colour, and a bad smell in the entire area.

The American aid organization, World Vision, which was part of OLS and had worked in the same area, reacted very strongly as well. The director Phillipe Guiton said that if there really was used poisonous gas in the area, it would have major consequences for the way the international aid community related to the regime in Khartoum.

UN's network for international aid to the whole of Sudan, OLS, confirmed that it had received reports about the attacks and that three UN workers in the area had become ill and were transported to the hospital for treatment.

But UN took their time getting into the area to take samples. Two days passed before the UN people went in. By then it was too late because the effect of the gas was gone. It almost looked like the UN was trying to avoid finding evidence.

When it came to the Ministry of Foreign Affairs in Oslo, the attacks came at a time when the Minister of Development Cooperation, Hilde Frafjord Johnson, was busy getting the MFA and her own government fully committed to the peace negotiations for Sudan. Therefore, it was not the best of times to start accusing Khartoum of gassing civilian targets in South Sudan.

But Hilde Frafjord Johnson and her staff did it anyway. Firstly, she asked key members of her own staff to check both with the UN and SPLM. They confirmed that there had been an attack, but they could not document that gas had been used. Then she brought the case before the authorities in Khartoum who denied all charges. The Ministry of Foreign Affairs therefore concluded that the charges were not sufficiently documented, and the case was closed. In NPA we were certain that gas had been used, but when MFA said no, we were at a loss because we ourselves did not yet have any concrete evidence.

What happened to the Samples?

The British had signed an agreement that they would report back to us, but they never did.

When it came to the USA, Lars Johan Johnsen was in the fall of 1999 invited to dinner at the American Embassy in Nairobi. During coffee, he was pulled aside by an American diplomat who was probably from the CIA. He said something like this:

"*You are probably interested to know what we found in the samples you gave us. The answer is that it was poisonous gas, but we can't say with certainty what kind of gas it was, because the samples* were small and old by the time we got them to the laboratory. But this has to be kept secret. *If you go home and say that we (CIA) have discovered gas, we will deny it because we want to try and find out where the gas was produced; Iraq, Iran or Sudan."*

We were back where we started. We knew it, but could not use the information. But then something interesting happened.

A Member of the Swedish Pentecostal Church enters the Scene

While we were still on this case, I received a phone call from a Swede somewhere outside Stockholm. He told me that he was an engineer, and that for the past few years he had worked on a water project for the Swedish Pentecostal Mission near Kajo Kaji in South Sudan. He was at work in the field on the day the Antonov planes dropped the special bombs near their project area. He confirmed that the bombs exploded in a very different way from cluster bombs. There was a muffled explosion, and immediately thereafter, there was an instant nauseating smell. People, animals and birds got sick and some died. He confirmed in full what NPA's doctor Gribani and our security people had reported.

Then he added: *"As an engineer, I know how to act in a situation like this, and I took my own samples from the area where the bombs had exploded and secured them as well as I could. Then, I put them in my travel bag and took a flight home to Sweden, and a few days ago, I turned them over to the Swedish Institute of Defence Research. They got very interested, and they wanted to have my samples and promised me a report about the results from their laboratory tests.*

I am an engineer and I took quite good quality samples. At the institute they said that the samples are so good and substantial in quantity that they can share it with the Norwegian Institute of Defence Research."

I thanked him profusely for the information, and I immediately thereafter called the Norwegian Institute of Defence Research. It took some minutes to get through to the right person, but eventually I was able to talk to someone who like his Swedish colleague got very interested, and it created added interest when I said that there was a possibility of working together with the Swedish institute. In the days following, a few of my NPA staff and I kept in touch both with the Swedish engineer and the Swedish Institute of Defence Research, and we had considerable expectations about the information we might receive.

Then, Silence, but why?

Days and weeks passed, and nothing happened. We called the Swedish engineer, who told us that the people at the Swedish institute had taken the case to their Director General. He had probably had some contacts to the Swedish government, and then he decided that no laboratory tests of the samples should be carried out. Instead, he ordered the destruction of the samples.

With that bad news, I immediately called the Norwegian Institute of Defence Research, and they had done the same thing. The case had been discussed at the level of the Director General, and the conclusion was that the case should be closed.

NPA was never from either institute given a proper explanation about this total change of attitude and opinion. Nobody would say anything.

We tried to find out what happened and finally came across a formal explanation. The UN- Convention on dangerous weapons, including chemical weapons, is very clear on how to collect samples, secure them and seal them. Then they are to be transported in a plane that is prepared in a certain way. Our people in Yei had done their best, but did not know the rules and had therefore broken them on several points. The Swedish engineer, without knowing it, had almost committed a crime when he took the samples home on a commercial flight without declaring what he had in his luggage. Transporting laboratory test material in this way is strictly forbidden.

But more important, none of the countries we had contacted, with the exception of the USA, wanted any political or diplomatic complications with the dictatorial regime in Khartoum. That was more important than trying to apply the UN Convention on the case.

In addition, Great Britain has at all times had a preference for Khartoum, no matter who was in power there, and they did not want any trouble this time either.

When it came to Norway and the reaction from the MFA, we had the impression that Norway's role in the peace negotiations made further investigations of the case difficult.

In Sweden, Lundin Oil was at that time a major partner in the oil business in Sudan, and this was an important consideration for the Swedish Government. In addition, NPA had repeatedly been exposed to accusations from Swedish missionary organizations for weapon smuggling in Sudan. And probably for the same reasons, SIDA had just cut its grants for our hospitals in South Sudan. The mood in Sweden when it came to NPA was not a favorable one.

However, when it comes to Netherland, it is still inconceivable to me why the diplomatic staff at Netherland's Embassy in Nairobi were as negative as they were. Netherland has as the Custodian of this UN-Convention a particular responsibility to respond in a totally different and positive manner on issues like this one. How could they be the custodian when they did not want to act? All of these governments with the exception of the USA, were cowards, and the Government of Netherlands was the most cowardly of them all.

In addition, could one reason also be that NPA supported the rebellion of the oppressed people of Sudan and cooperated closely with SPLM/A who in diplomatic language were still called the rebels? We were partisans and maybe we were not seen as credible because they believed that we wanted to dishonour the regime in Khartoum?

Two Meetings with CIA in Nairobi in the Fall of 2001

The events of September 11, 2001 with the terror attack and following mass death in New York and Washington will be remembered forever. Not just in the USA, but in the whole world.

I left NPA in May 2001, but in October the same year, I had a reporting assignment in Kenya. I stayed as usual at the Fairview Hotel, and had many meetings with old Kenyan friends and colleagues, with former colleagues in NPA, and key people in SPLM/A. I also had a long discussion with John Garang.

In one of these meetings I learned that a CIA representative working in Nairobi wanted to see me about the situation in the Horn of Africa. I said that if a CIA- agent wanted to meet with me to discuss islamic fundamentalism in Sudan and in other places on the Horn of Africa, then I also had a strong interest in meeting him. The next morning, the telephone rang. An American at the other end, introduced himself and said that he really wanted to meet with me. He came to the hotel just after breakfast and proved to be a knowledgeable and insightful man when it came to politics and social issues on the Horn of Africa.

We had an intriguing conversation, and I mentioned the poisonous gas attack in the summer of 1999. He became very interested, and I explained the circumstances. I also told him that the American Embassy in Nairobi (CIA) had been given samples, and that the answer they had given us, was to be kept secret. He was not familiar with any of this, but promised to find out and get back to me.

A couple of days later, he had checked out what they had on the case in Washington, and we had another meeting. Everything I had said, was correct. He added that the test had shown that the gas that was used was significantly stronger than tear gas, but not as strong as the very poisonous sarin gas. They could not determine anything else because the samples were not good enough.

Then I asked if I could use this information in public, and he said yes, as long as I did not use his name.

10
THE BUILDING OF DEMOCRATIC INSTITUTIONS SABOTAGED

Strong efforts were made in the period between 2005 and 2013 by patriotic and democratic, committed South Sudanese and supported by many of their international friends to create the legal and professional base for Freedom of Expression and free and Independent Media both in Sudan and South Sudan. Similar strong efforts were made to change SPLM from a liberation movement into a member based, democratic and progressive political party. But both efforts failed, because they were sabotaged by people in the highest office both of SPLM and the Government of South Sudan. I was part of the process and saw how the powers of destruction succeeded. In this chapter, I tell my story, about how, and why it happened.

The Concern of John Garang and the Beginning of the Building of Institutions for Democracy

When the Comprehensive Peace Agreement (CPA) was signed in 2005, the Right to Freedom of Expression and the foundation for free and independent media was non-existent in Sudan. In addition, four of every five people in South Sudan could not read or write. Only a very small number of people had ever seen a newspaper. This situation was the same in the majority African populated areas of Darfur, Kordofan/Nuba Mountains and the Red Sea hills in Northern Sudan.

The situation was however radically different with the Arab minority and the upper class in Sudan. Most, if not all of them, had been to school, and many had higher education.

Sudan in the period from independence in 1956 up to 2005 was dominated by military rule and dictatorships. There was no tradition of free media and freedom of expression. Therefore, if after the CPA in 2005, anyone wanted to establish the principles of democracy and basic human rights like Freedom of Expression in Sudan, they had to move quickly to create from scratch the democratic and legal foundation.

From my first meeting with John Garang in 1993 and up to his death in 2005, I had many interesting and rewarding conversations with him. Towards the end of the 1990s, he convinced me and other international political friends that the SPLM/A soon was going to be so strong, both politically and militarily that a political settlement to the conflict was going to be inevitable. He conveyed to me and others an intense concern about the challenges connected to the building of the principle institutions for a democratic society in the whole Sudan. His vision was: A new, secular and democratic Sudan. He was very engaged in trying to get people to understand how a democratic society functioned and that it entailed freedom of expression, free and independent media, and the freedom for journalists to conduct their profession in a democratic society. Therefore, he raised several times the issue with me about the need for SPLM to get support in order to get the training of media people started. After the end of my tenure with the NPA in the spring of 2001, he asked me once again if I could take a lead role in developing a project in support of Freedom of Expression and free and independent media for the whole of Sudan.

Journalists, from both Northern and Southern Sudan who were either refugees or had migrated to other countries, first and foremost to neighbouring Kenya and Uganda, were also quite concerned with the same issues. Nairobi became from 2002 the meeting venue with a growing number of activities related to freedom of expression and independent media. The Sudanese who spearheaded these ideas were mostly from South Sudan.

The NPA was asked to get involved in the project while local and National media organizations were emerging. For South Sudan, an organization called Association for Media Development in South Sudan (AMDISS), with the well-known writer Jacob Akol as the chair, was founded. For Northern Sudan, there was a consensus to use the Khartoum Centre for Human Rights and Environmental Development as the other key Sudanese partner in the activities evolving.

In the beginning, the NPA did not have any earmarked financial support from the NMFA for the work being done. It had for this reason to take the money from its framework agreement with Norad. The parties concerned also applied for support from DFID, the British Department for International Development, but got an outright rejection. Then in 2004 NPA forwarded a similar application to NMFA, but did not have any clarification on the matter until after the parliamentary elections in Norway in the fall of 2005 when a coalition of the Labour Party, the Left Socialists and the Centre Party formed the government.

On 9th January 2005, The Comprehensive Peace Agreement for Sudan (CPA) was signed during a big ceremony at Nayo stadium in Nairobi. The NPA delegation was composed of the Secretary General Eva Bjøreng and Head of Communication,

Ivar Christiansen. The former NPA Resident representative for the Sudan Programme, Sten Rino Bonsaksen, and I myself were invited by John Garang himself as official guests. After almost a whole day of celebrations at the Nayo stadium in Nairobi, SPLM in the evening hosted a big international reception at Hotel Continental. Towards the end of the reception one of the SPLM leaders the Late Samson Kwaje, came to me and said:

"Halle, it is now very urgent to come up with institution building for free and independent media in the new democracy that is going to emerge in the whole Sudan. You have already promised to us to take a special responsibility in doing that. Now we want you to act."

I responded that I was ready to start, but NPA already had taken an initiative on the matter, and I would therefore talk with the leadership of NPA about it, before I did anything more. I met with Eva Bjøreng and Ivar Christiansen later in the evening. We were all the next day travelling back to Norway, and Eva Bjøreng offered me a lift to the airport. I told Eva and Ivar about the inquiry from the SPLM, and that I felt it would look a bit stupid if I now tried to set up my own project since the NPA already had started working with AMDISS. Eva answered very friendly that she thought I ought to come back to NPA as an external media advisor and be a part of the media project. I did not hesitate, but accepted the offer on spot.

The Consortium for Freedom of Expression and the political Environment in South Sudan and Sudan (North)

A couple of weeks later I got an assignment as NPA's representative in the International Media Consortium composed of AMDISS, KCHRED, Article 19 in London, IMS, International Media Support in Copenhagen, the Olof Palme International Centre in Stockholm and NPA.

In the spring of 2005 and in the aftermath of the CPA, the Norwegian Government with Minister for Development Cooperation, Hilde Frafjord Johnson in charge of the event, hosted a big international donors conference for the whole Sudan in Oslo. Two civil society meetings with good representation from Northern Sudanese, South Sudanese and Norwegian civil society organizations were held in connection with the donor's conference.

NPA used the occasion to invite members of the consortium to Oslo. The funding of this meeting of the Consortium members was again secured from the NPA framework agreement with Norad. It was only after the change of government in Norway in the fall of 2005, that the Freedom of Expression project got its first allocation from the Ministry of Foreign Affairs.

In the late summer of 2005 the members of the consortium met in London and developed the first work plans. Article 19, which is a leading institution for both the protection of and advancement of the basic human right, Freedom of Expression, was to be the lead agency of the consortium. In the time that followed, we had continuous contact with the government in Juba through the Minister of Information, the late Samson Kwaje, who was both very encouraging and cooperative regarding our work.

In this regard, the situation with the government in Khartoum was totally opposite. The National Congress Party(NCP), which was the political party of the old islamists who made de coup'etat in 1989, had according to the CPA 52 per cent representation in the new National transition government. They had of course control over everything to do with culture, religion and information. Nobody in the NCP had a positive interest in the project. However, the consortium through AMDISS and its chair, Jacob Akol, had continuous contact both with the SPLM Chairman Salva Kiir who at that time was President of South Sudan and First Vice President of Sudan, and the SPLM first deputy and vice-president of South Sudan, Riek Machar. The consortium also had direct contact with the SPLM secretariat in Khartoum where the Secretary General Pa'gan Amum and his deputy, Yasir Arman, were important team players.

The first Meetings of the Consortium

The first meeting of the consortium was held in Rumbek in South Sudan in September 2005. Many International and regional media institutions now showed an interest and wanted to be associated with the project. I mention UNESCO, the AU, The BBC Trust, the Reuters Trust. The interest from other actors, especially from media institutions in the neighbouring African countries, was also considerable. Many participants therefore came for this first meeting. The Vice-President of South Sudan, Riek Machar, gave the opening speech. He told us that he and the new government in Juba were committed to the values and principles of democracy and human rights, and therefore would fully support the project. We had a very constructive meeting, and we left Rumbek very encouraged. The next meeting was scheduled for November 2005 and was to be held in Khartoum.

Monitored by the Intelligence in Khartoum

Shortly after I was appointed as International Director of NPA in the spring of 1992, I was declared persona non-grata by the regime in Khartoum and rejected entry visa to Sudan. I was therefore a little bit anxious, when in 2005 I applied for a visa to participate in the planned consortium meeting in Khartoum, but after some discussion and a few meetings at the Sudanese Embassy in Oslo, I got it.

When I one morning in November 2005 arrived in Khartoum, there was no checking of luggage or similar at the airport, but I soon discovered that someone kept following me like a shadow all the time I was there.

The International interest for this meeting was even greater than for the one in Rumbek. UNESCO was well represented, the World Association of Newspaper Publishers (WAN) sent a representative. She was stopped and delayed at the airport and searched by the Police. What specially attracted the interest of the security officers, were her many publications and pamphlets on Freedom of Expression, but finally, she was let in. BBC World Trust, Reuters Trust, UNICEF, The UN-Radio for Sudan and many other international and African media representatives participated.

The Consortium in the person of Jacob Akol had invited, the president of South Sudan and the Vice-President of Sudan, Salva Kiir, to give the opening speech, and other representatives of the Khartoum Government to attend and address the conference.

Salva Kiir put one condition in order to give the opening speech. Jacob Akol, the leader of AMDISS, should draft the text. Unfortunately, Salva Kiir was at the last minute hindered from coming to the seminar, but he sent one of his presidential advisors, Telar Deng. He read out the elegant and poetic tribute to freedom of expression and human rights that Jacob Akol had drafted, not a word was changed.

The National Congress Party, the main partner in the Government of National Unity, sent an old ambassador who warned against the excesses of freedom of expression, and he told us that freedom of expression was well safeguarded in Sudan. The speech was simply not only paradoxical, but very outdated and reactionary.

On the first day of the conference I noticed a cameraman with a sound recorder who was working very hard during the sessions. He took close-ups of me and the others, both foreign and national participants. I went during a coffee break to him and asked him whom he was working for. He responded without hesitation:

"I work for the National Security Service and my task during this conference is to make a full recording of all what is being said and done for my employer"!

As soon as we were in session again, I informed the others about my discovery, that we had an intelligence agent at work in the conference. The participants from South Sudan were furious and wanted to call off the meeting. The participants from Northern Sudan were embarrassed, afraid and ashamed at the same time. Those of us who came from abroad protested. We had another break to discuss the matter. A compromise was reached. The agent agreed not to move around, but do the recording from a fixed position in a corner of the room. He also agreed not to come back the next day.

The next day came, and the meeting continued. Now there was another cameraman active in the conference. I went to him as well and asked whom he was working for. He answered without hesitation:*" Khartoum Media Services." "And whom does Khartoum Media Services work for"* I asked. The man again answered without any hesitation: *"The National Security Services."* The participants protested again, and after a short while the agent left the meeting.

Back in Oslo, I made sure that NPA sent a report regarding our experience with the National Security Services in Khartoum to our Ministry of Foreign Affairs.

The Khartoum Experience

This experience from Khartoum can be compared with similar experiences in other countries under dictatorships. What struck me most was how those who gave lectures and were close to the regime spoke of a reality that did not exist. The former Director of Sudan's National Broadcasting Cooperation assured us that Sudan had the best technological facilities for radio and TV, and that there was almost full freedom to broadcast whatever opinion to be expressed. Similar claims also came from the Director of the National State Press Council. Both speakers were elderly men apparently quite convinced that they represented a regime of excellence and transparency while they at the same time were totally without knowledge or insight about how the situation was in other parts of the world.

That first Consortium meeting in Khartoum also became the last. When we applied for permission to hold another meeting in Khartoum in the spring of 2006, the application was rejected. The same was the case when we applied for visas. The reason given was that the regime could not guarantee the security of the participants, if they came for another meeting. In this way, it became impossible to hold any more meetings in Khartoum, so Nairobi and Juba in the months and the years following, became the sites for our meetings.

Meetings in Nairobi with secret Agents from the Khartoum Regime in the Shadow

In 2007and 2008 the Consortium had two meetings in Nairobi. It was at the time when Mwai Kibaki was the President in Kenya and the Rainbow Coalition had the government. Never, had the basic human right, Freedom of Expression, been more respected in Kenya than during Kibaki's reign. The meetings in Nairobi were very constructive, and we made great progress in our work. The participants from Khartoum experienced a degree of safety and freedom they never had at home. For this reason, they got more relaxed and talked more openly and trustfully about how extremely difficult the Human Rights situation was in the whole of Northern Sudan. Not only that, in Nairobi they enjoyed a kind of freedom they never had at home when going to restaurants in Khartoum. When dining, they had a few glasses of wine or beer, and some of them even tried out meals with pork meat.

But they should not have taken the risk to enjoy the freedom to drink whatever they liked during meals at restaurants in Nairobi. Immediately upon return to Khartoum, one of the female participants at the Nairobi meeting was arrested and interrogated. During the interrogation, she was told how many glasses of wine and beer she had been drinking while in Nairobi, and the interrogator also mentioned that they were informed that during one meal she had eaten pork meat. She was then told that she had broken the laws of the Koran and had thereby committed a crime for which there would be punishment. During a break in the interrogation, one policeman starred at her and said: *"You are divorced, aren't you"?* The woman confirmed, and the policeman continued: *"You are a good-looking woman, I shall try you out when we meet next".* To humiliate and create fear is part of the interrogation methods of the Khartoum regime.

Feisal Elbagir, a leading member of the Consortium and the Director of Khartoum Centre for Human Rights, Environment and Development (KCHRED) was also arrested and taken for interrogation. He never allowed himself to be scared. He stated very clearly during the interrogation that he was a communist and an atheist and that he ate and drank whatever he liked. The policeman strongly disliked Feisal's fearlessness and asked:*"What do you think of the SPLM"?*

Feisal answered:

"SPLM is the best thing that has ever happened in Sudan for a long time."

The policeman looked coldly at Feisal for some seconds before he said:

"We do not like types like you, and we may next time we meet, do like this to you."

He then put his finger to his throat and made the sign of cutting it.

Despite these experiences KCHRED, the Consortium's partner in Northern Sudan, tried to influence both the State authorities and the media environment in Khartoum to liberalize the existing media laws and regulations, but faced many obstacles. One came from UNDP which never liked what the Consortium was doing. UNDP turned down an invitation to participate in the meeting of the Consortium in Khartoum in November 2005 and established instead a cooperation with a foundation called

"Future Trends" which was the islamists' answer to the work of our consortium.

This foundation, Future Trends" nevertheless attempted to develop a proposal with a degree of liberalization of the media laws of 2004, but the proposal was rejected by the Government. The Minister of Justice made it very clear that the Government would not tolerate any proposal from outside aiming at liberalizing laws in favour of more Freedom of Expression and more independence and freedom for mass media.

In 2008 the Government in Khartoum in cooperation with the State Press Council came up with proposals for new laws for the press and other print media. The proposals had the following main points:

- All who wanted to become a journalist must have higher education and a license/approval from the State Press Council.
- Editorial self-censorship was deemed inadequate.
- The authorities should at any time have the right to interfere with the editorial work of any media institution and whenever necessary apply censorship on media institutions that would try to challenge the limits set by the law about what was allowed to print.
- It was unlawful to practise investigative journalism which could uncover critical aspects of the regime's way of doing things.
- It was forbidden to write anything critical about Islam
- The State Press Council had the right to fine publishing houses and publishers and editors of newspapers and magazines that broke the new media laws up to a sum of USD 15 000, -

The proposals for these new media laws which were presented four years after the signing of the CPA, were in complete violations of the democratic principles laid down in the CPA and the interim constitution both for Sudan and South Sudan. When the new laws came up for a vote in the National Assembly, the SPLM leadership in Khartoum led by Secretary General of SPLM for the whole of Sudan, Pa'gan Amum, and Secretary

General for SPLM Northern Sector, Yasir Arman, demonstrated outside the parliament building in an attempt to block the adoption of the laws. The demonstration resulted in both men being arrested and taken to a police station. Pa'gan Amum was released after a short time while Yasir Armen was kept in prison for some days.

SPLM voted against the new laws, but they were adopted with the established majority vote of NCP's 52 per cent in the house. Consequently, today Sudan has more repressive media laws than at any time since its independence in 1956.

Feisal Elbagir, the Director of KCHRD in Khartoum was a great driving force for a free and liberal society in Sudan North. However, it gradually became more and more difficult for him and his family to live and work in Khartoum.

One day he got a hint from a friend within the system.

"Feisal, they are coming to get you in a few days, and you will never get out again."

Feisal managed to escape to Kenya where he was taken care of by friends, and he later received political asylum in Kenya. He was, however, quite concerned about what could happen to his wife and children. Fortunately, after some months they managed to escape to Kenya, and the family is political refugees in Kenya today.

A little later, KCHRED was banned by the Khartoum regime. This ban may stand as a memory of what we tried to do to improve a little on the human rights situation in Sudan North. The regime made sure that our efforts ended in failure.

What happened in South Sudan?

The Consortium had a very satisfactory start of its work in South Sudan with the Rumbek meeting in the fall of 2005, and we met again in Juba in February 2006 for another successful get together. At the first meeting in Juba in February 2006 there was even greater international and regional interest and participation

*Jacob Acol, journalist and writer and a fighter for freedom of expression, the founding father of AMDISS.
Picture: Gurtong*

than what we had at the meeting in Khartoum. We were part of the friendly and human breeze from all over the world that at the time softly swept over the land and people of South Sudan.

Both the Vice-President, Riek Machar and the Minister of Information, Samson Kwaje, graced the meeting. During the meeting, we did a lot of good work, and towards the end of it, concrete proposals began to take form. A draft for a Journalist's Guide and another draft to advise editors on what stories deserved to be publish and not, were done. A first draft for a proposal for a set of new media laws for South Sudan based on the new laws in Ghana and Kenya, was done as well. We felt that we were making history in the sense that we were participating in the building of important pillars and institutions for democracy development in South Sudan.

On the last evening of the meeting, NPA invited participants, members of government and parliament, SPLM, UN, other international agencies and whatever else there was of media people in Juba for a big reception at one of the restaurants on the river bank of the Nile. Five ministers and a much higher number of deputy ministers and members of parliament and others, honoured the invitation. The atmosphere was great. The Minister of Information, Samson Kwaje, gave a speech in which he strongly encouraged us to continue the work. I also spoke and reminded all present that we were part of a big boost for democracy, freedom of expression and free and independent media. South Sudan was to be the next democracy in Africa, and the showcase counterpart to the dictatorship in Khartoum.

A Great Signal from the Government

In the fall of 2006 the Consortium had another meeting in Juba. A core group from the leadership of the Consortium was invited to a meeting with the Government in session and led by President Salva Kiir in order to present its work to the government members. The time frame, set for this meeting was originally 30 minutes, but it ended up being de facto a seminar on Freedom of Expression and related issues, lasting for two hours. All members of government showed great interest and took part in the discussion. Having this experience behind us, we became very enthusiastic, and felt that we really might be part of making history in South Sudan. The World Bank Resident Representative in South Sudan had a very pleasant comment regarding this meeting with the government, saying that he never had seen anything similar happening in none of the countries he had worked in.

The year 2007 passed in a similar manner. On the surface, democratic developments in South Sudan were apparently going on well, and we felt that the Consortium's goal of contributing to building democracy in South Sudan could be achieved.

2008, - some Chilly Head Wind

The year 2008 began in the same manner, but then something happened.

Samson Kwaje was very unexpectedly and contrary to his own will transferred, and became Minister of Agriculture. I have reflected quite a lot on why he was moved, and I have in recent times concluded that the President, Salva Kiir and his close confidants in the Presidency, thought he was too liberal minded and democratic in his politics and work manner. Some key people in the circles around the President did obviously no longer like Kwaje's close support for and cooperation with the Consortium. He was replaced by Changson Chang from the opposition party, the United Democratic Salvation Front (UDSF). Changson never took part in the liberation struggle, and he only had limited experience as a member of government. He had less self-confidence than Samson Kwaje who was a confidant of John Garang. Changson Chang nevertheless, came to our next meeting and supported the work of the Consortium in his opening speech.

A Hidden Message from Khartoum

However, we had in the same meeting a very unpleasant political experience. We had asked the Ministry of Information for a speaker to shed some light on the status quo regarding what media laws that for the time being, were being applied in South Sudan. A high-ranking representative from the Ministry of Justice with the title of senior legal advisor came to give the lecture.

He was a South Sudanese, but he had done his law studies at the University of Khartoum. Having completed his studies, he had been employed in the Ministry of Justice in Khartoum. He was one of the many South Sudanese who had got their education and work experience in the cultural climate provided for by the dictatorship in Khartoum. He had no experience whatsoever in democracy building, but had now come home to contribute in building South Sudan and had become a legal advisor in the Ministry of Justice.

He started lecturing, and the political message came fast. He said that South Sudan lacked legislation of its own in every area of society. For this reason, it was the laws that were adopted by the Khartoum regime before the 2005 CPA that were still valid and applicable for South Sudan until the National Assembly passed new laws. That also included the media laws of 2004 for Sudan which from its core was very undemocratic.

The speaker simply ignored the CPA and the interim Constitution as relevant documents for consideration although both documents guaranteed those basic freedoms.

This implied, if the legal advisor was correct, that until some day in the future, there was no legal space for freedom of expression and free and independent media in South Sudan. According to his interpretation, the people of South Sudan were still living under the laws of the dictatorship in Khartoum which they had fought for 22 years!

In the debate that ensued, many of the participants reacted critically to the views presented by the speaker. Many pointed out that both the CPA and the interim Constitution guaranteed that all basic human rights, including freedom of expression, were now valid for both South Sudan and Sudan North. The speaker rejected these views as relevant, and he repeated and emphasized that as long as new media bills were not passed, the old laws from 2004 were the only valid ones.

I was one of those who reacted strongly to his interpretation and concluded my comments with the following strong words:

"We in NPA as well as others supported the liberation struggle in South Sudan because the people fought for freedom and democracy. It is totally unacceptable that such views as yours, are now being advocated by a senior staff member of the administration of the new and democratic Government of South Sudan."

The government's legal advisor listened to me with an expressionless face and with eyes like ice, and then he left without a comment. It took us some time to compose ourselves before we could continue with the meeting. In the aftermath, I could only see the statements and views held by this legal advisor as a hidden message from Khartoum implying that they had their loyal representatives in the government of South Sudan and thereby also a continuing strong influence. Not only that, we gradually came to learn that some key members of SPLM itself held similar views.

Despite this incident, the cooperation with the Ministry of Information and the new Minister went well. In the summer of 2008 the Minister presented to Parliament a White Paper on Freedom of Expression and free and independent media in South Sudan. This Government Document in the main reflected the principles and values contained in the draft documents that the Consortium on request one year earlier had handed over to the Ministry. In the fall of 2009 the Minister of Information presented four draft bills on:

1. The Right to Information
2. A free public Service Broadcasting in line with the Principles and Values that Institutions like BBC and the Norwegian Broadcasting Corporation (NRK) are based on.
3. Regulations concerning the Right to conduct commercial Broadcasting
4. Rules governing the Relationship between the Government and free and independent Newspapers, Magazines and other Publications.

The consortium and all the others who had worked with us, especially the other South Sudanese partners, were happy and relieved that everything looked like that the work of the Consortium was meaningful and contributing to the growth of democracy.

The draft bills were sent to the Ministry of Parliamentary Affairs where Michael Makuei Leuth at the time was the Minister.

(Mr. Makuei Leuth is today the Minister of Information and Broadcasting in the present government that initially was formed

at the end of April 2016, but reshaped in July 2016, and which is supposed to rule South Sudan until new, free and fair elections are held within a period of 30 months counted from the beginning of 2016. Whether the latter will happen, is rather unlikely.)

Minister Lueth was obviously very unhappy with the liberal and democratic contents of the new proposed laws. The draft bills were therefore not acted upon, but put to rest until late 2011. Then, some very important amendments were made by the Minister without any consultations neither with his colleague, the Minister of Information, nor with us in the Consortium. These Amendments decisively weakened the democratic nature of the bills. Then the bills were sent to Parliament. The Chairperson of the Parliamentary Committee that was to finalize the bills before they were presented for a debate and a vote, shared the views of Minister Lueth. He also did not like the political contents of the original proposals that were presented by the Ministry of Information in the fall of 2009, and he was in favour of Minister Leuth's changes that decisively weakened the principled, democratic and political content of the proposal.

AMDISS, this time led by Dr. Hakim Moi, then in 2012 started a counter lobbying offensive with the parliamentarians aiming at reversing the undemocratic and negative changes that had been made with the bills now pending for a vote in Parliament. The lobbying was very successful, and during the spring and summer of 2012 the negative changes introduced by Minister Leuth, were reversed. Most MPs now concluded that they wanted to have the liberal and democratic media laws in South Sudan as they in the main had been proposed by the Minster of Information, and that was how it went. The parliament finally with a solid majority passed the bills with just a few minor amendments of a restrictive nature.

The four media bills were then sent to President Salva Kiir for signing. That was in the summer of 2012. Then, nothing happened for a very long time, and it was obvious that strong opponents of the bills were at work both in the Office of the

President and in the new government appointed in August 2013 with many ministers neither having fought in the liberation struggle nor being members of SPLM. These forces strongly advised the President not to sign the bills and thus making them laws of the land. In addition, having watched President Kiir's political behaviour and leadership since 2012, I am also convinced that the President himself gradually lost the interest he once had, in making South Sudan develop into a democratic society. He had for this reason in the latter part of 2012 and in the whole of 2013 not any longer any interest in seeing the bills made into laws of the land because they would be a hindrance for the political actions that were being planned by him and his close associates for the second half of 2013 and further.

According to some sources, the President nevertheless signed some press bills into law in the fall of 2014, but the bills have never been published anywhere. Therefore, no one outside the closed circles around the President knows what the final content is. In fact, the validity of the bills has been suspended for an indefinite period.

The formal status quo for media laws in South Sudan today is therefore that the media laws of the Khartoum regime of 2004 are the ones being applied in South Sudan. This is the situation 15 years after some concerned South Sudanese sat down with likeminded people from the region and from NPA in a meeting room in Nairobi with a dream that they should be part of a process that in the end, would make South Sudan a democratic society.

Therefore, in real terms the media laws in Sudan and South Sudan today are in the main, the same, but there is one very important difference. The regime that has ruled South Sudan from the fall of 2013 with Salva Kiir at the helm, is responsible for a very destructive political process that has made South Sudan an even more lawless society than that of the Sudan.

The violations of basic human rights like Freedom of Expression, are as common in South Sudan today as they are in Sudan.

The Assassinations of Journalists

Isaiah Abraham Chan was one of South Sudan's skilful and fearless journalists. Early in the morning of December 4th, 2012, a small group of men dressed in black and driving a car with tinted windows and no registration number plates, parked outside Isaiah's home in Juba. His wife opened the door, and they asked whether Isaiah was at home. The wife confirmed and told them Isaiah was inside the house. They told her to ask Isaiah to come out. He did, and they asked him to confirm his name, that he was a journalist and that he had written articles criticizing corruption and the government's handling of political issues. He confirmed that he had done so. They forced him to kneel, and then they murdered him point blank with shots to the back of his head.

There were massive and furious reactions against this horrible crime and murder both in Juba and abroad. The American Government reacted very sharply and sent police investigators to Juba, but in vain. The Government showed no willingness to cooperate.

However, everything pointed to the fact that Isaiah Abraham was murdered by criminals who were contracted assassins by orders from a local mafia in Juba. Many claim that this and other mafia groups, in Juba, are closely connected to Dinka clans with strong links both to the Dinka Council of Elders and the Government. The assassins of Isaiah are still free men in Juba because it serves the interests of those in power. But Isaiah is not the only journalist having been killed in South Sudan since December 2012. In 2015 alone, seven more were killed and the total number since December 2012 are more than twelve. None of the murders have been investigated. In addition, journalists risk being picked up at work by the National Security and then severely tortured before they are being dumped in a graveyard or at the roadside.

The Responsible Ones

The Head of Government, President Salva Kiir is, of course in the final analysis, the chief responsible for these criminal and deadly developments in South Sudan, but he has a minister who carries a more direct responsibility, the Minister of Information, Michael Makuei Leuth. He is in Salva Kiir's inner circle, and he was a key man in the group of leading politicians who opposed the proposed media bills in 2009 and finally succeeded in making them dead documents. He has since August 2013, when he was appointed Minister of Information, to the extent he has cared for any law, been using the media laws of Sudan from 2004, and they are not only anti-democratic, but makes a mockery of the concept of Press Freedom. Minister Makuei Leuth has since August 2013 cooperated with the Internal Security Branch of the Government and had newspapers closed, netsites closed, whole editions of papers confiscated, editors and journalists arrested, tortured and murdered. In short, Minister Makuei is in charge of a policy that is equal to the policy of the Khartoum regime when it comes to oppressing basic human rights as the Freedom of Expression.

Today, the two regimes are equally oppressive, and to the extent there is a difference, South Sudan is more unpredictable and therefore more dangerous than Sudan.

SPLM, FROM GUERRILLA MOVEMENT TO POLITICAL PARTY

The Message from the Minister of Information

During the meeting of the Consortium in Juba in February 2006, the Minister of Information, Samson Kwaje, asked for a confidential talk with me. He had two very important political issues to discuss. The first was that it was of greatest importance that Norway continued to finance the Consortium and the media programme.

The second was both urgent and even more important. SPLM was very weak both organizationally and politically, and the liberation movement needed both financial and organisational support in its efforts to transform itself from a liberation movement into a democratic, popular and progressive, political party. The SPLM leadership did not have any experience in doing things like that, and it therefore needed assistance. In short, SPLM wanted to start a party building project in cooperation with the Norwegian Labour Movement. I asked Samson Kwaje to write a letter to Erik Solheim, the Norwegian Minister for International Development Cooperation regarding continued support to the media project, and I told him that I personally as soon as I was back in Norway, would seek a meeting with Minister Erik Solheim to convey his request for support for a party building project.

When I arrived back in Norway in the beginning of March 2006, I called the Office of Minister Solheim, seeking an appointment with him to convey to him the messages from Minister Samson Kwaje. I easily got an appointment for March 14th at 11:00 am at the Minister's Office.

The day arrived. Solheim had gathered his team of Sudan- advisors. I was well received, and I handed over the letter while at the same time verbally presenting the message about the need for support to the party building project. Erik Solheim answered in a very pleasant way, and his words went almost exactly like this:

"Your messages both from the Government in Juba and the SPLM are very important ones. The issue regarding the extension of support to the media project is so obvious that we don't need to spend time on it.

The request for support for the transformation of SPLM into a democratic political party is even more important, and might be a decisive issue for the peace agreement to succeed. If the SPLM does not manage to stay together as one organization while at the same time develop into a political party with a popular support, all will be lost. The CPA agreement itself will be in great danger. This proje-

ct is no doubt of fundamental importance, and it will need financial and organizational support for a long time to come".

I was a bit overwhelmed when I expressed my thanks. The Minister had a kind of foresight that was impressive. I then asked him which Norwegian political party he thought could take up such a job.

Solheim answered:

"A Norwegian political party, no, that might be too complicated. This task has to go to NPA"!

After my meeting with Solheim, NPA got a confirmation from the Ministry that there would be fresh funds for the continuation of the media project. The Ministry also conveyed to NPA that it would welcome a request from NPA in cooperation with SPLM to start the new party building project.

The Making of SPLA and SPLM, a Look back at History

But what was the situation in the SPLM in terms of democratic structures and experience when the peace agreement was signed in 2005? What conditions existed to make a successful project? An important starting point is the year 1983 with the mutiny of soldiers in Bor and Ayod, John Garang becoming the first Chairman and Commander in Chief of SPLA. In a matter of few days the SPLA was founded with an authoritarian command structure. To the extent the SPLA had any ideology it was a kind of authoritarian socialism.

Garang had an impressive academic and military education, first and foremost from the United States of America while the other SPLA founding fathers were mostly illiterate. The ideological and political education of officers was almost non-existent.

SPLA was in the beginning in the main, a coalition of tribal leaders and their soldiers, making a guerrilla movement that hardly had any experience or understanding of the reality of democratic work.

The most important political and military ally during the first seven years of the liberation struggle was the communist dictator, Haile Mariam Mengistu of Ethiopia while the Soviet Union and to some extent East Germany (DDR) supported the struggle with arms. In short, it was a primitive kind of authoritarianism and a crude socialist political doctrine that marked the beginning of SPLA's existence. This also affected the relationship with the civilian population ,and the behaviour of the SPLA soldiers during military confrontations. There is no doubt that both SPLA officers and soldiers committed severe crimes ,and sometimes gross atrocities against their own population. SPLA had at the same time a mentor, the government forces of Khartoum, which was exceptionally brutal and violent both whenever fighting took place, and against the civilian population. The Khartoum regime incessantly funded and supplied militias in opposition to SPLM/A that were even more brutal and ruthless than the Khartoum forces themselves.

The Need for a political Organization – the making of SPLM

John Garang and some of the others in the SPLA leadership realized early in the struggle the need for a political superstructure. Hence, SPLM, the Sudan People's Liberation Movement was established in August 1983. Garang's grand vision was the liberation of the whole Sudan, not just South Sudan.

To begin with, a political platform was formed and used by SPLM that articulated a type of authoritarian socialist politics. But there was lack both of resources and time for political education, also perhaps, not enough political will. SPLM had not much to offer of human and political values and social understanding to its freedom fighters in the battlefield. It also turned out that the extremely brutal way SPLA behaved not only in the battlefield, but at large, also infected the SPLM. The political superstructure that should have been the overriding power over the military one, did not get sufficient priority. SPLM therefore from its very beginning has suffered from the infection of the militaristic and very authoritarian attitude that has characterized the SPLA.

Around 1990, as mentioned earlier, a global political paradigm shift took place with the collapse of the communist regimes and their ideologies of the Soviet Union and other East European countries. One of many consequences was that the support from the Soviet Union and GDR to the Mengistu communist dictatorship in Ethiopia came to an end. Another implication of all this was that Ethiopia's support to SPLM/A also ended. This was followed by the Nasir revolt in August 1991, and the failed attempt to remove Garang.

The Nasir revolt coupled with the global political paradigm shift, forced a new political orientation with the SPLM. The texts in pamphlets and similar that articulated an authoritarian form of socialism disappeared and were replaced by new concepts and texts on democracy, human rights and human dignity. The strength of the new political messages was, however, not strong enough to change the authoritarian legacy that had affected both the SPLM and the SPLA from their very beginning in 1983, and neither was there within SPLM much exercise in practising democracy.

However, the leadership of the SPM/A realized that there was a strong need to strengthen the SPLM as a political organization, and in 1992 the planning of SPLM's first Convention started. But holding a convention had again and again to be postponed due to hectic military activities and the sustained bombing raids from Khartoum against both military and civilian targets in the liberated areas. In addition, the SPLM/A of John Garang was severely weakened both militarily and politically because of the Nasir split in 1991.

SPLM's First Convention – 1994

The first Convention of the SPLM was finally held in Chukudum in March 1994. Both the NPA and the Norwegian Church Aid (NCA) contributed with money and food supplies. About 200 delegates and dozens of guests from Sudan, mainly elderly traditional leaders, came for the convention. Many of the delegates had travelled for very long distances on foot. The delegates from the Nuba Mountains and Upper Nile had walked for five months to reach the site of the convention, in itself a very strong demonstration of the hope and expectations that many people had in SPLM.

Several institutions and organizations from outside the Sudan and from east Africa were invited for the occasion but only two showed up; NPA's Resident Representative Helge Rohn and the Executive Director for the American Refugee Committee, Roger Winter. Both gave speeches during the convention.

John Garang gave a great and visionary speech and was lauded as the great leader. The delegates at the Convention passed many resolutions. The most important was the new political programme of the SPLM which had much in common with social democracy.

Land ownership and rights was a central political issue during the debate at the Convention. The rulers in Khartoum had for a long time back nationalized all land, and land was therefore state ownership. That principle was hated by most people. The SPLM in its new programme therefore stated that in the New Sudan, the land should belong to the people as it is in the African tradition. This made the SPLM very popular all over the country.

A resolution was also passed that invited for cooperation with the United Nations through Operation Lifeline Sudan (UN/OLS) after many years of tension and conflict. Another one dealt with the issue of those who had deserted the SPLA. They were declared free men and invited to come back to SPLA. Garang was unanimously elected as Chairman and Commander-in-Chief while Salva Kiir was elected deputy Chairman and deputy Commander-in-Chief.

The following year, the SPLM held another and even bigger meeting in Chukudum. This time civil society in the new secular and democratic Sudan was the main issue for discussion. SPLM considered civil society as a very important pillar of societal development both politically and socially in the New Sudan.

About 1000 participants came for this meeting from all over Sudan, and in addition several dozen came from exile abroad and from international organizations. Most of the UN's specialized organizations were represented. The World Council of Churches, Lutheran World Foundation and many other international organizations participated. Both NPA and NCA had contributed financially and provided food for the conference, and they as well had representatives at the meeting.

It was a comprehensive debate that covered many issues, and many resolutions were passed, a couple of them on guidelines for the role of civil society in the development of the New Sudan.

Several years passed by before the SPLM could call for its next convention. The second one was planned for the year 2000 but had to be postponed. The main reason for these continuous postponements was the war which all the time demanded the most of whatever resources SPLM had, while the leadership also had to give priority to conduct the war. At the same time, the peace negotiations under the umbrella of IGAD had dragged on for many years without any real progress. However, around year 2000 the negotiations picked up. They were intensified in 2002 with the signing of the Machakos Protocol, and were finally concluded with the signing of the Comprehensive Peace Agreement on 9th January 2005.

The peace negotiations were as well very demanding for the leadership group of SPLM and for the Chairman himself, John Garang, and at the same time there was a serious conflict between Garang and his deputy, Salva Kiir, on the surface, about the peace negotiations and the way forward for SPLM, but beneath, it reflected that people around Salva Kiir, like Bona Malwal, wanted to have him at the helm, not Garang.

With the CPA of 2005 it was everyone's expectation that John Garang would be the new great political leader of Sudan both during the six years' transition period and after, as he stood firm on his commitment for a new, secular and democratic Sudan and had become a very trusted and popular national leader all over the country. It was also expected that he would put a lot of effort into the development of the SPLM as a National, democratic and progressive political party with the active participation of its members. I knew Garang well and I know that he wanted a party with a social democratic programme.

However, no one knows what comes tomorrow. Three weeks after having been sworn in as Sudan's First Vice President during a big ceremony in Khartoum, and riding high all over Sudan as a very popular political leader, John Garang died in a helicopter crash on 30th July 2005. The SPLM was facing a deep crisis, but the leadership acted very fast. The SPLM leadership Council was able to hold a secret meeting in which it bridged over internal rivalries and conflicts and chose Salva Kiir as the new Chairman and Riek Machar as deputy Chairman.

The Party building Project begins

After Erik Solheim's go ahead signal in March 2006, the ball was in NPA's court. However, it took almost nine months for NPA to act, a very long time indeed. The application for funding for the project was only sent in the beginning of 2007, and then it also took some time for the NMFA to process the application and confirm the funding. The first payment of the grant was effected in the spring of 2007. A cooperation agreement was signed between the NPA and the SPLM during the official visit of Salva Kiir in his capacity as President for South Sudan and 1st Vice-President for Sudan to Norway in the beginning of June 2007.

In October 2007, the Secretary- General of SPLM, Pa'gan Amum, came on a working visit to Norway. He had meetings with Minster Erik Solheim and officials in the NMFA. He gave a public lecture and interviews. He also had several working sessions with the staff of NPA on the party building project that in the beginning in principle covered the SPLM for the whole Sudan while the practical work should begin in South Sudan.

Why only SPLM?

But why only the SPLM, and why didn't the project include the other political parties in South Sudan? This has an easy answer. In South Sudan in 2005 there were only two organized networks that covered the whole nation; one was Churches and their networks like South Sudan Council of Churches and the other was the SPLM. There were no others. Both networks included people from different ethnic groups. If one had to build a national political party with democratic content and including all the ethnic groups, then the SPLM was the only alternative.

NPA now started the preparation of the party building project, and Finn-Erik Thoresen who was NPA's Secretary General at the time, took a considerable interest in the project. The key elements that were identified for the first phase of the process were organization building, training of party officials, mobilization of women and the development of the Youth Organization of SPLM. Marit Haernes was in the summer of 2007 engaged as one of the managers of the project, and in September the same year, 18 months after Minister Erik Solheim's go head, the project started.

The NPA in coordination with the SPLM secretariat started with the mobilization and training of women in the SPLM. Marit Haernes as the project manager established the first contact with the Norwegian Labour Party. Very soon thereafter, a small groups of women from the Labour Party, most of whom from the Labour Party's Youth Wing (AUF) came to South Sudan to conduct the "Women Can" course. It soon attracted the interest of thousands of South Sudanese women, and the training courses turned out to be a great success. For most women, this was their first meeting with some form of formal adult education. It is estimated that until 2013 more than 150,000 women in one form or another took part in the "Women Can" course. No other training course in South Sudan had ever before gathered such a high number of participants.

Regarding the development of the Youth Organization of SPLM, NPA contacted the Youth Wing of the Norwegian Labour Party (AUF) that responded positively to the request, and the cooperation with the SPLM Youth League was immediately started.

SPLM's Second Convention – May 2008

The SPLM decision making organs decided sometime in 2007 to hold its second National Convention in May 2008. It was fourteen years after the first national convention in Chukudum in 2004.

The making of SPLM's first comprehensive political programme, which would be the political platform from which South Sudan and Sudan as nations and states should develop, was seen as the major priority of the convention. But the preparatory work started late and developed very slowly. There were many different reasons for this slow-go. The most important one was probably the lack of experience, not resources because the material and political support for the programme would come from the Norwegian Government as a grant through the Labour Party. Since SPLM hardly ever in the past had taken time and given priority to the development of its policies, internal political disagreements had been covered up. Now as the preparations for the convention began, these disagreements surfaced again.

Late in the winter of 2008, an alarming message came from Marit Hærnes, NPA's project manager in Juba. She reported serious delays in the preparation of the proposals for SPLMs first political programme. SPLM urgently needed external assistance to complete the proposals in time before the convention.

NPA had at that time concluded that it would assist with organization building in the SPLM, but not in the development of its political programme. The appeal for assistance to draft the proposal for a political programme therefore went to the Labour Party which agreed to assist. In a matter of few days a delegation of experienced Labour Party people was set up, and the members were Kjell Engebretsen, a former Norwegian Member of Parliament, Kathrine Raadim, International Secretary of the Labour Party, and Liv Torres, then on leave from the NPA, but from the summer of 2011 until the fall of 2015, the Secretary General of NPA.

I was also asked to be part of the delegation, but due to other obligations I could not make it.

The delegation had just a week available for the assignment which was all too short. But together with people from the SPLM secretariat, they managed to start the work. Having South Sudan's tragic history and Sudans miserable social conditions in mind, they together with people from the SPLM secretariat in my opinion drafted good policy papers in the areas of education, health, and social Policy. But time was not sufficient to look at the big challenges connected to responsible policies for key areas as economic policy, the management of natural resources, land and agriculture, water and fisheries, oil and minerals, a strategy for the development of new industries and many more.

The date for the opening of the Convention was set to be 10th of May, and I as a former Secretary General of NPA was invited as a guest of honour.

War instead of a National Convention

The day, the Convention was to begin, people in both Sudan and South Sudan woke up to the shocking news over radio and TV that there was an intense battle going on in Omdurman, Khartoum's twin city. The Justice and Equality Movement (JEM) is a political guerrilla movement with its main roots in Darfur. It had in the darkness of the night managed to drive some 300 military vehicles with some thousands of guerrilla soldiers through the desert and over 800 km unnoticed. The JEM units had attacked with full force and occupied part of the city, carrying out a lot of sabotage actions. The attack came shortly after President Omar Bashir had travelled on a pilgrimage to Mecca. Salva Kiir as First Vice President in Sudan, had immediately to travel to Khartoum to act as Head of State and Commander in Chief in the battles against the guerrilla units of JEM. The opening of the SPLM Convention was therefore postponed for two days.

Officially, the SPLM condemned the attacks, but there were few in Juba who could hide their glee at what had happened. Both delegates and guests listened to the news and used their time as best possible through the weekend while we waited for the Convention to start.

On Monday 12th May the JEM forces were driven out of Omdurman, and the Khartoum regime made an official announcement that the JEM guerrilla units had been destroyed. It was a clear lie. A few days later, The Al-Jazeera TV broadcasted a documentary that showed that the JEM forces just had a minimal loss. They had withdrawn from Omdurman in an orderly manner and reorganized themselves. The following night they drove back through the desert to their hiding places in Darfur.

Salva Kiir returned two days later to Juba. But instead of the Convention opening the next day,13th of May, news of yet another war came. Special forces loyal to the National Congress Party (NCP) of Sudan's President, Omar Bashir, had forcefully attacked Abyei, one of the three disputed areas in the CPA, and an area with significant oil reserves. The attackers burned villages and sent thousands of people to flee. The reactions in Juba and the whole of South Sudan were very strong, people were furious at was happening in Abyei. The same applied to the international community. Their condemnations of what had happened, were very strong, and the hostilities faded by Tuesday 14th May.

I used some of the waiting time to read the draft both for SPLM's first principle political manifesto and the proposal for the political action programme for the development of the society of South Sudan in the years to come, However, these proposals which should have been made public and available to delegates and others well in advance of the convention, were only made available during the waiting time because the NCA and NPA offices in Juba offered to print and distribute the draft proposals to the delegates and guests.

The draft for the principal political manifesto was, in my opinion, a fairly good one, while the draft action programme was far from anything that could be considered a comprehensive political programme for the development of the society of South Sudan. The chapters that dealt with education, health and social issues were fairly well done, but in my opinion, the rest of the proposals were totally unacceptable. There was nothing reflecting the necessary and very active and constructive role of the state and the government in the development of a very poor and underdeveloped society like South Sudan that had to start from scratch in the building of state, government and public institutions and infrastructure.

There was a chapter in the draft dealing with future Economic Policy written by a consultant who was a South Sudanese, educated in the United States and with working experience from the World bank. It was a paper full of neo-liberal phrases. The draft was so liberalistic that even members of neo-liberalist political parties in Europe would have had problems accepting its contents. It was of course also very far away from the historical development experience of the societies of Scandinavia which in the main is a Social-Democratic one. The contents in the chapters dealing with water, land, agriculture and fisheries had a similar content and laid the field open for large scale privatization and commercialization, very contrary to what SPLM decided at its first convention in Chukudum in 1994. There was almost nothing about the poor farmers and their need to own the land they lived of. The drafts dealing with oil production was a gift to Chinese and other oil companies that were already in business in South Sudan or waiting in the shadow. They were ready to start their totally irresponsible robbery of resources without any consideration for the people in the areas concerned or the environment. The programme proposals for these areas were in short, scandalously poor. I was more than worried regarding what would happen if they were offered for discussion and vote at the Convention. If they were to be passed, it would mark a quick end to any kind of cooperation with the Norwegian Labour Party and at the same time make things very difficult for NPA and NCA. In short, these proposals opened for a policy of selling South Sudan out.

Finally, the Convention

The convention finally opened on Wednesday 15th May. It was a great experience. We arrived at the site early in the morning and stood in long queues for some time before we got security clearance. But the mood was superb, and standing in the queue became a cheerful experience.

As the former Secretary General of NPA I received the tag Honorary Guest no.1, and I was later seated on seat no.1. That was a way of emphasizing NPA's contribution, status and significance during the liberation struggle.

The hall which is part of the University of Juba, is large and was beautifully decorated. At the opening session, there were around 2000 delegates in attendance, in addition about 400 guests from inside Sudan and from abroad. Just minutes before the opening, a burly man, dressed in a white robe and a turban, appeared at the entrance. It was the leader of the Sufi movement, a more than hundred years old religious sect, and a kind of a Muslim brotherhood in Sudan, who was arriving, being an honorary guest. He was invited, but had not sent any prior message of acceptance and participation. But within minutes the hosts prepared his accreditation, and the man got a name tag as Honorary Guest no. 0 and was placed on a seat to my left of me. He was more than two meters high and had a weight of more 130 kg. He greeted me kindly and tried to talk to me, but he could only speak Arabic which is a language outside my command, and he did not understand English. An old SPLA commander from the Nuba Mountains was seated to my right. He spoke very good English and was a very interesting man to talk with at the same time as he had very humoristic remarks. Two seats further away sat the Norwegian Government Representative, Consul General Jan Ledang.

There was a big group from USA among the guests. Some were Christian fundamentalists, others were politicians from "Black Caucus", others were just liberal members of the American Congress or from the US civil society. Among them was Roger Winter, formerly the Executive Director of the American Refugee Committee. He was from the beginning of NPA's activities in South Sudan in 1986, an old friend and supporter, now at the Convention as a special Envoy of the US Government.

The atmosphere in the hall was during the whole day like a fairy tale. The delegates, young and old, came from all corners of the Sudan, also the war-affected Darfur. The majority were men, but also many women were present. The course, "Women Can", had in an important way contributed to the participation of so many women.

Many of the delegates had walked on foot for weeks, even months, or travelled on buses for weeks to reach Juba. Many could neither read nor write. What most of them had in common was that it was their first time to participate in a national Convention of the SPLM. People were incredibly happy. They greeted and hugged each other in their friendly African way. A band played rhythmic and inciting African music in at the background. Again, and again, women ran to free floor area at the front table and danced in enthusiasm and happiness.

On the high table on the scene one man sat from early morning, 1st Deputy Chairman Riek Machar. He never said a word from the podium to the audience during the first day.

Then the Secretary General of SPLM, Pa'gan Amum, came on the stage. He has a great and strong voice that carries far. He is a very good orator, and he also sings very well. It was great to see him in action he made the atmosphere become almost electric.

Then we heard the shout: "The President is Coming!" There was complete silence. Everyone stood up and there came Salva Kiir. People clapped and there was great applause. Salva Kiir has little charisma and is a poor speaker but he could at the time convey authority and demand respect.

The opening of the Convention was like most other political conventions, there were songs, welcome speeches and greetings from invited guests. Two of the many speakers were the Sufi leader seated next to me and Jan Ledang, Norway's official representative.

The convention had very able chairs who made sure that the time table for the agenda was kept, so the first day went very well. As we were coming close to the end of the programme of the first day, the acting chair rose. He was Abel-Azziz Adam Al Hilu, a great political leader and guerrilla commander from the Nuba Mountains, and an old friend. He said:

"We still have some few more minutes of our time for today's programme, I shall therefore invite two particular good friends of the SPLM from the time of the liberation struggle to greet us."

I could instantly feel my nerves. I normally don't have the fear of a microphone or a podium and an audience, but this was something else. No one had given me any warning in advance, and I had not prepared myself for what might come.

Then I heard the chair say: "Roger Winter from USA will now greet us." Many people knew Roger Winter, and there was an immediate and big applause. Roger was well-prepared. He is a good orator and spoke for ten minutes which was followed by a song.

Then I heard the chair say:

"And now, Halle Jørn Hanssen, will address us."

There was silence with the audience and the chair added; "Uncle Halle, the former Secretary General of NPA." Now, the audience exploded and there was an almost tumultuous atmosphere when I came on the stage and looked at the audience.

I composed and concentrated myself like I used to do when I was a young athlete on the track ready for an 800-meter run. In my introduction, I reminded them of the days of struggle, and the suffering so many of them had been through. Freedom had come at a great price. I told them they were still surrounded by enemies who very much would wanted to divide them. Because divided you are weak, united you are strong. I further told them that I belonged to the Norwegian Labour Movement, and that we from our own history had bitter memories of what happens when divisive forces take over. One becomes the loser, and the enemy both from inside and outside who wants to divide and have split and rule, they become victorious. I therefore called on them to do their utmost to keep the SPLM united. Unity is strength! The audience responded with a thunderous applause.

It was easy to move among the delegates and the guests during the evening and the night. I talked with many, sometimes, I just listened to what was being said, and I with the help of friends, I picked up a lot of rumours. One rumour was that a big opposition was being organized against the re-election of Salva Kiir, and that he would not be re-elected. Others were very sure that Riek Machar would be thrown out from his position as the first Deputy Chairman because Salva Kiir didn't like him. The same was said about Pa'gan Amum. People said that Salva Kiir never had liked him, and that Kiir would prefer a Dinka for the position as SPLM Secretary General.

The next morning, I had breakfast together with an old friend, Alfred Taban, at the time, the editor of *Khartoum Monitor*. He was a delegate from Central Equatoria. He told me that the delegates from the three states of Equatoria had had a meeting the night before to discuss the rumours and the elections. Their resolution was crystal clear: No split, but full support for the re-election of the whole leadership. Alfred added that the delegates from the three states of Equatoria were almost equal to half the number of the total delegates. He was therefore sure that their proposal would carry the majority.

When the convention came to the agenda point on elections, the Election Committee had a simple proposal. It had captured the atmosphere of the Convention, and it proposed for the whole leadership to be re-elected, and so it happened with acclamation. The same also happened with the two deputy Secretaries Generals, Ann Itto for South Sudan and Yasir Arman for Sudan North, both were elected.

There were political debates during the sessions of the Convention on the proposed drafts for the political programmes, but luckily, the decision to finalize both the draft on the new political manifesto and the proposed programme of action was delegated to the Liberation Council of SPLM.

However, a very important resolution was passed unanimously. SPLM was committed to uphold the vision of John Garang: A united Sudan, secular, democratic and progressive.

In the months succeeding the convention, rumours related to what happened or did not happen at the convention continued to flow. During this same period, I had a few working visits to Juba, and I talked with many people. I came at the end to hold it for likely that what was being told about the preferences of Salva Kiir and his Dinka advisors (The Jieng Council) were true. If they at the Convention had felt sure that they had the power to do it, they would have kicked out both Riek Machar and Pa'gan Amum from the leadership group of SPLM.

Bumps on the Road

The party building project continued in the aftermath of the SPLM Convention. The training of women in organization-work was still a central task, but the project was extended to cover other issues, among others, the training of elected officers of the SPLM, staff members of the SPLM secretariat, the development of an SPLM Home Site and the use of the internet.

But both NPA and the Norwegian Labour Party experienced a standstill when it came to the training of elected officers. It had many explanations.

The last part of 2008 and the whole of 2009 was marked by the many and difficult conflicts that both the Government of South - Sudan and SPLM had with the regime in Khartoum. The SPLM Headquarters headed by Secretary General, Pa'gan Amum, was at the same time still in Khartoum. The vision was still a united but new, democratic and secular Sudan.

Pa'gan Amum was a politician with many assignments and obligations. Early in 2008 he was appointed Minister of Cabinet Affairs for the Government of National Unity in Khartoum, a key governmental position he held till the end of 2009. President Salva Kiir then appointed him as Minister of Reconciliation and Peace in South Sudan and the Implementation of CPA at large. He was at the same time appointed South Sudan's Chief Negotiator with the regime in Khartoum. However just after independence in July 2011, Pa'gan resigned as Minister because he did not feel that he had the trust and backing of his own President in his reconciliation and peace work. However he accepted to continue as South Sudan's Chief negotiator on the many outstanding issues with Khartoum both regarding the implementation of CPA and issues related to oil production and oil transportation.

Pa'gan Amum has an enormous capacity to work, but it was difficult for him to complete all the tasks in full. The SPLM Secretariat and the SPLM organization was to suffer most, and the cooperation project with NPA and the Labour Party suffered as well because the Secretary General of SPLM had too many tasks to carry out.

The second reason for the standstill and the delay was of a different nature. The party building project now had three Norwegian partner organizations that were working together. The NPA was dealing with the development of SPLM as an organization while The Labour Party was to contribute to the development of SPLM's National policies, and the improvement of the SPLM secretariat, communications and more. The Norwegian Labour Youth (AUF) had also started its cooperation with the SPLM Youth League. In the project, one was dealing with several concrete issues, first and foremost the training in organization development and the training of elected officers.

The first project grant from 2007 had been used, and NPA sent in 2009 a new application to NMFA while the Norwegian Labour Party and the Labour Youth sent separate applications for their parts of the project.

But to the very big surprise of everyone, NMFA refused to grant more money for the project. NMFA had forwarded the applications to the Norwegian Ambassador to South Sudan, Ingrid Ofstad. She was in principle against that type of support, and her response to NMFA in Oslo was very firm and very negative indeed. She on principle grounds strongly advised against the continuation of the project. NPA, the Labour Party and the Labour Youth should not be involved in that type of work in South Sudan. It was apparently of no relevance to the ambassador that her superior, The Minister himself, Erik Solheim in 2006 firmly had stated that this had to be a priority task and a long-term project. The project suddenly became a big internal controversy in the Foreign Ministry.

The controversy lasted for several months before it finally ended on the table of Development Minister Solheim with some positive comments from the bureaucrats at home in the NMFA, but also with the very critical remarks of Ambassador Ingrid Ofstad. Solheim had to use his prerogative as Minister to disregard the comments of the Ambassador, and then he approved a second phase of the project which by now had been delayed for several months. Without Erik Solheim's political firmness and foresight, the party building may have come to a halt at that point and long before any real impact could have been measured.

Pa'gan Amum led a big SPLM delegation that was invited to the Norwegian Labour Party Convention in the spring of 2009, and a new agreement was reached on the future running of the project. Fresh money from NMFA came in 2010, but again strange delays emerged, now on the side of SPLM.

Audun Herning who since late 2009 had been the NPA project leader, ended in 2012 his tenure, and Eskild Johansen, the Regional Secretary of the Labour Party in Troms, in Northern Norway became his successor.

The Booklet from Norway; "The elected Delegate/Officer"

A great emphasis was now laid on the training of delegates/elected officers in the SPLM. Part of the syllabus was a translation of an old training manual from the Norwegian Labour Movement, written by the young elected officer Einar Gerhardsen and had the Title: "The Elected Delegate". The booklet was first published in 1931 and has since then been updated and is still being used in the Norwegian labour movement as a basis for organization training. A relevant version, translated into English, has in the last decades been used for the same purpose internationally, and in 2011/12 also with SPLM in South Sudan.

The new NPA project manager, Eskild Johansen, had never had any international assignment before he came to South Sudan. But he was from Karlsøy in Troms, in Northern Norway and knew the local party history. In 1903 the Labour Party in Troms, Norway, had elected their first three representatives of the Labour Party ever to the Norwegian Parliament because of good organization and powerful grass root mobilization.

Eskild established close working relations with Jacob Atem, a member of the local NPA secretariat staff in Juba. Jacob was one of the thousands of children and youth, mainly males, who were in the big march from South Sudan to Ethiopia in the mid-1980s. Jacob, who was now member of the SPLM, became a spear- head for the NPA activities with the SPLM secretariat. This worked very well and made the kick-starting of the training of the elected delegates/representatives easy. From autumn 2012 to December 2013 about 2500 delegates of the SPLM from all the states of South Sudan undertook a basic course in organizational work based on the principles and experience laid down in the text of Mr. Gerhardsen's booklet. Concurrently women from the Labour Party continued to come to South Sudan for the "Women Can" course.

Under the circumstances, these results obtained in the joint party building project were quite impressive.

(Who was Mr. Einar Gerhardsen? Mr. Gerhardsen was in the late 1920s a blue-collar road construction worker who like many other young workers at the time became politically conscious. As a young worker and elected delegate, he was active in the Communist Party, but ran into opposition with the dogmas of the party, left the communists and joined the Labour Party. He rose quickly with the Labour Party and in 1923, only 26 years old, and elected Secretary General of the Labour Party.

He never had the money to get higher education, but read and studied a lot and gained knowledge and insight through the many training and educational courses that were organized and made available for members of the Labour Movement through the Labour Movement Adult Educational Organization. In 1931, he wrote the training manual mentioned above which is still in use in the Labour Movement in Norway.

At the beginning of the Second World War, Mr. Gerhardsen was for a brief time the Major of Oslo, but fell out with the German and Nazi occupying powers at the time. He was arrested, tortured and sent to a concentration camp in Germany. He survived that experience, and when he came back to Norway in 1945, the Labour Party made him its Chairman. In the fall of 1945, the Labour Party in the national elections won a solid majority in Parliament, and soon thereafter Mr. Gerhardsen became the Norwegian Prime Minister. He held the position as Prime Minister for almost 20 years. He is the most renowned of all Norwegian Prime Ministers after the Second

World War and is considered the father of the Norwegian welfare state.)

The SPLM Youth League becomes Part of the Party Building Project, but falls in its own Trap

The Labour Youth sent its first delegation to South Sudan in the autumn of 2007. It was led by Åsmund Aukrust who was by then a member of the Central Committee with responsibility for international cooperation. Åsmund who is now a Labour MP, shared with me his memories about the work in South Sudan:

"*We landed one day in the autumn of 2007 in excellent weather at Juba airport. When we came out of the plane, we were received by a welcoming delegation from the SPLM Youth League who was carrying large placards with words of welcome and slogans about the new cooperation with the Norwegian Labour Youth. We were of course flattered by the warm welcome. Afterwards, as we went around Juba, this positive impression was strengthened. A lot was happening in the capital of South Sudan. New roads were under construction, and new buildings were sprouting from everywhere. People were happy enjoying the new won freedom and waiting for the expected independence for South Sudan to come.*

Our first meeting with the leadership and membership of the youth league was characterized by the optimism and expectation of what the future would bring. We, in the Labour Youth, felt that we were involved in a cooperation project that was going to be interesting and exciting. We took note of the fact that some of the leaders of the SPLM Youth were well-educated, well aware of the challenges ahead and converse on issues of politics and social development, while other members never had had access to education.

The first group was the children of the country's elite and the second was youth from the outskirts of Juba and the faraway villages. The latter had little knowledge about politics and society but had clear views about what they expected from the youth league.

We were welcomed on the first day by Akol Paul Kordit, the Chairman of the SPLM Youth League. Akol was not an elected leader but was designated until a convention with elections would be conducted. In the beginning, he impressed us with his knowledge of politics and his apparent leadership skills. However, he soon left us with the impression of being very dominating in his behaviour almost authoritarian.

We invited in the summer of 2008 a delegation of the SPLM Youth League to the AUF Summer Camp at Utoya island, and they sent a delegation led by Akol Paul Kordit. When the delegation arrived at Utoya, they were accommodated together with our other international guests in some of the few and comfortable places we had indoors, but Akol gave notice to the fact that he was very dissatisfied with the standards of the accommodation, he had been offered at our summer camp. The other participants at the camp stayed in tents.

During the period between 2008 and 2011 we had several visits both ways. We were in South Sudan and worked with organization training, and they were in Norway to see how we in the Labour Youth worked. At the same time, they learned about the Norwegian society. Many bonds of friendship developed between the young people in the Labour Youth and the SPLM Youth League. When the great tragedy of the bombing of the Headquarters of the Norwegian Government in the centre of Oslo and the massacre at the AUF Summer Camp at Utoya on 22nd July 2011 hit, our friends from South Sudan were the first to send their condolences and message of solidarity.

But it looked like the leader of the SPLM Youth League Akol Paul Kordit, seemed increasingly less interested in the cooperation with the Labour Youth. He once at meeting pulled a pistol to demonstrate his point. He showed after a while little willingness to corporate and became less and less interested in taking part in a process that would lead to organizing a democratic convention of the SPLM Youth League which we in AUF considered of greatest importance to move the cooperation ahead."

In 2012 the Labour Youth got a message from the leadership of the SPLM Youth League that they no longer were interested in having AUF as cooperation partner in the development of their own organization.

What happened? During that time, a conflict developed between the Chairman of the SPLM Youth and the Secretary General of SPLM and the SPLM Secretariat. The SPLM Secretariat was insisting that a convention of the SPLM Youth League had to be convened. Furthermore, the SPLM Youth League would have to hold elections at such a convention to have an elected Chair Person and an elected National Board of the Youth League. That was rightly seen as a condition for the continuation of the cooperation with the Norwegian Labour Youth (AUF). Akol Paul rejected that demand and claimed he was the definite future leader of the SPLM Youth League and that there was no need for any elections. After that Akol rejected any further cooperation with the AUF.

It later came out that Akol Paul Kordit who was an electronic engineer by profession was designated as SPLM Youth leader by Martin Majut Yak.

How did that happen?

Martin Majut Yak is not just anybody in the power circles of South Sudan. He never took part in the liberation struggle, but was enjoying the good life in Canada. However, he is a close relative of Salva Kiir and has, for a long time, been an Executive Director in the Office of the President while he upon an appointment by Salva Kiir also has held and is holding a key position within the SPLM Secretariat as the person in charge of syndicalist organizations.

In short, Akol Paul Kordit was with Martin Majut Yak as the middleman, Salva Kiir's handpicked man to lead the SPLM Youth League. Martin Majut Yak was for this reason instructed by the SPLM Chairman Salva Kiir, on his behalf, to appoint Akol Paul Kordit as the Chairman of the SPLM Youth League.

In December 2013 Akol Paul Kordit supported the decisions that led to the attack and massacre of the nuers in Juba and the subsequent civil war that followed. He later became an open and uncompromising ally of Salva Kiir in the internal SPLM conflict, and he supported from the very beginning the views of the President in the civil war that started in December 2013. He wanted the detainees convicted and executed, and he was one of the leaders in the demonstrations in March 2014 who were calling for the dismissal of Hilde Frafjord Johnson from her position as the Special Representative of the UN Secretary-General and the Head of United Nations Mission in South Sudan (UNMISS). In the summer of 2016 he was appointed deputy Minister of Information with Mikael Makuei Leuth as his immediate superior. The two are now among the masterminds of the oppression of freedom of expression, the censorship and closure of newspapers, arrest, torture and murder of journalists in South Sudan.

The Political Will for Democratization of SPLM was destroyed

The SPLM Convention in May 2008 forwarded the proposed political manifesto and the programme of action to the National Liberation Council. From autumn 2008 to the spring of 2013 at least five formal requests were made by Secretary General Pa'gan Amum to convene meetings in the political Bureau and the Liberation Council so that the draft proposals from the Convention could be discussed and passed. But Salva Kiir as party Chairman, repeatedly rejected to endorse any request for the meetings, paralyzing SPLM's political organs in the period from May 2008 to December 2013 when on December 13th and 14th the catastrophic meeting took place that with the President and the Chairman, Salva Kiir, as the pusher, plunged the country into civil war.

From 2009 until 2011 the Labour Party project leader Mari Aaby and the staff of the SPLM secretariat cooperated on plans on how the organizational and political transformation of SPLM into a democratic and progressive political party could be speeded up, but little or nothing was achieved. Planned visits from Oslo and meetings in Juba for discussions and policy development were postponed time and time again.

In November 2012, the Labour Party sent Odin Adelsten Bohmann, the Vice - Chair of the Labour Party in the Telemark constituency of Norway, and me to Juba to try to expedite the process. Secretary General Pa'gan Amum was at the time of our arrival on his way home from an official visit to Cuba. His deputy, Ann Itto, was also out of Juba.

So, we hit a wall in the SPLM Secretariat. It was clear that with the absence of Pa'gan and Ann Itto from the secretariat, someone in the secretariat was trying to hinder the development of the project. We did, however, meet with staff members in the secretariat, during which I made it clear that if nothing happened, we from the Norwegian side will break off the cooperation with SPLM. We added that such a move from our side would have consequences not only for the relationship between the SPLM, the Labour Party and NPA, but could perhaps spill over and have a negative impact on the relations between Norway and South Sudan in general. That was our message the day before Pa'gan came back to Juba. There is no doubt that the staff members of the secretariat present, listened in frustration and despair to what I said, but for some reason, they could not respond.

But as soon as Pa'gan was back, the atmosphere changed completely. A friendly dinner was held the same night with leaders and staff from the SPLM secretariat. It was followed the next day in the morning with a meeting with many staff members and with Pa'gan in the front seat. We discussed in a very friendly manner, and new and concrete agreements were put in place for the future running of the project.

Towards the end of the first meeting they shared with us the results of an internal assessment study that had been conducted among SPLM members. A questionnaire had been given out where members were asked what expectations they had had to the SPLM and what their opinions were on the performance of the SPLM since the SPLM Convention in 2008. The response from the membership was hard and very critical. In short, the message from the members was that almost nothing had been done regarding national developments at large or with the activation of SPLM as a democratic membership organization. It must have been depressing reading for the management and staff of the SPLM secretariat as well as for the Chairman of SPLM and the Politburo, if the latter ever read it.

However, the fact that the result of the assessment was shared with us, I took it as a sign of trust. The Management and the staff of the SPLM secretariat by doing that, conveyed in my view, the message that they needed support and cooperation to be able to improve their performance.

In the afternoon, we held a new meeting with the SPLM Secretariat with about 30 staff members participating. It became a very interesting experience. In the beginning, only a few said anything, until one of the women staff members suddenly intervened with a strong and very critical statement on the state of affairs with SPLM. She was so powerful that she almost exploded in her criticism. It was about lack of any political and organizational development internally, lack of delegation of duties, etc.

After that it was almost a landslide. Everyone wanted to speak and, and all except one, spoke. They were all criticizing, but they were at the same very constructive in their discussion. There was no lack neither of analysis nor insight regarding how improvements could be made. After the meeting Odin and myself agreed that what happened in the meeting had been a very interesting and encouraging experience. We headed back to Norway in the belief that the misunderstandings that had caused delays, had been removed, and that the cooperation scheme with the Labour Party now would see real progress.

For the rest of 2012 the SPLM secretariat followed up on our agreements, and in the winter of 2013, a lot of important activities connected to the party building project took place. Early in January a delegation from the Labour Party travelled to Juba for a week. The visit started with a round-table conference with close to 100 participants. The participants were mainly ministers, SPLM secretariat officials, the Political Bureau, many members of the National Liberation Council and governors of all the ten states.

The round table conference was to start Monday 6th January at 10 am, but during breakfast we were told that the opening was postponed to 1pm. The President and Party Chairman Salva Kiir, himself wanted open the conference, and he had to have a meeting in Parliament before he could do the opening. A little later there was another postponement to 4 pm.

We were all gathered in the conference hall with Riek Machar in the chair of the meeting when President Salva Kiir arrived very punctually at 4 pm. He warmly greeted all in the Labour Party delegation, something we very much appreciated, During the meeting he talked to me twice, and he said that he would like to have a personal meeting with me. But, he never followed up. We had no meeting.

Salva Kiir made a politically constructive welcome speech. He said all the right things about the important role of an active state in a poor and undeveloped country like South Sudan. He also had a few constructive reflections on how to improve on the performance of SPLM.

Secretary General Pa'gan Amum had asked the Norwegian delegation to share some key points from the historical experience of Norway concerning nation building, national ownership, political administration, control of natural resources. It was left to me to do the presentation of that topic while Deputy Minister of Finance, Kjetil Lund, talked about the Norwegian management of natural resources since the discovery of oil and gas around 1970. The other members of the delegation supplemented, it became in political terms a wonderful afternoon.

The agenda for the following day covered a broad discussion on the political issues raised in our presentations the day before. Again, after a hesitant start, the debate almost exploded while it at the same time carried a very constructive tone. The participants were positive and enthusiastic in their many references to the Norwegian experience, in particular when it came to the issue of the role of the state regarding the ownership and management of vital National resources. It was highlighted again and again that this was of great relevance to South Sudan.

I remember one governor who had a few particularly strong words on the issues mentioned. He was hard in his criticism of the SPLM leadership concerning the absence of a political action programme. He talked for so long that the chair, Riek Machar, interrupted and asked him to conclude. The governor was quiet for a few seconds while he stared intensely at Riek Machar. Then he thundered:

"No, Mr. Vice Chairman, today you shall shut up while I speak, and I shall speak until I come to my end, and I have made my points."

Machar after that remained silent as criticism poured on him and the other leading members of the SPLM and the Government until the speaker came to his end.

The many other meetings which we had for the rest of the week, went very well. The meetings were well attended and there were good and constructive discussions. Several of the young and skillful advisors from the Norwegian Labour Party Secretariat and the Labour Parliamentary Group gave presentations on how to run the secretariat of a political party, how to work in a parliamentary group, how to keep track of membership records, communicate with members and more.

On the last day of the meetings I was asked to address the assembly with a few words. I reminded them of the days of the struggle, the suffering the people went through and the type of important tasks and challenges that now laid on the shoulders of the SPLM. Finally, I said:

"Now is about you staying united because divisions will be destructive."

After the big roundtable conference on 6th and 7th January 2013 attended by more than one hundred high level party members, the Labour Party delegation together with some of the central leaders in the SPLM Secretariat were invited for dinner, which as always, whenever SPLM was hosting, became a pleasant experience.

After the dinner, I experienced something that surprised me. The Secretary for Syndicated Organizations in the SPLM Secretariat, Martin Majut Yak, came to me, sat down beside me and said:

"Uncle Halle, do you know what will happen if the political and organizational developments you in the Norwegian Labour Party are suggesting for the SPLM, result in opposition to the Chairman, so that he may not be renominated for the elections as the SPLM Candidate for President? Do you know what will happen then?"

I answered no. Martin looked at me for a moment and said:

"Then there will be two SPLM, because we will never allow anyone to come in the way of the renomination of Salva Kiir as the SPLM Candidate for President at the forth coming elections."

It was a message that I on the spot did not fully understand. But as the political events unfolded in South Sudan in the year of 2013, I came to understand the message from Martin Majut Yak. He was the messenger conveying, on behalf of Salva Kiir, Paul Malong, the Jieng Council of Elders and other Dinka tribalists, the message that their priority at any cost was the reelection of Salva Kiir as President of South Sudan. SPLM becoming a democratic organization, and national elections being conducted in a free and fair political environment, were becoming irrelevant considerations.

The Party Building Project was destroyed by the destructive Events of 2013

I consider all our meetings on the project in January 2013 as constructive and successful. There were a couple of minor consultations meetings in March 2013 between the Labour Party and the SPLM that also were constructive. Then everything stalled.

The talk after March 2013 was all the time about the meetings of the Politburo and the National Liberation Council (NLC) that should be called to discuss and finalize the proposed political Manifesto and the political action programme. The proposals have been at rest since May 2008, and nine years had passed in between. The Government had been running the country without any political guidelines, rooted in democratic decision making in the political organs of the governing party SPLM.

In addition, the meetings to come in the Politburo and the National Liberation Council should also discuss other important matters that were linked to the call for the next SPLM Convention that, according to the rules, had to be held at latest in the summer of 2013. In the Norwegian Labour Party, we considered successful meetings in the two political organs of SPLM to be very important stepping stones forward for the party building project to continue.

But none of these very important meetings took place. According to my sources in SPLM who are several, the Secretary general, Pagan Amum formally and five times in the period between May 2008 and the spring of 2013 called on the Chairman, Salva Kiir, and asked for his approval and signature to call the meetings to be held. But every time the Chairman refused to approve and sign. For this and many other reasons related to Salva Kiir's poor conduct as Head of both the Government and the SPLM, a long time simmering conflict between the Chairman on one side, and the Secretary General and other members of the Politburo on the other side, on issues related to the forthcoming Convention, developed in a very serious manner. It related to the procedures for the local elections of delegates, the rules for the nomination of the SPLM candidate for the Presidency at the general elections to be held later that year and more.

The conflict peaked in July when Pa'gan Amum was suspended from his position as Secretary General, accused of insubordination against the chairman and critical utterances in public in violation of the SPLM Constitution. Pagan Amum was further accused of having taken a big amount of money from the SPLM treasury. He was also banned from expressing himself in public and from travelling outside Juba town. Both orders by the President were obvious violations of basic human rights and the interim Constitution of South Sudan.

Pa'gan Amum as Secretary General was the key link in SPLM regarding the cooperation with the Norwegian Labour Party. When he was removed from his position as Secretary General, the party building project consequently came to a halt.

The Transformation of SPLM into a Democratic Membership Organization

NPA was as already mentioned, the Norwegian counterpart to SPLM with regard to transforming SPLM into a membership organization with formal democratic structures at all levels from the village to the National level. The NPA project manager, Eskild Johansen, and his assistant Jacob Atem, continued to work with the SPLM secretariat through-out the fall of 2013 emphasizing the training of elected officers. This part of the party building project was particularly successful with around 2500 SPLM members being trained. But in December 2013 everything also stalled for this part of the project. The project leader, Eskild Johansen, had come to the end of his contract with NPA, and he returned to Norway just days ahead of the Juba massacre in the third week of December 2013. With Eskild's return to Norway, the whole party building project stopped even though there was a lot of goodwill within the Labour Party and NPA for the continuing cooperation with SPLM.

The Deathblow to the Project

However, the deathblow to the project was of course what happened in the meeting of the National Liberation Council on 13th and 14th December 2013, the speech of the Chairman Salva Kiir, the decisions that caused the witch hunt for those who no longer had confidence in Salva Kiir, peaking with the massacres of the nuers in the days following.

In fact, what happened in December 2013 in Juba and South Sudan was not only the deathblow to the party building project. It was the deathblow to the building of key institutions for the development of democracy in South Sudan and to SPLM as a politically unifying political organization for the people of the land.

What happened, could it have been avoided?

The party building project came to a halt due to the reasons stated above. Could something have been done differently from the Norwegian side? Yes, undoubtedly.

The actual work both with the media and party building project started late, media in 2001/2, the party building project only in 2008.

Key leaders within the SPLM knew long before the CPA in 2005 how bad the internal situation was both politically and organizationally. It was because of that, that John Garang in August 1998 asked me as the Secretary General of NPA to convey to the Norwegian Government that he saw a strong need for support for democracy training at all levels and thereby the need for democratic institution building in the liberated areas of South Sudan with civil society as a key ingredient of the whole. I brought the message home to Norway, but it fell on rocky grounds both in NMFA and among organizations that worked in South Sudan. In short, there was no political understanding and support for the message from John Garang. This was the case in Norway, and this was the case with all other donor countries.

Foresight was non-existent. NPA alone had no funds of its own to start a programme of this type.

If training in democratic work and the building of key institutions for democracy had started with SPLM in 1998 instead of 7 to 10 years later, maybe, the situation in South Sudan today would have been very contrary to the total failure we see today.

With regards to what happened in the party building project cooperation, discussed above that developed after CPA in 2005, things started late at home in Norway. The Minister Erik Solheim responded instantly and in a very positive manner in March 2006 to a request from SPLM. However, the Norwegian partners, NMFA and NPA spent about 18 months discussing and preparing, before anything happened from the Norwegian side. Then the NPA and the Labour youth both started working with SPLM. In 2009 there was a very unnecessary delay in the party building project because the Norwegian Ambassador to South Sudan disagreed on principle grounds and tried to stop the project that her superior, the Minister of Development Cooperation, Erik Solheim had given his go ahead in March 2006.

NPA had its own project manager in Juba for the party building project working together with local NPA staff and SPLM. The Labour Party had very able and committed people in the secretariat in Oslo, working on the project. But they had other assignments as well, and they could for this reason never give full time to the joint project for the transformation of SPLM. In short, there is in my view a lot to learn from the shortcomings we were part of with regards to the party building project with SPLM.

Hassan el Turabi, the ideological and religious leader behind the Coup d'état in Sudan in 1989.

Omar Bashir, President of Sudan.

David Hoile, director of ESCAP, and the spin doctor of Omar Bashir. Faximile from kenyans.europe.

11
DANGEROUS ENEMIES

The Regime in Khartoum and its religious and ideological Nature

Throughout history there have been many accounts of the conflict between the north and south in Sudan. In a news report three years after NPA began its humanitarian aid work in South Sudan, Gunnar Kopperud from the Oslo newspaper, Dagbladet, described the conflict as follows:

"*The civil war is a war with many layers. The top layer is the conflict between the Arabic-Muslim majority in the north and the African-Christian minority in the south. Thus, this war is the spearhead of Islam conversion in Africa, an Arab-African Islamic struggle for cultural, political and economic control and dominance.*

However, beneath the religious-ideological conflict lies a number of other conflicts; traditional and irreconcilable tribal differences, strategic interference from regional powers such as Libya, Egypt and Iraq, not to mention the economic struggle over South Sudan's vast natural resources of minerals, oil and most importantly water.

The Nile gathers here on its journey as the lifeline of North-Eastern Africa."

Even 28 years later, I think this quote from 1989 gives a picture about what the conflict is about.

The ideological Dimension intensifies the Conflict

On June 30th 1989 a group of young officers carried through a military coup in Sudan, removing the democratically elected, however incompetent, Prime Minister Sadiq al-Mahdi. Omar Bashir led the coup and was immediately made Head of State and the chairman of the Revolutionary Command Council for National Salvation (RCC). It was soon apparent that the new powers were collaborating closely with The National Islamic Front (NIF) and its leader Hassan al-Tourabi. The primary goal of al-Tourabi's organization was to convert all people in Sudan to Islam. To achieve this goal, the application of the Muslim Sharia Laws was to be intensified all over Sudan. At the same time the new powers entered an extensive and comprehensive collaboration with Iran and Iraq.

Al-Tourabi had great ambitions. An Islamic Sudan would be the beginning of the Islamic conversion of Africa. But to make Sudan capable of this, the rebellion in the south had to be destroyed. Consequently, the war against SPLM/A had to be intensified.

Sudan had many social, political and economic weaknesses. Nearly all the roads, bridges, airports, military bases were in a state of near collapse. Banking and financial institutions barely functioned. Both the physical and administrative infrastructure had to be radically improved before Sudan could be the bridgehead for the Islamic Conversion of Africa.

The Helper, Osama bin Laden

In 1991 al-Tourabi invited Osama bin Laden to Khartoum. He had proven himself a worthy engineer and a very able manager of major infrastructural projects in Saudi-Arabia and other places. Could he take the responsibility for the large development projects that the new regime wanted to implement? The first meeting with Obama bin Laden in Khartoum was very successful.

Some months later, in 1992, he was exiled from Saudi-Arabia after pressure from the USA. But Osama bin Laden had an easy escape. His new friends in Khartoum welcomed him with open arms, and he stayed in Sudan for four years. He completed many large infrastructural projects and he improved the banking system in the country.

But he did much more. He had frequent meetings with Hassan al-Tourabi, Omar Bashir and other powerful men within the new islamist elite groups in Khartoum. They had a new proposition for him. Could Osama bin Laden accept other leadership roles? The islamists in NIF had plans for the establishment of a global terrorist organization. But as far as Sudan was concerned, Africa was the focus. Bin Laden gladly accepted this additional assignment.

Officially, bin Laden had the responsibility for developing large agricultural projects both near Kassala and in other parts in the eastern regions of Sudan. These projects were, according to my sources which I consider very reliable, however, a facade for the other activity that was established in all secrecy, namely training camps for terrorists. Recruits from Sudan, the Middle East, Afghanistan, Pakistan and Muslim parts of Africa came to these camps. The years that bin Laden stayed and worked in Sudan were the formative years for the Al Quaida terrorist organization of which he later became the leader.

The goal was to destabilize the East African countries of Somalia, Kenya, Uganda, Tanzania, Rwanda and Burundi. The first target was Somalia, where their first and successful operations began in 1993-94. After which the focus was on Kenya, Tanzania and Uganda. In August 1998, the first major terrorist attacks hit the USA embassies in Kenya and Tanzania. In Kenya 213 innocent people were killed in the bomb attack while approximately 4000 were wounded, in Tanzania 11 lost their lives while 85 were wounded. In Uganda, the Lord's Resistance Army (LRA) was equipped by Khartoum with arms and instructors with the aim of carrying out terrorist activities in Uganda. Some of the terrorist activities we have seen in East African countries in recent years, stem from this activity initiated in the middle 1990ies by Hassan al-Tourabi, Omar Bashir and Osama bin Laden with advisors from Iran and other countries in the Middle East.

The Merchants of Death

For the regime in Sudan to achieve their goals, they needed more modern weapons. Khartoum's arms dealers found several countries willing to sell, and China became the most important arms supplier for the regime in Khartoum. The willingness China demonstrated, was connected to the oil fields that had had been discovered in Sudan in the 1980s and early 1990s, and the Chinese desire to position themselves as a major partner in oil production in Sudan.

Therefore, several arms contracts were made. One included the delivery of tens of thousands of the Chinese version of the Kalashnikov 47 rifles. Another included tanks, and a third, the combat aircraft Fantan (A-5) that is especially made for attacking ground targets.

Russia sold primarily combat aircrafts, and Sudan bought the most recent version of the highly advanced and costly MIG-29. It was specially adopted to the needs of the regime in Khartoum as a particularly efficient war plane for attacks against ground targets, in practice, SPLA units on the move. Both Russia and China sold the most advanced combat helicopters to Khartoum. Ukraine sold weapons for ground forces, and from 1989 and until recently, Iran sold weapons of various kinds. Now Iran is out in the cold while reactionary and dictatorial Saudi Arabia as well as the new and very authoritarian rulers in Egypt are warmly embraced in Khartoum.

Several of the countries mentioned above, produced and sold landmines, other types of mines and anti-personnel weapons.

Both sides in the war in Sudan used landmines, but only the regime in Khartoum used anti-personnel cluster bombs and a type of poisonous gas that was never fully specified.

The Khartoum regime's use of poisonous gas is narrated in chapter 9 of this book. The gas attacks were primarily aimed at civilian targets. Whether this gas was produced in Sudan or imported, has so far not been possible to determine, but poisonous gas was produced and stored in several Arabic countries.

The regime also used a type of gas that burned, possibly white phosphor, against both civilian and military targets in South Sudan. NPA former colleague, Ken Miller, was an eyewitness to these attacks:

"Halle, it was utterly horrible, indescribably horrible. I waded through burned down villages just after the attack with burning gas (phosphor) where people were either burned to death or were dying. They screamed in agony, and there was very little we could do to save lives. We had neither the medical equipment nor the capacity to help."

I have received confirmation from several SPLA officers that such attacks with burning gas took place several times while the international community remained silent.

The Sound of Terror

There was one dreaded sound during the long war of liberation that caused more fear and havoc in the civilian population in South Sudan than anything else, and that was the sound of an Antonov airplane. Not only did people fear the sound, but also domestic animals and birds recognized the sound and fled. The airplane was originally a Russian produced cargo plane of which the regime bought many. The Antonov plane was then modified to be a bomber and used in terror attacks against the civilian population. At the time, the Antonov was used mainly against targets in the south and in Darfur, now the plane is being used in attacks against the civilian population in the Nuba mountains.

In the early 1990s, the regime produced "home-made barrel bombs". Large metal containers were made and filled with explosives, metal bits, large nails and similar. When the bomb was ready it would weigh between 200 and 500 kilograms. Between 10 and 20 bombs were loaded into these Antonov planes. The plane had to fly at high altitudes to avoid SPLA's artillery fire. The primary targets were civilians, such as village markets, schools and hospitals. Whenever these bomb attacks took place, many civilians were killed instantly, and many others were injured without any possibility of getting hospital care. They therefore had to carry the shrapnel in their bodies for the rest of their lives.

There is no doubt that hospitals were primary targets when the Antonov planes attacked. NPAs hospital in Yei with a Red Cross insignia painted on the roof was bombed 52 times between 1998 and 2005. Sometimes the bombing was so inaccurate that it did not hit its primary target, but other where people were gathered, and many innocent civilians were killed or seriously injured during these brutal air raids.

Antonov planes often came at night. Sometimes they would just fly over villages to create fear and panic, and people in the middle of the night and in darkness would flee and run for cover.

Until around the year 2000, the bombs were rolled out the cargo door of the plane, and consequently the accuracy was less than perfect. After 2000, the regime bought new Antonov planes that were equipped with bomb sites and bomb hatches, and then the accuracy improved.

There are no statistics of the bombing raids carried out by Antonov planes against targets in South Sudan, but I would estimate an average of two to three raids per week over a period of 22 years, yielding about 3000 bomb attacks. Nobody knows for certain how many bombs were dropped, but probably somewhere between 20 000 and 30 000. Since 2011 bomb attacks have intensified against targets in Darfur and the Nuba Mountains where the liberation struggle continues.

Crimes without Punishment

The regime in Khartoum has always and systematically broken the international Red Cross conventions of warfare and treatment of prisoners. In relation to other and newer conventions, the regime has committed serious war crimes. The International Criminal Court (ICC) reacted in response to the crimes in Darfur, but not regarding the crimes against the civilian population in South Sudan and the Nuba Mountains. The regime broke international conventions against production and use of landmines, and the convention forbidding use of cluster bombs. NPA together with many other civil society and human rights groups have lobbied and been successful both in Norway and with partners internationally to have these horrible weapons banned. Finally, Khartoum has also violated the Convention that deals with chemical warfare.

The regime in Khartoum, now in its 28th year, was charged by the UN for it crimes against humanity in Darfur, and in July 2008 the ICC released an arrest warrant for president Omar Bashir. Three of his closest colleagues had been placed under an arrest warrant by ICC the year before.

In December 2014, the UN and international human rights organizations accused government forces of mass rape of 200 women in Darfur. Bashir in contempt refuted these allegations and claimed that the UN people were lying, and expelled one of the key UN leaders from Sudan.

On December 12, 2014, the ICCs prosecutor Fatou Bensouda informed the UN Security Council that the investigation on President Bashir had had to be discontinued due to lack of cooperation from central member states of the UN.

Bensouda concluded her speech by reminding the members of the UN Security Council of the mass rape of 200 women in Darfur. She added that the actions were so brutal that the members of the Security Council should feel obliged to act. Nobody doubted whom the message was meant for; China, Russia and several African countries including South Sudan. Salva Kiir has joined the club of ICC bashers, and he has on several occasions been critical of the ICC since he was elected as president of South Sudan in 2011, but especially after the outbreak of the civil war in December 2013.

Why did the UN and the world never react to the crimes committed against the civilian population in South Sudan between 1983 and 2005? Perhaps because during the first ten years of the liberation struggle SPLM/A was perceived by the West to be a kind of a Marxist movement allied to the dictatorial Mengistu regime in Ethiopia. However, after the split in Nasir in 1991, there was some minor criticism of Khartoum. But this changed when Bill Clinton became president in the USA. In 1994 Sudan was put on the list of terrorist countries and had some painful sanctions added at the same time. Sudan has remained on that list ever since even though President Obama to the regret of many, in his last days of his presidency softened the sanctions against Sudan.

When the peace negotiations began in 1999, it was not possible to accuse the regime in Khartoum of crimes, and at the same time hope that the negotiations would succeed.

In the middle of April 2015 elections were held in Sudan. It was not a free and fair election, and the opposition boycotted it. Newspapers that were critical of the Bashir and his regime, were censured or closed. Students and others who were critical, were arrested, beaten and tortured. On April 27th, the official results were announced; Omar Bashir was re-elected with 94 percent of the vote. The official election participation percentage was 46 percent and much lower in the capital of Khartoum, only 37 percent. Most Sudan's voters remained at home in silent protest.

Sudan continues to have a dictatorship even though the April elections in 2015 on the surface were made to look democratic. Omar Bashir, who has been the dictator since the summer of 1989, will continue until the summer of 2020, and the crimes without punishment committed by the regime will certainly continue until 2020. I doubt whether there will ever be any change for the better for peoples of Sudan, but I strongly hope that I shall be mistaken on that point.

Glimpses from a Journey into Starvation and Death

One day in August 1998 I went with some colleagues from NPA and Norwegian and international press far into South Sudan. Tomm Kristiansen from NRK was one of the reporters. It was in the middle of the drought and the famine that had been made worse by the war ravaging the land.

Firstly, we went to see our own local NPA staff who was helping starving and dying people in an area around Akot. Our small staff did as well as they could, but in relation to what was needed, it was too little. It was a painful experience to witness all the suffering.

In the afternoon, we flew west and landed on an airstrip near a large camp of internally displaced persons and a field hospital run by Doctors Without Borders (MSF). We had our own tents and equipment and we were invited to set up our own little camp inside the MSF camp area.

In the evening Tomm Krisitiansen from NRK approached me with tears in his eyes and told me that he had spoken with a woman who had had a very traumatic experience. He asked me to come and talk with her. She told the following story:

"*The government forces attacked our village. I was alone with our five children. My husband is fighting with SPLA. We all had to flee, and I have had nothing to eat or drink except what we found on the road, and all of my children died of starvation.*"

Tomm commented: "*But you have a child with you.*"

"*Yes, all my children died on the road. First one died, and I dug a grave for him. But when the next one died I was so tired, I didn't have the strength to dig a grave so I threw him into the Nile. I had to try and save myself and keep strength to save the other children. But they died as well, and I had to throw them into the Nile. At*

the end of the long march I found two children who were still alive, alone on the bank of the river, their mother was dead. I decided to try and save them and take care of them as if they were my own. We managed to make it here, and here is one of the children."
"Where is the other one?"
"Over there," and the woman pointed at the hospital tent.

We walked over to the tent and saw the child. It was completely emaciated with a blank stare. A nurse from Doctors Without Borders was treating the child. We asked if she thought the child would make it and she was not sure. I cried as I walked out.

The next morning, we went back to the tent. The child was alive. The treatment had worked, and the child would most likely survive.

Then, Tomm and I went for a walk outside the camp. We heard a beautiful song, children's voices singing as only Africans can. Under a tree a short distance away, we met a group of children. There were maybe 30 children and a young man, and I asked what they were doing. This is our school, said the young man. He had three books; the Bible, a Psalm book and an old reader. That was it. We spoke with the teacher who was quite an impressive young man. He talked about the war, and why they fought, but he hoped for peace to come, and then it would be important that the children could read and write.

Then, as it so often happens during the monsoon season in the tropics, heavy clouds gathered, and it rained for hours. The airstrip was turned into mud. It was impossible to fly that evening, August 7th, 1998.

Using his satellite telephone, Tomm Kristiansen prepared for a direct radio broadcast to listeners in Norway. But a big and very frightening piece of news came in his way. His editors in Oslo told him that there was no time and space for his piece on the starving and dying people of Southern Sudan because there had been terrorist attacks on the American embassies in Nairobi and Dar we Salaam with many causalities.

The rain continued to pour down. A couple of our colleagues had to get up in the middle of the night, and they had to dig ditches around our tents to lead the water away. I thought about the thousands of refugees in the camp next to us. They had little food, many were sick, and they did not have the opportunity to dig ditches around their tents to lead the water away. The water therefore flooded into the tents.

The rain stopped at some point during the night. A powerful and very warm morning sun dried the airstrip and we could leave for Nairobi late that morning.

At the Site of the Terrorist Attack in Nairobi

When we landed in Nairobi, I contacted NPAs Head of Security, Charles Aloo, a former officer with the Kenyan armed forces. He agreed to take me to the American Embassy that had been attacked and turned into a big ruin by islamic terrorists. Through Charles' former colleagues, the Kenyan security officers, we were allowed to get close to the ruins. It was an awful sight. Kenyan aid workers worked frantically, and many dug with their bare hands, looking for possible survivors. While we were there, 24 hours after the attack, they found a young woman, seriously injured, but alive.

I cried, and many around me cried, and I said to myself that the scoundrels in Khartoum had something to do with this horrible crime and massacre.

During the terrorist attack in Nairobi, August 7th, 212 people lost their lives, almost all Kenyans, and about 4000 were injured. Nevertheless, the attack was not successful. If it had succeeded according to plan, the 60 tons of diesel in the basement of the embassy would have exploded, destroying large areas of Nairobi's center and killing thousands of innocent people. The responsible ones for the attack was Al Qaida and their leader Osama bin Laden, and I am sure there was jubilation also in the islamist circles in Khartoum of what was perceived as a successful operation.

"You shall kill all the infidels and everyone in the international organizations that support them!"

This was the Muslim mantra from al-Tourabi and his likeminded that was frequently repeated in the middle of the 1990s. It was to be perceived as an order, especially for officers and soldiers fighting against SPLA. Not only that, international organizations that supported the war for liberation in Sudan were named explicitly. NPA's workers were obvious targets of this jihad.

Strict Security Measures

The first two NPA resident representatives, Egil Hagen and Helge Rohn, were trained as officers and had graduated from the Norwegian Military Academy in Oslo. Intelligence and security were part of their curriculum. Therefore, both made security in the relief operations a priority from day one. NPA's vehicles and food transport trucks never crossed the border into South Sudan before it was deemed secure.

There were many challenges; communication technology in the early 1990s was not as sophisticated and accessible as it is today. Radio was expensive and required constant updating with new investments, for which the donors often were not willing to grant support. In addition, everything connected to the use of radio communication had to be cleared with the Kenyan authorities. At the same time NPA had continuous communication with SRRA and SPLA's intelligence units regarding everything related to security.

Fortunately, radio and other communication technology was constantly developing, and NPA despite reservations by donors, could make use of that newest technology. Thus, NPA contrary to the conventional belief in UN and OLS circles, had very good and reliable security in its operations.

Last, but not least, we had very capable and reliable heads of security at our main office in Nairobi, most of whom were South Sudanese, and we had security people in the field, all of them Africans and mostly South Sudanese. In addition, all NPA staff had high security awareness.

I worked with our two heads of security. The first was Charles Aloo, who was NPA's Head of Security for eight years before he became president Kibaki's special advisor for Sudan. The other was Chaat Paul, who came from SPLM/A's inner circle and was a confidant of John Garang himself.

The Fate of Chaat Paul

After the CPA in 2005, Chaat Paul became member of the of security group for John Garang. After Garang's death he was transferred to Salva Kiir's office in Khartoum for a while, and then at independence of South Sudan in 2011, he was transferred to the Office of the President in Juba and made Director of Communications.

Then in late 2015, 16 staff in the Office of the President were arrested and accused of corruption, among them the former NPA Head of Security, Chaat Paul. In the winter and spring of 2016 a strange case against the accused was performed in the High Court of South Sudan. The prosecutor, a military officer from Internal Security, presented a case that to most people seemed utterly weak and with very little substance. The defense lawyers refused the evidence presented, and the accused stated their innocence, some claiming their arrest was a means to cover up the real corruption that was taking place in the Office of the President. But in vain, the prosecutor demanded life in prison for all the accused, and the judge followed the demand.

I have personally for some 15 years had a close cooperation with Chaat Paul. His not only a former NPA colleague, but a very decent person and a friend. I do not believe that he is guilty, and to my great joy, I now see that legal groups in South Sudan, East Africa and internationally, that work on the case of Chaat Paul and the others convicted, state that the evidence brought against the accused were false. Chaat Paul, like the others, became necessary scapegoats for the vast scale corruption that since Salva Kiir took office in Juba in 2005, has taken place in the Office of the President and in the ministries with the President himself sometimes in charge of the corruption activities, other times condoning what his confidants in corruption were doing. All this has been documented and revealed in detail in many reports. (see chapter 20)

My friend, the freedom fighter Chaat Paul and the others convicted, have been rottening in the prison cells of Salva Kiir. But to the surprise of many, Chaat Paul and three of his fellow comrades in prison, were pardoned and set free in early August 2017.

The faith of the other twelwe, still in prison for life, is uncertain.

More on NPA and the Security in the Field

Between 1986 and 2005 NPA vehicles crossed the border to South Sudan many thousands of times, traveling hundreds of thousands of kilometers in roadless South Sudan. Of course, we had accidents, but nothing serious. In hindsight, we were so lucky that it is as if a stronger hand was protecting us.

The fear of attack from the government forces or the militia groups financed and equipped by Khartoum was always present. In 1998 some of our vehicles crossed the border into Kenya in a convoy together with cars from several other humanitarian organizations. Vehicle after vehicle passed through the same point on the road without anything happening. However, when the NPA's cars passed through, clearly marked with NPA's insignia, they were attacked with heavy fire for several minutes. Two local workers in the truck were killed. No one doubted that Khartoum was behind the attack. But they were not successful in other attempts because of our security arrangements worked.

12 000 Flights, two deadly Incidents

Between 1986 and 2005 NPA had close to 12000 flights between Kenya and Uganda and airstrips in Sudan, as well as flights between airstrips inside Sudan. In 1988 we had an accident due to bad weather, killing the two people on board.

In 1993 there was a tragic accident in Nakuru which I have narrated in chapter 5. But apart from these two, NPA had no major plane accidents in Sudan, even though the planes we hired, were shot at many times. After a mission, a bullet hole or several were sometimes discovered in the body of the plane, but they never hit the vital part or pilots or passengers.

All flights followed strict security procedures. Here are two examples:

Once in 1998, we were to fly from Wilson Airport in Nairobi to Yei in South Sudan. Nils Røhne, NPA's new International Director was travelling with me in the group. Before departure, the pilot explained that we would land in Loki in Turkana. There, he would give us some safety instructions before we continued. We stopped as planned at Loki airport in Turkana to get our passports and other documents stamped by the Kenyan Authorities. Then we were ready to continue, and the pilot gave the following announcement, which was similar for all our other flights into Sudan:

"We are now flying into enemy territory. The Khartoum forces have anti-aircraft guns that can hit us if we are unlucky. They have Russian MIG-19 fighter jets stationed in Juba that can reach us in four minutes if they see us on the radar. That's why we always fly low, so that we have the hills and mountains above us. Thus, the radar in Juba cannot see us. When we fly over areas controlled by SPLA, there is no danger of being shot at from the ground.

When we land in Yei, you have three minutes to get out of the plane with your baggage and cargo. If you use more time and there is a spy in the area, he can signal to the intelligence unit of Khartoum in Juba. Then a fighter jet might be in the airspace here before I can take off. In the worst case, it may be able to destroy my plane while still on the runway."

Then he added:

"We have an agreement that I will pick you up tomorrow at 12 o'clock. You must be ready on time at the airstrip. If you are late, I will take off immediately to make sure that fighter jets cannot reach me. If you are ready, you have three minutes to board with luggage and cargo. Then we will take off. If a fighter jet does come after us, we have one minute to enter Ugandan airspace."

This was the standard procedure for all flights during that period between 1986 and 2005. It is nothing, but a miracle that NPA did not have any other fatal accidents than those already narrated in the book, during this long period.

The flight that day to Yei became an experience. The airplane floated as if on waves, a little up, a little down, following the hills, ridges and mountains. Sometimes almost touching the tree tops, but we were always under Juba's radar. No fighter jets came. We landed in Yei, off –loaded in less than three minutes. Then we carried out our visits and had our appointments with NPA staff at the hospital as well as the local heads of SRRA and SPLM/A, and then had a quiet night at our staff house in Yei. The next day we were on the airstrip as scheduled. After a few minutes, we could hear the hum of the airplane engine, coming to pick us up. We used less than three minutes to board, and then it was full speed back to Kenya.

However, only an hour after we left Yei, the dreaded Antonov-bombers attacked and bombed the hospital and the town of Yei. The x-ray department was destroyed as well as other hospital buildings. A few patients were injured, but no one was killed. However, several people were killed in town. The news reached us when we landed in Nairobi. I vowed to act on the matter, and I decided that we were flying back to Yei early the next morning in a show of solidarity with the victims of the attack, and at the same time to have a view of the destruction that was caused at the hospital.

Upon arrival in Yei the next day, we gathered our staff at the hospital, all patients who could walk, with or without crutches, all SRRA, SPLM and SPLA people who could come and people from Yei. Then I gave a speech against the regime in Khartoum, saying:

"The NPA are not scared by the terror bombing from Khartoum. We continue to stand with you in solidarity. I promise, here and now, that the damage to the hospital will be repaired within a year from now."

Nils Røhne looked at me and said. *"But what about the money, Halle?"* I knew we at that moment did not have the money to support my promise. We would have to raise it. The hospital was rebuilt one year later.

The Chairman of the Board of Directors of NPA was bombed in Yei

As mentioned in chapter 5, I had suggested to the Chairman of the NPA Board of Directors, Harald Øveraas that we should invite the Chairman of SPLM, John Garang with a small delegation as guests of honour to the NPA National Convention in the summer of 1999. Harald Øveraas listened to my proposal, hesitated a bit and then he said: *"Before we decide anything, I would like to go to Sudan and see how our operations work in practice."*

I was put in charge of putting together a delegation. I felt that there was a need within the Norwegian Labour Party and the Labour Movement at large, to gain a better understanding of the NPA Sudan programme. I therefore decided to invite Kjell Engebretsen, who was the Chair of the Labour Party in the Akershus Constituency, a member of parliament and a member of the Foreign Affairs Committee of the Parliament, and Anniken Huitfeldt who was the Chair of the Norwegian Labour Party Youth. Both said yes without hesitation. From the NPA Head Office, Head of Information, Ivar Christiansen and the NPA Resident Representative for the Sudan Programme, Lars Johan Johnsen joined the delegation.

One early morning in January 1999 the delegation arrived in Nairobi. Shortly upon arrival, they met with John and Rebecca Garang, and other leading SPLM members. Then, the next day the journey took them to NPAs camp in Loki on the way to the hospital in Yei.

Ivar Christiansen narrated the following from the journey:

"*Harald was the Head of Delegation, but since I spoke better English and had been in the fields of Sudan before, I became in practical terms the head of the delegation. I carried a satellite telephone and had an agreement with NRK to report immediately if anything happened.*

Then the day came when we were to fly to Yei. Having boarded the plane, the pilot explained that when we flew over Sudanese territory, he would fly low, in the shadow of the landscape and mountains, so we could avoid Khartoum's radar and fighter jets stationed in Juba. When we landed, we had to be ready to disembark within three minutes because of the same reason. Anniken did not like to fly, and this announcement did not help. Therefore, the flight to Yei was a little bit special. We flew concealed in the contours of the landscape and when we landed in Yei, we had the three minutes to get off. Then the plane took off and disappeared in the direction of Kenya.

We were welcomed by both the local NPA workers led by Dr. Gribani, Head of the hospital, and the local leaders of SRRA and SPLM/A. And of course, we had SPLA guards with us everywhere. After a tour of the town, we were brought to the hospital where we were shown around before we met with the staff and members of SRRA and SPLM to discuss matters of common interest.

Then we heard the sound of some engine, but what was that? A strange sound, high and weak at the same time. However, the locals immediately knew what it was, Antonov planes on their way to bomb Yei. The alarm howled. We were going to be bombed, and we knew that they most likely would use 500-kilogram barrel bombs full of explosives, nails and bit of metal in the attack. The roof of the hospital had a large Red Cross flag painted as a kind of protection.

All the patients had to be evacuated. Those who could walk, went to a clearing in the woods. The bed-ridden were carried out on stretchers. Everything happened very quickly.

We were taken care of by the SPLA guard and driven to an area some little distance away. Then, we were told to jump into the ready-made trenches named foxholes, and pull the metal sheeting over us. Kjell stood by his hole and with some hesitation asked me. "What is the point of doing this?" I said that if the bomb hit the hole or nearby, we didn't have a chance. But if it hit further away, then the shrapnel and air pressure will go over us. "Jump in!" I yelled to Kjell and the others, and they disappeared in their holes.

Then, there was a new sound, a whining of bombs falling, with an increasing intensity. We waited in silence in our holes, seconds passed. Then we heard the thunder of exploding bombs, first one, then another and another. The sound of the planes faded, and it was replaced by silence for a little while, complete silence. Then we heard the signal, marking the end of the air strike.

We crawled out of the holes and were told that the planes had aimed at the hospital, but the wind had been so strong that the bombs were carried off course. The bombs that were dropped from 4000 meters, drifted with the wind a couple of hundred meters away from the hospital area before they hit the ground and exploded. Two people were killed and several were injured. In what was a typical terror bomb attack that the people in South Sudan experienced hundreds of times every year during the 20-year long war."

This experience made a strong impression on the members of the delegation. There was no doubt that the authorities in Khartoum had learnt about the visit, and no doubt, they had been bombing to kill the NPA delegation if possible.

As soon as the attack was over, Ivar Christiansen quickly put up his satellite phone, contacted NRK in Oslo and reported live on the news broadcast that the NPA delegation in Yei, and the hospital and the people of Yei had just survived a deadly bomb attack by Khartoum.

Sudan's Foreign Minister attacks NPA during an official Visit in Norway

Two months later, the Sudanese Foreign Minister was on an official visit to Norway, and he wished to meet representatives from the Norwegian civil society organizations that operated in Sudan and the Horn of Africa. The Foreign Ministry responded to his wish and invited for a meeting with relevant NGO representatives, NPA included. I was not able to attend the meeting so our Administrative Director Paal Giortz took my place.

As soon as the meeting had started, the Sudanese Foreign Minister launched a strong attack at NPA, accusing us, among other things, of gun running. Paal, who was not prepared for this, attempted nevertheless, but unsuccessfully, to dismiss the allegations. The next day I met with Ola Metliaas, Secretary -General of the Norwegian Refugee Council (NRC). He said he had been at the meeting together with Magne Barth from the Red Norwegian Cross. After the meeting had ended, they, on their way back to office, had discussed what the foreign minister had said and agreed that there might be something behind the allegations against NPA:

Where there's smoke, there's fire, he said.

I got very angry at him, and I asked him why he was unable to have a more critical attitude to the foreign minister's baseless accusations. I then proceeded to explain to him about the work NPA did in Sudan. He turned out to be quite ignorant about the whole thing.

The following day, the Sudanese Foreign Minister met with the Foreign Affairs Committee of the Norwegian Parliament. The former Norwegian Prime Minister, Thorbjørn Jagland, as the Chair of the Committee, opened the meeting and welcomed Sudan's Foreign Minister who immediately took the floor. After some polite introductory comments, he made it his priority issue to direct a severe attack at NPA, accusing us of smuggling weapons. It took less than a minute before Kjell Engebretsen stood up and banged his fist on the table and said:

"Mister Chairman, I shall not sit here and listen to this crap from this liar. I have recently been to the fields of misery, war and death in South Sudan and seen the inhuman conditions your people live under, while you, Mister Foreign Minister, and your government bomb and kill people every single day. Not only that, you tried to kill me and my friends in the NPA delegation when you bombed us in Yei last January. Mister Chairman, I am leaving this meeting in protest of the fact that Sudan's Foreign Minister is here and lying about NPA. Good- bye!"

This was a very unexpected turn of events. The Sudanese foreign minister had least of all expected anything like this to happen, and for the members of the Committee present it was also an unexpected turn of events. MP Engebretsen's furious outburst came to be the end of that meeting in the Foreign Affairs Committee.

The accusations of NPA's weapon smuggling was repeated by officials in Khartoum and their lackeys in other places several times every year throughout the 20 years from 1986 to 2005. As Minister of Development Cooperation in the Norwegian Government, Hilde Frafjord Johnson faced these accusations several times, and as a rule she replied the following:

"Almost every time I spoke with Sudan's Foreign Minister Mustafa Osman Ismail, especially on the telephone, he complained about NPA. Often, the core of his complaints was weapon smuggling. I responded by saying that I have heard this from you before. You must provide me with concrete documentation, if not, I shall have to consider the accusations as baseless. However, no such documentation ever appeared. These accusations became a ritual. They mocked the NPA calling them the Norwegian People's Army. It started in 1998, but it calmed down when the peace negotiations around 2001 started making progress.

DAVID HOILE – OMAR BASHIR'S BRITISH SPIN DOCTOR AND THE MAN WHO WANTED TO DESTROY NPA

Prelude, a meeting with Lord Avebury in London

An elderly and very friendly man with long grey hair and old fashioned glasses leaned over the table and said: "*Mr. Hanssen, are you aware of what is being written about you and NPA regarding Sudan?*"

The grey-haired man was a British politician. His name was Eric Lubbock, 4th Baron Avebury. He was a Member of Parliament for the Liberal Party from 1962 to 1970. In 1970 he inherited his title and his seat in the House of Lords, now known as Lord Avebury.

I was advised by some good international friends who were concerned with NPAs reputation and the constant accusations of weapon smuggling, to contact him next time on visit in London.

One day in the winter of 1998 I sat in his little, old fashioned house in the center of London. The Lord's home office was cluttered with books and papers, appearing haphazard and chaotic, but I came to learn that that was a wrong perception, everything was in its place.

We had a long and friendly conversation, first and foremost on the situation in Sudan. Lord Avebury was mostly concerned with the Khartoum- regime's violations of human rights and the brutal war that was waged against the people in the south. But he was also very interested in what programmes and activities NPA had in South Sudan. I explained a little about what we did, and I added also some comments why NPA had taken a stand in solidarity with the liberation struggle of the people in Sudan. At that point he asked me the question:

"*Mr. Hanssen, are you aware of what is being written about you and NPA regarding Sudan?*"

He got up and without hesitation pulled a piece of paper off the bookshelf that he showed to me and said:

"*This kind of message about you appears every time something happens in Sudan. Hundreds of parliamentarians, diplomats and bureaucrats all over Europe get the same message. These messages are often used in many European countries as the basis for media coverage of NPA, also here in Great Britain.*"

The content was most shocking with heavy accusations as to NPAs involvement in what was named the terrorist organization SPLM/A, accusations of weapon smuggling and other serious offences committed in Sudan. It was completely disastrous for NPA's reputation. I was shaken because this was totally new to me, I had no advance knowledge of this.

I looked at the letter head, and it said: "The British – Sudanese Public Affairs Council. BSPAC". The press announcement was signed by David Hoile.

"*What am I supposed to do with this?*" I asked Lord Avebury. "*Well, you should find out more about both the man and the institution and take it from there,*" was his response.

We ended the meeting on a very friendly note, and I left the British Lord who very clearly promised to fight harder in the House of Lords for Human Rights for the people of Sudan and to be more active and critical of British Policy towards the holders of power in Khartoum.

I stood out in the grey cold London air for a minute quite shaken and thought: "*What do I do now*"? I had heard and read of such accusations many times, but had never seen such accusations in print on the sender's stationary. I had at the time no concrete knowledge of the powers that operated in the international arena specializing in smear campaigns, lies and destruction of others' reputation, now having NPA as an important target and spreading lies about NPA's involvement in Sudan.

Journalist Contacts in London

During my 13 years from the fall of 1969 to the fall of 1982 as a foreign news reporter in NRK, I had several interesting journalistic assignments. In the fall of 1972 I was for instance for a few months the stand in for the London Correspondent on sick leave. From 1978 to 1982 I was the African Correspondent, based in Nairobi. During these 13 years, I established contact with many British colleagues and became a personal friend of some of them. Many of them had substantial reporting experience from countries in Africa.

I decided to contact two of them. One of them was The *Guardian's* Victoria Brittain, at the time the assistant foreign news editor and The *Guardian's* former Africa Correspondent stationed in Nairobi at the same time as myself. The other was the well-known film maker, former BBC colleague and all the time, the Sudan expert Julie Flint.

I met them both and they had a lot to say about the British Sudanese Public Affairs Council (BSPAC) and The European-Sudanese Public Affairs Council (ESPAC)and David Hoile, both institutions were in fact the same one, only with different letter heads. Both Julie and Victoria were unequivocally negative about the institution, and the man who was being paid to destroy NPA.

The story they told, in addition to what I have gathered from other colleagues and read about in the extensive documentation about ESPAC on the institution's own homepage and otherwise on the Internet and other places, are summarized in the following pages.

ESPAC– A Propaganda Machine

The name of the institution in 1998 was "The British Sudanese Public Affairs Council". A few years later it changed the name, and it was called "The European–Sudanese Public Affairs Council". The director has always been David Hoile.

In addition to this institution, David Hoile's name is connected to high ranking positions in a number of political institutions on the extreme right in Great Britain and globally. The ideological core for these institutions is "libertarian". But ESPAC and David Hoile are on the main propagating strong anti-European and anti-democratic views, and in my view, with a strong tendency towards racism and fascism.

David Hoile was born and grew up in the old Southern Rhodesia. As a youth, he was a member of The Rhodesian Front. He enlisted towards the end of the 1970s as a commando soldier in Ian Smith's forces, fighting against the liberation movements in Zimbabwe.

The Guardian published at the time several articles about David Hoile. In the early 1980s he was an extreme right wing activist, fighting for continued apartheid in South Africa. On more than one occasion he was pictured with a sticker on his tie with a picture of Nelson Mandela and the text: "*Hang Nelson Mandela and all ANC Terrorists!*"

Hoile was a very active member of the ultra-right Conservative Students Union and a staunch supporter of Margaret Thatcher and her neo liberal policies. For a time, he was a member of the Board of Directors of the Conservative Party and active in the party.

Before this, he had a rather formidable list as an extreme right wing activist in several international contexts. The following is a brief selection of his participation in such activities.

While Hoile was still a student activist, he established a close relationship to the South African Apartheid regime, as well as establishing good contacts within the INKATHA Freedom Party (IFP) and their leader Mangosuthu Buthelezi. Hoile was one of the apartheid regime's many supporters who strongly objected to the boycott of South Africa.

NPA supported the boycott, and between 1976 and 1986 we also were the secret channel for the Norwegian Labour Movement's support to ANC. From 1986 NPA was chosen as the Norwegian channel for humanitarian support to ANC in exile and in South Africa. About 350 million NOK, (approx. 40 million USD) mainly government funding, were channeled through NPA to ANC.

From 1987 Hoile was an active member of the Washington based right wing International Freedom Foundation (IFF) that among many other activities carried out smear campaigns against ANC. Hoile collaborated closely with the Conservative parliamentarian John Carlisle, who was also a staunch supporter of the old apartheid regime. The activities of IFF were not limited to South Africa, but also included support to The National Union for the Total Independence of Angola (UNITA), The Mozambican National Resistance(RENAMO) in Mozambique and Mujahedin in Afghanistan (the forerunner to Taliban).

NPA supported The Mozambique Liberation Front (FRELIMO) and The People's Movement for the Liberation of Angola (MPLA), strong political opponents of both RENAMO and UNITA. NPA was critical of Mujahedin in Afghanistan.

South Africa was Hoile's focus in the 1980s and the apartheid regime provided substantial financial and political support to Hoile's activities. According to my sources, the Apartheid regime as late as in 1991-92 transferred approx. two million USD for his activities. They both held the view that if ANC gained political power in South Africa, South Africa would become a Marxist stronghold on the African continent.

In the middle of the 1980s Hoile formed the "Committee for a Free Nicaragua" as a propaganda forum for the Contras, and he himself fought with the Contras forces for shorter periods as they battled against the Government Sandinista forces.

NPA was an active critic of the Contras, it had a strong solidarity support for the Sandinista government at the time and has since continued its development programmes in the country.

Hoile's support for the apartheid regime in South Africa was in vain. Likewise, was his participation in the other reactionary movements, except for Nicaragua.

Hoile with all his political failures and defeats, had therefore a need to readdress his involvement to other areas in Africa. In 1994 he visited Khartoum as the guest of President Omar Bashir. Sudan became Hoile's new project. This coincided with Osama bin Laden's presence in Sudan.

Following Hoile's visit, some form of an agreement was reached with the regime in Khartoum, where the task was to improve the international reputation of the Bashir regime. Payment was to be transferred through existing channels controlled by Hoile, namely ESPAC and the consulting firm Westminster Associates. Considering the prolific information and travel activity by Hoile and his associates since 1994, the payments from the regime in Khartoum to ESPAC might have run into several million US dollars. During the whole period since the 1994 agreement in Khartoum, David Hoile has de facto been serving Omar Bashir as his spin doctor, and as far as I know, he still does.

Hoile became a very loyal propagandist for the regime in Khartoum. In addition to improving the regime's reputation, Hoile was also given the task of conducting smear campaigns against critics of the regime in Khartoum. During the liberation war in Sudan, SPLM and SPLA were after 1994 the most central targets for Hoile's smear campaigns. Both were systematically described as terrorist organizations by ESPAC and accused of horrendous offences and breaches of human rights. In that context, it became very important to carry out smear campaigns aimed at bringing NPA in disrepute. The following is one of many similar quotes:

"NPA, – An Organization supporting International Terrorism

From 1994 until 2005/8 several hundred messages was produced by ESPAC about NPA's so-called support for terrorists in South Sudan. They contained all kind of accusations and lies about NPAs activities, first in South Sudan, and later even in Sri Lanka. The goal was to destroy NPAs reputation and credibility.

ESPAC and others who used ESPAC as a source accused NPA multiple times for gun running in South Sudan. Towards the end of the war, a video about gun running in Sudan was broadcast on Arabic TV-stations with a picture of NPA's Dan Eiffe manipulated into the video. Dan's face was placed on a body in uniform in an arms store supposed to be a NPA store, handing out weapons to SPLA soldiers. The video had no producer, but appeared to be part of an ESPAC-production.

In November 1999 NRK broadcasted two documentaries on the war in Sudan made by the editorial staff of a documentary unit named "Brennpunkt" (Focal Point). The responsible producer was Ola Flyum, and he used documentation from ESPAC.

In the 1990s the Khartoum regime had several agents in Norway. One of them was a South Sudanese man who had learnt Norwegian amazingly quickly. He moved with ease around in various social circles and was always well dressed. He often called me with strange questions about what NPA did in Sudan. He left Norway shortly after the CPA in 2005.

Shortly after the so-called documentaries by NRK/Brennpunkt had been broadcast, the same agent ensured that a copy was brought to ESPAC in London. The transcript was translated in full into English. Then, ESPAC produced its own video copies with David Hoile as the editor and NRK as the main source, and with a four-page article attached with the headlines:

Norwegian People's Aid extends Conflicts and prolongs Oppression
Norwegian People's Aid and the Militarization of Aid in Sudan

Both the two videos and the articles contain tirades of accusations and lies regarding the NPA activities in South Sudan.

For many years, David Hoile has used his different positions to promote his extreme right wing views. He was also one of the managers in the consulting firm Westminster Associates in London. During the Sudan peace negotiations in Kenya from 2001 to 2005, he presented himself as a kind of free-lance advisor while he was working for the Khartoum regime, staying partly in Nairobi and partly in Khartoum. During a diplomatic reception in Khartoum, in 2002, he met a high-ranking Norwegian diplomat. Hoile offered to be an advisor for the Norwegian delegation during the negotiations, but the offer was politely turned down.

Hoile, USA and Darfur

There is little doubt that the Reagan administration in USA and the Thatcher administration in Great Britain agreed with much of what Hoile did in Central America and the southern parts of Africa.

However, the situation was different when it came to the USA and Sudan. During Bush senior's time as President of USA, the USA critique of Khartoum's regime increased.

In 1993 NPA was chosen as a channel for US emergency aid and assistance for the liberated areas in South Sudan.

Consequently, ESPAC and Hoile found themselves in an antagonistic relationship with USA. It began with Bush senior, intensified during the Clinton administration and became even stronger during Bush junior's administration.

The close cooperation that developed between NPA and USAID, American politicians, diplomats and NGO leaders, made it gradually more difficult for Hoile to continue his smear campaign against NPA.

In terms of the conflict in Darfur, Hoile supported from the very beginning the regime in Khartoum in their brutal handling of the conflict. The liberation fighters in Darfur saw the root of the conflict in part as being the extremely uneven distribution of resources and goods between the Khartoum region on one side and the rest of the country on the other side, and in part, the systematic and continuing oppression of the African ethnic groups in Darfur. Thus, the conflict dimensions in Darfur and South Sudan were very similar.

Hoile consistently and strongly opposed these views, held by the freedom fighters. Instead, he claimed that the root of the

Darfur conflict was ethnic, and he at several occasions characterized the conflict and war in Darfur since 2003 as a traditional African tribal war.

But David Hoile has been awarded for his support for and loyalty to the Bashir regime in Khartoum. The university of Nyala in Darfur has awarded him with academic credit for his many books and articles and employed him as a professor of peace studies. He is also a professor at the Institute for African and Asian studies at the University of Khartoum.

Hoile – Sri Lanka and NPA

In 2002 during the temporary peace truce in Sri Lanka, the Norwegian Foreign Ministry after consultations with the Sri Lanka government requested NPA to start a mine clearing programme in Sri Lanka. The programme went well for quite a while until some political disagreements with the government developed.

NPA was suddenly and without any justification accused of supporting the rebel group The Liberation Tigers of Tamil Eelam (**LTTE**). In addition, strong accusations of weapon smuggling to LTTE came suddenly out of the blue.

On July 27th, 2008, the spokesman and chief propagandist of the Sri Lankan Ministry of Defence, Walter Jayawardhana, published a long and very critical article on NPA entitled:

"Norwegian NGO used by LTTE also supplied Arms for an Insurgency in Sudan".

In the introduction, Mr. Jayawardhana had a reference to what NPA had been doing in Sri Lanka followed by some quotes from NPA s By-Laws. However, the main content of the article derived from the article by ESCAP which was written based on the NRK/Brennpunkt documentaries. The article was cited by several media institutions in Asia and of course damaged NPA's reputation in Sri Lanka and other Asian countries.

Hoile Condemned the International Criminal Court, ICC

Since the establishment of the ICC in 2002 David Hoile has been one of the court's harshest critics. This applies particularly to the position of ICC on the war crimes in Darfur. In 2005 Hoile wrote the book "Darfur in Perspective". He in the book criticizes everything and everyone who was critical to the Khartoum's regime way of dealing with the Darfur conflict. The American Government was not only accused of collaboration with Al Qaida in Darfur, but also for financing parts of the rebellion in Darfur against Khartoum.

Hoile's criticism was reinforced when the ICC in July 2008, accused Omar Bashir of being a war criminal and for crimes against humanity and issued an arrest warrant for Bashir.

Hoile has in recent years published several critical articles against ICC in African political magazines like "New African", and he has given several lectures in different fora in many African countries strongly attacking the ICC and perpetuating the view that ICC is anti-African. In Europe and America no one takes David Hoile seriously any more.

In Hoile's many writings and statements, it was not only the NPA that was targeted. USA during the Clinton administration and later during Bush Juniors administration, was also heavily criticized. The well-known American Sudan-researcher and activist, Eric Reeves, was accused of lack of objectivity and ability to analyze and do research. Not only that, Hoile called Eric Reeves a source of continuous disinformation on Sudan and Darfur.

Furthermore, he accused international media such as the *New York Times*, *Washington Post*, the *Guardian*, the *Independent*, the *Observer*, The *Economist*, *Financial Times* and the BBC, among others, for being dogmatic and unreliable.

A unique Defamation Campaign

It is both strange and reprehensible that Hoile and his institutions in many African fora and countries continue to be perceived as a serious and credible source of information. The NRK Brennpunkt editors used him uncritically as a source in their infamous documentary from 1999; "THE GUN RUNNERS". Not only that, in the media political battle that followed, the Brennpunkt editors presented Hoile as a respectable British academic in a letter to the Norwegian Press Complaints Commission.

When one views the role, ESPAC has played as a propaganda machine for the Khartoum regime in the conflict in Sudan over a time span of 15 years, it is rather amazing that NPA did not sustain more damage. But in the 1990s, when the ESPAC smear campaigns were at their worst, there was more than one close call.

NRK – BRENNPUNKT
(THE FOCAL POINT, the name of the programme in english)

NRK– new Accusations of Gun Running

Early in the winter of 1999, I received the first confidential messages from staff members in Nairobi that reporters from the NRK/Brennpunkt Programme were in Nairobi, trying to get into South Sudan. Their mission was to document NPA as a gun runner in South Sudan. The NRK reporters had neither in advance nor on mission contacted neither NPA in Oslo nor in Nairobi. The head of the NRK reporting team was Ola Flyum.

I had been working as an international reporter with NRK for 13 years, and I was NRK's first Africa-Correspondent ever in the period 1978-82, based in Nairobi. I had therefore some substantive experience and knowledge of the African political landscape. I decided to watch the NRK reporting team at work, very closely.

The management group of NPA and the staff at the Information Department were informed in all confidence about what was in the making from NRK. During 1999, I made several trips to Nairobi and in close cooperation with key members of our staff in Nairobi, we could trace quite in detail the footsteps of the reporting team. We from that work, learnt a lot about what the NRK team had been and was doing, their working methods as well as a lot about their sources. Therefore, we were well prepared for the NRKs first programme documentary that was broadcast on November 10, 1999. It carried the title:

"A DISGUISED GENOCIDE"
"Aid relief is prolonging the war"

This TV broadcast was made and aired 18 years ago, so there is no reason to go into detail about the contents in the documentary. But the main impression remains.

The so-called documentary lacked facts. It gave no factual information about Sudan and the many layers of conflict that existed. It contained nothing about the history of oppression and humiliation of the African ethnic groups, especially those in South Sudan. The leaders of the liberation movement were not interviewed. Their views on why they were fighting a freedom war, were absent.

On the homepage of NRK in 2017, we still find the title of the above-mentioned documentary, as well as the quote from the South Sudanese Bishop Paride Taban:

"Aid relief is like fattening the cow before it is slaughtered!"

The NRK reporter, Ola Flyum added the following:

"This brutal comment regarding the largest aid relief operation of our time in Sudan, comes from Bishop Paride Taban. He, as well as others, believe that as long as the 16-year-old civil war continues, there is little point with aid relief because it is the war that creates the constant starvation catastrophes."

The bishop was the main witness in the documentary. He was a church leader, but not a historian or a politician, and he in 1999 had for a long time been opposed to Garang and SPLM/A. However, the bishop did not have any answers as to how to make the tyrants in Khartoum respect human dignity and rights, the only mean to stop the war.

The broadcast of the so-called NRK documentary from 1999 coincided with the political trends of the 1990s. Critics, particularly on the conservative right side in the political debate in Western Europe and North America, argued that supporting liberation struggles and freedom fighters, was the same as contributing to keeping wars going and being part of genocide. Several European politically conservative writers advocated this simplified view.

The next NRK/Brennpunkt Programme was broadcast on November 17th, 1999 and carried the rather infamous title:

"THE GUN RUNNERS"

There was no question mark, only a statement that was made to appear as factual. NPA was then introduced as an organization dealing with gun running. There was absolutely nothing about NPA's humanitarian and development work in the liberated areas. It was considered irrelevant by the producer.

Still in 2017 we find the following statement on NRKs homepage:

"NPA has repeatedly been accused of transporting weapons to the rebels in South Sudan. The organization has repeatedly denied these allegations."

However, the Minister of Development Cooperation at the time, Hilde Frafjord Johnson, made the following comment in the broadcast:

"I am certain that there is no truth in these rumours."

She also personally requested that Sudan's Minister of Foreign Affairs to provide evidence to support his allegations that NPA was smuggling weapons which he never responded to.

Before the documentary was broadcast, I was in the capacity of Secretary General of NPA interviewed by the NRK reporter

Ola Flyum. He seemed uncertain and poorly prepared, and after a few questions he asked for a break in the recording to review his questions. During this break the camera was still recording without my knowledge, and I was filmed as I yawned and looked rather frustrated and irritated. This footage was used in the programme with the intention to portray me in such a way that my facial expression was my reaction to the accusations of weapon smuggling while it was my very visible reaction to a very poorly prepared reporter and his unsubstantiated accusations against and lies about NPA.

The uninformed viewer could hardly perceive the content of the programme as anything but alarming. It would be devastating for NPA and its reputation if people believed what was presented. The responsible reporters and editors in NRK had gone to great lengths with a clear intention to portray NPA as gun runners. Several film clips from so-called independent sources were used, and the programme was edited in a tendentious manner.

NPA brought a Complain before the Broadcasting Council and the Norwegian Press Complain Commission

The press immediately wanted comments. I was clear in my response and dismissed everything, and criticized NRKs poor journalism and skewing of the facts. NPA immediately reported the programme to both the Broadcasting Council and the Norwegian Press Complaints Commission.

The complaint was handled a few weeks later in a meeting of the Broadcasting Council. I represented NPA with a few colleagues. Brennpunkt' chief editor strongly protested at our presence. He said that our presence would weaken the Council's ability to remain impartial in its judgement, and thereby weaken NRKs integrity and reputation. The Chair of the Council Ivan Kristoffersen rejected the criticism.

The debate in that meeting of the Council was extensive, long and with a clear tendency of supporting the NPA complain. At the end, except for the Chair of the Council, all other members voted in favour of the proposal that criticized the editor in chief and the reporters behind the programme for undocumented and poor journalistic work.

There was also a debate in the Norwegian Press Complaints Commission, but they concluded very differently even though there in that meeting as well were critical voices. The commission concluded that there was insufficient basis for criticism against the editor in chief and the reporters who were responsible for the programme.

After the programme had been aired, NPA carried out an opinion poll to assess NPAs reputation and credibility and if it had been weakened by the infamous programme.

The opinion poll produced several interesting results. Among those who previously had strongly believed in NPA, their support fell by five percent, which was much less than anticipated. However, among those who in the past had showed little or no support for NPA, the support had substantially increased, and that was a big and pleasant surprise.

NRK's Sources

NRK used ESPAC and David Hoile as an important source. Whatever else they used as source material I do not fully know, but I and a few fellow NPA staff knew extremely well some of NRK's key informants. The following has not been reported before, and the details are made anonymous to protect my numerous sources.

At some point in the 1980s, a Norwegian professional pilot employed by a bigger European Aviation Company was caught in the act of smuggling drugs. He was sacked, taken to court, found guilty and convicted of drug smuggling and sentenced to several years in prison. While in prison, he behaved himself very well, and he was therefore given leave to see his wife and family after a brief imprisonment. However, well in advance of the visit, the wife who was also a pilot, had planned in detail their escape route. So as soon as the prisoner was with his family, the whole family escaped to California. The USA had and has no extradition agreements with Norway, as it does not have with most other countries, so the family was in safe surroundings far away from the Norwegian prison.

In California, they started a small, commercial aviation company. They bought several old Dakota planes, known for their durability. They are solidly constructed, safe in the air, do not require much landing space and can land on hard flat surfaces such as in the desert, on the savanna or on the tundra. The couple specialized in selling air transport services to the American film industry for transport of personal and equipment for shooting of films in areas like the desert, the savanna or the mountains. They were increasingly successful in their business activities.

After a while, as their son grew, he too became a pilot. But he was restless with an acting out behavior and lifestyle. His parents became rather worried, and after some family discussion, they proposed for the young man to go to Nairobi and seek employment as a pilot with one of the many small aviation companies at Wilson Airport. The young man listened to his parents, and he around 1993 went to Nairobi and Wilson Airport in search of a job.

One of the companies, SKYWAYS, flew at the time relief assistance to the Nuba mountains in a covert operation for a consortium of humanitarian organizations led by NPA. The missions were dangerous and it was difficult to find willing pilots. So, the young Norwegian man turned American from California, got the chance to be part of the crew, carrying out the covert emergency flight operations into the Nuba mountains. Sometimes he was an assistant, and a couple of times he flew as second pilot. He filmed some of what he saw and experienced during these flights.

Whenever the young man had time off, he was a frequent guest at Nairobi's many bars, nightclubs and brothels, and he developed a serious alcohol problem. The missions to Nuba Mountains departed at five o'clock in the morning, and often he was in no condition to fly. One morning when he was very much needed because of sickness with other crew members, he did not report to work. SKYWAYS had suddenly a difficult problem. The director called the hotel which he used to stay in and had the rather shocking news that the young man from California had been thrown out of the hotel because of violent behavior towards women. He had been arrested that same morning charged with a very violent and bloody rape of a woman who had agreed to come with him to his room. (The director of the hotel concerned, has personally told me this story).

The director of SKYWAYs had a very big problem with absent pilots. He needed the man for some urgent missions and negotiated a temporary bail with the Police in Nairobi.

One day the young pilot from California was on a mission with a plane from SKYWAYS to a small village in South Sudan, and had landed on an airstrip that was short. When he was to take off for his return to Nairobi, he overlooked the procedures for starting the engines and burned one of the two engines and failed to take off. The plane remained on the airstrip, while the pilot had to get a ride back to Nairobi.

When he told his employer about the accident, it turned out to be the last straw. The director got extremely angry, and the young pilot was fired on the spot and was told to leave Kenya as quickly as possible. If not, the director would immediately take him back to the police. The young man read the situation right and took the first flight back to California.

During Christmas 1998, he and his family in California had visitors from Norway. One evening the young man showed some of his film clips from Kenya. One of them was from his participation on missions to the Nuba Mountains, and he claimed that he had been part of gun running to the Nuba mountains with NPA in charge of the airlifts. The relatives from Norway got a copy of the film and according to my sources, gave it to a staff member at NRK/Brennpunkt in the early winter of 1999. That was the starting point, and the reporter Ola Flyum was put in charge of the project to make the story about NPA as the gun runner.

In the programme there was another so-called main witness who stated that he had been part of gun running with NPA, having flown guns to the Nuba mountains. He was a Norwegian as well, and had a past both as a missionary and a missionary pilot. Several decades ago, he and his wife were sent to a country in Africa and stationed at its capital as pilots serving the needs of mission organizations. His mission bought a plane that he was supposed to use to bring people and goods to the mission stations in the outskirts of the country far away from the capital. Everything ran smoothly in the beginning. The missionary couple and the male spouse pilot, upheld their Christian belief and made many flights for a very poor salary to the mission stations in the outskirts, certainly serving the needs of very poor and often very ill people.

But one day the country's dictator heard about the pilot, and decided that he needed a man like him to do some work for him. So, he decided to apply his charisma and charm to seduce the young couple who were working for a very low salary.

During a short time, the dictator and his aids again and again invited the young couple for parties and dinners, letting them in the beginning in small portions have the taste of dolce vita, or sweet life in Africa. The seduction project was very successful. After some time, the pilot was not flying for the missionaries any more, but for the dictator and his salary and payment was far better. The lives of the pilot and his wife had become very different. Suddenly they were a rich couple living in opulence.

However, in the mid-late 1990s the dictator, who for so long had believed that he was invulnerable, ran into very serious problems like dictators usually do despite what they believe when are at the peak of power. The dictator had to flee for his life and settled as a refugee in another African country. So, it was no longer safe for the pilot and his wife, being friends of the dictator, to stay in the capital. They lost their income and their dolce vita and decided to move to Kenya. But in Kenya it became difficult for the now, not so rich Norwegian to get any work, and certainly, to find job as a pilot was very difficult.

I knew the man when he was a young missionary pilot, but for a long time, I knew nothing about his life in the service of the dictator. One summer in the mid-1990s the couple was back in Oslo on holiday. I happened one day to meet them in the street, and I was taken by their very expensive dress. They told me that they had moved to Kenya, and that he had an interest in commissioned work for NPA in Nairobi and Sudan. I advised him to seek contact with the people in charge of our Nairobi office. He did so and was given a mission in 1994 to fly medical supplies to Rwanda. However, the mission was carried out in such a way that the NPA Nairobi office stopped its cooperation with him.

But SKYWAYS that flew relief assistance to the Nuba Mountains for the secret consortium was often looking for pilots. Therefore, the Norwegian, having been the dictator's friend, was commissioned as a co-pilot on a couple of missions to the Nuba mountains.

The pilot and his wife held a grudge against NPA because we had refused to give him any more work. I believe that that was a contributing factor as to why he could so easily lie about NPA in the NRK/Brennpunkt TV documentary. In addition, he was in my view, already at the time when the NRK documentary was broadcast, a totally demoralized person.

12

COMPETITORS, NETWORKS AND RELATIONS

NORWEGIAN CHURCH AID AND NORWEGIAN PEOPLE'S AID, COMPETITORS IN SUDAN

In hindsight, it might be easy to criticize the way and approach Norwegian Church Aid (NCA) initiated and carried out in its development programmes in South Sudan from 1973-1983, but there is no doubt that they did a lot of good work as well. Tens of thousands of people were lifted out of illiteracy. Health institutions became available for many people for the first time. Agriculture improved substantially, and infrastructure was built.

However, there was at the political level, three issues that made NCA's association with SPLM and its Chairman and SPLA's Commander in Chief, John Garang, and thereby NPA difficult. During the long war, this distance only increased. John Garang broached that subject several times in our conversations.

Firstly, SPLM/A had a revolutionary ideology during their first years, which many viewed as tantamount to Communism, and NCA did not approve. This was one reason why NCA supported the internal rebellion against John Garang in 1991, as it manifested itself during the split in Nasir in August 1991.

Secondly, NCA had built many alliances to the old regime in Juba. Many key actors of that regime did not support SPLM/A's leadership at that time.

Thirdly, NCA had a substantial amount of programme activity in the North of Sudan that was controlled from NCA's office in Khartoum, and NCA wanted to protect it. In addition, NCA maintained an office in the government held garrison town of Juba during the whole liberation war. To keep up the latter, they had to maintain a working relationship with the regime in Khartoum; the same regime that had declared NPA an enemy.

NCA's opposition to NPA being present in Sudan

The fact that NPA came in as a new Norwegian actor in relief and development work in South Sudan in 1986 under the leadership of Egil Hagen, was not seen to be in NCA's interest. This is described very clearly in Bibiana Dahle Piene's well-documented, well-written, and very interesting book from 2014: *Norge i Sudan (Norway in Sudan)* in the chapter entitled "The Fighting Roosters" (Kamphanene). On page 157 in the book the author reveals a piece of history from the time of 1986/87 that was unknown to me and most others until it was published in 2014. NPA had in the summer of 1987 applied to the NMFA for a grant of NOK 20 million for humanitarian assistance to the peoples of South Sudan. Even before NPA had applied, key staff of NCA started lobbying key staff in the Foreign Ministry with the aim to block any decision in support of a grant to NPA, and they were successful. In Bibiana's book on page 157 one finds the following quote from the chief administrator for emergency relief in the Foreign Ministry, carrying the title:

"VERY IMPORTANT!
Regarding the situation in South Sudan and the need for emergency aid, it is obvious that NCA with its many hundred locally employed staff has a major advantage (compared with NPA) when it comes to assisting local people in need. The emergency situation in the field of South Sudan is not of a magnitude that may justify a disregard of all political reservations which should be linked to a government funding for projects being carried out by somebody (NPA) that has formalized its cooperation with the rebel movement SPLA."

(The parenthesis in the quote above has been inserted by this author.)

In the Foreign Ministry as I have already described in chapter 3, THE BEGINNING, the NCA lobbyists continued their successful work. In the beginning of 1987 the attitude of the top officials in the Foreign Ministry was one of a total rejection of the NPA application for a grant for humanitarian assistance and any other NPA involvement in South Sudan. The principle argument being that NPA had taken a stand in support of what was named the rebellion. The political concept of a liberation war was disregarded, and the civil war seen as a power struggle between two major groups fighting for power in Khartoum.

The dominant view with the NMFA was that Norwegian government grants for humanitarian aid to Sudan should be channeled through UN and NGOs like NCA that stayed neutral in the conflict.

But a de facto argument in favour of a new policy was building up in the field. UN and NGOs like NCA had since the early fall of 1986 been working hard to establish an emergency operation to be named "**Operation Rainbow**" with airlifts out of Khartoum and drops of food in areas with people in desperate need. However, the Khartoum regime had refused to give its go ahead, because SPLM/A was demanding that part of the emergency food and medicines should be dropped in areas they controlled. If not, then, SPLA threatened to shoot down the planes. In Khartoum, NCA's strong and outspoken Secretary

General, Jan P Erichsen together with people like Mother Teresa were active in the corridors trying to persuade the government to let the operation start. But they all tried in vain. While all this dragged on, the people suffered from severe hunger and died by the tens of thousands.

The stalemate in Khartoum between UN and the regime became more and more embarrassing for UN and the International community. At the end, they gave up the whole idea of "Operation Rainbow". The NCA Secretary General Erichsen who used to consider the regime in Khartoum as trustworthy, returned to Oslo deeply disappointed. Not only that, he called Trond Bakkevig, the political advisor to Foreign Minister Thorvald Stoltenberg and told him that NCA no longer would oppose that NPA would get a grant for its Sudan programme.

In the fall of 1987, there was a big meeting of church organizations in Geneva, discussing the war, the draught and the famines killing the people of Sudan. At that meeting NPA became a topic, and mainly because it had taken a stand in support of the liberation war. There were many African representatives at the meeting, among them the renowned Kenyan church leader and diplomat, Bethuel Kiplagat. He was already at the time a friend of NPA, and he addressed the meeting on the conflict, why there was a liberation war and what the churches should do. He, of course, named and praised NPA. The political fallout from the meeting was that NPA was to be considered a worthy partner to support.

The Murder of Helge Hummelvoll and three Aid Workers

In September 1992, the Norwegian photographer Helge Hummelvoll was on assignment in South Sudan. On Sunday, September 27th, he was on his way out of South Sudan, travelling in a UN-car and accompanied by three aid workers. The car was caught in a crossfire between SPLA soldiers and defectors belonging to Riek Machar's group. Helge Hummelvoll and a Philippian aid worker were shot from behind when they tried to escape into the surrounding forest. The others were taken prisoner and later shot.

NCA held SPLA and John Garang responsible for this terrible and tragic event. Both NCA and the UN heavily criticized SPLA, and both the UN and NCA, as well as all the other OLS member organizations, in protest pulled out of South Sudan for a period.

After a long meeting with John Garang, NPA's Resident Representative for the Sudan programme, Helge Rohn, was convinced that SPLM/A was not guilty of the murders and dismissed the accusations against SPLA. NPA therefore decided to stay on in Sudan, and this made the relationship with NCA at all levels, and particularly in Nairobi, even worse.

This tragedy is described in detail in Bibiana Piene's book from 2014, *Norge i Sudan* (*Norway in Sudan*); in the chapter "The murders that Turned the Time" (Drapene som snudde tiden) pages 184 to 197.

The Conflict between SPLM and the Churches in South Sudan

NCA had a close relationship with the Sudan Council of Churches (SCC), which was established in 1965 with its headquarters in Khartoum. After the rebellion in 1983 the SCC had great difficulty in operating in South Sudan, especially in the areas controlled by SPLM/A. NCA cooperated with SCC, while SPLM/A never had a good relationship with them. I believe that this relationship influenced SPLM's attitude towards NCA and vice a versa.

To decrease the tension with SPLM, the church leaders in South Sudan took the initiative in 1989 to form the New Sudan Council of Churches (NSCC), with Bishop Paride Taban as leader. SPLM invited NSCC to work together, and they held a conference that was viewed as successful. During the first years, NSCC worked successfully in the liberated areas.

But then there was the rebellion against Garang and the split of SPLM into two factions in Nasir in 1991. This also divided the NSCC. Many church leaders agreed with the criticism against SPLM/A regarding the authoritarian leadership of John Garang and the many violations of basic human rights for which SPLA was responsible. Some church leaders, however, chose to remain on the same side as Garang and SPLM/A Mainstream, while others sided with Riek Machar and Lam Akol. NCA's leadership chose the latter, and the Secretary General, Jan P. Erichsen brought Lam Akol to Oslo.

At first, NPA in Oslo hesitated to take a side after the split in Nasir, but eventually the leaders were convinced by Dan Eiffe's reports from Nasir and Bor (see chapter 4). NPA therefore decided to support Garang and SPLM/A Mainstream.

The splitting up of SPLM/A, the Bor-massacre and the many military defeats suffered by SPLM/A Mainstream in the years following the events in Nasir, did not improve the relationship between NSCC and SPLM/A. At the same time there was an ever increasing tension building up within NSCC. In a desperate attempt to find a solution, Bishop Paride Taban suggested that both John Garang and Riek Machar should step down as leaders of the two SPLM/A factions and be replaced by church leaders.

The leaders of NSCC then decided to arrange a mediation conference between SPLM/Mainstream and the defectors in Nasir. SPLM made NSCC aware of the fact that the defectors from Nasir had close political and military bonds with Khartoum. The church leaders refused to believe it. The mediation conference lead by one of Kenya's highest church leaders, failed.

As this was happening, I had several meetings with John Garang. I asked what he thought about the mediation meeting. He distanced himself from the meeting and was very critical to the fact that NCA had funded and actively participated in it.

The bad relationship between SPLM and NSCC continued for several years. Not until the mediation conference between the two parties in Yei in 1997 did the situation improve.

Everything that happened between SPLM and NSCC contributed to the tension between NCA and NPA. The tension was present at all levels, both at home and abroad.

However, this is a long time ago. Almost all of us who were in the middle of this conflict and rivalry between two Norwegian NGOs working in Sudan, are now retired. A new generation has taken over, and I am happy to know that NCA and NPA share a good working relationship in the current very difficult times in South Sudan.

NPA'S RELATIONS TO SWEDEN

During my time in NPA, the relationship to Sweden and many of our Swedish partners in development cooperation and relief aid, was quite problematic. Sweden was known both for having a substantial development cooperation programme and for having the political courage of supporting in places where others hesitated. Unfortunately, when it came to NPA in Sudan, Sweden hesitated.

I was several times with Sida in Stockholm, trying to mobilize support for our Sudan programme. I was always well-received, but there was a constant ambivalence. NPA had sided with the rebels in the South, and there were rumours of weapon smuggling. At the same time, there was a brutal war and massive human suffering.

However, NPA was met with considerable political good will from the Social-Democratic "Olof Palme International Centre", Sweden's closest parallel organization to NPA. They, however, had limited resources and other political priorities in their international cooperation.

In 1997, NPA finally received a positive reply from Sida. They were willing to support the NPA health programme with funding for the four hospitals NPA was running in South Sudan.

Lundin Oil

We were aware that NPA in Sweden had an almost invisible, but powerful political adversary in Lundin Oil. This Swedish company had for a long time had its eye on the possibility of being a partner in exploiting Sudan's oil reserves.

The same year that NPA received support from Sida, Lundin Oil, as a partner in an international consortium of oil companies, was given the right to drill for oil, in what was called Block 5, just over the border in South Sudan. In the years that followed, Lundin Oil through their cooperation with the regime in Khartoum, was accused of being responsible for displacing tens of thousands of people from the land in the areas they were drilling. The local people in these areas was forced to leave their homes and chased away and left in utter poverty, and many died.

I do not know what political arrangements Lundin Oil had with the Government of Sudan or the Government of Sweden, but there was, of course, political communication and thereby a political relationship of some substance. The way I see it, Lundin Oil was a loyal partner with the regime in Khartoum. It had all the information necessary about the conflict. Not in any source I have had access to, did the representatives of Lundin Oil convey any real concern for human rights violations and people dying from famine and war. Lundin Oil was one of many international oil companies that were bed fellows in the brutal war that Khartoum carried out against the people in the South fighting for their freedom. Lundin Oil's people also had a close relationship to Riek Machar while Machar was a partner to and a member of the government in Khartoum. The Lundin Oil people also had a highly critical view of SPLM/A and its Chairman, John Garang.

Carl Bildt

Carl Bildt has held many high-ranking positions in Swedish and international politics. He was the leader for the Moderates, Sweden's conservative political party, Prime Minister, Peace Negotiator in the Balkans and Foreign Minister.

In the year 2000 he became a board member for Lundin Oil. A short while later he was put in charge of a group within Lundin Oil that was to consider the challenges associated with oil production in Sudan.

In the spring of 2002 Carl Bildt as a board member, was on a business trip to Khartoum and Nairobi. Riek Machar was at that particular time staying in Nairobi. He was in the final phase of this negotiations with the leadership of SPLM regarding the conditions for his return to SPLM/A Mainstream.

Carl Bildt one day invited Machar for lunch to discuss the peace negotiations and Lundin Oil's possibility of oil production in Sudan and South Sudan. The next day Carl Bildt invited the Norwegian diplomat, Halvor Aschjem, to lunch. He was the Norwegian Special Envoy on Sudan, closely associated with the Norwegian Minister of Development Cooperation, Hilde Frafjord Johnson, and seconded by his government to the Peace Negotiations on Sudan.

Carl Bildt and Halvor Aschjem had an enjoyable lunch, discussing many pertinent issues related to the possibility of peace in Sudan, oil exploration in Sudan and South Sudan, the Horn of Africa and other issues. Bildt told Aschjem about his lunch meeting with Riek Machar, which he had found very interesting; particularly the part about Lundin Oil and the possibility of future oil production in Sudan.

Aschjem listened with great interest. Then he asked whether Bildt had any plans to see John Garang. Bildt looked at Achjem for a while, and then he said:

"John Garang, is he a potential future leader in Sudan?"

Aschjem allowed himself a small pause before answering:

"I believe that Garang has a very important future role to play as leader in Sudan. You must never make the mistake of underestimating John Garang. My advice is that you invite him for a meeting as soon as possible."

But Carl Bildt did not meet with John Garang. Probably because in the opinion of certain so-called international experts on Sudan, they believed that Garang did not have the support of the people and therefore could not win in an open election in Sudan.

I have this information from Aschjem himself. I was frequently in Nairobi during the period the peace negotiations lasted, and Aschjem and I had our informal and discreet meetings during breakfast at Fairview Hotel in Nairobi whenever I was there. Halvor and I certainly enjoyed some 20 breakfasts talks together.

The Swedish Church and Missionary Organizations

Throughout most of the 1990s, NPA faced another very critical political environment in Sweden; the church and missionary organizations with activities in Sudan and on the Horn of Africa. Most of them heavily criticized both SPLM/A and NPA. The young radical theologian Anna Karin Hammar was one of several and without doubt the leading critic. She is the sister of Karl Gustav Hilding Hammar, who was at that time the Archbishop in Uppsala.

When it came to SPLM/A, the criticism revolved around what was said to be their brutal warfare, and further more accusations of torture of war prisoners and cruel treatment of the civilian population in areas where the war front was moving.

When it came to NPA, the criticism revolved around that NPA had taken a political stand in support of the liberation struggle and that NPA thereby was indirectly responsible for SPLM/A's crimes. In addition, the accusation against NPA of weapon smuggling was a standard repeat in these political circles in Sweden.

In the spring of 1999 the Swedish Church together with many missionary organizations called a meeting about Sudan in Uppsala. Anna Karin Hammar played a central role in organizing the meeting, and she was to be a main speaker. I heard about the meeting from the SPLM Representative in the Nordic countries, John Duku, who was invited. I immediately wrote to the organizer and explained about NPA's programme work in Sudan and why we had taken a political stand in support of the liberation struggle. I then asked if it was possible for me to be invited to participate in the meeting. I received a curt reply in which the organizer stated that I was not wanted.

A little later Sida without any advance warning abruptly cancelled their support to our health programme in Sudan. The reason given was that we had insufficient documentation of what we did at the hospitals, lack of financial control and insufficient reporting on it all. The issue of documentation was sheer nonsense. We had solid documentation regarding our activities at the hospitals. For the rest, if there was any shortcoming, we could have worked together with Sida to improve our reporting.

The reasons given by Sida was in my view, nothing but a kind of plastering over political problems in Sweden. I think Sida was under political pressure first and foremost from Lundin Oil, and strangely enough also the progressive Church leader Anna Karin Hammar and Swedish missionary organizations.

The consequences of losing the support from Sida were dramatic. We were not able to find new donors, and we for this reason had to cut down both on the numbers of hospitals we ran, and the number of people we could treat. Thousands of innocent people who desperately needed medical assistance could not get it and died. I was with NPA colleagues in Stockholm a few times, trying to convince Sida to reverse its decision and come back as a donor, but it was all in vain.

Kenya, Uganda, Ethiopia and Eritrea

NPA could not have accomplished anything in South Sudan without the friendly understanding and political support we had from government authorities in the neighboring countries on the Horn of Africa.

When Egil Hagen arrived in Kenya in 1986, he met with the Ministry of Foreign Affairs' powerful Permanent Secretary, Bethuel Kiplagat. During their first discussions, Egil secured a trust and support from Kiplagat that came to be of utmost importance for NPA.

When I in the spring of 1987 was in South Sudan on assignment for NPA, Egil Hagen and Vegard Bye from NPA introduced me to Kiplagat. At the meeting, he confirmed that the Kenyan Government strongly supported NPA's work in South Sudan, while having the NPA headquarters in Nairobi.

Later during the fall of 1990, when Norway was thrown out of Kenya, NPA had some problems with the State Office for international and national volunteer organizations in Kenya. They had some concerns about us. NPA had an office in Nairobi, but no development projects in Kenya. They wanted some. We replied that it was not that easy, because Kenya had broken the diplomatic relations with Norway.

We emphasized that NPA's office in Nairobi had many Kenyan employees. Every year, large amounts of food and other aid relief was unloaded in Mombasa heading for South Sudan, and the transportation companies were primarily Kenyan, who earned considerable money on the transport. Finally, we emphasized that we made most of our purchases in Kenya, running into millions of US dollars every year. In short, NPA spent a considerable amount of money in Kenya that benefited the economy at large.

But despite all this documentation from our side, our relationship to the Kenyan NGO Office remained tense and difficult for some years to come.

Apart from this experience with the Kenyan NGO Office, and the story narrated in chapter 8 about the conflict we had with the Tax and Revenue Authority about taxes, Kenya was for the main, and when it came to the political context, a reliable host country for NPA during the difficult period of 20 years between 1986 and 2006. Then NPA moved to Juba.

Regarding Uganda, Dan Eiffe and Ken Miller were the main intermediaries to the authorities. NPA had a large transit base in Koboko, in north-west Uganda and a small office in Kampala. The authorities in Uganda were all the time updated on our activities and had a good overview of what we did. We felt that we had the full support of the Government of Uganda for what we did in South Sudan. In addition, president Museveni and the SPLM Chairman John Garang, were personal friends.

In Ethiopia, the context was more delicate, but changed for the better. When the dictator Mengistu was in power, NPA had nothing to do with the regime. Then, there was a revolutionary power shift in 1991, when the ragged army of young boys and girls from the Tigrayan People's Liberation Front (TPLF), marched in to Addis Ababa, and chased the dictator and his lackeys out of the country.

NPA and The Norwegian Development Fund had for many years a cooperation with the Relief Society of Tigray (REST), the humanitarian wing of the TPLF. NPA was pleased when TPLF in 1991 was able to remove the old communist dictatorship.

However, the new regime in Ethiopia chased SPLM/A and all the refugees from Sudan out of Ethiopia. More than 200 000 homeless and destitute refugees had to begin a difficult and dangerous journey back to their homeland in South Sudan.

Bol wek Agoth, South Sudan's Ambassador to Norway until the fall of 2014, was among some 30 000 - 40 000 youth who during the 1980s, walked, sometimes for several months, to join the SPLA in Ethiopia. He was in Ethiopia as a young officer when TPLF took power. He was part of the forced exodus from Ethiopia, and he shared some of his memories with me:

"When it became commonly known that the TPLF-army was marching on Addis Ababa and that they would conquer the capital, the Ethiopian Government Army had mass desertions of soldiers. Even high-ranking officers who worked with SPLA deserted. After TPLF took power in Addis, they ordered all Sudanese to leave Ethiopia immediately. Troops from the new National government came from Gambella to make sure that we obeyed orders and left. But I need to add that in my memory, we did not experience any real hostility from the new government troops. Everything went orderly, without major incident, no shooting. They shoved us out with a gentle hand."

NPA's secret ways through Sudan into Tigray in Ethiopia

The SPLM/A leadership was not aware that NPA and The Norwegian Development Fund for many years had had a close cooperation with REST, the humanitarian wing of TPLF. NPA also supported the liberation struggle in Eritrea.

Our cooperation with REST in Tigray was in political terms an easy one, but making the cooperation possible in practical terms was very difficult. It was of course not possible to reach the areas of Tigray where the liberation struggle was raging via the capital in Ethiopia. Unorthodox and alternative roads had to be used.

Fortunately for us, until the power shift in Ethiopia in the summer of 1991, the relationship between Sudan and Ethiopia was very bad. Therefore, the authorities in Sudan looked the other way whenever NPA and our colleagues from the Norwegian Development Fund used Sudan and Khartoum as ports of entry into Tigray.

But staff members from NPA in Oslo on their way to Tigray had to keep the fact that they were NPA staff a total secret whenever they applied for a visa to Sudan. While we had solidarity programmes in Tigray, NPA did the same in the territories liberated by SPLM/A in South Sudan. The Khartoum regime considered as we have already learnt in previous chapters, NPA an enemy in the fields of South Sudan.

After the coup d'état in 1989 in Sudan, the new military and Islamic regime was extremely preoccupied with identifying potential enemies. For this reason, whenever staff from NPA and The Development Fund came to Sudan, an entry visa was not enough. They had to apply for a new travel permit every time they traveled from one town in Sudan to another.

There was an incident once. Svein Olsen from NPA arrived in Sudan. He had his entry visa, but did not have all the permits he needed for travelling from one town to another. He was checked by the local security in one of the towns, he had no permit for travelling through that town, and he was taken back to the airport in Khartoum and sent out of the country.

Friends in Tigray

The cooperation with REST created an atmosphere of trust. NPA's staff on working visits in the field, were invited for informal meetings with TPLF's undisputed leader Meles Zenawi, who after the takeover in the summer of 1991 became Ethiopia's Prime Minister, a position he held until he died from cancer in the summer of 2012. He was very familiar with NPA's work both in Tigray and South Sudan.

In addition, there was an intermediary that NPA HQ in Oslo was not aware of, a striking, intelligent American journalist named Gayle Smith. She was an active participant in the liberation struggle and stayed in Tigray for many years. She met with NPA staff in the field, and she was very familiar with our work in Tigray. She was also a close friend of Meles Zenawi. In the USA she belonged to the Democratic Party.

After TPLF took power in Ethiopia and Meles Zenawi became Prime Minister, Gayle Smith, while Bill Clinton was the President of USA, worked systematically to improve relations between Ethiopia and the USA.

The relationship between the leaders in SPLM/A led by John Garang and the new leaders in Ethiopia gradually changed for the better, and in 1993-94 SPLM/A once again received political and military support from Ethiopia.

Eritrea, another friend in the Horn of Africa

When it came to Eritrea, in 1984 the leaders of the Eritrean People's Liberation Front (EPLF) requested NPA to bring food relief into the liberated areas of Eritrea. Egil Hagen and Terje Skavdal headed the first mission into Eritrea which was also supported by NPA's 'sister' organizations in Denmark and Germany. Hagen and Skavdal in cooperation with people from EPLF were in the fields for three weeks distributing food in the liberated areas. During this time, they met both with Isaias Afwerki and other leaders in the EPLF, thus contributing to the development of good relations with NPA.

After the independence of Eritrea in 1993, the new government granted SPLM permission to establish a main office in the capital, Asmara. Later this was expanded to include all democratic opposition groups in Sudan organized under the umbrella of the National Democratic Alliance (NDA).

NPA had thus during the 1980s and 1990s established and developed a rather unique, political solidarity cluster of networks in the Horn of Africa and in East Africa that was tied to the liberation struggles in Ethiopia, Eritrea and Sudan/South Sudan. In the years to follow, NPA benefitted greatly from this, because it provided NPA with channels of political influence that other NGOs did not have.

Meles Zenawi was Head of TPLF, the Tigray People's Liberation Front when NPA staff first met him in the field of Tigray in the 1880ies, in the midst of the liberation struggle. He later became the Prime Minster of Ethiopia and from around 1992 a close supporter of the liberation struggle in South Sudan. Picture from Wikimedia commons

Isaias Afwerki was the Head of EPLF, the Eritrean People's Liberation Front, and later the President of Eritrea. I once when reporting for NRK in 1981, met him in the field in the midst of the liberation struggle. He made an impression as a very strong and tough leader and Commander in Chief. Picture from Wikipedia

13

SOME OF NPA'S KEY SUPPORTERS

"THE LOST BOYS OF SUDAN."
THE LONG MARCH TO ETHIOPIA
THE TALE OF ONE BOY

The liberation war in South Sudan is a war with a lot of tragedies. The story of 30-40 000 young boys who walked to Ethiopia in large groups between 1984 and 1988 is one of these. The marches lasted for several months and those taking part, have been given the name "The Lost Boys of Sudan". According to SPLM, approximately 28 000 survived these marches, while others claim only 20 000 did.

Today, the stories from these marches are told by tens of thousands of families in South Sudan. Since 2005 many documentaries, TV-series, films and books have been made based on these children's stories. Most of them are produced in USA.

One of these books; "What *is the What*," is written by the American author Dave Eggers. It is a great book, based on the story of Valentino Achak Deng, one of the boys who survived the march. It is a touching story. They walked without water or food for several days, many became ill and many died. Most of the boys were between seven and fifteen years old, while some were older. There were also some young girls.

Some were captured by the militia groups who worked for the regime in Khartoum and sold as slaves. Amazingly enough, some of them managed to escape slavery and make their way to Ethiopia. Some of their experiences are told in the novel.

Bol wek Agoth, South Sudan's ambassador to Norway from the summer 2011 to the fall 2013, was one of them. He told me about his experience during the march to Ethiopia, here is an excerpt:

"*I come from the same region as Salva Kiir. When I was 19 years old and had just finished school, I decided to become a freedom fighter. This was in 1984. We were a group of boys from my village and the surrounding area, who began to walk. After a while, there were many of us, about 12 000, mostly boys. We walked every day and several nights for a month before we reached Ethiopia. During our march, we were attacked by Khartoum's soldiers, both from the air and on the ground. Sometimes animals attacked us at night. Many were sick and dying. It was a very difficult march.*"

Yet, many did reach Ethiopia. They lived in large camps and went to school. Then, because of the revolution in Ethiopia during the summer of 1991, the young boys and the hundreds of thousands of other refugees from South Sudan were deported. The retreat march was in many ways even more demanding. Several times the fleeing flocks of people were attacked by Ethiopian military as well as Southern Sudanese militia groups, paid by the regime in Khartoum. Again, many thousands lost their lives. NPA provided food and medicine for the refugees and the young boys on their way back to South Sudan.

Some of the youth started to work on NPA's projects and received support to go to school and to study. One of them I know well. His name is Jacob Atem Anyieth Atem. He is now in his late 30s, has a family and works for NPA in Juba. He shared his experience in a letter he wrote to me, and which I could share with my readers:

"I was eleven years when I one day in 1987 left my village in Bor with a few of my friends at the request of the zonal Commander who was Kuol Manyang Juuk. We were told that the purpose of the march was to take us to school in Ethiopia. On my arrival in Maar which was the assembly center, it was late evening, we found a large number of boys mostly from the neighboring villages of Ajuong, Nyuak, Kongor and Nyaruweng. There were so many boys resting that they covered a large field. I could hardly understand their words although they too spoke our indigenous Dinka language. Their pronunciation was so different that I could not understand what they said. It was strange, and it was frightening, not to be able to understand people who spoke my own language. We spent one night in Maar and left the next morning for the land area of Bor. There, we met another huge number of boys mostly from Barel Gazel and Bentiu in Baidit, the headquarter of Commander Kuol Manyang Juuk. Our number increased to about 26,000 boys. In addition, some families were marching as well.

We walked through the thick bushes of Bor on our way to Pibor, and we walked for six days before we reached Pibor town. We rested there until the dry season made it possible to walk to Ethiopia. As we marched, we saw human skulls and other remains scattered in the semi-desert between Bor and Pibor. We were told that all these bones were from physically and mentally weak boys who could not stand the strain of previous marches, but had succumbed to thirst and hunger and then died. This served as a warning to us. We understood that we had to strengthen ourselves and develop a very strong will to overcome thirst and starvation. We succeeded, and we could walk for three to four days without food and water. We normally only got food and water when we rested at SPLA Camps.

Crossing swollen rivers was another hurdle for us. A few of us who grew up along the riverside, could swim to the other side of the river, but most boys needed help from friends and SPLA escort units, though some of them, despite the assistance rendered, drowned in the deep rivers. On our arrival to Pinyundo – a camp in Ethiopia, we spent a week without food. The only source of food was wild fruits in the bush, but since we were very many, the available wild fruits in the nearby bushes were gone in less than two days. Two tractors that brought bags of Maize from Itang, a refugee camp a long distance away in Central Ethiopia, became our rescue. These few bags were distributed among us, and we had to really economize with the maize to make it last for at least a week. We were then expecting food supplies from UNCHR. This period was a very critical one, and a significant number of my fellow boys died of hunger and other related diseases. I remember that we had to bury more than 15 people each day in my (Battalion) group only. The UNHCR finally delivered a lot of food to the camp; this was in form of maize, beans, lentils and oil, and our days got better.

After two months in the camps, Dr. John Garang came on visit. He told us that we were the seeds of South Sudan, and as schools would be opened soon, we should study hard to be able to serve our country well. After Dr. John Garang left, we were later organized into 16 groups, each group composed of 1,800 boys, making a total of roughly 28,000 boys. The number had increased as we met other boys on our way who joined us in the camps. We were instructed to build our school-buildings ourselves, using grass, woods and poles that we cut from the forest. All schools were built in three months. Then, another problem emerged, we lacked discipline and respect for each other as we all came from different regions and tribes. The only solution for this was to take us to military training centres to instill some discipline in us and develop some ability to work together. The training was organized in two phases, and each phase lasted for four months.

After the military training, we all returned to our original camps, and schools were opened. I started school for the first time in my life in 1987, 11 years old. This was the turning point in my life. I must admit that had I not been part of the march to Ethiopia, I would not have known the value of education. It was thanks to the SPLM leadership at the time and Dr. John Garang, that we, the young children of Southern Sudan, got this rare opportunity to go to school in the bush. I stayed in Ethiopia from 1987 to 1991.

We had to leave Ethiopia in 1991 when Mengistu, the former president of Ethiopia and a strong supporter of SPLM/A, was overthrown. We, the first few days, walked back to Pochalla, a town on the Ethiopian-South Sudan border. Then, I and other colleagues in the red Army were recruited into the SPLA combat units. I was 15 years and had finished Primary five at the time. We moved from Pochalla to Kapoeta where I was trained how to operate a radio. I became a radio operator in the headquarters of some SPLA commando units that went on the offensive under the name; "Bright star Campaign" (BSC). We defended Kapoeta until it was recaptured by the Sudan Armed Forces in 1992. This defeat was a great loss to SPLA, but we were asked to join another SPLA unit that was positioned at Jebellen along Juba-Nimule road. I ended this time up in the headquarters of General Oyai Deng Ajak.

He is one of the people who has greatly contributed to the betterment my life. Oyai sent me and some young boys from the Nuba Mountain to the displaced persons camp at Labone. From there, I found my way to a new camp in Northern Uganda where I could get back to school. After finishing Ordinary level (O Level) in Uganda, I came back to the camp at Labone, where NPA had a centre for the distribution of food and other emergency items. NPA was running the Labone Hospital as well. I got employed by NPA in 1999 as a nursing aid. I worked for two years before attending a medical school in Chukudum and subsequently Yei. After three years, I graduated from Yei Medical Training School as a Laboratory Technician with a certificate. I then continued working with the NPA health programme until December 2009. Then, I was asked to be a staff member on the NPA/SPLM Party Building Project. However, I had already before that, enrolled in a Bachelor Programme at Kampala International University (KIU), on a distant learning programme. NPA covered tuition while I continued working on the NPA/SPLM Party Building Project. I am currently undertaking a master programme in Project Planning and Management at Cavendish University, Uganda.

This is in brief my story as one of the Lost Boys of Sudan which also became my way of getting education and establishing the first contacts with NPA. There has been many ups and downs in my life on the way to what I am today."

Bethuel Kiplagat, the rock fast friend of NPA in Kenya

NPA's relationship with Bethuel Kiplagat began with the founding father of the NPA Sudan Programme, Egil Hagen. They met shortly upon Egil's arrival in Kenya in January 1986. How they met, I do not know in detail. But Bethuel Kiplagat had at the time a powerful position in the Government Administration as he was the Permanent Secretary in the Ministry of Foreign Affairs, and it is certain that one main topic at their first meeting, was the liberation struggle in Sudan and whether Egil Hagen could operate some emergency projects from Nairobi through Turkana and into South Sudan.

Kiplagat was 27 years old at the time of Kenya's independence in 1963. He as one of the few young Kenyans who before that had had the opportunity to qualify for academic studies. He was admitted to the only university in East Africa at the time, the Makerere University in Kampala, where he studied physical science. Upon graduation, he got a scholarship to study the Sociology of Religion at the famous Sorbonne University in Paris.

When he returned to Kenya, he was involved in the work of the National Christian Council of Churches in Kenya, and in 1971 he was appointed its Deputy Secretary General. Both before that and during his time with the Council, he developed a strong interest for social justice, human rights, conflict resolution and related themes. He has been involved in the search for solutions to the problems of the peoples of Sudan since the early 1970s. He was for a period the Director of Relief, Rehabilitation and Development Programme of the Sudan Council of

Churches in South Sudan, and he has been a longtime advisor to IGAD on Sudan and other conflict issues on the Horn of Africa.

In 1978, he was asked to become Kenya's Ambassador to France, and three years later he was moved to London as Kenya's Ambassador to Great Britain.

In 1983, he was appointed the Secretary General of the KMFA, a position he held until 1991 when he fell out of favour with his authoritarian President, Daniel arap Moi.

Kiplagat became during his time as the Permanent Secretary in the Ministry of Foreign Affairs a very important partner for NPA in Kenya. When he had his first meetings with Egil Hagen in the winter of 1986, he welcomed NPA to Kenya. When NPA's Secretary General and International Director were on a mission in Kenya in the summer of 1986 to assess the work of Egil Hagen, and update themselves on the conflict in Sudan, Kiplagat strongly encouraged them to increase NPA's role in South Sudan with the aim to stay in South Sudan for a long time.

When I headed the NPA Assessment Mission into South Sudan in the spring of 1987, I met with Kiplagat and had his strong support for both my mission and the work of NPA.

In 1998, NPA had as narrated in chapter 8, a difficult conflict with the Kenyan Government's administration on tax issues, how to register in Kenya and more. When the Kenyan Government then asked us to have appointed a local board of Kenyans for NPA in Kenya, the NPA staff in Nairobi came up with a proposal, we in Oslo immediately endorsed. They proposed for Kiplagat to become the chairman of the board and to let him have a say, who should be the board members.

Kiplagat said yes, proposed for other board members with a good reputation, and we appointed accordingly and reported the outcome to the relevant government office. They did of course, not like our way of handling the issue, but there was nothing they could say. We had followed their guidelines, but we surprised them with the appointment of Bethuel Kiplagat as the NPA Chairman in Kenya. They did not like the appointment of

Kiplagat who had a very good reputation for honesty, fairness and transparency. He was such a strong personality with a lot of political influence that there was nothing they could do.

Kiplagat was an excellent chairman for NPA in Kenya from 1998 until 2003. He steered NPA away from troubled seas, and he gave a lot of very valuable political advice both regarding the situation in Kenya and the liberation struggle in Sudan, a struggle which he passionately supported.

With the change of regime in Kenya in 2002, and the Kibaki government in power, introducing new and easier rules for NGOs in Kenya, the need for a local NPA Board was no longer justified, and with the consent of Kiplagat, it was dissolved.

Both before and after his role with NPA, Kiplagat has continued to serve many good courses in Kenya and Africa. He was a longtime advisor for the civil society of Kenya and East Africa on peaceful conflict resolution. He mediated in the conflict in Uganda in 1985/86, and he did the same in Ethiopia in the conflict around 1990/92. He chaired for many years the International Commission for Reconciliation and Peace in Somalia.

He was for a long period the Chairman of the Board of Directors of AMREF. He was one of the founding fathers and mothers of the International Peace Academy, and he was until late the Chancellor of Egerton University and the Director of the African Peace Forum. Bethuel Kiplagat passed away on 14th July 2017.

Roger Winter, – A Pillar of Rock Support for NPA in USA

Roger Winter met Egil Hagen for the first time in Nairobi in 1986, just after Egil had started his work in South Sudan. In a very short time, they developed an extraordinary, good relationship, and Roger Winter became the most important support link for NPA in relation to American authorities. He facilitated contacts in Congress, the State department and USAID. When Egil died, and Helge Rohn became the new Resident Representative, the cooperation developed even further. Roger Winter was certainly instrumental in initiating the discussions between State Department and NPA in the summer of 1993 that led to USA choosing NPA as its bilateral channel for humanitarian assistance to the peoples behind the frontlines in South Sudan.

Roger Winter is an American activist. During his youth, he joined the Salvation Army and the Civil Rights Movement in USA. He is married to an African-American woman and has always been strongly involved in African affairs. In 1981, he was appointed the Executive Director of the U.S. Committee for Refugees.

Politically, he is a democrat. As the Executive Director of the U.S. Committee for Refugees, he travelled widely and reported back to U.S. audiences on the massive refugee tragedies in many parts of the world, primarily in Africa. In 2003, he was appointed Assistant USAID Administrator with a special responsibility for Sudan. Later he was part of a State Department team for South Sudan. Between 2006 and 2013 he was a volunteer advisor and goodwill ambassador for the Government in South Sudan.

But in July 2013 Roger Winter along with three other leading American supporters of the liberation of South Sudan, Eric Reeves, John Prendergast and Ted Dagne, wrote an open letter to President Salva Kiir, strongly criticizing the many violations of human rights and acts of corruption committed by members of the government, the government administration and SPLA. They strongly warned against the development of an authoritarian regime in South Sudan and against escalating the conflict within SPLM.

When I read the letter a day after it was published, I had a few instant reactions. Firstly, I agreed with everything my four American friends wrote. Secondly, I felt as they did, great pain at what was happening in South Sudan. I thought of the time of the liberation struggle, how committed my own NPA staff was in their contribution and even more, our African staff. I thought of our American friends and how committed they were. Lastly and mostly, I thought of the liberation fighters who gave their lives in the struggle, and I thought of the poor people of South Sudan. They had suffered so much for so long. They had such great expectations to what independence and freedom would mean to their everyday lives. But already in the summer of 2013 it was evident, to all who could see. The people of South Sudan was being let down by a key group of their own former liberators, a key group led by the President himself, Salva Kiir. These men had turned themselves into killers and cleptokrats and were destroying the people and the land they once said they liberated.

After the publication of the letter, I understand that Roger Winter was no longer welcome as advisor and goodwill ambassador for South Sudan.

Through the years, Roger Winter has had considerable political influence regarding USAs African policies. He worked hard to get Susan Rice's appointment as Assistant Secretary of State for African Affairs during the Clinton administration. She visited the Horn of Africa and Sudan several times, and she was well-acquainted with NPAs work in South Sudan.

Roger Winter was several times with NPA in South Sudan and the Nuba Mountains. He facilitated meetings in Washington for NPA. Roger Winter was a guest of honour at NPAs National Convention in August 1999.

Regarding Sudan and the regime in Khartoum, Roger Winter has been a scathing critic of the egregious oppression Bashir's regime represents, and he has been an advocate for American military intervention to remove the Khartoum regime.

An American observer, Eliza Griswold, described Roger Winter this way, in the New York Times on June 15th, 2008:

"*It's not evenhandedness that makes him effective; it's his total commitment to the people of South Sudan and a conviction, which has only grown with the years, that the government in Khartoum is, a brutal cabal. After two decades of fighting for their rights at negotiating tables, he has gained the southerners' complete trust.*"

In the same article Eliza Griswold quotes one of the intellectuals from South Sudan:
"He's simple and clear," Edward Lino, the southern government's chairman in Abyei, told me. "He doesn't mince words. He's a great man" who also "has great, great push."

Roger Winter is a morally and politically dedicated person, who promotes his cause with fervor. With his warm and energetic personality; it is easy to like Roger Winter.

Jan Pronk, the Dutch Minister of Development Cooperation on visit with NPA in South Sudan

Early one cold winter morning in 1993, the telephone rang in my NPA office. When I answered it, I heard a voice say:

"Hello, my name is Jan Pronk. I am the Minster for Development Cooperation in the Dutch Government. I am calling you to say that I in Nairobi have met with your Resident Representative Helge Rohn and his colleagues. They are great guys, and they organized a trip for me into South Sudan. I saw your humanitarian work under very difficult conditions, and I am impressed, very impressed.

The reason why I am calling you now is to say that our government will grant 20 mill NOK to NPA's work in South Sudan and the Nuba Mountains. But there is one condition, the Norwegian Ministry of Foreign Affairs must increase their grant to match our grant. If your Ministry does not do that, then our grant will only be 10 million NOK."

For a moment I was speechless, but I managed to stutter a thank you. Pronk also asked me to have NPA organize the necessary administrative work to have the grant released. He further told me to keep him informed about the response from the Norwegian Foreign Ministry. We were overwhelmed by this surprise news, and I immediately called Helge Rohn to tell him the good news. Helge said that Pronk had come on visit at short notice, and he added:

"A Dutch reporter, Erst Temmermann, came to see us in Nairobi. She represented one of the largest newspapers in Netherlands and

wanted to do a comprehensive article about NPA in the field. We agreed, and Dan Eiffe accompanied her. Dan is, as you know, not only very good at promoting the cause, but he is also a very charming man. He therefore skillfully exposed the Dutch journalist to a difficult and conflict-ridden political landscape.

Erst Temmermann went back to the Netherlands and wrote a two-page article with pictures in one of the Netherland's largest newspapers which provided NPA with a rare and great publicity in Netherlands. Pronk read the article, and that was part of the reason why he asked us to facilitate a visit to the fields of South Sudan so that he with his own eyes could see the immense sufferings the people were exposed to."

Jan Pronk is one of the most fascinating European politicians I have ever met, and he has had a long and devoted relationship to Sudan.

He was born 77 years ago, and both his parents were teachers. He studied economics at the famous Erasmus School of Economy in Rotterdam and did very well as a student. In his spare time, he was actively involved in student politics and social work with the Protestant Church.

In 1965, he joined the Labour Party in The Netherlands and immersed himself in political work. He was particularly concerned with international solidarity work. At the same time, he worked with the famous Dutch economist Jan Tinbergen, winner of the Nobel Peace Prize in Economics, and the EU politician Sicco Mansholt. The three of them were particularly interested in The Club of Rome's book *Limits to Growth* and the consequences it would have, if practiced in The Netherlands.

Jan Pronk with several others pulled the Labour Party in the 1960s towards the left. In 1971, he was elected member of parliament, and in 1973 he was appointed the Minister for Development Co-operation. He was a very active minister and worked very closely with among others, the Norwegian Minister of Foreign Affairs, Thorvald Stoltenberg, to establish a New International Economic Order (NIEO). But as we remember, they and the leaders of the developing countries failed in their efforts. Instead we got the Ronald Reagan and Margareth Thatcher's version of a world order letting the forces of the market free.

Two years after Pronk became a minister, the government passed a budget for international development cooperation that allocated 1.5 percent of the Gross National Product (GNP), the largest of any West-European country.

Dutch aid went to many countries, also communist countries such as Northern Yemen and Cuba. Pronk was a harsh critic of the apartheid system in South Africa, and he and the Dutch government supported the liberation struggles both in Sudan and South Africa.

Pronk was an exciting politician and a man of principle. When he spoke, he could ignite an audience. He was known to work very hard and for long hours. He held prominent positions with academic institutions and international organizations, while being a minister. For these reasons, when cabinet meetings ran late into the evening, he often fell asleep. He was a minister in various governments for 17 years. Prime Minister Kok from the Labour Party was very fond of his enthusiastic and highly competent minister. He gave Pronk two nicknames "Minister for the National Conscience" and "Minister by Profession".

Jan Pronk held many international positions. He was a board member of the World Bank, he led the UNs first conference on Climate Change in 2002 and he was the special UN Envoy to the World Summit on Sustainable Development in Tokyo in 2002.

When the report of the Srebrenica massacre in Bosnia was published in 2002, Pronk said that as a Dutch politician, he felt a moral and political responsibility for the fact that the Dutch military forces present in Srebrenica, did not prevent the massacre, and he resigned as a minister.

In 2004 the UN Secretary General Kofi Anan appointed Jan Pronk as the UN Secretary General's Special Envoy to Sudan. He was extensively involved as the UN Representative in the conflict in Darfur, and he criticized the regime in Khartoum for the attacks of the government forces on the civilian population in Darfur. However, it was not long before his criticism collided with the views of Sudan's President Omar Bashir. He was furious with what he called Pronk's psychological war fare against him and his government. He then ordered for the expulsion of Jan Pronk who was given 72 hours to leave Sudan.

Pronk was one of the deputy chairmen in the Labour Party. In 2007, he decided to run for the position as Chairman of the Labour Party with a promise to take the party to the left if he won. But he lost the election and retired from politics. In 2013, he left the Labour Party after 48 years of membership, stating that the party had become too conservative.

Pronk was colorful both as a politician and socially. One last example, in 1984 he was arrested for driving while under the influence of alcohol. He admitted to his crime and vowed to abstain from alcohol, and he did. At the same time, he began long distance running.

Gayle Smith, a beautiful American Woman on the Political Scene in the Horn of Africa

The American journalist, activist and politician Gayle Smith has had an active involvement in the Horn of Africa since the end of the 1970s. Helge Rohn said the following about his first meeting with her:

"During the hectic years of 1993-94 with heavy involvement by NPA both in South Sudan and the Nuba Mountains, an American woman unexpectedly joined one of our meetings of the secret consortium providing humanitarian aid to the Nuba Mountains. Her name was Gayle Smith. She was stunningly beautiful and had an unusually good political understanding of the political complexity of the Horn of Africa. She told us that she had worked in the area for a long time, and that she now was a special representative of the US Government. We later learnt that she also carried the special name of "The First Lady of Ethiopia".

She knew quite a lot about NPAs work in South Sudan and the Nuba Mountains, and she spoke very favorably about it. She, at the same time, assured us that she would do her best to secure more American support for our work. And she did. We received more funding, and NPA brought many important Americans to the Nuba Mountains.

One day, I asked her if she would like to meet John Garang, and she readily accepted. We contacted SPLM/A that on short notice arranged for a meeting. We flew to an airstrip in South Sudan, and then we drove by car through the bush for several hours before we arrived at the secret place where Garang was staying. The meeting started in the late evening. The two developed quickly a very good political chemistry, and they shared many common ideas and views. The talk between the two lasted long into the dark night. I sat up with them, listening to their fascinating talk about politics and society, and political leaders in East Africa. I did not have much that I could add, but I had a most fascinating night."

Svein Olsen, who is a senior staff member with NPA, has been deeply involved in the programmes of NPA in the Horn of Africa. He got to know Gayle Smith at a very early stage:

"She came to Tigray in the middle of the 1980s during a very difficult period in the liberation war. I met her then for the first time, and I got the impression that she had some ties with the American Embassy in Ethiopia. She was a good friend of Martine Billanou, who was the coordinator for the consortium for aid relief and development in Tigray (REST) of which NPA also was a member. Furthermore, I also met her frequently in Eritrea during the time of the national referendum for independence in April 1993. When Gayle was part of more informal gatherings, she sometimes could boast about having been a freedom fighter in Tigray.

Personally, I was impressed by Gayle Smith. She moved with a pure and distinguished kind of dignity. She was good at promoting herself and her history, and it was obvious that she had connections all the way to the top of American politics."

Svein Olsen also had good memories of the Tigrean People's Liberation Front (TPLF) and its opposing ideological sides. He saw Gayle Smith as a cautious, but active conversation partner for many of the leaders of TPLF regarding which ideological choices that needed to be made for the future. In the middle of all this, she worked for a period at the local office of Norwegian Church Aid in Tigray.

Gayle Smith was born and raised in Ethiopia, but had a USA citizenship. As a young woman, she went back to USA for education and studies. Upon completion of her studies in the middle of the 1970s, she worked as a journalist and reported from the countries on the Horn of Africa for almost 20 years. She had a reputation of being a very able journalist, and she worked for companies such as BBC, AP, Reuters, Boston Globe, London Observer and the Financial Times. She also worked as a consultant for some international NGOs working in the Horn of Africa.

She supported from the time of her arrival in the Horn, the liberation movements both in Tigray and in Eritrea, and later also the struggle of SPLM/A Mainstream. She was particularly involved with the liberation struggle in Tigray. It is well known that she developed a personal relationship with the famous leader of TPLF, Meles Zenawi, who in 1991 became Ethiopia's Prime Minister. Gayle Smith led the US-Government's delegation at Meles Zenawi's funeral in the summer 2012, and she spoke on behalf of the American Government at the ceremony.

The reason why this story is narrated in this book is simple. There were two Norwegian NGOs that took a stand in support of the liberation struggle in Tigray and later in Ethiopia; Norwegian People's Aid and the Norwegian Development Fund. NPA worked closely with TPLFs humanitarian branch, the Relief Society of Tigray (REST), and NPA staff had direct contact with the leader Meles Zenawi.

When Gayle Smith came to the meetings of NPA and their partners in 1993-94, she was on a special assignment for USAID. When the assignment was completed, she was appointed as Chief of Staff for USAID. In 1998, she was made President Clinton's personal assistant and Director for Africa in USAs National Security Council.

When President Barack Obama was elected president in 2008, he appointed Gayle Smith as a Special Assistant and Senior Director for Development and Democracy at the National Security Council. In May 2015, Obama nominated Gayle Smith as the new Chief Administrator of USAID. President Obama, in announcing Smith's nomination, stated:

"Today, I am proud to nominate Gayle E. Smith as our next Administrator of the U.S. Agency for International Development (USAID). I've worked closely with Gayle for nearly a decade, and for the past six years Gayle has served as a senior leader on international development, humanitarian crisis response, and democracy issues on my National Security Council staff. Gayle's energy and passion have been instrumental in guiding America's international development policy, responding to a record number of humanitarian crises worldwide, and ensuring that development remains at the forefront of the national security agenda at a time when USAID is more indispensable than ever. Gayle has my full confidence, and I have no doubt that she will prove to be an outstanding leader for the tireless men and women of USAID as they work to improve lives around the world. I urge the Senate to act quickly on this nomination."

The world-famous photographer Sebastiao Salgado decides to support NPA

Early in 1994, Helge Rohn as the NPA Residential Representative received an interesting call from the Nairobi office of the French Doctors Without Borders (MSF). They told Helge that they had a request from the world renowned Brazilian photographer Sebastiao Salgado to assist him in getting into South Sudan to take pictures of the people who for so long had been exposed to severe oppression, war and starvation. However, the MSF Nairobi felt that NPA, with its large programme behind the frontlines, was a better suited to assist Salgado. So, MSF wanted to hand over the request to NPA. It was a very welcome request, and NPA agreed to host Salgado's visit.

Helge Rohn decided personally to accompany Salgado into the field, and the NPA staff prepared for the visit. Salgado had the permission from SPLM/A to take all the pictures he wanted. Having stayed with Salgado in the field for a few days, Helge returned to Nairobi, while Salgado stayed behind and worked for some weeks in South Sudan. SPLM/A understood the importance of the visit, and they did their best to make it as successful as possible. Helge had this to say about Salgado's visit:

"*It was a rare and extraordinary experience to see the world-renowned Salgado in action with his camera. Salgado was a very political person, and he often expressed his solidarity with the people of South Sudan during his stay. We also managed to get a meeting with Garang.*"

When Salgado returned to Nairobi he was satisfied with the work he had been able to do. He was also very grateful for the way, the trip had been organized, and he invited Helge Rohn and his family out for dinner. During the dinner, he conveyed his gratitude in this way:

"*I greatly appreciate the help you in NPA have given me, and I would therefore like to give NPA some of my best pictures from South Sudan and other places where people are fighting for their dignity and their rights. You can use the pictures as you see fit in your work to create a better understanding for the lives of the oppressed.*"

This is how NPA was given access to some of Salgado's best pictures. In 1994, NPA was granted the annual televised National Fundraising Campaign organized by Norwegian Broadcasting Corporation (NRK), and NPA used many of Salgado's pictures during that campaign period. Salgado's pictures have later frequently been used by NPA in other funding raising campaigns. Some of Salgado's pictures also figure in this book.

A naked boy arrives at a refugee camp and is being helped by his new comrades. Picture by Sebastiao Salgado.

Jacob Atem, one of the many who took part in the march to Ethiopia.

Jan Pronk

Gayle Smith

Sebastiao Salgado

14
EGIL HAGEN, THE FOUNDING FATHER OF NPA'S SUDAN PROGRAMME

Egil Hagen was on his death bed. Christmas 1991 was only a few days away. Cancer had been diagnosed earlier that year, and Egil returned to Norway in the spring of 1991. The doctors at the National Cancer Hospital in Oslo did everything they could. Firstly, they carried out emergency surgery only to discover that the cancer had spread. Then they tried chemotherapy and radiation therapy, but in vain.

The Secretary General of NPA, Odd Wivegh was visiting Egil for the last time. As they talked, Egil, raised on his elbow with what little strength he had left, and whispered:

"*Odd, I want Helge Rohn, my old friend from the Norwegian Military Academy, to be my successor in Nairobi, and I want you* to ask Halle Jørn Hanssen to apply for the position as Head of International Development for NPA when it is advertised. Can you promise me that?"

Odd Wivegh looked at Egil Hagen and said: "*I promise.*"

Egil whispered a thank you and slipped into sleep.

The day before Christmas Eve in 1991 I went to see my close friend Egil. He did not look good, but for a moment, his eyes lit up, and he turned to me and said:

"*If I get better, my wife and I, we have tickets for Nairobi, and we leave on New Year's Eve.*"

Then reality hit him. We talked about the Sudan programme, the cancer, and that he might die soon. He also told me that he had asked Odd Wivegh to get Helge Rohn to take over as the Head of the Sudan Programme and that he asked Odd to ask me to apply for the position as Head of International Development. He added that Wivegh had agreed to this.

Egil passed away on Boxing Day. The funeral was held in the church of his home town of Drøbak. I was in my capacity as Head of Information of Norad, asked by my superior in the Ministry of Foreign Affairs to speak at the funeral, conveying on behalf of the Ministry, our condolences and greetings to the family and the audience. I took pride in the opportunity to say something important about both my friend and fellow human being, Egil Hagen and the values he represented.

Egil and I first met in Norway while he was a military officer.

Then some years later when he was on a mission for the Red Cross in Kenya in the fall of 1981, we met again. I was then working as the Africa Correspondent of the Norwegian Broadcasting Corporation. We got along easily, and we quickly developed a close friendship.

We met every time he came to Nairobi from his work with the Pokot people in the mountains near Turkana, where there was drought and famine. Egil was in charge of a relief project, drilling water holes and providing food for the many thousands in need.

Two stories about Egil Hagen

I was working in my Nairobi office when someone, one day late in the fall of 1981 knocked on the door. Egil came in smiling and said:

"*Good Morning. I have a good story for you.*"

Then he continued:

"*You see, for a long time, I have seen that the children of the Pokot people are very frail, even though they get food. I figured that it was due to a lack of protein and vitamins, and I contacted the people at the Norad fishery project in Turkana. They have a supply of dried fish that they have not been able to sell. I brought some of the dried fish to the Pokot people, but they will not eat fish. They said it tasted like snake meat.*

As you know, every morning I do exercises to keep fit. Firstly, I run about 10 kilometers and then I do some weight training with 70 kilo weights. A couple of weeks ago, I had just come in from my daily run and had started weight training. A group of young men appeared, all about the same age. They had been out in the bush for some weeks as part of the traditional initiation exercise to become adults. They had to survive on what they could find and if possible they had to kill a lion, so they would be accepted as real men.

They laughed as they came over to me, pointing to the weights and wanted to try them. The first one tried, but could not lift it, then another and another. Nobody could lift it. "Ok, we can't do this, but come over here and try to do something we can do, and then we will see who is best."

I was led to the edge of the woods. They brought out spears and said that we would have a spear throwing contest. "Ok", I said. They believed that this was not something I was good at. One of them threw a spear, and it went far. Then it was my turn. I threw farther, much farther. They tried again, but no one could throw as far as I did.

At this point, many people had gathered around to see what was going on, some were hinting that I had some kind of magic power or witchcraft that enabled me to do this. Then I got an idea. I asked everyone to come to the store with dry fish. There I rolled up my sleeves and showed the bulging upper arm muscle, as I pointed to the dry fish and said: "FISHPOWER"!

It was quiet. Then the elders, my local staff and I, discussed the power that was in the dry fish. After that they decided that from that day dry fish would be mixed in with the corn porridge. Halle, do you know what has happened? I had to increase the amount of dry fish we bought from 60 kilos to 600 kilos per month. Everyone now eats corn porridge with dry fish, and the children have become much healthier."

What the young Pokot men did not know when they invited Egil for the competition, was that Egil back in Norway was a known decathlon athlete, and one of the exercises in decathlon is to throw the spear.

When his 6 months' contract with the Red Cross came to an end, Egil came to my office in Nairobi for a last visit before travelling back home. He then shared the following story:

"*You see Halle, as I was leaving the camp yesterday morning, a group of elders came over to me to thank me for everything I had done. They had a bucket with very beautiful precious stones that you find in the area where the Pokots live. I thanked them, and I put the stones in two old boots, put them in the car and drove to Kitale where I stayed overnight at the Kitale Country Club.*

But this morning when I was going to leave, I stood there looking at the boots with all the stones and thought: "These will cause a lot of trouble going through customs. So, I threw all the stones in the garbage can, except these small ones here."

Then he showed me a handful of small precious gems.

I said to him: "*Egil, are you crazy, do you know what you have done? You have thrown away precious gems worth several hundred thousand NOK, maybe more. The mountain people thanked you in the nicest way they could.*"

Egil became a little embarrassed and asked:

"*Do you think I may exchange these stones for a beautiful piece of jewelry with a jeweler in Nairobi*"?

I answered: "*I think so, on the ground floor in this building there is an Indian jeweler's store that might have something for you.*"

Egil followed my advice, and came back after a while and showed me a gorgeous bracelet. He had asked the old man in the store if they could trade. The old man had looked at the stones and said: "*For this you can take anything here.*" Egil had found the bracelet and asked if he could take it. The old man had nodded enthusiastically and wrapped the gift.

Egil traveled home to Norway the same evening. He had helped the Pokot people and saved thousands of lives through his ingenious idea to relate the cause of his male physical strength with the eating of dry fish, and the people had thanked him in the most beautiful way they could.

The next day I went to see the Indian shop owner, and I asked him what the bracelet cost. He said it cost 20 000 NOK (Approx. USD 1 500, -). If the price of the bracelet is anything to go by, then Egil had unknowingly thrown away precious gems worth more than one million NOK on the market in Europe.

I can only hope that some poor cleaning lady at the Kitale County Club was the first to find the gems and understood their value. Who knows? Maybe the stones changed her and her family's life for the better.

Who was Egil Hagen?

He was born and grew up in Drøbak, a small town near Oslo. His father was a carpenter, while his mother was a housewife. The parents were members of the local Labour Party branch. During the Second World War, his father had been active in the Norwegian Resistance Movement (Milorg). He was a very respected person, a prominent local politician and the Mayor of the Municipality for a period.

While a young boy, Egil was active in athletics and football during the summer, and skiing and ice hockey during the winter. Later boxing became his passion, and after that motorcycles and motor cross while he kept up his physical training to stay fit and strong.

He wanted to join the Norwegian National Defence Forces and become an officer. After High School, he was in 1967 admitted as a student at the Norwegian Military Academy. He did well in his studies. At the Academy, he chose to write about Mao Zedong's philosophy of guerrilla warfare for his thesis. This gave him insight into Marxism and the reasoning behind liberation movements such as Mau Mau in Kenya, the National Liberation Front (FNL) in Vietnam and FLN in Algeria. But he at the same time remained an outspoken anti-communist, and he was in favour of Norway being a member of NATO.

After the graduation from the Norwegian Military Academy, he was stationed with the Northern Brigade in a military camp close to the town of Harstad. His family joined him, and he enjoyed his work as an officer even if he did not always like the military pickiness.

Egil stayed with the Northern Brigade for four years, and he was promoted to Captain in the Infantery.

However, when he returned home to Drøbak in the summer of 1974, sad news awaited him. His mother was seriously ill and dying. His father had borrowed a large amount from the local bank and invested it in a housing construction site, anticipating that the housing market would continue to grow. Unfortunately, the housing market did not continue to grow, but collapsed. There was no return on his investments. His father was unable to service the loan in the bank, and he was on the verge of bankruptcy when Egil returned home. Egil tried everything to save his father from bankruptcy, as well as save his childhood home, but in vain. He was met with a cold shoulder from the bank manager. His childhood home was auctioned. It was very painful both personally and politically for Egil and his family, leaving Egil with an extremely critical view of banks and the way capitalism worked. He took an oath that he would make enough money in the future to buy his childhood home back.

Norway had at the time struck oil in the North Sea. Big investments both from the state and from private companies were being made. The age of oil and oil capitalism was rapidly developing. Egil decided to give up his military career, and he took up work as a high-level manager with the French Oil Company, ELF, now operating offshore on the Norwegian shelfs in the North Sea. Egil's salary was substantial, and after a short time he managed to buy his family a house in the new oil town of Stavanger. Then, after a couple of years, he bought back his childhood home in Drøbak.

But Egil was growing tired of working in the oil industry, while at the same time developing strong political objections to what he experienced, and he once said to me:

"*Halle, this is an awful experience. My colleagues are only concerned with how they can cheat the Norwegian government for taxes. I cannot take this anymore. I am going to quit.*"

Corruption in the National Skiing Association

The Norwegian Skiing Association advertised in 1979 a new leader position for the newly established Skipool Norway, which organized sponsors for elite ski athletes. Egil applied and got the position. However, he soon realized that the system was corrupt, and that the corruption was directed from the top itself, the elected President of the Association.

Egil was furious and resigned in protest. Having done that, he wrote a letter which he made public, exposing the corruption managed by the President himself. The media exposed the corruption scandal. It turned into a drama. There was a court case that Egil won while the President landed in jail.

But Egil had to pay a high price for his honesty and outspokenness. He had stepped on many toes in the higher ranks of Norwegian Sports and the Norwegian businesses and banks. Before the corruption scandal got public, Egil was promised a job with the very renowned ski-producer Madhus, but then failed to get it. Egil discovered that he was no longer welcome in the business world in Norway.

He was met with a cold front. Nobody in that world wanted to have anything to do with him. That was the price he paid for being a whistle blower on corruption.

Egil Hagen joins the World of International Humanitarian Assistance

Therefore, he decided to do something completely different. He wanted to work in the field of international development and emergency relief.

In the fall of 1979 Uganda's dictator Idi Amin ordered the invasion of neighbouring Tanzania and occupied a part of its territory. The Government of Tanzania held back for a while, but then early in 1980, launched a powerful counter-attack, and let Amin and the world know that they would not stop until Amin was removed from power. The Tanzanian forces surprised the world with their efficiency. In April of 1980 they marched with very little opposition to the capital of Kampala while Amin and his gang fled north. Then, the Tanzanian offensive stopped.

From that point onward, the law of the jungle took over in the northern parts of the Uganda. Many civilians were killed in clashes between forces who were still loyal to Amin, and military groups that now supported the new holders of power in Kampala.

Egil Hagen was then for the first time employed by the Norwegian Red Cross. His assignment was in Uganda, and he was sent into the areas of the conflicts and clashes in the Northern part of the country. There was death and destruction everywhere. Egil and his Red Cross team could do some humanitarian emergency work in the areas concerned, but only at great personal risk. The conflict was extremely intense and quite anarchistic in nature. In the end, Egil and his team had to flee, barely escaping alive.

After his terrifying experiences in Uganda, Egil was home with his family in Drøbak for some weeks, but he needed to work and earn money. He was still blacklisted by the Norwegian business community.

Therefore, he decided to return to the military ranks. In the summer of 1980 he took a job as a UN-Officer in the United Nations Interim Force in Lebanon (UNIFIL). He was given the command of a UN Company that primarily consisted of soldiers from Ghana. The company had operational responsibility for a conflict-ridden area with PLO-soldiers on the one side and Israeli forces in cooperation with Lebanese Christian militia on the other side. The time with the UN in Lebanon was an arduous experience for Egil. He did a good job, but after six months he chose to resign and return to his family and Norway.

In the fall of 1981 he was contracted for a new assignment with the Red Cross, this time with the Pokot People in Kenya, which I have already narrated in the introduction of this chapter.

Egil Hagen joins NPA

One evening in the middle of the winter of 1983, Mr. Thorvald Stoltenberg called me. He was the Chair of the Labour Movement Committee for International Solidarity Work. They were in the process of employing a new Resident Representative for NPA in Lebanon, and they had someone named Egil Hagen from Drøbak on the list of applicants. Did I know him, and what could I say about him? I gave Egil the recommendation he deserved, and the next day the Committee decided to employ Egil Hagen as the new NPA Resident Representative in Lebanon. Egil knew Lebanon from his time as a UN Officer. The political situation in the country was extremely difficult, riddled as Lebanon was by civil and religious sectarian conflicts.

At that time, the relationship between foreign aid workers and the authorities was especially strained. Aid workers were seen as left-wing radicals who only had sympathy for the Palestinians. Most of them did not get their work permits renewed. Some were forced to leave the country.

Egil was known for his professional competence, his honesty and rectitude. But he did not have much of a reputation as a diplomat, and NPA's presence was also in danger. However, Egil managed the situation very well. He cleaned up in the internal administrative chaos, which was a result of a major shortage of staff. People had to work day and night out in the field because there was a lot of heavy fighting and many causalities, and they therefore could not manage to do the necessary administrative work as well.

During a short time, Egil managed to form a workable relationship with the authorities and the different political factions and militias. He was in Lebanon for two years, and NPA developed an important and effective humanitarian presence in the country that since has remained a very important programme. The many stories, still being told about Egil's many risky and dangerous operations from these years in Lebanon, belong somewhere else.

In the winter of 1985, Egil changed his employer, and went to UNICEF in Khartoum. The first field operations took him to the Red Sea Mountains in Sudan. Egil discovered quickly that it was difficult to operate emergency relief in Sudan. The UN-bureaucracy was slow at best, but navigating the intricacies of the Sudanese bureaucracy was much worse. Corruption permeated all levels, and the political willingness, at the level of the government bureaucracy, to do anything about hunger and poverty was non-existent.

Egil worked for a short period under extremely difficult conditions in the Red Sea Mountains before he was given a new assignment in South Sudan. He soon experienced that the authorities in Khartoum did not permit emergency relief delivery to those who were hit by the drought, war and hunger in the southern parts of the country.

SPLM/A had been carrying out its liberation war for two years and had made major military progress. Egil had at that time limited knowledge of the situation in Sudan, and especially when it came to the southern regions. At this point, SPLA/M defined itself as a socialistic and revolutionary liberation movement.

Egil was a social democrat and in the beginning, he did not approve of what the SPLM/A stood for.

However, when he experienced the Khartoum's regime active discrimination of the black people who constituted the majority in the country, and the total unwillingness of the Khartoum regime to let emergency relief supplies reach the starving and ill people in camps in the Southern regions of the country, he changed his mind.

At the same time, he became acquainted with a retired Major, Niconorah. He was a Southerner and a former officer in the Sudanese government forces. He had served under Nimeiri's regime, but had ended up in the opposition. He and others had attempted a military rebellion, but had failed. Niconorah and the other rebels were tried in court and sentenced to death. But they were pardoned in an amnesty that was granted by a later regime.

Niconorah was concerned with the refugees from South Sudan who lived under inhuman conditions in camps just outside of the capital. He asked UNICEF and Egil if they could do something. Norway's ambassador to Egypt was also accredited to Sudan. Ambassador Botnen, came on a routine business visit to Khartoum. He and Egil met, and Egil brought him to the refugee camps. Botnen was shocked by what he saw. When he left, Egil thought he had been given a kind of authorization to act. Together with Niconorah he started with support from UNICEF, a substantial aid operation to the displaced peoples in the camps. It went well for a time, until the authorities discovered it and ordered an immediate halt of the activity.

His experience in Khartoum with the Sudanese Government's systematic discrimination of its own black, African population and the political weakness of the UN system, made Egil conclude that he had to get away from all this.

Egil made up his mind. He wanted to be in charge of an emergency operation that directly benefitted the oppressed peoples in South Sudan.

In the fall of 1985 he went, as mentioned in chapter 3, The Beginning, on a private and secret trip to Addis Ababa for talks with the leaders of SPLM/A. After that meeting he returned to Khartoum and resigned from his position in UNICEF. A few weeks before Christmas in 1985 he went home to Norway.

During his residence, both as a UN-officer and as the Head of NPA's work in Lebanon, Egil developed a considerable contact network with Americans in Lebanon. Some were officers, including CIA, others came from different political affiliations in USA, some were representatives of US NGOs and some were just rich American do-gooders who came along, wanting to do some relief work in Lebanon.

When he in the winter of 1986 arrived in Nairobi and started working, he reactivated parts of his network of professionals and friends in USA who might have some interest in the fate of the suffering people in Sudan. Egil's had a strong persuasion ability, and he was successful with his contacts in USA. They soon started to provide some emergency aid in kind, medicine and food for Egil's new project.

Egil Hagen, a Legend in South Sudan

Egil Hagen had a strong personality with some particular features. He was almost absolute in terms of his understanding of what was right and wrong both in everyday life and in politics. He did not tolerate indifference, and he held the view that there was too much indifference in organizations working with humanitarian assistance, first and foremost in the UN-system. For this reason, he did not sugar-coat his words whenever he criticized the UN, whether it was in interviews on CNN, in conversations with Norwegian journalists or privately. This created, of course, problems for both himself, for NPA and sometimes even NMFA, but he at the same time commanded a lot respect for his honorable character, and the way he worked and conducted himself.

Ivar Christiansen, who came to NPA as the new Head of Information in the summer of 1989, was immediately sent on mission to Sudan. It was his African debut, and in Nairobi he was well received by Egil, and the two travelled into South Sudan. Ivar shared the following from that journey:

"*It was a fantastic journey, just meeting Egil Hagen! His reputation was mythical. Mostly when he talked, he talked quietly, with a hoarse voice, but he also had an enormous talent as an orator, and he had a very strong persuasion power. Whenever he talked, people listened. When I met him, he had just been visiting USA, addressing several US fora, including committees in the US Congress, on the liberation war in Sudan. He had given a couple of interviews on CNN. Not only that, he personally knew people high up in the US Administration, in State Department and in the Congress,*

I was very fortunate to be allowed to go with him into Sudan. We met John Garang once. We were in the bush somewhere, not far from Nimule. It was late evening and very dark, just the flickering from the fire, as it was slowly ebbing out. Suddenly someone tapped me on the shoulder. I turned, looking into a black, smiling face: "NPA I presume. My name is John Garang." He came out of nowhere. Khartoum was constantly searching for him, and he could not let them catch him. Garang sat down and began talking and said: "This is going to be a very long war. But we will prevail because of you." He looked at Egil and me. It was an intense encounter that I still very vividly remember and carry with me".

"*How would you characterize the person Egil Hagen*", I asked Ivar, and he answered:

"*He had a particular strong sense of justice. He got angry whenever he experienced injustice and wanted to do something about it.*"

I asked his friend and successor in NPA's Sudan Programme, Helge Rohn, the same question:

"At school, he was incredibly good at drawing and had an artistic flare. He was also a good story teller. Whenever he spoke, people listened. But his unquestionable and strong personal integrity was realized best when he was working for poor with emergency relief and aid. Then, he was great."

The late Torolf Elster, who was a renowned Norwegian journalist and writer, and he was for many years the Director-General of the Norwegian Broadcasting Corporation while I worked with the institution. When he retired, he wrote two politically very important books, the first one; *Hjem til familien*, (Home to the Family) which was a narration of international development cooperation, while the second book had the title *Verden brenner* (The World is Afire), a narration about the refugee problems of the world. He met Egil Hagen on one of his travels while writing the book; The World is Afire. In that book, he wrote the following about Egil Hagen:

"Hagen was quite a remarkable man. He appears to be reckless, but he takes no unnecessary chances. The strange thing about Hagen is his ability to relate to people and always have an overview of the situation. While I met with him, so many came to him to get advice. He relates very well both with the authorities and guerilla leaders."

15
JOHN GARANG - THE LIBERATOR AND THE LEGEND

A very gifted, but poor Boy who rose to become the Liberator

John Garang was born in 1945, the sixth of seven siblings in a poor Dinka family in a village close the town of Bor in Jonglei in South Sudan. He experienced the hardship of poverty all through his childhood. At the age of ten, his father died, and one of his uncles took care of him. The uncle soon understood that he had responsibility for an exceptionally gifted little boy. But there was no primary school in the village, and to get John Garang to school, the uncle had to send the little boy to a neighbouring village that was a few days walk away on foot. The uncle made sure that John could complete primary school before he was admitted to a missionary, secondary school in Rumbek. Garang did extremely well at school, and he developed a strong political interest at a very early age. He was a radical, and he engaged in political discussion whenever there was an opportunity both at school and outside. The central themes for discussion already at this early stage, was the oppressive nature of the Khartoum regime and the need for a liberation struggle.

He became the leader of a pupils' rebellion against the curriculum at the school in Rumbek that spread to many other schools in South Sudan. Garang was expelled from the school and was refused admittance at any other school in South Sudan.

All this made him even more rebellious, and he, 17 years old, sought contact with leaders of the Anyanya liberation movement. He became a guerilla soldier and a freedom fighter, but some of the commanders of Anyanya saw the very talented young boy and got worried that he might be wounded or killed in the struggle. They sat down with the young man. After a long talk, in which the elders argued that he needed to get more education so that he could serve his people better, they persuaded him to leave the fighting.

Garang was by then a persona non-grata in South Sudan. He fled 18 years old together with a small group of other youngsters, and they walked for approximately 500 km before they crossed the border to Ethiopia.

But Ethiopia in 1963 was in disarray, and Garang saw no future in the country. He began another refugee walk, this time in the direction of Kenya.

The Refugee Boy and his Way to Tanzania

Kenya in 1963 was about to get its independence. John Garang arrived in a country where the people had suffered extremely under British Colonial rule. The Mau-Mau liberation war in the 1950s was marked by extreme violence by the British and their Kenyan lackeys. However, the young refugee from Sudan who came walking into Kenya, was well received by Kenyans who took him as their friend. He was given shelter, and he took a job in a kiosk in the Kibera slum area in Nairobi. While in Kenya, he continued his political engagement and his outspokenness. Because of that, he one day ran into serious trouble. The British colonizers who still were present in Kenya, had their agents at work. One day an agent overheard the radical refugee from Sudan talking politics with some people standing around him. The agent immediately reported to his superior that there was a dangerous youngster refugee from Sudan at work in Kibera. The superior, being a British Police Officer, drew an instant conclusion and the order was:

"Arrest the guy and we will hand him over to the authorities in Khartoum!"

However, there were some young and politically conscious Kenyans present, aspiring to be policemen in independent Kenya. They had access to one of Kenya's great liberation leaders, Jaramogi Oginga Odinga, and they reported the arrest order to him. Odinga was at the time about to be appointed the Vice-President of independent Kenya. He acted instantly and had Garang picked up and taken to his house before the colonial police could arrest him. Oginga protected Garang and kept him as a friend of the family while he contacted his Tanzanian friend, President Julius Nyerere. They agreed that Garang should come to Tanzania. Nyerere would in the meantime contact some of his missionary friends and see to it that Garang was admitted to school again.

Some days later, Garang together with some other refugee boys from Sudan, were placed on a truck, loaded with sacks of coffee beans. The boys hid among the sacks as they crossed the border to Tanzania, and in Tanzania they were well received by people sent by Nyerere.

Nyerere had in advance of Garang's arrival, contacted his American friends, the missionary couple Robins at the American Missionary Secondary School in Magamba in the south-eastern part of Tanzania, and they had agreed to admit Garang to the school. Not only that, they had also contacted a local parish in Minnesota that agreed to give a scholarship to Garang.

John Garang in Tanzania and USA

At the new school Garang met with a very different environment and mood from what he was used to at home in Sudan, and as a refugee in Ethiopia and Kenya. Tanzania was at the time enjoying its new born freedom and independence. Julius Nyerere was a socialist and a beloved President. The spirits were high, and at the school Garang met with teachers from USA, Norway, Tanzania and other African countries or colonies on their way to independence, and Garang met students from Tanzania and many other African countries.

Garang was a hardworking student and performed very well at school while he with his friendly personality easily established good relations with his teachers and his fellow students. One of the teachers with whom he established particularly good relations and a personal friendship that lasted for life, was a Norwegian, Mr. Arvid Bøe from Romsdal in Western Norway. They had many conversations about Christianity, other religions and on the issue, whether to believe or not. Garang also told me that they also talked a lot about politics and societal developments. Once Garang asked Mr. Bøe whether he thought the Bible was a good guide for political work, Mr. Bøe looked at him, for a little while and then answered:

"*My dear John. The Bible is a revolutionary book; it is like dynamite in politics*".

Garang did exceptionally well at school in Tanzania, and he was for this reason allowed to do a short cut. He did two years of study in one year, and he graduated with top grades in all subjects.

At the end of the year and with the exams results in his pocket, he went back to now independent Kenya and was employed as a teacher in mathematics at Gatunganga Secondary School in the Central Province. While teaching in Kenya, he got the good news that he had received the Thomas Watson scholarship for studies in the USA.

Garang arrived in USA in 1965 and studied for a while at Berkeley University in California before he moved to the Mid-West. He was admitted for studies at Grinell College in Iowa and had

Copied from Minnesota Globe, 16. 9. 1968.

his BA degree in economics with excellent grades. He won a new scholarship for continued studies at the University of California. However, his longing for Africa was too strong, and he got permission to use his American scholarship to continue his studies of agricultural economics at the University of Dar es Salaam in Tanzania. While a student in Dar es Salaam, he joined the University Students' African Revolutionary Front, and he became a very active member of that association. The founding father of the University Students' African Revolutionary Front in Dar es Salaam, was Yoveri Museveni, today the President of Uganda.

Back in Sudan

Having passed his exams at the University of Dar es Salaam and obtained his MA in Economics, John Garang went back to South Sudan to join the unit of the Anyanya liberation movement commanded by Gordon Muortat Mayen. Having fought for a while, he was picked for further military training and sent to Israel. Upon return to South Sudan, he was promoted to Captain of the Anyanya Liberation Army.

Shortly after having returned to South Sudan to continue the liberation struggle, there was a ceasefire, and peace negotiations were to start in Addis Ababa. Garang was very skeptical of the whole approach of the delegation from Anyanya, the South Sudan Liberation Movement in the negotiations. He wrote a letter to the Head of the Anyanya Delegation, General Joseph Lagu, with both some critical comments and some clear advice on how to conduct the negotiations.

I have for the English edition of this book chosen to publish the letter in full as it reflects John Garang political thinking already in 1972 at the age of 27, being a young Captain in the Anyanya Liberation Army. The letter is in my view also very interesting when one looks at the key points in the letter and compare with the key points in the CPA of 2005, the Comprehensive Peace Agreement between SPLM/A and the Government of Sudan. There are many similarities.

The letter:

The General Headquarters
Anyanya National Armed Forces
South Sudan
January 24, 1972
The Commander in chief
Anyanya National Armed Forces
Leader of the South Sudan Liberation Movement
Members of the Anyanya SSLM Negotiation Committee

Dear compatriots:
That we are strong, growing in force and a power to be reckoned with in Sudanese politics, status and future is evidenced by the fact that the Khartoum administration is now interested in negotiating a peace settlement directly with the Anyanya.

We must take a firm stand all the way in the coming talks. The Numeiry regime is a sick administration ripe to collapse any time. We must not be tricked into committing suicide to lay down our instruments of liberation, our arms, by a withering and dying regime just for the purpose of lengthening its own days of breath or just that some opportunistic Southerners find a means of employment in the blood of our people.

We are already at war and we are growing stronger everyday while sooner or later the Numeiry regime will go, but nothing will ever defeat us if we persist in the war. Let no one among you or among the enemy have the mistaken and opportunist's view that these talks are the last chance of peace for South Sudanese people. Let no one have the incorrect view that if these talks collapse and fail war will break out. We are already at war for the last nine to seventeen years. The Anyanya and South Sudanese people are capable and ready to fight on for another nine years or more if no correct and acceptable solution is found.

Any solution within the context of a New United Sudan must first and foremost recognize the Anyanya as the legitimate army of the South Sudanese people. The implementation of whatever degree of merging agreed by the negotiating armies and administrations to the United New Sudan must take not less than ten years; during this time, the two armies and administrations must maintain separate identities while conditions for their gradual merging into United New Sudan are being created by both sides. This is the only procedure that guarantees the future and interests of the South Sudanese people in a United New Sudan and the objective indication that both sides are sincere in seeking the cessation of belligerency, peaceful settlement and life in a United Sudan.

Following is a more comprehensive presentation of guidelines to the spirit, objectives and strategy which should be adopted at the talks and which, if followed, could possibly lead to a solution acceptable to the rank-and-file of the Anyanya and the South Sudanese People.

A: THE OBJECTIVE REALITIES:
1. The Central Problem in the Sudanese war is the dominance of Arab Nationalism. It is historically a universal law that in whatever multi-nationality country where one of the nationalities is economically and politically (and therefore socially and culturally) dominant over other nationalities, that country is pregnant with instability, discontent and crisis eventually erupting in warfare. Such has been the case in the Sudan.
2. The South Sudanese people, in conformity with historical necessity, took up arms against the glaring oppression and neglect meted on them by the forces of Arab Nationalism, an oppression and neglect which were as glaring as they were cruel, reckless and raking as they were arrogant. It was only after the virtual exhaustion of all peaceful constitutional possibilities of multi-national coexistence with a United Progressive Sudan that the disaffecti-

on and indignation of the South Sudanese People reached their human boundaries and war broke out, war had to break out.
3. Constitutional guarantees against exactions and barbarities of Arab Nationalism, accommodations and adjustments to the mal-practices of Arab Chauvinism have all failed the past to be respected and to meet the aspirations of the South Sudanese People. This is why war had to break out in the first place.
4. There is no reason, absolutely no objective reason for clearheaded Southerners and Northerners alike to believe after eight years and more of continuous warfare and the repeated failures of some forms of constitutional guarantees that paper constitutional guarantees are now going to solve the war in the Sudan. Any Southerner who holds the mistaken view that Arab Nationalism now sincere, now means good business, now gives the South local autonomy in good faith and that this autonomy will be guaranteed by a few phrases scribbled on some sheets of paper stapled and bound together and christened " The Constitution", that Southerner either suffers from acute historical myopia or else advocates the treasonable stand of opportunism, national subjugation and continued Arab Chauvinism and domination; in short, such Southerner calls for surrender in a camouflaged form.
5. It is historically evident that unless a correct consistent Social Democratic solution is found to the Central Question, i.e., to the problem of economic and political domination of Arab Nationalism over other nationalities, then, any attempts at solving the war in Sudan, no matter how refined and logical on paper, will always end in certain failure.
6. There is no objective indication that the Khartoum-based Arab nationalist administration is capable of concluding a consistent social democratic solution to the National Question in the Sudan. Arab Nationalism in the Sudan, consistent with its predatory nature, proposes and declares solutions such as "local autonomy" within the context of a United Arab Sudan. Such muddle-headedness returns us back to 1963 and1955 and is an objective indication that the necessary mutation which

would enable ruling Northerners to face up to the objective realities of the Sudan has not yet taken root.
7. There are only two possible ways for resolving the Sudanese crises: The birth of two nation-states out of the present (geographical) Sudan or political autonomy for both the South and the North (and/or any other part that so demands) in a federated United New Sudan. Political Autonomy in this usage means that the autonomous regions have adequate political power, in terms of armed forces, to protect the region against the encroachment by the federation or by one of the regions in the federation, and, furthermore, that a region retains the right to secede from the federation if its interests are not adequately served by the federation.(It must be clear to Southerners that the retention of the right to secede from such a federation must be guaranteed by the federal constitution and by the existence of a physical Southern Armed Forces.)
8. We cannot dwell on the status of matters regarding the super-structure such as judicial system, fundamental rights and freedoms, personal liberty, freedom of religion and conscience, freedom of minority to use their language and develop their culture, education, tele-communications, census, etc., etc. (all contained in Mading de Garang's proposed constitution for the democratic republic of Sudan). The status of these and others will ultimately depend on either the solution is two nation-states or political autonomy (as defined above) for the two regions (or more) in a federated (NEW) Sudan. These peripheral issues must not be allowed to detract the deliberations of the talks, nota bene para VII above.

B: THE NECESSARY CONDITIONS, OBJECTIVES AND STRATEGY FOR THE TALKS

It is imperative that the basis and necessary conditions be created and for these basis and conditions to be developed and mature so as to objectively arrive at a United (NEW) and lasting peace. This approach is to start from the objective realities of the

Sudan. It is chauvinistic and naive to start with assumption of a United (ARAB) Sudan and then turn around and try to force the contradictory objective realities to conform to the subjective naïve assumption and wishes of a United Arab Sudan. Hence it follows from the objective facts in section (A) that for a United New Sudan the following conditions must be met:

1. Arab Nationalism in the Sudan must be categorically renounced. This concretely means that Arab Nationalism must no longer be neither an internal (therefore) nor an external policy and practice in the United New Sudan.
2. There at present two armies, the Anyanya and the army of the Khartoum administration; these armies are now at war in the Sudan. This point we hope is recognized by all as an objective existence for that is precisely why there are negotiations. Well, if the Sudan is to be a one United Country, if this is the interests of both Northerners and Southerners, then, which of these two warring armies will be the army of the New Sudan the Anyanya, the army of the Khartoum administration or both and how and/or why?
3. The Anyanya thus must firstly be accepted by the Khartoum administration as the arm of the South Sudan. Failure to recognize the Anyanya the legitimate army of the South would amount to denial or refusal to admit a physical existence, and the result of such naïveté would be the inevitable collapse of the negotiations and the continuation of the war whether anybody likes it or not.
4. The solution to the war and for the United NEW Sudan must be viewed as a synthesis of two armies (the Anyanya and the army of the Khartoum rulers) and the formation of a new type of army consistent with the particularity of the NEW Sudan. The solution must not be looked at or hoped to be (as is always the case) the ABSORPTION of one army the Anyanya into other (the army of the Khartoum Arab Administration), but rather as we said as a SYNTHESIS of two warring armies. Whether such synthesis is possible depends on whether the necessary mutation within the forces of the

Arab Nationalism and within the Anyanya exists. I am not aware that there has been such an objective necessary mutation, but I am only assuming its implied existence for otherwise there would be no objective grounds for the negotiations! And the originators of these negotiations could legitimately be charged with treasonable political scheming and racketeering against the beloved people.

5. A minimum period of five years must initially be allowed for the creation and maturation of necessary conditions and mutations required by the merging of the two belligerent armies and administrations into the New Sudan divorced of belligerency and of the basic cause of belligerence, Arab Nationalism. The armies and administrations of the Anyanya and of the Khartoum dictatorship must maintain separate identities during these five years of groundwork of conditions for Unity.
6. After the first initial five years of groundwork another minimum period of five years must be allowed for the actualization of the agreed degree of merging by the two armies and administrations. Merging and the actual objective formation of the NEW Sudan will be rapid in the second five years' period, since the necessary conditions and mutations for a United NEW Sudan will have been created in the first five years of groundwork.
7. We have made the above recommendations (guidelines) after a brief presentation of the objective political realities of the Sudan, not a bene Section (A) above. We have made these recommendations without fear of intimidation and with sincerity, objectivity and to the best interests of the Peoples of South Sudan, Africa and the world. We strongly believe that a United NEW Sudan and lasting peace and progress can be arrived at only through ACTION and not through PAPER declarations, resolutions and mechanical scheming. If the solution is sought within the spirit and logic of the above facts and recommendations, then, peace, progress and a United (NEW) Sudan are possible objectives to realize. But if, on the contrary hand, a solution is sought within the spirit

of Arab Nationalism and the context of a United Arab Sudan, then, gentlemen of the negotiations, instability, crisis and continued warfare are the only invited options and the Anyanya consistent with its historical and historic task of African liberation will take these options so mercilessly and mercifully placed upon its shoulders by blood thirsty Arab Chauvinism.

Captain John Garang de Mabior
The General Headquarters
Anyanya National Armed Forces
South Sudan
January 24, 1972

(This letter by John Garang from 1972 has been copied from the website Nyamilepedia)

In the Aftermath of the Addis Ababa Agreement

When the Addis Ababa Peace Agreement was made public a few months later, John Garang was critical of the outcome, but decided to go along with it. Consequently, he accepted an offer to become a Captain in the new Sudan National Forces, and he moved to Khartoum.

Shortly after having settled in Khartoum, he married Rebecca Nyadeng whom he had met during their stay in USA some years earlier. While Garang was Commander in Chief of SPLA, his wife Rebecca was both wife and a liberation fighter. In the beginning of the struggle she often stayed with him at front.

I have known Rebecca and John Garang from many meetings during the time of the struggle, and I have since my first meetings with them in the early 1990s seen them as my friends. While they both were alive, they were a beloved couple with six children. One of them, Mabior Garang de Mabior has taken up the Mantle of his father, now fighting with SPLM/A in Opposition for the hope of a return to a sane, human, democratic and peaceful political situation in South Sudan.

As an officer in Khartoum in the 1970s, John Garang continued to express his dissatisfaction with the Addis Ababa Agreement. His many political utterances became at the end so difficult and embarrassing for Abel Alier, Joseph Lagu and other old Anyanya leaders, that they provided a scholarship and persuaded Garang to go back to USA for further studies.

Garang accepted the offer and went back to USA towards the end of 1970s and was admitted to the famous US Fort Benning War Academy. As usual, he did extremely well and graduated number three out of 200 officers. He prolonged his stay in USA and went back to Iowa State University where he in 1981 completed his PHD in agricultural economics.

A year later he was back in Sudan and was immediately promoted to be a colonel and ordered to serve at the Military Headquarters of the National Armed Forces while he also on part time basis, held a position as Professor at the Agricultural Faculty of the University of Khartoum.

Not only that, soon upon his return to Sudan, Garang in secret founded a small group of likeminded officers with the name: "The Progressive Officers' Network". Their secret aim was to launch a National rebellion against the regime in Khartoum on 18th August 1983.

Garang's Norwegian Friend

While Garang in the latter part of 1960s studied at Grinell College, he was as a foreign student invited to visit the Hippi family whose forefathers had come from Ireland. The Hippi family at the time had a Norwegian student staying with them as their contribution to the US International Students' Exchange Programme. Her name is Haldis Drabløs Vonstad from the town of Aalesund on the North-Western Coast of Norway. She arrived in Minnesota in the fall of 1965 and returned to Norway in 1968. She shared this story with me:

"It was a very exciting experience for me coming from Norway, to meet with John Garang from Sudan. He represented a historical and cultural legacy so different from what I represented. John was a very friendly and polite young man, and he was very, very gifted and knowledgeable.

He was a great story teller as well and he really kept us awake, telling about the peoples of Sudan, their different backgrounds, the oppression of the Arab rulers. He was concerned with the problem of injustice. He was very clear in his opinion about the need to fight for liberation to get rid of oppression and poverty. He was at the same time very aware of the fact that international assistance and solidarity was needed for the liberation struggle to succeed, so that the peoples of Sudan could have a better future.

Halle:
Did he at any time share with you his reflections about his own role as a leader in the liberation struggle?
Haldis:
Yes, he often talked about his role and contribution. Once, while we had such a discussion, our host-mother made the following comment: John, when you get back to Sudan, you will either become the president, or they will arrest you and put you in jail. I do sincerely hope that the latter does not happen!

Mary was one of the daughters in the Hippi host family. She, Haldis and John Garang developed a very close friendship, and the two female students brought John Garang with them when there were traditional celebrations in the Irish and Norwegian immigrant communities. Once there was a big Christmas party with the Norwegians, and the participants as the tradition is, walked in circles around the Christmas Tree while singing old Christmas songs. Haldis told me the following story:

John Garang was present, but felt that this was a too strange tradition for him to participate. So, he remained sitting on a chair on one side of the big hall, watching the others and their walk and songs.

On the other side of the hall, there was a very old Norwegian male immigrant sitting. He was very old, and he had some difficulties when he had to walk. So, he was also sitting, watching. Then his eyes fell on John Garang. He stared for a while, then got on his feet and trudged across the floor to Garang. The old man starred again at Garang for a while and said:

"Tell me, what part of the country do you come from?"

John Garang also had an enjoyable memory of this episode and laughed as he told me this story.

There are many other stories from Garang's time as a student in USA that Haldis and others have shared with me. He was a very friendly and well-behaved young man who easily made friends in different social environments. He always studied and worked very hard, and he always did exceptionally well whenever he sat for exams. During his leisure time, he read literature, novels and poetry, philosophy, history and religion. Thus, he became a very learned man.

During holidays, he always worked to earn extra money which he sent back to poor and gifted Sudanese youngsters who could not otherwise afford to go to school.

The friendship established between Mary, Haldis and John Garang while they were students in Minnesota and Iowa, was expanded to include their spouses when they later married. When John Garang died in July 2005, the friendship between the others remained and continues to grow.

Stateless, wanted Asylum in Norway

Haldis Drabløs Vonstad told me during our many conversations about John Garang in USA also about their later family relationship:

"It was a sad day, the day in 1968 I left Minnesota at the end of my studies and had to say good-bye to Mary and John. But all the time after, John continued to send me greetings, sometimes only a postcard, sometimes a letter, sometimes they came by post, sometimes they were brought by Norwegian Staff members, first of NCA, then of NPA working in Sudan.

Once in 1969 I got a letter from his host family in Iowa. They told me that John had just completed his MA in agricultural economics. But as he was immensely disliked by the Khartoum regime because of his political stand and statements while he was a student both in Tanzania and USA, they had not only cancelled his passport but also made him stateless. Now, being a stateless person without a passport, the US authorities were unable to grant him permission to stay in the USA.

Garang needed help, and the question was whether we in my family could assist in the process of Garang coming to Norway as a political refugee and seek political asylum in Norway. My parents immediately responded that John could stay with us. However, when we sought for advice in our political environment about whether it was feasible that John could get asylum, the response was negative. Norway at the time had a centre-right government headed by Prime Minister Per Borten. The Minister of Justice at the time was Mrs. Elisabeth Schweigaard Selmer from the Conservative Party. She was a hardliner on issues related to asylum seekers. The conclusion was that it would be a risky affair trying to apply. However, the same political contacts advised to propose to John to apply for asylum in Sweden as Sweden with the young Olof Palme as an upcoming political leader had a very liberal policy towards asylum seekers.

However, the end of the story was that the American authorities had some contact with the authorities in Khartoum. They reversed their decision, reinstated John Garang as a Sudanese citizen and gave him his passport back."

Halle: *"When did you get acquainted with Rebecca Garang?"*

Haldis: *"Rebecca was an exchange student in USA, and she and John got to know each other during their stay in USA, but this happened after I had left USA.*

They married in 1981 just before they left for USA for John's second study visit, this time both at Fort Benning and the Iowa State University.

Then, there was quite a lot of contact at the family level. John's American host family met with him and Rebecca in Tanzania in 1989. John was then in Dar es Salaam for talks with the leadership of ANC.

He invited Mary and me to visit Rebecca and him in Nairobi in 1990, but we were at the same time informed that we had to plan our travel in secret and be very careful upon entry into Kenya, not mentioning his name etc. because he was a wanted guerilla leader who was hunted by his enemies.

We arrived in Nairobi one day in 1990 and reported as agreed in advance at the SPLM Office. We then were told that we could not see John in Nairobi, and that we for this reason had to travel to Addis Ababa to see him there. We did as advised, and travelled to Addis Ababa."

The story above fits into a story about Garang's experience with President Moi at the time which I would like to add. Garang and SPLM/A from the beginning in 1983 until the Nasir split in 1991, had as its political guideline a rather crude socialistic policy. In 1990 SPLM still had its Headquarters in Gambella in Ethiopia while they had an office in Nairobi.

Kenya both under Jomo Kenyatta and his successor President Moi in the economic field pursued a free market policy. They at the same time de facto maintained a kind of political dictatorship while they in their foreign policy favoured Western Europe and the USA.

Moi disliked immensely SPLM's socialist policy while he at the same time had sympathy for the liberation struggle. The presence in Kenya of both SPLM and John Garang was only tolerated while the leading members of SPLM/A were being closely watched.

Around 1990 SPLM in Kenya once acted in a way that made President Moi very furious, and he ordered for all SPLM personell and all refugees from South Sudan immediately to be expelled from Kenya. Garang was in despair, seeing a political catastrophe coming. He asked for an audience with Moi which was granted. When he entered the office of Moi, he was immediately struck by the continuing anger of the President.

Garang saw no option, but to kneel and pray to Moi for forgiveness for all mistakes committed by SPLM and himself, while at the same time pleading for the right for both SPLM and the refugees to stay in Kenya.

Moi listened, looked at Garang in silence for a little while, then he rose from his chair and said: "*You are forgiven. SPLM and the refugees may continue to stay in Kenya.*"

Haldis now continues her story about the 1990 visit:

Rebecca was waiting for us at the airport in Addis Ababa, and in the days following we stayed with her and the children in their house in Addis. I remember that there were Ethiopian guards outside the house and SPLM guards inside.

Shortly after our arrival, we received the news from John who was in Gambella, that he wanted us to travel to Gambella so that we could meet there. Departure was planned for the next morning, but when the driver went by the Police to get the permission to travel to Gambella the request from SPLM had been turned down. The political situation in Ethiopia at the time was extremely tense with daily demonstrations and clashes. A curfew was introduced, and we could not travel.

While we strived, trying to find solutions to our problems so that we could see John Garang, Nelson Mandela came on a state visit to Ethiopia. If anything, the visit of the great South African liberator and statesman only increased tension in the capital and in the country. The Police and the Military were on high alert and wanted to control everyone and everything.

The SPLM people who took care of us, tried and tried to get permission for us to drive by car to Gambella, but in vain. Our visit ended in Addis Ababa, and the big advantage was that we developed our friendship with Rebecca and he family a lot. This friendship has since only grown stronger and stronger."

Halle: "*After this journey to Nairobi and Addis Ababa, when did you next meet with John Garang?*"

Haldis: "*As far as I remember, it must have been in 1996. I got a message from the SPLM secretariat that John and Rebecca would come on visit to me and my family in Aalesund in connection with* a working visit John had at the CMI Centre at the University of Bergen (Bergen is the second biggest city in Norway, situated on the Western Coast). Rebecca and John not only wanted to see me and my family, but also Mr. Arvid Bøe, his old teacher from the days at the secondary school in Tanzania. Arvid was then in his late 70s, and he was extremely happy to learn that John soon was on his way to see him at his village in Romsdal (Arvid Bøe had then retired from his job as a missionary teacher in Tanzania and had moved back to his home village in Norway).

Unfortunately, John got so busy with his meetings in Bergen that he had to cancel his visit to Aalesund and Romsdal. Arvid then travelled to Bergen and saw John here. Arvid was so happy with that meeting, and he on his return from the meetings with John, said to me that he felt that John for sure was to become a great political leader not only in Sudan, but on the African Continent.

However, while John had his meetings in Bergen, Rebecca came on visit to Aalesund, and we had some wonderful days together. We then travelled together to Oslo, and I met with John during his stay in Oslo before he left for Kenya and the battlefields of Sudan".

The year after, Haldis and Mary on an invitation by Rebecca and John Garang, travelled to Nairobi and stayed with the family for a few days.

NPA was in 1999 both celebrating its 60 years' anniversary and having its Convention. John Garang and Rebecca were invited as guests of honour at the Convention. Two other guests were Haldis Drabløs and her husband Einar Vonstad. The four met a few times in private during the days of the NPA Convention.

In 2004 Haldis and Einar again visited the Garang family, first in Nairobi, and then they were flown into New Site in South Sudan and spent a few days with the Garang family at their home in New Site in South Sudan.

Haldis' friend from her time in USA, Mary Hippi was trained as a health worker, and she like Haldis maintained a strong solidarity engagement for the peoples of South Sudan. When Mary's children were grown up, she decided to leave her family to work as health worker with SPLM/A behind the frontlines in South Sudan. She worked hard and did well very well, and NPA decided in the late 1990 to employ Mary as a leading nurse at one of the hospitals we were in charge of in South Sudan. During the period from 2000 to 2003, Mary was in charge of the NPA Health Programme in South Sudan.

In addition to the visits and meetings mentioned, John and Rebecca have paid at least one visit to Haldis' family in Aalesund, and Haldis has been on visits to Nairobi.

In Aalesund in the late 1980s the Haldis and Einar Vonstad family together with solidarity friends in Aalesund and its surroundings, established a local solidarity club that annually collected approx. 10 000 to 15 000 USD that was used for health work for children in South Sudan. During my time as Secretary General of NPA, the leadership of the local club in Aalesund and NPA agreed to make the club part of the NPA National Association. Since then I have had many visits to Aalesund, given speeches on the situation in South Sudan and spent many pleasant evenings with the Vonstad family.

John Garang's many Enimies

John Garang had throughout his life as a liberation leader, many enemies. As soon as he in 1983 had been chosen the Commander in Chief of SPLA and the Chairman of SPLM, the Khartoum regime declared him their arch enemy. Consequently, they had a continuous hunt for him throughout the whole war of liberation from 1983 until around 2002/3. If they could have him killed, it would be so much easier to quell what they saw as a rebellion in the South. In addition, there were a few Southerners as well who hated him and would rather see him dead.

After the Nasir split in 1991, both Riek Machar and Lam Akol belonged to that group, and both developed close cooperation with the regime in Khartoum to have Garang killed and the SPLM/A/ Mainstream destroyed. Militia commanders from South Sudan like

Peter Gadet and Paulino Matiep, had with orders from Khartoum the liquidation of Garang as a permanent point on their agenda.

Within the leadership of SPLM/A there was from time to time risky tension and conflict, caused by internal disagreement and rivalry. Three of those causing difficult internal conflicts, were Arok Thon, William Nyuon and Kerubino Nyuon. The three were illiterates, and they were extremely authoritarian and brutal in their dealing both with SPLA soldiers and the local civilian population.

In the end, Garang had no choice but to degrade and exclude them from SPLM/A. Their immediate response was to contact Khartoum to declare their loyalty and their willingness to serve the interests of Khartoum. The task given to them by Khartoum was to assassinate Garang.

Bona Malwal, a Man of Political Destruction who hated Garang

Bona Malwal is a Dinka leader and an intellectual, born in 1938, who had his education in journalism and thereafter worked as journalist. He was a member of the Government in South Sudan during the peace time 1972-1983. Since then he has spent part of his time in Khartoum and part in Oxford, Great Britain. He, from the very beginning of the founding of SPLA and SPLM in 1983, developed a political opposition to Garang that at the end of Garang's life turned into a personal hatred, and Bona Malwal is known to have had spitting comments about Garang in the aftermath of his death.

Bona Malwal, while being a member of the Jieng Council of Elders, has in recent years developed a kind of racist ideological belief that the Dinka people are superior to the other ethnic groups in South Sudan. He is a close friend of Salva Kiir and an intimate political advisor as well. He was, according to my sources, advising Kiir in the summer of 2013 about the changes Kiir should carry out both with his government and within SPLM. He has stayed on as a close advisor to Kiir during the time of the civil war from December 2013 until the present. In the winter of

2015 he undertook a lecture tour in USA as an Envoy of Present Salva Kiir, preaching the superiority of the Dinkas while ridiculing the Nuers and the other ethnic groups in South Sudan as being inferior and not fit to govern South Sudan. Bona Malwal carries a large responsibility for the hatred of Garang that has developed with some of the Dinka elite in South Sudan. As a political advisor with a very strong influence with President Salva Kiir, he also carries a heavy responsibility for the destruction of South Sudan that has taken place from the summer of 2013.

Kerubino, another of Garang's bitter Enemies on a special Mission in Nairobi

All the enemies of Garang made his everyday life difficult. While on mission in the field he from 1983 until the establishment of New Site in 2002 could hardly stay one night in the same shelter. While travelling in the battlefields, he and his guards always had to look for agents who might have penetrated the inner circles of confidants with the mission to assassinate. They had furthermore to look out for snipers, mines and air attacks. During visits abroad, he always had to look out for mercenaries who had been paid to kill him.

I do not have the full overview of all the failed attempts at Garang's life, but Elliah Malok writes the following in his book; "The South Sudan Struggle for Liberty":

"A lot is still not known about all the times John Garang had a narrow escape from death both at the front and in other situations. However, only in the short period between 1996 and 2000 Garang's car hit a landmine several times, but Garang like a miracle escaped unhurt every time."

I have been told about two other narrow escapes, of which the last one is still surrounded with a lot of mystery.

As I have already narrated in chapter 8, NPA had in the years 1998 – 2001 problems with the Kenyan Tax and Revenue Authority. They wanted to investigate our accounting system and the way we paid salaries to our staff. We in NPA did not believe that this request was made in good faith, but rather was stimulated by agents of Khartoum who again and again tried to corrupt politicians and officials in the Kenyan public service to have things done their way.

While the NPA had these problems, Kerubino who many years earlier had been expelled from SPLM/A because of his brutal conduct of war and his equally brutal behavior towards civilians, came on a special mission to Nairobi. This was in the late summer of 1999, and he made it known that he had an interest in seeking a rapprochement with Garang because he wanted to get back to SPLM/A. However, the SPLA intelligence agents in Nairobi had at the time received advanced spy technology, and they were watching Kerubino's movements in town. They soon discovered that he paid frequent visits to the Sudanese Embassy. They tapped the conversations that took place inside while Kerubino was on a visit, and they soon picked up that the real mission of Kerubino was to assassinate Garang. Garang was at the time, staying in his residence in Nairobi, and the plan was for a small group of well-trained and armed special soldiers to attack at the residence and kill Garang. The evening came, the attack began, but the attackers met stiff resistance as a SPLA unit was waiting and fighting back. Most of the attackers were killed, but one survived and escaped, Kerubino.

But Kerubino's mission had a part II, and that was the same evening to have a gang of bandits carry out an attack on NPA's Office in Nairobi in order to destroy it. As planned, a gang of bandits armed with sticks and iron tools attacked the NPA gate, trying to break it. The gate was of iron and locked with big locks. To try and break it was hard work. Our night guards (askaris) on duty immediately called the nearest police station, and the Kenyan Police responded within minutes with a speed and a forcefulness unheard of. A small, but very efficient unit of security officers and soldiers came apparently from nowhere, beat down the bandits, arrested all of them and drove away. The NPA management in Nairobi was in the aftermath of what happened that night, only vaguely told about the background for the attack. I later picked up more.

What lesson did NPA learn from this experience? Firstly, it was another confirmation that Khartoum viewed NPA as enemy. Secondly, the efficient way the Kenyan Police dealt with the attempted break in, we read as a message from Kenya: *We keep an eye on you, and we protect you when necessary.*

What happened to Kerubino? He hurried back to Khartoum and again declared that his service was available, and he ended up joining the Southern militia group, named the South Sudan United Forces, headed by the infamous Paulino Matip. There are conflicting reports about the end saga of Kerubino, but according to my sources, Khartoum was tired of Kerubino, and he was led into an ambush one day in September 1999 and killed. In style with the tradition of South Sudanese militia leaders and similar, he had several wives and at least 20 children who suddenly lost their bread winner who had made his income from brutality, war and death.

Another narrow Escape for Garang

In February 2000, I stayed for a few days in Nairobi on one of many missions into South Sudan. John Duku, the SPLM Resident to the Nordic countries, was in Nairobi at the same time, and the two of us had an informal meeting with John Garang and Rebecca at their residence in Nairobi. They were both in excellent spirits. We talked about the political and military situation in Sudan, about the growing international push for peace negotiations to take off and the role being played by the Norwegian Minister of Development Cooperation, Hilde Frafjord Johnson. And we of course talked about NPA, our work in the field, the problems we had had, and the fact that we felt the Government of Kenya was protecting our presence in the country.

The informal meeting came to an end, and we said good bye. As we came out, there were so many people gathered and a few of them were priests in their gowns. I asked one of them why they were gathering, and the priest being extremely serious, told the following story:

"We are here having a service to thank our God and Father for again having saved the life of John Garang."

A staff member of the Garang inner circle told me a bit later about the background for the gathering.

John Garang had for a while planned to pay a working visit to one of his close friends in Black Africa, the former President of Nigeria, Olusegun Obasanjo, and they wanted to combine that visit with one to another friend in Black Africa, the President of the Ivory Coast. The day for the travel arrived, and Garang and two close aides left for the Nairobi International Airport. They checked in and were about to board the plane when suddenly a Kenyan security officer appeared from nowhere, asking to see their travel documents. He had a quick glance at them and in a very affirmative tone said:

You do not have proper travel documents, and you are therefore not allowed to travel. He then told them to return to their residences in Nairobi. No other explanation.

The KQ flight no 431 took off for Lagos. But as it approached Lagos, the weather conditions were too bad to land. The Harmattan wind was blowing heavily from the Sahara Desert, and the visibility was poor. The experienced captain therefore decided to continue to Abidjan. Having waited for some hours in Abidjan, the weather conditions in Lagos improved, and the captain decided to return to Lagos. But shortly after takeoff, the plane crashed into the seas off Abidjan. Only ten of the 179 passengers and crew survived. The cause of the accident was most likely a technical one. Of the 169 who died in the crash, the authorities were able to identify all passengers, but one.

But what reason was behind the order of the Kenyan security officer for Garang and his aids not to travel? The order may in some way or other have come from somebody with higher authority.

My Meetings with John Garang

My first meeting with John Garang was at NPA in Oslo in the winter of 1993 and my last was in Oslo during the Donor Conference in the Spring of 2005. In the time span of these 12 years we met, mostly in Nairobi and sometimes in the field. In addition, I met him during the peace negotiations in Naivasha.

I have in chapter six told my story from February 2003 about an NPA flight via Kigali into Akot, and the night we spent at the airstrip in Akot. On our return the day after, we had a stop at New Site to see John Garang and Rebecca. This time we travelled together with the SPLA officer who had been in charge of the guard at the airstrip the night before. The weather was bright with high visibility as we flew down, and the young SPLA officer and I stood side by side looking out through the window on the landscape below while he pointed out areas of battles he had taken part in. He was one of the many young men and women of South Sudan who had been fighting for liberty, human dignity and human rights, and then in the winter of 2003 as the peace negotiations were approaching their final stages, was hoping for peace, freedom and development.

When we landed at New Site, John Garang and Rebecca were waiting at the airstrip for me and my NPA colleague and friend, Ken Miller. We had a talk about the peace negotiations that at that point in time were at a cross road.

But it was also in one of the rare situations one could meet with Rebecca and John Garang in a very relaxed and informal setting. It was a quiet and warm afternoon with a soft wind passing by, and the most dominant sound came from birds, singing in the trees around the village. Rebecca and John were in excellent spirits, talking laughing and joking, holding each other's hands as if they were two youngsters who had just fallen in love. They took us on a sight-seeing walk through the village, and John left it for Rebecca to be our guide. There was a lot of activities, a primary school for children, an adult education centre for women, a house where women did handicraft. The whole thing was impressive.

They also showed us the SPLM Guest House. It was a nice house, but simple in its structure. John was laughing as he told us that it did not hold the standard of Hilton Hotel or similar. Sometimes when high level politicians, diplomats or special envoys from abroad came on a working visit, they had difficulties accepting and adopting to the little comfort available.

Both on this trip and in one other, I picked up this amusing story below from visits of dignitaries in New Site.

John Danforth in New Site

In 2002 President George Bush appointed Senator John Danforth as his Special Envoy for Sudan. Danforth who was a very experienced politician on US affairs, had only limited insight into the complexities of African politics. He travelled first to Khartoum to see representatives of the Khartoum regime and discuss with them the ongoing peace negotiations and problems related to them.

Most Khartoum governments have been known for their great hospitality towards their foreign guests. They treat and entertain them greatly to benefit politically at the end. So they treated Danforth very well indeed, and he, according to my sources, came to enjoy both his stay and some of the views held by members of the government.

Then, Danforth travelled to New Site to see Garang and other members of the SPLM leadership group. Danforth was invited to stay in the best guest room in the SPLM Guest House. I have seen the room. It was nice, but simple, and the menu that could be provided for Danforth at New Site could not meet the lavish standard of Khartoum

So, when Danforth and Garang met for their first round of discussion ever, Danforth was in somewhat bad mood when he delivered his message which he ended with the following:

"Mr. Garang, if you do not understand the implications of what I have said, I shall bury you."

Garang looked quietly at him. He thanked Danforth for coming the long way to New Site to see him, and he asked Danforth to convey to President Bush how happy he was with the fact that the US President had appointed him as the Special Envoy for Sudan. Then, Garang elaborated on the SPLM policies and their positions and demands in the ongoing peace negotiations, and said: *"So, Mr. Danforth. If you do not understand what I have told you now and the implications thereof, I shall bury you."*

My sources told me that Danforth did not expect Garang to reply in the way he did. Danforth was silent for a little while before he came back into the discussion with a very different and softer approach.

More from my Meetings with John Garang

As mentioned, the relationship between Rebecca and John Garang was always very loving and very special. Rebecca was like her husband a very political human being. She had throughout the struggle stood firmly besides her husband, the SPLM Chairman and the SPLA Commander in Chief. She like many other young liberation fighters had had their guerilla training in Cuba. She had been in battle zones with her gun, but during battles had mostly taken care of wounded soldiers, softened their pains and provided food.

John Garang himself was a very impressive personality. Sometimes when I came to see him, I tended to believe that the struggle was such an uphill battle, that it was difficult to predict a victorious outcome. John Garang always had another and much better analysis of what was going on. Whenever I and other solidarity comrades left him, John Garang had convinced us that the outcome would be victorious. Garang never said that SPLA would win a military victory. He always stressed the following:

"We in SPLM/A shall at the end create a combined military and political situation that shall force Khartoum to negotiate a peace agreement."

The content of this sentence, Garang stated again and again in our many meetings during the 12 years we met.

It was always both very exciting and very rewarding to talk with John Garang. He was always an optimist, also when times were dark.

He had a very good PHD from Ohio State University in Agricultural Economics, and he was a military graduate with superb grades from Fort Benning in USA. In addition, in his extremely pressed everyday life he had taken time to read literature and philosophy. He was not only a brilliant intellectual, but in the very meaning of the word, a very learned man who could talk about any subject with insight and authority.

Whenever we met, John Garang wanted to talk about the African political awakening in Sudan. He always reminded us that there was an African majority in the country, and that a significant minority of them were muslims. They had in common that they for so long had been oppressed by the Arab elite in Khartoum, for so long had been exposed to the oppressive religious and cultural propaganda of the same Arab elite, that they had come to believe that they were Muslims first and Africans second. What mattered now was to make them politically and culturally conscious of the fact that they were Africans first and muslims second. This consideration was first and foremost directed towards the peoples of the North, first and foremost, the African peoples of Darfur, The Red Sea Mountains and the Nuba Mountains.

Another frequent topic was Islam. John Garang was very seasoned on that topic. He was utterly critical of Islamist fundamentalism and the court around the Khartoum dictator Omar Bashir who were islamists. He said that they sometimes talked in ways that may make one believe that they were in favour of human rights and equal rights for women, and then he added with a strong emphasis:

"You must never trust what they say. They will always have an interpretation or meaning of what they say that is very different from what you believe that they say. One must never allow for these people to gain dominant political power and influence because then

they become very dangerous. They must always be controlled by a democratic majority of a secular state".

On this point Garang held an absolute view. In the eyes of the most conservative islamists Garang was not only a dangerous man, but a man who had to dye because of his views.

Ken Miller who was the NPA manager for emergency and food aid into South Sudan and did outstanding work during the time of the liberation struggle, knew John Garang very well. He had this to say about Garang:

"He was a very strong and able leader. He was so knowledgeable and sure of himself. He was like a magnet for other people, they were drawn to him, and the best of them became his confidants and very close staff members. He was very disciplined, and he worked very hard. His working day began often around 4 to 5 o'clock in the morning and ended very late at night."

Throughout the struggle, again and again complaints came about SPLA violating human rights and human dignity by abusing and mistreating their fellow-people in South Sudan. There is no doubt that this happened from time to time.

In NPA we brought up this matter of violating human rights in our talks with John Garang and other leading people in SPLM. They listened and said that our complaints would be considered, and if some commander was found guilty, he would be punished. I know that our complaints sometimes were followed up.

John Garang's Appeal for Support for the Building of democratic Institutions

John Garang, once in a meeting we had in Nairobi in early August 1998, raised an important matter for discussion. In the main, this was what he said:

SPLM/SPLA is now in physical control of most of the land area of South Sudan. We have to prepare ourselves for the fact that we soon shall have the political power to govern the people of the land, but we are ill prepared for this challenge.

> Our officers and soldiers need education and training in the conduct of war as it is laid down in the Geneva Conventions. We now need to develop a military behavior that ends the reasons for the many complaints about us violating human rights and the Geneva Conventions. We shall soon have to establish a civil law enforcement authority at the level of our villages, but we have no cadres who are trained to do such a job.
>
> We shall also soon have to establish a civilian administration that is based on the principles and values that govern a democratic society in the areas liberated, but we have very few people trained for this task and with an experience to do it.
>
> For all this we need international assistance. Can you in NPA and can Norway assist us in all this?"

As soon as I returned to Oslo, I held a well-attended press conference where I shared with the media and civil society my experience from the fields of South Sudan with people starving and dying because of drought, hunger and war and the continuing big need for humanitarian assistance. I also explicitly shared with the audience the message from John Garang about the need for international assistance both with regards to democracy building and the training of officers and soldiers in the conduct of war according to the rules laid down in the Geneva Conventions.

It was summer time, and on that day, the Norwegian Broadcasting Corporation (NRK) sent a young and inexperienced holiday substitute to report on what I had to tell. She concluded from my statements that it was unheard of and immoral of Garang to ask for international assistance to begin laying the basis for democratic development of the society of South Sudan in a situation when people were dying from hunger and war.

When the NRK TV news were broadcast in the evening, this was the top story; The indifferent and immoral John Garang who did ask for support for democracy building while his people were dying.

Hilde Frafjord Johnson who then in the summer of 1998 still was a relatively new and inexperienced Minister of Development and Human Rights, was called to the newsroom and interviewed in a very partial way by the same reporter about Garang's indifference. The Minister responded the way the reporter wanted. She said that Garang's message was untimely and would therefore not be considered.

The Minister and myself in the days following, had a few hard rounds debating in radio and in the newspapers about Garang's message which I of course strongly defended and supported. NPA alone did not have the financial base to support Garang's proposal in a big way, but we did the little we could. No other international donor would either support Garang's request. It fell on deaf ears.

In the aftermath of this and with the destructive events in South Sudan in the last couple of years with a dictatorial government, led by President Kiir, murdering its own people, I have from time to time reflected on Garang's message from August 1998. I considered it, not only very important, but foresighted and visionary. If the international donor community in 1998 had listened and come to the aid of SPLM and the emerging civil society in South Sudan and started the building of the democratic foundations so desperately needed, maybe South Sudan today would have been a young, peaceful and emerging democracy instead of being what it is, the place for horror and death and the systematic violations of human rights and human dignity.

John Garang and Hilde Frafjord Johnson and their Encounters

In the spring of 1998, Hilde Frafjord Johnson as a young and ambitious Minister, made her first careful moves to get going the stalled peace negotiations for Sudan.

I met Garang in the field in South Sudan just shortly before Hilde Frafjord Johnson came to see him for the first time, and I asked him what he thought about the news that had arrived about a new Norwegian peace initiative.

He said that he could not care less, and that he felt that there were a few Norwegian Church Aid people who dreamt about getting the Nobel Peace Award.

Hilde Frafjord Johnson travelled shortly after my visit to Kenya and South Sudan to see John Garang for the first time. NPA got the task to get the appointment in place, and thereafter to provide for air transport. The meeting was to be held in Chukudum where NPA had a rather comprehensive project activity.

I talked with Hilde Frafjord Johnson sometime after that meeting, and she said:

"NPA facilitated my first meeting with John Garang, and Halvor Aschjem, one of the former leaders of NCA, was accompanying me. The first part of the flight was to Loki in Turkana where we stayed overnight at the NPA Camp. The day after, we continued to Chukudum and first visited the polytechnic school NPA had in Chukudum.

Then we met with John Garang. I felt that I could establish a very good communication with him. He was a very impressive personality. He had self-confidence, and he was a strong leader. We had in my view a very good first meeting."

A couple of months later I was again on mission in South Sudan, I met John Garang anew, and I asked him about the first meeting with Hilde Frafjord Johnson.

He brightened up, smiled and said:

"Oh, Hilde, she's almost like one of us. We have set the tune. She speaks Kiswahili, and she knows us Africans. I really like her, and I look forward to our coming meetings with great expectations."

Then from 1998 and until 2005 I met with John Garang many times. We talked about the NPA activities in the field, the liberation struggle, the peace negotiations and about Hilde Frafjord Johnson.

John Garang had on that matter a consistent view:

"Hilde is outstanding. We have full confidence in each other, and she does a marvelous job to push the peace process forward."

Those of us who followed the peace negotiations know that this special relationship lasted until the death of John Garang on

30th July 2005. Both Hilde and I were guests at Garang's funeral. We met in Nairobi the night after, and she said:

"Halle, I have cried and cried all the time since this happened. What has happened is so terrible, and it is such an enormous loss for the peoples of South Sudan."

Garang welcomed as the victorious in Khartoum

John Garang was in the period after the signing of the CPA in Nairobi on 9th January 2005, travelling almost day and night across South Sudan to tell the people about the peace. The people came walking or on bikes or mules or in buses in their tens of thousands to the meetings to listen to their great liberator.

At the same time Garang was very busy getting the implementation of the CPA started. With the signature of the CPA, John Garang became the President of South Sudan and the 1st Vice-President of Sudan. A constitution for the transition period of six years had to be worked out while the new public administration for South Sudan had to be established from scratch. There was no end to what had to be done.

However, the most important and at the same time, the most unpredictable of all things that had to be done, was the ceremony in Khartoum on 9th July 2005 when John Garang was to be inaugurated as the 1st Vice-president of Sudan.

The negotiations between the NCP Government in Khartoum and SPLM about how the ceremony was to be conducted, were very difficult and dragging out in time. President Omar Bashir and his government wanted a minimalist ceremony, SPLM the opposite, a big one. One of the SPLM top leaders from the North, Yassir Arman, was in charge of the negotiations, and he told me that it was only late in the night just a few hours away from the morning when the ceremony was to take place, that they finally had a compromise.

The unknown question was all the time; how many people would come for the ceremony. The NCP government was hoping for less and had planned for a maximum of 100 000 attending.

However, even before dawn, hundreds of thousands of the poor and the black people of Khartoum were on the move towards the square where the ceremony was to take place. At the end, the assessment was that more than a million people turned out to celebrate that John Garang, the great liberator, had become the 1st Vice-President of Sudan.

The presence of this mass of people was of great encouragement for John Garang and SPLM. It confirmed that he and SPLM had a large popular political support also in the North. If free and fair elections were to be held in the whole of Sudan which was an essential part of the CPA, John Garang stood a good chance to be the victorious and the first President of the new Sudan. If that were to happen, the road was open to realize his lifelong political dream and vision:

"The new Sudan, secular and democratic with respect for human dignity and human rights".

The helicopter accident, John Garang dies

The present holders of political power in Khartoum, got their power through a military coup d'état in 1989. The ideological and religious foundation for the new regime was Islamism. The man in charge of the coup was the young officer, Omar Bashir, the present President an de facto dictator in Sudan.

Bashir and his court reacted in disbelief and fear to the mass manifestation of support for Garang. They read it the only way possible; If free and fair elections were to be held as was stated in the CPA, Garang might win and they would lose. Such a result would not only carry far reaching consequences of a personal nature for Bashir and his court. Much more important, they would lose political power and they would not any longer be able to operate as oppressive cleptokrats exploiting the economy of Sudan for their own benefits. Last, but not least, the Arab minority in Sudan would lose the very privileged position they had enjoyed economically, socially and culturally in Sudan for almost 70 years.

This outlook was grim and it had to be destroyed, one way or another.

In the days following the ceremony in Khartoum, John Garang travelled far and wide across Sudan, meeting large crowds everywhere who wanted to listen and learn about the time of peace that was ahead.

On 29th July the President of Uganda, Yoweri Museveni, invited him for a private get together at his farm south of Entebbe. John Garang honoured the invitation and stayed overnight at the farm. What they talked about, only Museveni knows.

Early in the morning of 30th July the Norwegian Ambassador to Uganda, Tore Gjøs got a call from Museveni inviting him and the other Nordic ambassadors for lunch together with him and Garang. The Nordic ambassadors had only one thing to do, it was to honour the invitation.

According to Gjøs, who told me the story during a visit I had to Kampala in the fall of 2005, Museveni was a bit reserved during their informal talks while Garang was in an excellent mood. Many items were discussed, the relationship between Uganda and Sudan in the aftermath of the liberation war and the CPA. No in-depth analysis or discussion of any matter, but a pleasant get-together in a friendly atmosphere.

Garang had promised his wife Rebecca to come home to New Site in South Sudan on 30th July, and he wanted very much to keep his promise. Museveni had made available for him one of his helicopters, and as soon as the luncheon had come to an end, Garang wanted to leave. However, the weather forecast for that afternoon for the eastern part of South Sudan was bad, thunder showers and wind, but Garang was determined. He wanted to go.

Garang had usually a very tight security. He had a few security intelligence officers who were very close to him and absolutely loyal. They always kept an iron-ring of security around Garang.

But two of the leading officers were missing on 30th of July. Garang had sent them on a very important secret mission inside Sudan. They were to meet and negotiate with one of the most brutal and notorious militia commanders in South Sudan, the nuer warlord, Paulino Matiep Nhial, the commander of the SSDF, the South Sudan Defence Forces. The task of Garang's confidants was to negotiate with Paulino Matiep about SSDF agreeing to join and integrate with the SPLA, the new National Army of South Sudan.

South Sudanese friends of mine who knew the security routines around Garang, say that they are convinced that if the two security officers who were on this secret mission in South Sudan, had been present and taken part in the security discussion that afternoon in Uganda, they would never have, under the prevailing weather conditions, allowed Garang to fly that afternoon.

The helicopter had a stopover at Entebbe before it continued in the direction of New Site. There were thunder showers and heavy wind. Rebecca Garang said that she heard the helicopter and left the house to look for it. High up in the skies she could see its lights, and she expected it to land. But suddenly the landing procedure seemed to be interrupted, and the helicopter disappeared into the skies.

A few moments later it crashed into a mountain peak, and all onboard lost their lives.

The news about the helicopter that had disappeared was soon picked up by the Khartoum Intelligence Services, and they quickly announced that an accident had taken place. From Uganda, there was no news. However, SPLM/A replied immediately to the news from Khartoum that they were wrong. The helicopter had had an emergency landing at an airstrip in South Sudan, but everyone onboard were safe.

This was a false piece of news planted by the SPLM leadership, but why? They knew that an accident had happened and that John Garang and the others onboard most likely had died. They also knew that when the news became known, there would be strong popular reactions in South Sudan, but also in the whole of the country and that the acting leadership of SPLM/A could be put under severe pressure. It could lead to an internal split in the movement, and the CPA agreement would obviously be in great danger. They of course also knew that many within the NCP in Khartoum and in the Bashir Government had expressed their disagreement with the CPA. They wanted it dead and buried.

The false piece of news from SPLM/A gave the leadership sufficient time to call a meeting of the National Liberation Council in Rumbek that for the time being was the capital of South Sudan. The meeting of the NLC took place, the members learnt about the tragedy that had happened. There was a short discussion. Then some members of the NLC proposed that Salva Kiir should be elected as Garang's successor, holding both the Chair of SPLM and being the Commander in Chief of SPLA. This also meant that Salva Kiir automatically would take over the positions as the President of South Sudan and the 1st Vice-President of Sudan. Furthermore, the CPA was no longer threatened to the same extent.

Then the SPLM/A leadership announced that they had been mistaken about the landing of the helicopter on an airstrip in South Sudan, and that an accident had taken place in which John Garang and all the others onboard the helicopter, had died. They further conveyed their feeling of sorrow and loss to the peoples of Sudan and South Sudan, and then they announced that the NLC had met and elected Salva Kiir as John Garang's successor in all positions he had held.

Those in Sudan and in other places who wished Garang dead, won the first round, but they failed in their wish to see SPLM/A split and for the time being to see the CPA dead and buried.

The black box of the helicopter was found shortly after the accident. An International Commission of Investigation was set up with participation from SPLM/A, The Khartoum Government, Uganda, USA and Russia and headed by the South Sudanese/Sudanese old statesman, Abel Allier. They worked for some weeks, and then the report was made public. The conclusion was that the helicopter had come to close to the mountain range and lost control. The pilot was to blame, the crash was attributed to human error.

An Accident or an Assassination?

John Garang was a friend, and I have talked with many people about what happened. Some were outstanding East African journalists, others were East African politicians, international diplomats or military officers with a long experience from the conflict-ridden areas in the Horn of Africa, some were pilots with a long experience from flying in South Sudan.

Most of those I have talked to, many of them being South Sudanese and some of them leading members of the SPLM/A that was, others being East Africans and a very few Europeans and North Americans, continue to believe that it was a very well designed and planned assassination of the man who threatened the established and dictatorial political order of Sudan.

As time passes, I like them have come to believe the same, that John Garang was assassinated in an extremely well-planned plot.

However, while I was writing this book, I also have talked to people who have had access to the members of the International Commission that made the investigation, and a few of them have read the report from the Commission and listened to the tape from the black box. They are convinced that it was an accident. This is still the official view.

Whatever it was, the peoples of Sudan and South Sudan and the peoples of Africa, lost a very great leader and a learned man with great visions for the future for the peoples of Sudan and of Africa.

The cost of his death is today very visible in the two failed states of Sudan, first and foremost, the new and totally failed state of dictatorial South Sudan, but also the failed state of the dictatorship in Khartoum.

16
DINNER GUESTS AT HOME IN OSLO

1992. Salva Kiir with a Delegation on their Way for Meetings in Bergen in Norway

I was still in the fall of 1992 new as the International Director of NPA. One day in November we had the news from our office in Nairobi that Salva Kiir and three other high ranking leaders of SPLM/A were on their way for meetings in Bergen.

The delegation would have a night stop-over in Oslo, and they wanted to have a meeting with the NPA about our work in South Sudan.

But why were they going to Bergen? The University of Bergen, UoB, had in 1992 had an academic cooperation programme with the University of Khartoum that had lasted for almost 30 years. There were many both Sudanese and Norwegian students and scholars specializing on topics in Sudan that had been working both in Bergen and in Khartoum. UoB had for some time developed a reputation of being an International Centre of Excellence when it came to studies of topics related to Sudan. The Director General of UoB at the time was Magne Lerheim. He had a strong political interest and an equally strong interest for cooperation among academic institutions in the North and the South. Lerheim had a strong working partner in Gunnar Sorbø who at the time was the new Director of the Centre for International Development Studies at UoB, and a fellow at the Internationally well-known CMI Institute that was linked to UoB.

They wanted to talk with the top leadership of SPLM/A about the possibility of using UoB as the Norwegian bridge head for peace talks, trying to find a way to stop the ongoing war in Sudan.

I had during my mission to South Sudan on behalf of NPA in the spring of 1987 learnt quite a lot from Egil Hagen about the SPLM/A leadership, and I had met a few of the second in command during my field trip. But this time it would be the first meeting, face to face, with some of the top leaders. The delegation had as members, Salva Kiir, then the deputy Chairman of SPLM and the deputy Commander in Chief of SPLA, Yusif Kuwa Meeki the SPLM/A leader and Commander from the Nuba Mountains, Martin Okerruk, the SPLM official Spokesman at the time and John Duku, the SPLM Resident Representative to the Nordic countries, based in Copenhagen.

A few of the NPA staff went over to the hotel in Oslo to meet the delegation and guide them to the NPA offices. They arrived and had a very friendly welcome. However, when they entered the NPA meeting room, I took note of the fact that they all were very poorly dressed for the Norwegian winter. They had inexpensive summer suits bought in Nairobi for a tropical climate and light shoes, but nor scarfs nor coats. In Oslo, it was cold with a humid and frosty air. It was obvious that our Sudanese guests felt the cold and did not like the weather in Oslo.

The meeting started, and we talked about the conflict. They told us very frankly that it was difficult times with many setbacks both militarily and politically. SPLM/A was still suffering from the Nasir Split in August 1991 and the combined offensive of Khartoum government forces and the forces of Riek Machar and Lam Akol. The military coup d'état in Khartoum in 1989 had brought to power an Islamic group headed by colonel Omar Bashir. The new rulers in Khartoum had both rejected any proposals for peace negotiations, and they had made it very clear that the war against the infidels would be stepped up. About the same time, there had been a violent shift of power in Addis Ababa. The dictatorial Marxist regime of Colonel Mengistu had been defeated by the forces of the Tigray Peoples Liberation front. The new rulers had abandoned the agreement SPLM/A had with the former regime about military training camps, refugee camps, youth camps and more, and they had then forced SPLM/A and all refugees to leave Ethiopian soil.

We then discussed the NPA contribution in the field of humanitarian assistance and the possibility of enlarging our programme.

At the end of the meeting, we in NPA repeated our political solidarity stand with the peoples of Sudan and South Sudan in their struggle for liberation while we promised to do our utmost to try and expand our programme so that more food and medicine could be available for the peoples behind the frontlines.

What struck both me and my NPA colleagues during our meeting, was the politeness, friendliness and relaxed mood that our guests conveyed. They certainly contributed to a very pleasant atmosphere in our meeting.

At the end of the meeting I asked our visitors whether they had any commitment for the coming evening. They said they were free. I then asked them whether they would like to come home to my wife Marit and me for dinner. They answered with a happy yes. I gave directions to our home and asked them to take a taxi that NPA would refund.

They arrived as agreed around 7 pm. Outside it was dark and cold with a frosty air, and as they entered the house it was easy to see that the November weather had an impact. They were all a bit frozen, and a few had already caught a cold.

In our home, the fireplace provided warmth and the candle lights were burning. All of them were pleased to have a glass of wine or beer except Yusif Kuwa who was a Muslim and wanted something non-alcoholic. The mood was informal and pleasant. We soon invited our guests to the table where a casserole with lamb meat was waiting. We had a very enjoyable meal.

After a while Yusif, the commander from the Nuba Mountains, wanted to say something about the ongoing war. He had from the very beginning a way of talking that was very convincing. He combined charisma and a low and friendly voice with authority. Firstly, he emphasised that the peoples of the Nuba Mountains were Africans, but they had been oppressed and humiliated for so long by the oppressors in Khartoum that they had converted to the same religion, Islam.

However, he had established contacts with John Garang, and they had had many talks about the situation in the Nuba Mountains. Garang had again and again emphasised that most of the peoples in Sudan North were Africans, and that it in particular related to the Nuba Mountains. Yusif Kuwa further told that Garang in their discussions had underlined the need to make the majority of the peoples of Sudan North conscientious of the fact that they were Africans first and Muslims second. Garang called it "the African Awakening in Sudan". The talks with Garang had made Yusif convinced that Garang's analysis and message was right. He and his people in the Nuba Mountains were Africans first and were the carriers of an African cultural tradition.

When all this was in place in Yusif's mind, he had got a new political foundation for his resistance to the oppressors in Khartoum. He had decided to join SPLM/A in full, take up arms and accept the responsibility as the regional Commander in Chief in the liberation struggle. The others of us at the table listened in silence, but with greatest interest to what Yusif told us. What Marit and I did not learn that evening was that Yusif Kuwa as and SPLM leader and SPLA Commander was loved by the people for his humane behaviour and at the same time his rare qualities as a leader. For the enemy, the situation was the opposite, they feared Yusif Kuwa more than any other SPLM/A commander in the region.

Yusif then stopped talking for a while, and I saw that Salva Kiir was looking quite intensely to our bookshelf in which there were many books on Africa. He pointed to one of the books and said: "*Halle, may I have a look at it?*"

It was the great picture book; THE PEOPLES OF KAU, made by the very famous, but also very controversial German photographer, Leni Riefenstahl. She was once the Nazi-dictator Hitler's most important film maker and photographer. She was in the aftermath of the Second World War imprisoned for 4 years, but no further case was made against her. However, she became an outcast in post-war German and European film industry, and she decided to do good as an art photographer in Africa. She went to the Nuba Mountains and made the famous book.

We others now watched Salva Kiir as he got completely taken by the pictures in the book. Several minutes passed, and then he said:

"*Halle, you have to give this book to me.*"

I answered that this was the only copy I had, but as soon as I got back to Nairobi, I promised to find a copy for him as well.

He accepted, and our talk around the table continued.

The evening was a very pleasant one, and the time ran fast. As our guests were about to leave, my wife Marit asked:

The clothes you carry, is that all you have for your stay in Norway?

The answer was yes. Then Marit told them to wait for a while, and she went to our store room and came back with four sweaters, winter coats, scarfs and four pair of winter shoes, all second hand but still good for use. Then, the guests were trying out what they were offered, and at the end all four had been equipped to stand the Norwegian winter. Marit then went to the medicine box and found some tablets that would ease the effects of the cold.

The guests left and walked down the road to the taxi while Marit and I through the window looked at the freedom fighters now dressed for the Norwegian winter.

A few days later, I was at the Oslo Airport waiting for the SPLM delegation on their way back from Bergen and in transit for Nairobi in Oslo. We met and had a joyful talk as they took off the second-hand winter clothes and handed them back to me.

A couple of weeks later I was in Nairobi and South Sudan on mission. I had given Salva Kiir a promise I had to honour, the book; THE PEOPLE OF KAU. I believed it would be easy to find the book in a bookshop in Nairobi, but I walked from one to another, and none of them had it. Finally, I came to a small one, a bit hidden away from the main streets that had the book. I bought it and had handed over to Salva Kiir.

Many years passed, and Salva Kiir and I met a few times either in Nairobi or in the battlefields of South Sudan, and we developed a good chemistry.

In June 2007 Salva Kiir as the President of South Sudan and the 1st Vice-President of Sudan came on an official visit to Norway. However, his arrival in Oslo was delayed for a couple of days because President Omar Bashir had protocol problems related to Salva Kiir's travel to Norway.

I was to see him during the visit, but his delayed arrival made it difficult for me to see him as I had other commitments outside Oslo. But the SPLM advance delegation that came to prepare for the President's visit, insisted that I had to see him. Only one possibility was available, it was to meet him at his hotel the same evening that he arrived in Oslo.

I was at the hotel at the time agreed and was soon guided by his aids to his hotel suite. There he was, the old liberation fighter, tall and slim with his hat on. We embraced each other and sat down, only the two of us.

We talked a little about the programme for his stay in Norway, and I shared some advice on the matter. Then I gave him a small gift, a picture book with English text showing Helgeland, the part of Norway where I grew up. I said: *"This is the picture of my home village."* It was a beautiful one with houses, cattle grazing in green fields, mountains and fjords.

Salva Kiir looked at me and then he said: *"Halle, just a few days before I travelled to Norway, I went to see my own home village from the time when I was a child. But there was nothing, but skulls and burnt out houses."*

We looked at each other for a few seconds, then tears flowed from our eyes. We embraced again. Then, ambassador John Duku knocked at the door and came in and said:

"The visit is over, Ambassador Vraalsen is waiting."

I then met Salva Kiir shortly at the SPLM Convention in Juba in May 2008, and then again in January 2013 when a rather big delegation from the Norwegian Labour Party was in Juba to take part in a Round Table Conference and a series of workshops on the party building project. Salva Kiir came to open the Round Table, and as he passed by me, he stopped and greeted me and said that he wanted to see me before I went back to Norway. As he left the conference hall after his speech, he again came by and reminded me that he wanted to see me. But he or his aids never followed up.

My final Meeting with Sala Kiir

My last meeting with Salva Kiir was on Monday 21st October 2013. He had invited me to Juba to try and mediate in the conflict within SPLM.

I was picked up in the morning for the meeting that was supposed to take place at 10 am. I waited about two hours, and then I was invited in for a talk. The president was fairly reserved in the beginning, but after a while, he opened up, and we had a frank and at the same time amicable discussion. When I left, he said to me:

"Halle, I am short of time today, but you must come for a private dinner with only me, one of the next few evenings. I will send for you."

When I left the Office of the President that morning, I felt discouraged. The President had left me with the impression of a person who had changed from being an even-handed man who would listen to the views of others and be open for compromise, into a person who was becoming dictatorial.

He had no analysis of the basic causes of the conflict. He was only angry with those who had been critical or in opposition to his way of governing. His hatred for Pa'gan Amum, the Secretary General of SPLM, whom he had sacked a short time ago, was shocking, and he told me stories about Pa'gan Amum that were flagrant lies. He accused Kosti Manibe, the Minister of Finance whom he had also sacked a short time ago, for being corrupt. Everyone else in Juba those days, told me that if there was one clean person in the SPLM hierarchy, it was Kosti Manibe.

I could see that the Chairman of SPLM and the President of South Sudan had gone a long way in alienating himself from his former comrades in arms in the liberation struggle. Not only that, it was obvious that he in the Office of the President and its immediate environment was in the process of surrounding himself with formal and informal advisors who had little or no background from the liberation struggle, but rather had their experience from their work for the dictatorial regime in Khartoum. Furthermore, there was a dominant presence of Dinka elders around in the office.

During my visit in Juba, I stayed at the residence of the Norwegian Ambassador. I had daily communication with somebody in the Office of the President. Every time I asked whether they had any news about the indicated dinner invitation. They answered every time; not tonight, but tomorrow night. My conclusion was that there were people at work in the Office of the President who were very determined to make sure that the dinner invitation would not come.

During my stay, I also met and discussed with some 40 people inside and outside SPLM about the crisis, some few were supporting the actions of the President while most were very critical. One of them suddenly burst in tears and stuttered: *"I am afraid we are going to lose everything we fought for in the struggle."*

I left Juba for Nairobi on the 29th of October 2013, and I spent the following week in Nairobi writing my report. It had 20 pages, and the conclusion was simple:

I stated very firmly that if nothing was done by the International Community to take measures that would deescalate the SPLM conflict, South Sudan could be thrown into violent conflict and war again.

I sent the report to NPA and the Norwegian Labour Party, and a copy was sent to the NMFA.

I had a quick response from the Secretary General of the Labour Party thanking me for an interesting report, but there was no follow up at all from the Labour Party. I heard nothing from NPA, and I was never invited by the NPA management to discuss the report and my recommendations. The lack of interest was staggering. I was however invited to the NMFA for a briefing a few days before Christmas in 2013, but then the war was on and the massacre of the Nuers in Juba had taken place.

Six weeks after I had sent the report, the meeting of the NLC of SPLM took place. The opening and very belligerent speech of the SPLM Chairman, Salva Kiir, killed any possibility of mending fences and making compromise to save SPLM, the country and the people from a new war.

My relationship with Salva Kiir started on a very friendly note in the fall of 1992. We then for 20 years maintained a friendly political relationship. That relationship came to an end during my visit to Juba in October 2013.

I have since held Salva Kiir and his court in Juba the main responsible for the destruction of South Sudan (More on the matter in Chapter 20).

Rebecca and John Garang for dinner

Another memory of South Sudanese guests in our home that is still vivid and pleasant, is the evening, when John and Rebecca Garang and aides came for dinner.

John Garang and Rebecca were guests of honour at the NPA Convention in August 1999 when NPA at the same time celebrated its 60th Anniversary. They came for dinner the day after the Convention. We could only seat 20 guests in our living room, and we had some difficult problems in choosing who to invite because so many NPA staff wanted to take part.

Our house is situated in a small hill and surrounded by a garden with large trees. When John Garang came up the stairs and saw the garden and the trees, he smiled and said: *"Halle, I think I feel safe here, but to be on the safe side, I do hope you have some marksmen in the treetops who can provide security."*

I answered that we had all reasons to feel safe because the Norwegian Security Police before his arrival in the country, had come for talks and discussed the security for him and his delegation during his stay in Norway. I added that I did not know where they were, but probably somewhere in the neighbourhood.

Thereafter, we all had a good laugh, and John Garang added with another big laugh:

"Oh, that is very good because it is very rare that I have the privilege of being provided security by the Police in the countries I visit."

It turned out to be a very pleasant dinner. It was a relaxed and warm atmosphere. There were a few short speeches while a lot of good stories were told from the fields of South Sudan and elsewhere that again and again triggered outbursts of laughter.

At the end, Rebecca insisted to take part in cleaning the table and doing the dishwashing. She is an impressive personality. During the time of the struggle she was both the loyal spouse of the Chairman and the Commander in Chief while at the same time taking part in the struggle. In the aftermath of the catastrophe in December 2013 and the civil war that followed, she has been a consistent spokeswoman for reconciliation and peace.

Samson Kwaje with an aching Back on Visit at the Oslo University Hospital

Samson Kwaje had many leadership positions within SPLM/A. He was one of John Garang's confidants, and he was for a period the leader of SRRA. He was many times on working visits to NPA in Oslo, and he came for many dinners at my home.

Early in the summer of 1998 we received the message from our Nairobi Office that Samson soon would be on his way to Oslo.

He had severely hurt his back in a car accident in the battlefield. Was it possible for NPA to assist so that he could undergo a surgery at a hospital in Norway?

We contacted the Oslo University Hospital. They were very cooperative and gave us a time for Samson to visit. Samson arrived in Oslo. We received him and assisted him to the hotel. He was obviously in pain and used pain killers. He used a stick and limped as he walked, and he was in a bad mood as he feared that he could not continue in the freedom struggle. He was also convinced that the only thing that could bring him back to full health, was surgery on his back. He went to the hospital and had a thorough examination. Then he was called to the doctor who gave him the following message and advice:

"You do not need surgery, but you need to start exercising as soon as possible because your pains come from a back that is gradually collapsing because of lack of exercise."

Samson came for dinner the same evening, and to put it briefly; He was angry with the doctor and everything. No surgery, but a list with a detailed overview of what exercises to do to rebuild his back muscles and thereby his strength. Samson had little or no confidence in such a solution. I, on the other hand, with a past as an athlete and with periods of back pains, strongly supported the view of the doctor. At the end of the dinner conversation Samson agreed that he would make use of the training programme suggested when he returned to Nairobi.

A couple of months later I was back in Nairobi on a mission, and I as usual had to see Samson. I met him, and he had a big smile and the following opening remark:

"Halle, you see, no stick, no limping. The doctor was right. I have followed his advice, and I have not only fully recovered, but I feel better than I have done for a very long time, and I am very fit for fight."

In the aftermath of the CPA in January 2005, Samson was appointed Minister of Information in the first Government of Salva Kiir. He was a true democrat who strongly wanted to see South Sudan develop into a free and democratic society in strong contrast to the dictatorship in Khartoum. For this reason, he as a Minister was a key supporter of the NPA and AMDISS project: Freedom of Expression and free and independent media in South Sudan.

A few years later, he was appointed Minister of Agriculture. One day he had a very small accident and had a wound on his leg. He received some very poor medical treatment in Juba. The wound got infected and blood poisoning developed. Samson was brought to a good hospital in Nairobi, but it was too late. He died from an infected wound that should have easily healed if only proper medical attention had been given in time.

June 2007, the Preparation for Salva Kiir's visit in Norway

Early in 2007, the Norwegian government invited Salva Kiir, as President of South Sudan and 1st Vice-president of Sudan on an official visit to Norway and he came in June.

One Sunday afternoon, two days ahead of the visit, I got a telephone call from John Duku. He was calling from the Copenhagen Airport, telling me that he was part of a four-man delegation travelling in advance of the President to finalize the programme for the meeting. And he added: "*We need to discuss all this with you, so we are coming for dinner tonight.*"

That was a challenge. In Norway shops are closed on Sundays, but there was a migrant's shop in the neigbourhood with a good assortment of vegetables that was open, and we had some meat in the freezer. The guests would be coming straight from the airport. The time was short, only a couple of hours for preparation.

Upon arrival, they declared with lots of laughter accompanying that whenever a SPLM or GOSS delegation came on visit, dinner with us at home was considered a necessity as part of the preparation for the working visit to follow.

It was another great dinner. It was still peace time in South Sudan. There was a lot of hope for the future. Basic healthcare and education for all would be provided. A new infrastructure would be constructed. South Sudan would be the opposite of the Sudan North; the new shining star in Africa, democratic, progressive, inclusive, transparent and peaceful.

We discussed the programme for Salva Kiir's visit. The NPA part of the programme was good, but the government part still had some missing points. A visit to the King and the Royal Family which in Norway is a very important part of protocol whenever heads of states are visiting, was for instance missing.

We discussed how the delegation could improve their programme with the NMFA, and at the least get to meet the Royal family.

The next day while the delegation sat in discussion with their counterparts in the NMFA, a telephone call came from the Royal Castle, inviting President Salva Kiir to pay a courtesy visit. It became a very successful visit. The King and the Queen were very well briefed and impressed the President and his delegation with many pointed questions about the situation in South Sudan and Sudan.

Dr. Sharif Harir, born in Darfur, studied and worked at the University of Bergen, was a Freedom Fighter in Sudan, now retired and a Resident Norwegian Citizen

Sharif Harir is an old friend. He now lives in my neighbouring municipality of Asker, and he has been at home for many dinners. He has an exciting story to tell.

During 1970s the young Norwegian social anthropologist Gunnar Sorbø from the University of Bergen was doing some field work in Darfur. In a break from the field, Gunnar was back in Khartoum for some rest and recreation at the American Club in Khartoum which had a nice swimming pool. The two, Gunnar and Sharif met one day at the pool side, and they developed good contact and became friends.

When Gunnar was back at UoB, he provided a NORAD scholarship for Sharif Harir for studies at UoB.

One day in 1978 Sharif Harir arrived at the Oslo Airport on his way to Bergen. He had great expectations about what waited for him in Bergen, but at the Oslo Airport had to pass the immigration control. He gave his passport, and the police man looked at it and said:

"*Where is your visa that gives you the permission to enter Norway?*"

"*Visa?*" Sharif said. "*What is that? I have never heard anything about a need for a visa.*"

"*If you do not have a visa, you cannot enter Norway,*" the policeman answered.

"*But I am on my way to Bergen for studies*", Sharif answered, a bit in desperation.

Do you have any paper from the University of Bergen that confirms that it is so, the police man asked?

No, I have no paper from the University, but I have a letter from NORAD.

Let me see, the police man said. He read the letter, and then told Sharif to follow him to the duty officer.

The duty officer also read the letter from NORAD, and then he said:

"*This is OK. I will give you a temporary visa that is valid for three days, but as soon as you arrive in Bergen, you have to report to the Police Office there and immediately apply for a long-term visa.*"

That was how Sharif Harir arrived in Norway. Whenever any similar situation occurs at our international airports today, the person concerned would immediately be sent back to his country of origin. There is no more flexibility.

Sharif was a very good student at UoB. He did his MA in social anthropology with excellent grades. I was the Director of Information with NORAD at the time, and I met Sharif for the first time then.

Having finished his MA, he went back to Khartoum and became a teacher at the Institute for Social Anthropology at the UoK.

Sharif was invited back to UoB to do his PHD in social anthropology. Gunnar Sørbø became his academic advisor, and

Sharif defended his PHD and his academic title in 1987. He then went back to UoK. When the coup d'état took place in 1989, Sharif became very critical of the regime and the very oppressive political developments that followed.

A couple of years passed. The regime became increasingly oppressive, and it persecuted its critics, arrested, tortured and killed them.

Magne Lerheim was a long-time Director General of the UoB. In the early 1990s, he left that position and was appointed the Secretary General of the National University Council for International Cooperation. He was in that capacity on a mission to South Africa to establish cooperation between Norwegian universities and South African ones, and he was also participating in an International conference of African academics in South Africa.

He was one evening approached by a professor from the UoK who asked for a private talk. He told Magne that he was a close friend of Sharif, and that just before his departure to South Africa, he had read a secret list of Sudanese academics who were to be sacked from the university and arrested because of their criticism of the regime. Sharif Harir was high up on the list, and the professor asked Magne to do his utmost to get an invitation for Sharif to return to Bergen for work.

Magne was a man of action, and he acted fast. A couple of days later, Sharif had the invitation he needed, and he quickly got his visa from the Norwegian Embassy and travelled to Bergen.

In Bergen, he met with his old friends, Gunnar Sorbø and Magne Lerheim. They were both very concerned about the political developments in Sudan and the sufferings caused by the ongoing liberation war. They also feared that the academic cooperation that for a long time had been developed between the UoK and UoB could suffer.

They knew Sharif's previous excellent academic work at both UoB and UoK well. They welcomed him back to Bergen, and Sharif was offered a position as a senior researcher at UoB. In the years that followed, Sharif did some excellent academic work in the field of social anthropology that received wide international recognition.

In Bergen, Sharif had married and had his own family. One day in 1998 he suddenly got a surprise message from the leadership of SLM, The Sudanese Liberation Movement in Darfur. They asked him to report at their HQ and join the liberation struggle as soon as possible.

When Sharif told me this story, I asked why he, with a family and a permanent academic position in Bergen, left it all behind and went back to take part in the liberation struggle.

He answered with the following:

"Halle, when you are faced with a situation like the one I was faced with in my homeland Darfur, I as an African had no choice. It was a situation with severe oppression, mass arrest and massacres of my own people. You feel a moral duty, and you must do what you have to do."

So, Sharif travelled and reported to the SLM HQ. He was given two major tasks. As a politician, he should move to Asmara in Eritrea and join the newly established secretariat of NDA, the National Democratic Alliance. His superior as Secretary General was Pa'gan Amum. As a freedom fighter, he should join the joint forces of NDA on the eastern front as one of the deputy commanders under the command of Pa'gan Amum. Pa'gan and Sharif worked closely together for six years. Then the CPA came in January 2005, and the conflict in Darfur was not part of the agreement.

John Garang strongly wanted Darfur to be part of the CPA, but the answer from the government in Khartoum was the following: **You can choose between a peace agreement that excludes Darfur and no agreement.**

With the death of John Garang in July 2005 the political developments both in the whole of Sudan and in South Sudan took a course very different from what was the vision of Garang and the priority in the CPA document, a new, secular and democratic Sudan.

South Sudan made use of the clause in the CPA that allowed for a referendum on independence, and the people voted massively in favour of independence. With all that happening, the base for the continued existence of NDA disappeared.

Sharif continued for a while in the liberation struggle for Darfur. But the hard years in the field had taken their toll. Sharif's health started to deteriorate. In Norway, a wife and a young son were waiting. He travelled back to Norway and joined his family in Asker. He is still of course a Norwegian citizen. He is writing his memoirs, and we are both active senior members in the Labour Party of the Akershus Constituency.

Yasir Arman, a Liberation Fighter from the North

Yasir Arman is one of around 30 freedom fighters from Sudan and South Sudan who has been with us for dinner. He visited Oslo both in January 2015 and January 2017. In 2015, he gave a lecture at PRIO on: "Will 2015 be the Year of Peace in Sudan?" He gave a resounding no the question, and he added that as long as Omar Bashir and his Islamist government was holding power in Sudan, peace could not come to Sudan.

At the dinner in our house the same evening Yasir Arman was in great spirits. We talked about the liberation struggle in the North and more concrete in the Nuba Mountains, in the Red Sea Hills and in Darfur and what kind of oppressive means the regime in Khartoum applied to stay in power.

When he came to Oslo in January 2017, he held many meetings, gave lectures and he had on the whole, a most successful visit with big audiences. Again, we had a dinner at our house with long talks about both the miserable state of affairs in the two states of Sudan and the liberation struggle in the Nuba Mountains.

Yasir Arman was born in Khartoum in 1961 by Arab-Muslim parents. During his childhood, there was little talk about politics at home. His parents had more than enough to do to make ends meet and keep their children at school.

However, when Yasir became a youth, he also became politically conscious, and he joined the Communist Party in Sudan. When he became a student at the university, he was elected Chairman of the Young Communists. He wanted to reform and democratise the Communist Party while he remained a bitter critic of Nimeiri's regime. The latter led to frequent arrests, and he was almost every time beaten up by the Police. In the Communist Party, there was no support for his reformist ideas. He was expelled and stayed in the political cold for a while. In 1987, he met for the first time with John Garang. He got enthusiastic about Garang's vision for e new, secular and democratic Sudan, and he joined the SPLM/A. He then decided to do guerrilla training with SPLA, and he became a very able guerrilla and liberation fighter. Having completed the training period, he was made commander of the SPLA forces in the Nuba Mountains and the Blue Nile.

Yasir became one of John Garang's confidants and was made member of the inner circle, the so-called Garang Boys, and he was part of the delegation that negotiated the CPA in 2005. When SPLM in the aftermath of the CPA was reorganised for the peaceful and democratic struggle for political power, Yasir Arman was made Secretary General of SPLM North and based in Khartoum. His immediate superior was his old friend, Pa'gan Amum, the Secretary General of SPLM for the whole country. They had also worked very closely together during the period when the NDA had its HQ in Asmara in Eritrea.

When Garang died, the separatists within SPLM led by Salva Kiir who wanted independence for South Sudan, got the upper hand in the organisation. Yasir saw his position and influence within SPLM fade away even though he remained the Secretary General of SPLM North. He decided to take a break from politics, and he went to USA. He joined the Ohio State University, the same one as John Garang studied at, for studies in 2007/08.

As stated in the CPA, the first elections for President and for Parliament, had to take place latest in 2010 in Sudan and South Sudan. Salva Kiir did not want to run as the SPLM candidate for President in the whole of Sudan and in that way challenge President Omar Bashir. He decided instead only to stand as the SPLM candidate for President in South Sudan.

SPLM then decided to nominate Yasir Arman as their candidate for President in Sudan. The election campaign started, and in the North the usual things from all previous election was repeated. Candidates from the opposition were harassed in all possible ways, and Yasir Arman suffered most from this harassment. He decided in the end in protest against the harassment to withdraw from the campaign.

However, his name remained on the lists of candidates, and on election day he won 22 percent of the votes, under the circumstances, a very good result.

In the aftermath of the overwhelming yes vote for independence in the referendum in January 2011 in South Sudan, SPLM was split into two organisations, SPLM North and SPLM South.

While SPLM South contrary to all expectations now in 2017 lies in ruins, SPLM North has survived and is very active both politically and militarily in particular in the Nuba Mountains and the Blue Nile. SPLM North has joined an alliance of opposition parties in Sudan under the umbrella of The Sudanese Revolutionary Front.

Yasir Arman remains a convinced supporter of Garang's vision of a new, secular and democratic Sudan. He is very critical of the view that the conflict in Sudan is an ethnic one between Arabs and black Africans. He argues that even though there are many lines of conflict in the Sudanese society, one main line of conflict goes between the small minority of very rich people regardless of ethnic background and the steadily growing majority of increasingly poor people. Another important conflict line goes between the centre and the periphery. He was against the splitting of Sudan into two states. He says that as soon as the Bashir regime is removed, he will work for a political and economic union with South Sudan.

His critic of the Bashir regime is very strong, and in an interview with the South African Daily Maverick on 30th October 2012 he said the following:

"There is in Khartoum an Islamic African university that indoctrinates students from black African countries. Some of black Africa's most dangerous Islamist leaders have studied at that university, among them the leaders of Boko Haram and Al Schabaab. The teachers at the university further encourage students and groups from countries like Kenya and Tanzania to go back home and create tension and conflict in their home countries. Khartoum is the centre that spreads the message about religious violence across all of Africa."

In Oslo in January 2017 he repeated this critic of the role plaid by the Islamic African University in Khartoum. The existence and work of this institution is a fact that is almost unknown in the Northern hemisphere, and I believe also in most countries in Black Africa.

Topics at the Dinner Table

There were so many people from Sudan and South Sudan and others with an interest for the two countries who came for dinner from the late 1980s until today. I resigned from my position as Secretary general of NPA at the end of my contract in May 2001 and left the organisation, but the requests for informal dinners with political discussions continued to come. For people from SPLM who came on working visit, it was irrelevant whether I was an official NPA leader or not.

Whenever they came, they called in advance, sometime from Nairobi, sometimes from Brussels or London or Copenhagen, saying that they wanted to come for dinner as there were some political issues to be discussed and sorted out before the meetings with officials in Oslo started up.

What did we eat? I enjoy making food, and I at an early stage made up a recipe for lamb and vegetables in the casserole and named it the SPLM casserole. It became a very popular dish.

In April 2005, three months after the signing of the CPA in Nairobi, the Norwegian Government hosted the first and big international donors' conference on South Sudan and Sudan in Oslo. One of those evenings we had an informal dinner with Pa'gan Amum, Abdul Aziz, Luka Biong and John Duku from the SPLM delegation. Pa'gan had in advance told me that he came from the Shilluk people and had fish as his favourite dish. He wanted Norwegian salmon for dinner. They all came, and I told them that I was fulfilling Pa'gan's wish and was serving salmon for dinner. All except Abdul Aziz seemed happy. Abdul just said: *"I am a man from the mountains and I like meat, not fish."*

Marit and I had to improvise, and we found in the fridge some good, marinated and dried lamb meat, made from a very old and traditional Norwegian recipe.

The evening became another very enjoyable one. We talked about the CPA, the donors' conference and all the promises given. We were hopeful and happy as we talked about all the challenges that were ahead when it came to the implementation of the CPA. It was peace time, and the democratic development for the societies of South Sudan and Sudan, so ravaged by conflict and war, lay ahead. Optimism dominated, but at the same time there was an undercurrent of fear that the forces of evil and destruction again should get the upper hand.

I do not have the numbers of dinners hosted, but from 1992 until present, at least some 70 - 80 dinners. From the very beginning, there were a few major themes being discussed. Until 2002 the liberation war and the role of NPA and other agencies, the neighbouring countries and political developments in Norway were primary topics.

At certain periods, some special problems arose. Upon my departure from NPA in the spring of 2001, the NPA President at the time Reiulf Steen and my successor, the new Secretary General, Eva Bjøreng, proposed to terminate the NPA Sudan programme and outsource it to other Norwegian NGOs like NCA and Save the Children. The reaction from SPLM/A to this surprising news was one of disbelief and fear, and they protested. I take it that there were messages conveyed both from the NMFA and the US State Department with a similar content. Many staff members in Oslo and all staff in Nairobi and in the field protested. To terminate the NPA Sudan programme just as the peace negotiations were making substantial progress, was seen by the other interested parties as an insensitive and destructive political act. Whenever we had dinners with guests from SPLM and like-minded from the spring and early summer of 2001, this was of course a topic for serious discussion. Fortunately, after some weeks the proposal disappeared and was never mentioned again.

Whenever we met for dinner, we also discussed the situation and the political attitude towards SPLM and NPA prevailing with the NMFA. What diplomatic staff had most influence, who were difficult ones to deal with? Who were possible middlemen? What MPs to talk with?

Furthermore, the situation in the neighbouring countries of Ethiopia, Kenya and Uganda was frequently analysed.

Political developments in other European countries and in USA towards the conflict in Sudan and towards SPLM/A, were other frequent topics. It was well known that EU officially had a kind of neutrality line towards the conflict in Sudan. However, in practise and to a large extent, policies pushed by the former colonial powers Great Britain and France until the end of the 1990s favoured Khartoum.

However, during the IGAD led peace negotiations around the year 2000, EU gradually changed its attitude. It became more critical towards Khartoum while it at the same time developed an understanding for the cause of the liberation war. The Norwegian Minister of Development at the time, Hilde Frafjord Johnson played an important role in this regard. She developed a political tool for this purpose. It happened to be so around the year 2000 that four European countries, Great Britain, Germany, Netherlands and Norway, had female ministers of development. Hilde Frafjord Johnson invited the four for a meeting at a former monastery in Western Norway, called Utstein Monastery. The war in Sudan and the ongoing peace negotiations were key topics in the meeting. The four female ministers decided to form a pressure group of their own in support of the peace negotiations. They travelled together to Sudan and South Sudan and talked with the leaders on each side in the conflict. Then they went back to their governments that were all centre-left, and the three ministers of the EU countries, Great Britain, Germany and Netherlands played important roles in the political process that led to a change of the EU policies regarding the conflict in Sudan.

A dinner at home one evening in April 2013 with South Sudanese friends and staff members from Norwegian Peoples Aid.

This picture is from the same dinner. Pa'gan Amum, to the left, was still the Secretary General of the SPLM. In the middle, Bol Wek Agoth, the Ambassador of South Sudan to Norway at the time, and the author. One important topic at the dinner was the party building project. 18 months later, Pa'gan Amum was in house arrest, banned by his own President from appearing and speaking in public. And the party building project had collapsed.

17
A FREEDOM FIGHTER BANNED FROM HIS COUNTRY

Suzanna and Pa'gan Amum at our Cottage in the Valdres Mountains

During the visit of President Salva Kiir in June 2007 the cooperation agreement between NPA and SPLM on the party building project was discussed, but another visit of the SPLM Secretary General, Pa'gan Amum, was necessary to sign the agreement and to start the implementation. He came together with his wife Suzanna in October 2007. I had in advance agreed with NPA as part of Pa'gan's programme, to take responsibility for a weekend tour to our cottage in the Valdres Mountains, not far from Jotunheimen, the mountain home of the famous Norwegian trolls. The visit was planned from Friday afternoon until Sunday night.

My wife Marit was already at the cottage preparing for the visit. She called me Friday morning saying: *"Halle, we have to cancel the visit. The weather is very bad, it is fog, snowing and the air is cold and icy."*

I replied: *It is too late to cancel now. They are waiting at the hotel. I shall pick them up in a couple of hours and start driving for the mountains.*

Marit heaved a deep sigh and said:

"OK, we then have to make the best out of the situation."

I picked up Suzanna and Pa'gan as agreed, and we started the 200-km. long trip. The weather in Oslo as well was very bad, rainy, foggy and windy. On the way, up one of the very first hills just some 30 km. away from Oslo, Suzanna suddenly felt bad, and I had to make a stop so that she could vomit. I felt despair. The mountain trip was a fiasco almost before it had started. I composed myself before I turned to Suzanna and Pa'gan to propose that we cancelled the trip and returned to the hotel. But they were smiling, and Pa'gan said: *"Don't worry Halle. We are pretty sure that this is a very good omen. Suzanna is pregnant. Just continue driving."*

What a relief. The drive up to the mountain town of Fagernes went well, and I started the climb towards the high mountains. Then the troubles started. The fog was so thick that we could hardly see five meters ahead. I had to drive on 1st gear. It was getting dark, the weather was terrible, and it was impossible to see anything of the nature around. My guests were so silent, and I did not know what to say even though I knew that we would shortly reach the cottage. It was a depressing situation. Later Pa'gan commented that he was grossly immersed in thoughts and dreams about how they in South Sudan would build the infrastructure of roads bridges and dams like those he had seen on the way to the mountains before the fog made it impossible to see anything.

Finally, we arrived. The outside light was on, Marit was there, welcoming the way only she can. Inside, candles were burning, and the warmth flowed from the open fire place in a living room modernized, but carrying the basic structure from the first time the timbre was used in the first house that was put up some 300 hundred years ago. We have a living room with timber walls that are 300 years old and with the golden colour that only very old timbre gives. The guests started relaxing and soon found comfort in the situation.

While sitting at the fire place, I talked about the Norwegian historical development experience of the last couple of hundred years. From the time, we were so poor that hundreds of thousands migrated mainly to North America because they saw no hope for any future at home, and until today when Norway is one of the best developed societies on earth with the most equal distribution of income and common good. We had thereafter some discussion about how it all came about, and what relevance our experience may have for South Sudan. We continued with the situation in South Sudan, and I expressed my joy over the fact that the cooperation agreement between NPA and SPLM on the party building project now was to be implemented.

Marit had made a real mountain dinner from the meat of reindeer, mushrooms, vegetables and potatoes. The talk at the dinner table was light and pleasant. Suzanna shared with us from her time as a student at the medical faculty in Juba where she obtained her first degrees in medicine before she had to flee through Egypt to USA. She continued her medical studies there and specialized in surgery. Having completed her studies, she worked as medical doctor at a local hospital in Denver in USA.

But the day was long, so we went early to bed.

Weather changes quickly in the mountains of Norway. When we got up the next day, the sky was blue, and the sun was shining. The mountain landscape appeared in all its beauty. We decided to look at the way the big lakes and rivers are dammed and regulated in the mountain areas of Norway, and we drove up to mountain range of Jotunheimen and the Valdres mountain plateau. Nature in these areas is impressive. High mountain peaks sometimes seeming to disappear in the clouds, deep valleys, big lakes and rivers. Norway gets around 95 percent of its electric power from hydropower, and some of the big centres of water gathering and hydropower production are to be found in rivers originating in the Jotunheimen mountains.

Pa'gan and Suzanna got a good impression of how it is all done, and they could certainly pick some ideas for future developments in South Sudan. We also met with local people and mountain guards who briefed us on both the conservation policies aiming at securing the big variety of mountain fauna and flora while having a sustainable use of other natural resources in the mountain areas like game and wild deer. Norway has a big and growing number of moose, deer and reindeer in its mountains and big woods. During the hunting season in the fall every year at least some 60 000 moose and deer are hunted and sold for food, and still the numbers of moose and deer are growing.

In my view, we have an important experience to share with countries in Africa when it comes to the sustainable management of mountain and forest flora and fauna.

We were back at the cottage late in the afternoon, and soon another dinner meal was on the table.

After dinner, at the open fire place Pa'gan started talking about his time as a student at the University of Khartoum. He and other students organized an underground Freedom Movement and study groups that turned into a rebellion and became one of the first fighting groups in South Sudan before SPLM/A. He also told about his time in Cuba and his life as a guerilla commander in Sudan. He shared with us some of the principles he applied in building good relations among the soldiers across ethnic lines before organizing the forces for a surprise attack. He and his forces shocked the world when they in the winter of 2000 organized a major surprise attack and conquered the garrison towns of Kassala and Hamushkoreb in Eastern Sudan and held it for two days while they emptied all military stores.

Pa'gan always had multi-ethnic guerilla groups. He considered it as very important for the guerilla soldiers to be able to see that they were fighting for something that was more important and larger than their tribe, or region. They shared goals and visions across ethnic divisions. He felt that it would be a small but important contribution to the unification of Sudan and South Sudan across ethnic lines of division.

A very important part of everyday life for a guerilla soldier in the battle field was to be able to hide so well that the enemy did not see him, and that was only possible when one developed a good and trustful relationship with the local people in a given area. The liberation army had to be the people's army.

Pa'gan has another feature with him which is not so well known by most people. He has a talent for song and music, and he loves music, European classic music and opera. He shared with us the following story from the time of the struggle:

"While I was commanding the guerilla units hiding in the forests or the swamplands or being in liberated areas, I once got a tape player and a small satellite radio with earphones. At the time, there was a wealthy Ethiopian living in USA, who had been able to buy the right to broadcast under the name of **The World Space Radio** *from a satellite in the space. This radio had many channels, and one carried classic music and opera.*

I brought that radio with me on several battle missions, and it happened many times in the lull between battles while watching the movement of the enemy that I at the same time was listening to Carnival Rusticana, the Barber of Seville, The four Seasons and other beautiful classic music.

It was quite magic that evening to sit in front of the open fire place and listen to Pa'gan's and Suzanna's stories.

I have talked with many, many people, South Sudanese, other East Africans and Africans, international politicians, diplomats and journalists who know Pa'gan Amum. Most of them had a common viewpoint on him. They considered him a particularly gifted person with rare political qualities, and they saw him as a future President of South Sudan.

SALVA KIIR AND PA'GAN AMUM, AND PA'GAN AMUM'S LIFE SINCE THE SUMMER OF 2013

Salva Kiir, a weak and failed leader

Salva Kiir has had a rough life experience, and in my and many others' view, the consequences of this experience have become increasingly visible in recent years. He has always been a soldier, and he started as a child soldier with Anyanya in the 1960s. He never had any proper education. He is no intellectual, but increasingly a sly traditionalist. He has travelled little outside Sudan and Africa. He never had a holiday. He has no charisma and is a very poor speaker. His health is poor and in decline.

John Garang was the big contrast. Garang had a PhD in economics from Ohio State University and a top grade as an officer from Fort Benning in USA. Garang was a man of the world with a personality and a charisma that impressed all who met him. Garang was a great speaker. He had in his inner circle not only Kiir, but his wife Rebecca and many young men and a few women with solid education from academic institutions both in Khartoum and abroad. In their company Kiir nourished an inferiority complex.

It has during his Presidency had many different utterances. When for instance Kiir was on his first official visit to the USA in 2006 and met President George Bush in the White House, he was hardly able to speak and left the talking to the accompanying members of his delegation.

When the UN Secretary General during Salva Kiir's first travel to the UN HQ in New York hosted a luncheon in his honour, Salva Kiir did not turn up. There are many similar stories.

Salva Kiir never liked Pa'gan Amum who like Garang has a solid education and is well read. And like Garang, Pa'gan has a strong personality with a lot of charisma. He is an excellent speaker and he has a beautiful voice when he sings, and he can rally an audience when he sings revolutionary songs. That was one of many reasons why he was the Master of Ceremony both at the funeral of John Garang in Juba in August 2005 and at Independence Day for South Sudan on 9th of July 2011.

But more important, Salva Kiir and Pa'gan Amum developed serious political differences. Pa'gan came in the early 1980s from the revolutionary left and became a left-orientated social-democrat within SPLM while Kiir strongly influenced by the Jieng Council and their likeminded, has moved with increasing speed to the political right. While doing that, Kiir, at the same time, developed an increasingly authoritarian personality.

Kiir tried after Garang's death to get rid of Pa'gan Amum the same way that he got rid of so many others who were considered "the Garang boys." People like Abdul Aziz, Edward Lino and Nihal Deng were chased into the cold after Garang's death. But he failed in his efforts to chase away Pa'gan Amum, and Pa'gan became the Secretary General of SPLM. At the SPLM Convention in May 2008 in Juba, Kiir and his Dinka likeminded, tried again to get rid of Pa'gan Amum as Secretary General of SPLM, but failed.

All this made the cooperation between the two men both within the SPLM leadership Group and the Government increasingly difficult. Pa'gan Amum as Secretary General in the period between May 2008 and the early summer of 2013, informally many times and formally and in writing five times proposed for Salva Kiir to call meetings of the Politburo and the National Liberation Council to discuss matters of highest political urgency for SPLM and the Government, but Salva Kiir refused to call the meetings.

In the spring of 2013 it developed into a full-blown conflict, and Salva Kiir decided to get rid of Pa'gan Amum. Kiir on 23rd July accused him of having violated the SPLM Constitution because he had criticized government policies and thereby the President. He was also accused of having mismanaged both the organization and the economy of SPLM and taken money for himself. Salva Kiir on this basis and without consulting the members of the SPLM Politburo suspended him from his position as Secretary General of SPLM.

Salva Kiir in flagrant violations both of the Constitution of South Sudan and the UN Declaration on Human Rights in addition placed Pa'gan Amum under house arrest and banned him from expressing any opinion in public and from travelling outside Juba. When Pa'gan Amum's father who was the Paramount Chief of the Ubuar Clan of the Shilluk people, fell sick, and as the tradition demanded, had to be taken to his home village, Pa'gan was denied this traditional right to bring his father home. When his father died shortly after the banning of Pa'gan, and he was to be buried in Malakal, Pa'gan Amum was prevented from taking part in his father's funeral.

In addition, The President/SPLM Chairman without calling a meeting of the Politburo, appointed in August 2013 a special committee headed by the then Speaker of the Parliament who was later appointed Vice-President, James Wani Igga, with the mandate to document Pa'gan's political statements that were seen to be critical of the President and in violation of the SPLM Constitution. The committee should further uncover all the corruption and mishandling of the SPLM's economy that Pa'gan Amum was accused of being responsible for.

The Vice-President is a true loyalist of the President while he for reasons like Kiir's, never has liked Pa'gan Amum. The other members of the committee had a similar relationship to Kiir, and as an advance gratitude, they were all promised to be appointed member of the new government.

I asked James Wani Igga, then Vice-President, when I was in Juba in October 2013, how the work of the committee was proceeding. He told that they were doing fine, and Pa'gan Amum had come to all meetings he had been called to, but had left at the last, shouting: *This is witch-hunt*! I then asked whether they had found any money, and Wani Igga replied that they had, but there were only minor withdrawals, and they had found nothing substantial that made it possible to accuse Pa'gan Amum for corruption. But the committee did what the SPLM Chairman, Salva Kiir, expected them to do. They wrote a report that should add to the ongoing process of destroying Pa'gan Amum's good name and reputation.

I have read the report in detail. It is evil in its intent which is to destroy the good name of Pa'gan Amum and the trust that many people had in him. It is shallow and one-sided both in its analysis and in its discussion of matters of relevance, and it carries no concrete evidence whatsoever related to the accusations made against Pa'gan Amum.

When I visited Juba in October 2013 and paid a visit to the President, I was told that Pa'gan Amum had been unable to take his sacking and banning and was roaming around on a drinking spree in the bars of Juba. Not only that, he had also become a "Born again Christian". The story was told with an unhidden evil joy.

But the story was a flagrant lie. Pa'gan Amum was in the fall of 2013 never drinking, but was spending a lot of time on basically three interlinked activities. He read a lot of books and articles, he did Yoga and he did a lot of swimming and other physical exercise. I met him, and I have never seen him so fit and well.

When I met Pa'gan Amum in Juba in October 2013, I shared with him what the President had told me about his drinking sprees in town and that he also had become a Born again Christian.

On the latter, Pa'gan Amum answered the following:

"Halle, I have for the last 30 years been an atheist, but in recent times, Suzanna and I have involved ourselves in reflections and discussions on the cardinal question of all times: The primacy of the matter of spirit, taking into consideration the philosophical implications of the latest scientific discoveries in fields of pure mathematics, astronomy, quantum physics as well as widening our understanding of the western idealist philosophy and eastern spirituality and the impact of all this on the meaning and purpose of life, on ethics and morality, and on religious issues. After a while, we joined a charismatic church of Apostle Sabino Daniel that is non-denominational and non-religious but spiritual one in a poor part of Juba. You may tell the President that I am a "Born again Christian", who have come to believe in the core message of Jesus Christ: Love. To love my enemies as I love myself".

Rumor Mongers in Juba, Pa'gan Amum and Norwegian People's Aid

During the spring and summer of 2013, I, while staying in Oslo, picked up a lot of rumours about central SPLM leaders and mainly non-Dinka. I knew that they were deeply disappointed with Salva Kiir's poor leadership both at the level of state and with SPLM. The common purpose, of these rumours, was that they were made to destroy the good name and reputation of the people named. I and others came to believe that somebody in Juba was producing these stories.

Seen with Norwegian eyes, there was in the spring and the summer of 2013 a very special story that developed around Pa'gan Amum. He was in April 2013 an official guest, representing SPLM, at the Convention of the Norwegian Labour Party. Just some weeks before Pa'gan Amum left for Oslo, NPA had finally got the go ahead to start the construction of their own administration building in Juba on a plot provided by the government.

While Pa'gan Amum was in Oslo, NPA in Juba suddenly had a visit from some official who told them that the construction had to stop as they were using a plot that was meant for other purposes. In the beginning, no reason for the stop-order was given, but then the rumor started flying that it was Pa'gan Amum who was behind the order to stop the construction. He wanted to use his position as Secretary General of SPLM, the rumor said, to secure the plot for a deal with a very wealthy Chinese businessman who wanted to construct a hotel on the plot. The rumor further said that Pa'gan Amum was promised big corruption money as soon as the deal was final.

When Pa'gan Amum came back from Oslo, the NPA management in Juba approached him on the matter. The way they saw it, he was unable to give good answers and for this reason, Pa'gan left the impression with some that the rumours were true.

One NPA leader in South Sudan said the following to me: *"Halle, you are naïve if you believe Pa'gan Amum is clean. He is* undertaken to find out what was happening to him, and he, probably because of this action, was later transferred to the house where the other detainees were being held.

When seven of the eleven detainees after the intervention of the President of Kenya, Uhuru Kenyatta, were being released in February 2014 and taken to Nairobi, the other four, Pa'gan Amum, Oyai Deng Ajak, Majok D'Agoot and Ezekiel Lol Guthuok, were kept in prison and now accused of high treason.

While the four were kept in prison, at least five attempts to assassinate them, took place, but the guards protecting them, were able to fight back the attempts

When the trial against the four, which lasted for six weeks, began, the Minister of Information Michael Leuth went public with a statement that for the four guilty; if they were found guilty, there was only one form of punishment available, death. The question for the court was to decide how they should die; either by hanging or the execution squad.

However, at the trial the accused defended themselves very well and rejected all accusations. Pa'gan who was the last to defend himself, began his speech at 9 o'clock in the morning. At noon, the Chief Judge asked whether he soon would finish. The answer was no. The Chief Judge then asked for a break. After 30 minutes Pa'gan continued until 14,30 in the afternoon. In other words, he defended himself in a speech that lasted for five hours. Then he finished. The Chief Judge then stated that he had no questions to raise, and he asked the chief prosecutor whether he would like to question the accused, but the answer was no. The Judge then asked the chief defence lawyer whether he would like to raise any questions. Again, the answer was no. What then happened towards the end of the trial was that the evidence provided by the Government Prosecutor collapsed, and to the surprise of everyone, the Government in the name of the Minister of Justice withdrew the case.

The four were acquitted and released in late April 2014, and a few days later they forcibly were exiled to Nairobi to join the other members of the group now, named the SPLM leaders, former political detainees. They then made it very clear that they were strongly against the civil war that was ravaging the people and land of South Sudan, and that they for this reason rejected a call from Riek Machar's SPLM in Opposition to join them in the armed conflict with the government forces. The members of the group then travelled to Addis Ababa and for the rest of 2014 and the first half of 2015, they as an independent group, naming themselves, SPLM/L/FD, rejecting the use of arms and violence, took actively part in the IGAD led peace negotiations.

In the winter and spring of 2015 a kind of parallel peace process started in Arusha in Tanzania. The idea was to solve the conflict through the reunification of the different factions of SPLM in conflict with each other. At the end of this negotiation process, the different factions of SPLM agreed and signed a document in which they committed themselves to reunite SPLM. I was one of many who thought there was an agreement.

Th reunification of SPLM and the new process of home-based reconciliation and peacemaking was stipulated to start in the early summer of 2015. A key element in the whole, was the reappointment of Pa'gan Amum as the Secretary General of SPLM. Pa'gan Amum, having been living in forced exile in Kenya and Ethiopia for more than a year, travelled in good faith and in the company of the Kenyan Minister of Defence, Raychelle Awour Omamo who was his protector, on 22nd June 2015 back to Juba for the reinstatement as Secretary General, followed by an oath taking ceremony. The meeting of the National Liberation Council that formally had to approve the reappointment, took place the following day. A member of the Politburo, never elected, but appointed by Salva Kiir, Akol Paul Chordit, a true enemy of Pa'gan Amum, was the spokesman that day. He told the audience that;

"*the Arusha Reunification Agreement has now born fruits.*"

In the afternoon of 23rd June at 5 o'clock the oath taking ceremony took place in the presence of the President/SPLM Chairman, Salva Kiir, and many local and international dignitaries, and with the President's religious advisor, Lauren Khor Bandi, as the Master of Ceremony.

Pa'gan Amum then shook hands with the President/SPLM Chairman Salva Kiir, and made a short speech in which he promised to do his utmost as the reinstated Secretary General to stop the war and initiate a national process of reconciliation and peacemaking.

I spoke to him on the 24th June, and he sounded like a happy man. He told me that Salva Kiir had promised to form a government of National Unity and spearhead a campaign to ask for forgiveness and plead for reconciliation and peace.

However, when Pa'gan Amum in the days following, wanted to start his work as the Secretary General, he met some very strange hindrances of different kinds. After another few days, he discovered that a plot was under way, apparently approved by the President, to have him assassinated. For the rest of the group of former detainees, (FPD) the plan was to keep them as a kind of prisoners and never let them leave Juba again.

Pa'gan Amum decided to meet Salva Kiir and confront him with this plot. Kiir, according to my sources, admitted that a meeting on the matter had taken place, but that his statements on the matters discussed, had been taken out of context. Kiir then allowed Pa'gan Amum and the delegation of FPD to travel to Addis Ababa to sign the peace agreement ARCISS. So, on the surface, for Pa'gan Amum and his colleagues, the travel to Addis Ababa appeared safe, but they still needed security and protection to leave Juba International Airport.

The 23rd June Events made the End of the Arusha Agreement.

Pa'gan Amum then stayed in Addis Ababa for a while and was part of the final negotiations for "the Agreement on the Resolution of the Conflict in South Sudan (ARCISS), and he signed on behalf of the FPD. As we remember, the two belligerent parties; SPLM inO with Riek Machar in charge, had problems, but signed while SPLM inG with Salva Kiir in charge had even bigger problems. The President and his government, now exposed to heavy international pressure, nevertheless delayed the process for almost two weeks before they signed, but then only with many reservations.

In the months that followed, Pa'gan Amum and other members of the group FPD, felt that they no longer had any real security anywhere in East Africa because the agents of the Government in Juba were operating in the neighbouring countries with a mandate to kill.

Pa'gan Amum and his wife and children then decided to travel to USA as political refugees and temporarily settle in Denver. While staying in USA, the government in Juba has cancelled his South Sudanese passport, and not only that, it has also tried to make him stateless by cancelling his citizenship in South Sudan. However, for the latter, they failed in their efforts.

Pa'gan and his family arrived in Denver in August 2015, and they had a difficult time as refugees in the USA. Suzanna who is a medical doctor, had not practiced for a while and had for that reason lost her right to work as a medical doctor. She had to do different refreshment courses befor she in March 2017 got her medical license back. Pa'gan was not allowed to do any kind of paid work until he and the whole family in April 2017 got the necessary refugee documents to stay and work in USA and travel abroad.

I told once in the late fall of 2016 an old friend of mine living in East Africa who has worked closely with SPLM/A and Pa'gan Amum for the last 25 years, about the fate of Pa'gan Amum and his family. He was silent for a little while and then he said: *"What a waste of talent. He was one of the very few who never took anything for himself."*

18
RIEK MACHAR, A FREEDOM FIGHTER OR WHEELER-DEALER?

A gifted and very ambitious Man

Riek Machar is 65 years old and comes from a traditional chief's family and clan with the Nuer people. When he grew up, he went to a school belonging to the Presbyterian Church in South Sudan.

He was a clever young boy who did well at school. Having completed secondary school, he studied engineering at the University of Khartoum. He then went to Great Britain for studies, and he took a Ph. D in philosophy and strategic studies at the University of Bradford.

On his return to Sudan in 1984, he joined the SPLM/A under Garang's leadership, and he was a commander of a large guerilla unit.

Seven years later, in August 1991 he together with Lam Akol led the rebellion in Nazir against Garang that split the SPLM/A into two factions; Garang's SPLM/A Mainstream and Machar's SPLM/A United. The justification for the rebellion was the authoritarian leadership style of Garang, but as important was a main political difference; Garang wanted a new, democratic and secular Sudan while Machar wanted independence for South Sudan.

Immediately after the rebellion, Khartoum came in with political, financial and military support for the rebels. This was followed by a military alliance between the forces of the regime in Khartoum and SPLM/A United, the alliance force now under the command of Riek Machar. In the battlefield, the alliance again and again defeated the SPLM/A Mainstream.

The first shocking news about the brutality of the war after the Nazir split came with the news broken by NPA's field worker, Dan Eiffe (see chapter 4, A Turning Point) about the Bor massacre in November 1991.

Shortly after the massacre in Bor, Machar was on a PR visit in Nairobi, giving a press conference at Pan Afrique Hotel. A young British aidworker, Emma McCune, was in the audience. The two met, had an instant love affair ending in bed the same night. They married shortly after, and Emma became a very important partner for Riek Machar until she died in a car accident in Nairobi in 1993. Emma's life story and her love affair and marriage with Riek Machar is eminently narrated in the book; *Emma's War*, by Deborah Scroggins, that was published in 2003.

Riek Machar, Khartoum's Man

In the period between the late fall of 1991 and 1994 many hundred thousand of South Sudanese lost their lives while as many were maimed for life because of the fierce fighting between Garang's SPLM/A on one side, and the alliance of Machar's/Lam Akol's forces and forces of the Khartoum regime on the other side. Several attempts at mediation were undertaken in 1993/94 to try and stop the war and make the two sides reconcile, but all efforts failed first and foremost because Machar refused to accept John Garang as the Chairman of SPLM and the Commander in Chief of SPLA.

Machar in 1994 reorganized his military force and renamed it SSIM/A, the South Sudan Independence Movement and Army ,while he at the same time had confirmed his continuing support of money and arms from Khartoum.

Machar gained many advantages from his cooperation with the Khartoum regime. In 1996, he signed a far-reaching cooperation agreement with the regime, and in 1997, the two parties signed a peace agreement of their own for South Sudan. Following these agreements, Machar was appointed a special advisor to Sudan's President Omar Bashir. He was made the President of the Khartoum based Council for the States of South Sudan. Furthermore, he was also appointed Commander in Chief of his own forces and all militsia forces, operating in the territory of South Sudan and fighting Garang's SPLM/A with political, financial and military support from the Khartoum regime.

In the period of the mid 1990s Machar spent long periods in Khartoum working closely with the government with the aim to defeat Garang's SPLM/A. During the same period, he also actively advised many multinational oil companies on business visits in Khartoum, how best to strategize to get permission to exploit oil in the areas of South Sudan where oil was deposits had been documented. It is commonly known that Riek Machar received very good payments for the advice he rendered to the companies concerned, One of them was Lundin Oil in Sweden.

However, between 1999 and 2002 Machar lost influence with the regime in Khartoum, and he had to start a difficult and complex process of negotiations with Garang's SPLM/A to get back into the father house. There were of course very many leaders, officers and soldiers in Garang's SPLM/A who because of the war experience, had very hard feelings against Machar and did not want him back. But Garang and his key advisors had to take a wider perspective. Without the reunification with 's organization and armed units, the ongoing peace negotiations in Nairobi would be hard to conclude in a successful way.

NPA given the Task of facilitating Machar's Return to SPLM/A

The leaders of NPAs Nairobi Office, Sten Rino Bonsaksen and Ken Miller, were secret partners in the efforts to make reunification possible. However, the impression left with my former colleagues with NPA in Nairobi is that Riek Machar is not a man you should trust.

Nevertheless, the negotiations between Garang's SPLM/A and Machar's organization were successful, and in 2002 Machar was back as number three in the SPLM/A hierarchy after Garang and Kiir.

There was never, at any point in time, a relationship marked by trust or cooperation between Salva Kiir and Riek Machar. I have a story from the secret meeting of the SPLM National Liberation Council held in Rumbak the day after Garang's death in July 2005 which is likely to be true. Kiir was then unanimously elected the Chairman and Commander in Chief with Riek Machar his deputy.

When the elections were over, congratulations and greetings were extended. Salva Kiir crossed the floor and went up to Riek Machar and congratulated him, Then, he stared at him for a moment and said:

"I do not like you. I do not trust you, and I shall follow you."

When the two shortly thereafter moved into the Office of the President, they immediately started a development that came to nourish the reciprocal suspicion of each other. They started the development of two separate administration units, one for the

President and one for the Vice-President. This had two decisive impacts. It widened the gap of mistrust that existed in advance between the two, and it increasingly created an unhealthy administrative situation in the Office of the President.

A hard-working Vice-President

However, Riek Machar was a very hardworking Vice-President. He was informal and easy to approach. He travelled widely in the country and talked with many people. His working style made it easy also for international partners to establish communication with him, see him and have him come to open meetings of different kinds.

We, the partners of the International Consortium on Freedom of Expression and free and independent media in South Sudan, had him come to give the opening speech at two of our meetings, one in Rumbak in the fall of 2005 and one in Juba I February 2006. Riek Machar spoke very well about the need for South Sudan to secure a political environment that made free speech a fundamental right for all citizens and about what was needed at large to secure a democratic development of the society.

The uneasy relationship between the President and the Vice-President grew in the year 2013 into an open political conflict. Machar in the winter of 2013 declared his intention to stand as a candidate for the Chairmanship of SPLM at the forthcoming Convention and then seek the nomination for the Presidency. This increased the conflict, and on 23rd July President Salva Kiir unilaterally without any consultation with Parliament and therefore in violation of the Constitution, sacked both the Vice-President and the whole cabinet.

I do not know what was on the mind of the President when he did all this. But his finger feelings of politics and the way democratic processes work, are poorly developed. The same goes for his understanding of how human beings, like his own ministers, would react to being degraded and humiliated. How could he believe that he could treat the core of the SPLM leaders from the time of the liberation struggle who were in government with him, the way he did and believe that there would be no reaction to it?

The Conflict between the Chairman and the Majority of the SPLM Politburo

The conflict between not only Machar and the President but most of the members of the Politburo, the National Liberation Council and the President escalated during the fall of 2013, and it exploded as I have already written about, into open conflict in the meeting of the National Liberation Council on 13th and 14th December 2013.

On the 15th of December 2013, the planned massacre of the Nuer people living in Juba, began. It became the beginning of the civil war that since has destroyed South Sudan.

In the morning of 16th December, a unit from SPLA with tanks and other heavy armory, surrounded the residence of Riek Machar in Juba. The aim was to destroy his house and kill all those inside. Riek Machar and his wife Angelina escaped through a backdoor and jumped into a car waiting in the backyard.

For the rest of the people present, most of them were killed on the spot and the house, a state-owned building, was turned into ruins.

Bishop Paride Taban, in a meeting in Oslo sometime after Christmas 2013, told me that he was present with Riek Machar and his wife Angelina in the house on Sunday evening 14th December. They discussed the growing crisis in the country that was to follow the disastrous decisions taken at the meeting of the National Liberation Council the same day.

In this discussion, Riek Machar and his wife Angelina promised the bishop that they would not be the first to take up arms if an armed conflict should come.

But on the day Machar and his wife escaped the assassination, special units of SPLA and the newly established Presidential

Guard had already for a day and a night, been in action in Juba carrying out the massacres of Nuers. No one will never know for sure how many Nuers and other people were murdered in Juba in this dark week proceeding Christmas 2013, but the indications are up to 20 000 people massacred. The two ones carrying the major responsibility for this, is of course the ones who gave the orders to kill, first and foremost the President, Salva Kiir and his key Dinka ally, Paul Malong.

With all this being done against the Nuer people of South Sudan, I do understand that Riek Machar and other Nuer leaders did not have much of a choice but to take up arms trying to defend themselves.

My Meetings with Riek Machar

I have only met Riek Machar a couple of times.

In the winter of 1993, John Garang had just been in Oslo on a working visit, and we had met at NPA for our first discussions. I promised then on behalf of NPA that we were standing with our commitments regarding the political and humanitarian support for SPLM/A Mainstream.

Riek Machar came to Oslo two weeks later, and he sought a meeting with me at NPA. We met, and Machar then demanded from NPA the same treatment for his SPLM/A United as we were providing for Garang's SPLM/A Mainstream.

I answered the following:

"Norwegian People's Aid is the humanitarian branch of the Norwegian Labour Movement, and the Labour Movement has a tradition of not honouring those who try for a policy of split and rule. So, the answer is no."

Riek Machar got very angry with my answer. He rose instantly, uttered some unpleasant remarks and left.

Almost 13 years passed, before we met again. The International Consortium on Freedom of Expression had its first meeting inside South Sudan in Rumbak in the fall of 2005. Riek Machar had as Vice-President accepted an invitation to be the key note speaker at the opening of our meeting. I, as the former Secretary General of NPA, was asked to be part of the delegation that would welcome Riek Machar at the airport. Machar arrived, he was in great spirits and greeted warmly all members of the delegation except me. He totally overlooked me because he remembered me from our meeting in Oslo. During his speech and the discussion afterwards, he never looked at me or caught my eyes.

Our next meeting was on 6th January 2013. I was then a member of the Labour Party delegation that was in Juba for a week to take part in meetings related to the party building project. I was one of the lecturers, and I was welcome by so many attending the first major meeting, who remembered me as uncle Halle from NPA. At that meeting Riek Machar paid attention to me and greeted me as well. He probably felt it to be opportune to do it then.

A Future for Riek Machar in South Sudan?

There is still no evidence and there will never be any evidence to the claim by President Salva Kiir and his confidants, that Riek Machar on 13th-14th December 2013 had any ready-made plan for a military rebellion. He and other Nuer leaders who were not arrested or killed at the time, had in my view no other option but to improvise an organized and armed resistance to the onslaught by the Kiir and Malong forces against the Nuer people from 15th December 2013. This armed struggle in the form of a very bloody and destructive civil war, has lasted since. There is no doubt that Machar to get arms to his soldiers, has reopened his old channels of cooperation with the Khartoum regime.

He has in that respect for long been successful. Khartoum has in the period since early 2014 supplied a lot of arms for his forces, but the supplies have of late come to a stand still.

There has since January 2014 been many cease fires negotiated by IGAD, and there have been quite a few peace agreements negotiated by IGAD that have all been broken by both parties, but first and foremost by the forces of the Government in Juba. The present ARCISS that was signed in August 2015 has also been broken so many times, again first and foremost by the government in Juba, that it no longer neither has any trust nor any validity.

The Final Collapse of Trust.
The Events in Juba on 8th July 2016

On 8th July 2016, there was a clash between the guards of President Salva Kiir and the guards of the Vice-President Riek Machar who by then had returned to juba as part of the ARCISS. Many of the soldiers on both sides were killed. The clash took place as the President and the Vice-President were having a meeting. The claim is that there was a plan to assassinate Riek Machar that failed.

What happened in Juba on the same day and the days following, gives support to the view that there might have been a plan to assassinate Riek Machar. Military units belonging to Kiir/Malong's SPLA and units belonging to Machar's side fought in Juba for a little while before Machar ordered his troops out of Juba. The Kiir/Malong units, then went on a rampage and killing spree in Juba, murdering non-Dinka people. Not only that, they also attacked the Terrain Hotel which provided housing for many international humanitarian workers, many of them European and North American. The Kiir/Malong soldiers then raped female aid workers at gun point, some of them being raped by at least 15 soldiers in a row.

Then the Kiir/Malong units went south and into the three states of Equatoria, looting, rampaging and killing whoever they thought was supporting Riek Machar. This looting and killing in the three states has lasted through out the whole fall of 2016 and is still on.

There have been claims by both independent observers in Juba and by spokespersons for Riek Machar that the Kiir/Malong Government forces in the hunt for Riek Machar in July and August 2016 hired mercenary logistic and military support from FSG, Frontier Services Group, headed by Eric Prince, the former Director of the infamous US private Mercenary Company, Blackwater. These claims have not yet been documented, but it is a known fact that Salva Kiir, as President and Commander in Chief in South Sudan, since 2008 has had a commercial cooperation with the said company.

All this has again undermined the popularity and standing of the President and his loyalists both among the people of the three states of Equatoria and of the people of most other states in South Sudan to the extent that there now are many indications to the fact that Riek Machar for the first time in his life may be a more popular leader in South Sudan than Salva Kiir and his group.

As I am writing the present text, Riek Machar is staying in South Africa while he still is the Chairman of the SPLM inO and the Commander in Chief of SPLA inO. His statute in South Africa seems unclear, but all indications point to the fact that he is de facto detained in South Africa. The story further goes that this detainment is based on an agreement between Salva Kiir and his Government and the Government of South Africa, and supported by IGAD Kiir and his court in Juba are said to be paying the expenses related to Machar's stay. Riek Machar cannot freely communicate with the outside world, and he can only move outside the house according to what his driver allows for.

To me, and I guess most others, this situation seems quite absurd. How can anyone believe that one meaningfully can create peace in Sudan while keeping the Vice- President of the Republic and the Nuer Leader a kind of prisoner in South Africa?

Riek Machar, an ambitious and at the same time, a very controvercial political leader. As I finalize the script of this book, he is still in a kind of political detention in South Africa. However, international efforts are now being undertaken to bring and end to this absurd and shameful situation, in order to bring Riek Machar back as a free man to the political landscape of South Sudan.

Fredrik Barth, a world famous Norwegian Professor of Social Anthropology, (1928 – 2016) laid in the early 1950ies the groundwork for the academic cooperation between Norway and Sudan.

Hilde Frafjord Johnson, the Norwegian Minister of Development Cooperation from 1997 to 2005 and later the Special Representative of the Secretary General of UN to South Sudan and Head of UNMISS. She has plaid a role of historical dimensions in developing the relations between South Sudan and Norway as this relationship stood in 2012.

19
THREADS IN THE WEB BETWEEN NORWAY, SUDAN AND SOUTH SUDAN

The First Thread

In 1954, the young Norwegian social anthropologist Fredrik Barth travelled to Sudan, to study the societies of Darfur as his goal. He had a fellowship from the University of Oslo. Upon return to Norway, Fredrik Barth received an appointment as researcher at the University of Bergen.

When professor Fredrik Barth passed away in January 2016, he was 87 years and considered one of the great social anthropologists of the world.

However, Barth's journey to Sudan in 1954 marked the beginning of an academic cooperation between the two countries; The University of Bergen was the initiator with Fredrik Barth as the driving force. The cooperation between UoB and the University of Khartoum was formalized in 1963, and it has with some periods of stagnation due to political hindrances by the regime in Khartoum, developed gradually and has become very important for both universities. In addition, the cooperation has been extended to other academic institutions in other parts of Sudan. Many dozens of students and researchers from the two countries have done their field work and studies in Norway and Sudan. Several of the foremost Norwegian academics in Social Anthropology and other study fields have much of their research tied to Sudan, not only Fredrik Barth, but Gunnar Haaland, Gunnar Sørbø, Leif Manger, Terje Tvedt and many others.

When the political oppression was at its worst in Sudan around 1991 and free and independent academic work was not possible, the formal cooperation was put on hold, and only picked up again about ten years ago, while the CPA was being negotiated.

The University of Bergen has in recent years also tried to establish cooperation with the University in Juba, but unfortunately ,progress has been slow because of the political violence and the lack of academic freedom in the country.

The University of Bergen is considered an "Academic Centre of Excellence" when it comes to Sudan.

The University College of Oslo has in the last 15 years, developed a substantial fellowship programme for students from South Sudan and Sudan, as well as paving the way for the possibility of future cooperation with other academic institutions in South Sudan. Unfortunately, also this very important cooperation for the academic institutions of South Sudan has as well come to a standstill because of the political violence, the terrible corruption and the lack of governement that marks the society of South Sudan today.

Norwegian Church Aid, a Norwegian Pioneer with many Threads

The Norwegian Broadcasting Company's **(NRK)** reporter Øystein Stabrun is probably the person in Norway who contributed most to raising the interest for Sudan in Norway (cf. Bibiana Piene's book). His reports from Sudan and the Anyanya War at the end of the 1960s, beginning of the 1970s, revealing the immense sufferings of an innocent people, had a strong impact on public opinion. In 1973, Norwegian Church Aid's (NCA) appointed him the first Country Director for its new development programme in South Sudan. He took charge of the programme under very difficult circumstances and stayed on for four years.

In the summer of 1972 there was another Norwegian TV (NRK) team in Sudan reporting both on the after effects of the war and the Peace Agreement that recently had been signed in Addis Ababa, as well as what challenges and possibilities that existed for peace and development.

Leading people from NCA, the World Council of Churches and the Lutheran World Federation were lobbying hard behind the scene in Addis Ababa in support of the peace negotiations. A political fact that contributed to the agreement being signed, were the many promises from countries in the North for development assistance, first and foremost to the totally underdeveloped South Sudan, but also promises for the North.

The Norwegian Government took its commitment seriously, and instructed Norad to engage in the development efforts in Sudan. Norad, for the first time ever, decided to delegate the responsibility for Norwegian development assistance to a Norwegian NGO, the Norwegian Church Aid. NCA then signed a long-term contract with Norad with an initial annual allocation of approx. 40 Mill. NOK.

The ideological foundation for NCA's work was the ideas embodied in Christian Brotherhood and International Solidarity, and its emergency and development programmes were rooted in these ideas. The foundation of the NCA programme in both

South Sudan and in the North, was laid early in 1973. The first expatriates, most of them devoted Christians mostly from Norway and on a low salary, were in place only a few months later. In the decade that followed, more than two hundred Norwegian expatriates were on contract for NCA in South Sudan, and between 1973 and 1983 only the United Nations had a larger development programme in South Sudan than NCA.

NCA's bilateral development programme in South Sudan in the 1970s and early 1980s with a focus on poverty ridden Eastern Equatoria was the largest Norwegian development programme run by a Norwegian NGO in an African country during a time of peace. During that period Norad allocated close to 1 billion NOK to the programme. Many of the Norwegian expatriates had families with them. During the whole period, about one thousand Norwegians stayed in South Sudan and got to know the people, their everyday life and their dreams for the future. For most of these Norwegians, it was their first African experience. It had a great impact with many of them who for the rest of their lives have continued to uphold a strong personal interest for the fate of the people of South Sudan.

Towards the end of the programme period in 1982/83, around 2000 South Sudanese were employed in the programmes and projects. NCA ran at the time 13 different development projects, and 119 agricultural cooperatives were in operation, with about 2000 farmers as members. Both health and education were priority areas.

Criticism has been raised against NCA, because they used too many Norwegians, and that the transfer of knowledge to the South Sudanese was not sufficiently emphasized. There is some truth in the critique, but what was really worth criticizing had very little to do with NCA.

The big political and developmental problem for Sudan and South Sudan at the time of the Addis Ababa Peace Agreement in 1972 and in the years, that followed, was that most countries that had promised to provide development assistance, did not keep their promises. If they had kept their promises and contributed to development at the same level as Norway and NCA did, then we might have been able to avoid the rebellion in 1983 and the very destructive wars that followed since.

There is no doubt, NCA with its strong and continuing involvement in South Sudan and Sudan throughout the past 50 years has created many strong political and human ties to Norway

The first political contacts between Norway and Sudan and threads, they created

The NRK-team's reports between 1966 and 1972 created both political concern and interest for Sudan in Norway. The academic cooperation, initiated in 1954 and led by the University in Bergen also contributed to interest and attention.

In 1973 the Labour Party formed the government with Trygve Bratteli as Prime Minister. Knut Frydenlund became the minister of foreign affairs with Thorvald Stoltenberg as his state secretary. Both Frydenlund and Stoltenberg were concerned with the new international political challenges such as the proposal for a new International Economic Order, the challenges in Norway's policies for International Development Cooperation and political development in the new states in Africa.

In the spring of 1974, the new Sudanese Minister of Foreign Affairs Mansour Khalid paid a working visit to Norway. He was a new member of the Nimeiri government which was in the process of changing its foreign policy orientation from Moscow to Washington. The Addis Ababa Peace Agreement for Sudan was in place, and Sudan needed new friends internationally. The Norwegian NGO, NCA; was in the process of establishing a comprehensive development programme in the southern part of Sudan.

Mansour Khalid was not just anybody. He came from an upper-class Muslim family in Khartoum, with a solid academic education and enough self-confidence to go with it. He was a Muslim, but religiously moderate, and politically he was in many ways leaning towards the left.

Knut Frydenlund liked the man who came to see him. The two ministers enjoyed each other's company and spoke easily and at length about different world problems. They continued to keep in touch, and Khalid invited Frydenlund to visit Sudan at the turn of the year 1974/75. Frydenlund accepted. The Frydenlund family decided to make use of the invitation to also have their first African experience together at Christmas 1974 in Kenya. After Christmas day, Frydenlund went to Khartoum on official business while the family remained behind in Kenya. The Sudan Government and the political establishment surrounding it, was known for its hospitality and ability to make official guests feel at home. Frydenlund had a politically most rewarding and socially most enjoyable time in Khartoum.

One day, he received an unexpected message about a change in his programme schedule. He should visit NCA's development programme in South Sudan. The NCA Country Director, Øystein Stabrun had persuaded the protocol people at the Ministry of Foreign Affairs in Khartoum to insert into the programme a visit to the NCA programme areas in the South. The visit was very successful. Frydenlund, like other guests at NCA at the time, was impressed by NCA's work for the betterment of the living conditions for poor people in the country.

Mansour Khalid stayed on as the Foreign Minister of Sudan for a while, but fell out with his increasingly dictatorial president Nymeiri, and he was sacked.

Gro Harlem Brundtland and Mansour Khalid and their threads in the Web

The former longtime Norwegian Prime Minister and leader of the Labour Party, Mrs. Gro Harlem Brundtland was in 1984 appointed Chairperson of the World Commission on Environment and Development (WCED), and she was looking for a deputy chairman from the South whom she could work with. Khalid who then was in conflict with the holders of power in Khartoum, was one of the strong candidates. Gro Harlem Brundtland wanted to see him before he was finally appointed, and Khalid as well wanted to see the Chairman, a woman from the North, as there was little tradition in Muslim societies for female chairmen. They met in Nairobi one day in the spring of 1984 and had a long conversation on the balcony of the residence of the Norwegian Ambassador to Kenya, and during the meeting Khalid accepted the nomination as the deputy chairman of WCED. They worked closely together for three years and then the Commission published the widely-acknowledged report; Our Common Future.

Mansour Khalid met with John Garang in 1986 while he was still the deputy chairman of WCED. The two soon found common political ground and became friends. Khalid who then was both a very scholared person and an experienced politician, advanced quickly into the leadership group of SPLM. He and Garang worked closely together, and Khalid published already in 1987, the book: *John Garang Speaks*, where he wrote an introduction to a collection of John Garang's political speeches.

Mansour Khalid was part of the SPLM negotiating group at the peace negotiations in Kenya from 2001 until 2005. When Garang died in July 2005, he was one of the many who were disliked by SPLM's new chairman, Salva Kiir, and named one of the Garang boys.

He pulled out of active participation in the liberation struggle and in politics, and he has since worked as an independent intellectual, academic and writer and published many books on a variety of political subjects mainly related to Africa.

Mansour Khalid was as Foreign Minister in Sudan in 1973 and onwards, instrumental in providing political support for NCA's development work in South Sudan. As a leading member of SPLM he came to learn about NPA's political support for the liberation struggle and NPA's humanitarian work in the South Sudan. Both I and other leading staff of NPA at the time have met Mansour Khalid many times.

The Visit of the Chairman of the Norwegian Conservative Party, an important Thread in the Web

In the 1970s, Norad introduced, as part of its education and communication programme for Norwegian citizens, an earmarked allocation in the budget where the educational associations of the political parties could apply for travel grants for its members to study development work in Norway's partner countries in the South.

Erling Norvik, the Chairman of the Conservative Party at the time, decided to participate in a such a study trip. NCA invited him to Sudan, and in the fall of 1980 he together with Bjørn Johannessen, a senior staff member from Norad went through Kenya into South Sudan. I as the Africa Correspondent of Norwegian Broadcasting Corporation, was invited to join them.

We met early one morning at Wilson Airport. Our pilot was a charming white Kenyan woman. We flew first to La Fonne, a small cluster of mountain peaks in Eastern Equatoria, where a small tribe was living, and with whom NCA had some projects. A group of elders was waiting at the airstrip and welcomed us most heartily. They wanted to introduce us to their traditional African governing system that had some obvious democratic features. They had a rather big traditional and beautiful house, a kind of parliament building, in which they met for discussions and resolutions.

We were taken there, but just as we were about to enter, an unexpected problem arose. The Kenyan pilot, whom we considered as part of our delegation, was not allowed into the parliament building. Only men could enter. The elders withdrew, gathered and discussed what to do while we were waiting. After a while, they reached a decision. Since the woman pilot wore trousers, she was declared to be an honorary man for the day. African pragmatism at its best.

Travelling with Erling Norvik was a wonderful experience. He was very interested both in what views the Africans had on development and what views NCA had. He never complained, he was always in good spirits, approachable and apparently never tired. I have hardly ever met a person with such great capacity to talk with people, to acquire new knowledge and instill confidence and trust. If anyone in Norway, it would be Thorvald Stoltenberg.

The day before we were going to leave, we were invited to a traditional African lunch feast in a village. We were a little anxious. But it was a fantastic food experience, with some of the best African, Arabic and Ethiopian dishes. There were meat and fish prepared in different ways, (there is plenty of good fish in South Sudan's lakes and rivers), various herbs and vegetables as well as fruit, all in all, there were about 30 courses. Everything was wonderful, and we let our appetites loose. I will never forget that lunch.

Tomm Kristiansen, President Salva Kiir's Communication Advisor, another Thread

Tomm Kristiansen is still a senior reporter/editor with Norwegian Broadcasting Corporation and one of the very best in Norway on reporting Africa. He has played a unique role in South Sudan in its process towards becoming an independent country. He was in 2006 appointed President Salva Kiir's Communication Advisor. The appointment was under the auspices of the United Nations Development Programme (UNDP), but there was also a Norwegian influence behind the appointment.

Hilde Frafjord Johnson was concerned about how South Sudan's first President, Salva Kiir who for so many years had been SPLA's Head of Intelligence with the ability to keep silent, being his most important deed, was going to communicate with his people. She knew Tomm Kristiansen, and she liked him and the way he was reporting Africa. For these reasons, she believed that he would be a good advisor to President Salva Kiir.

Tomm arrived at a workplace that was brand new and untested. The South Sudanese working at the President's office had never done anything like this before. During the liberation struggle, they were either soldiers or refugees somewhere abroad. Last, but not least, the total lack of experience in running a President's Office simply because this was the first time there was a real President's Office was in South Sudan.

Not only did Tomm Kristiansen survive in his job, but under difficult conditions he together with other staff did a good job.

When Tomm finished his contract, he wrote a book, *Presidentens mann, oppdrag Sør-Sudan* (The President's Man, assignment South Sudan). I hold the view that Tomm is even-handed and constructive in narrating his very special experience.

The Norwegian Support Group for Peace in Sudan and South Sudan, (NSGPSS) a special thread in the Web

Norwegian Church Aid (NCA) employed a couple of hundred Norwegians in South Sudan between 1973 and 1985. When their family members are added, the numbers run into approximately one thousand.

After the SPLM split in Nasir in 1991 and the extremely violent conflict that followed, some of the most devoted former staff members of NCA in 1993 formed a Support group for Peace in Sudan (SGPS). The group expanded gradually to include people from NPA, various academic institutions such as the University of Bergen and University College in Akershus and Oslo, as well as staff members from Norad and the Ministry of Foreign Affairs (MFA).

As the peace process developed between 2001 and 2005, SGPS became an open forum for discussion and debate about the many conflicts and their causes, the war and possibilities for lasting peace. In 1999 SGPS had its first meeting with John Garang when he was the guest of honour at NPA's National Convention. Parallel to this, SGPS began working with the Sudanese refugee groups in Norway.

NSGPS strongly supported the peace negotiations in Kenya, and it equally strongly endorsed CPA when it was signed in January 2005. In April 2005, the Norwegian government in cooperation with UN hosted an official donor conference for Sudan and South Sudan in Oslo. SGPS, then with the support from the Norwegian government, hosted two civil society conferences that drew a wide range of participants from civil society groups both in North and South Sudan, one with the participation of both sexes, the other for women only. A similar conference was held in Juba in June 2007. However, after 2007 and to the great disappointment of SGPSS, the political developments first in Sudan north and then also in South Sudan have taken a direction that is not compatible with a grass-root based and free development of civil society in neither country. SGPS was nevertheless renamed in 2011 to be called the Norwegian Support Group for Peace in Sudan and South Sudan (NSGPSS).

NSGPSS continues despite the present and politically very hostile environment to real and lasting peace in both countries as a bridge building institution between Norway and the two Sudanese countries. SGPSS is also a bridge builder between the Sudanese and South Sudanese communities in Norway.

SPS is a non-profit NGO whose activities for 90 percent of the budget is based on membership fees and voluntary work, but NMFA/Norad has at times given support for smaller project activities.

The Sudan Forum

The Sudan Forum is an informal, but politically an important forum that is about 15 years old. Norwegian NGOs that have activities in Sudan and South Sudan are members Its meets usually once a month and as a rule, senior representatives from NMFA and Norad take part in the meetings that are held in the tradition of the Chatham House rules. The list of members includes; the Adventist Development and Relief Agency (ADRA), Amnesty International, Norwegian Peoples Aid, the National Association for Heart and Lung Disease (LHL), Norwegian Refugee Council (NRC), Norwegian Church Aid, Doctors Without Borders, Save the Children, Red Cross, Support Group for Peace in Sudan and South Sudan, The Solidarity Council for Africa and representatives from MFA, Norad and research institutions. The discussions taking place at the meetings of the Sudan Forum, are very open and may at times be very frank when it comes to discussing events and developments in the two countries and the policies of Norway and the Troika towards the same. It is my view that without Sudan Forum, Norway's commitment to peace and development in the two states easily could have evaporated.

IGAD, PARTNER FOR NORWAY

In 1986 the countries on the Horn of Africa formed a regional collaborative organization called the Intergovernmental Authority on Drought and Development (IGAD). Its primary purpose was to work on issues related to developing semi-desert and desert areas. Later the mandate was expanded to also include work on conflict resolution and peace negotiations and "Drought" was deleted from the name.

Starting in 1993-94, IGAD with financial support from Norway and others donors, provided the framework for peace negotiations in Sudan. The negotiations had a rocky start in 1994 with Kenya proposing some guiding principles for the negotiating process. It took three years before a first partial agreement was reached. The primary point of contention was whether South Sudan in a referendum should have the right to choose between independence or remaining in union with the rest of Sudan.

It was not until 1998-99 that the negotiations really took off.

This was first and foremost due to Al Quaida's attacks on the American embassies in Nairobi and Dar er Salaam. Khartoum was rightly accused of having provided training grounds for the terrorists, and to avoid the wrath of the USA, the Khartoum regime took a political turn around, declared its willingness to fight terrorism and proposed to send representatives to participate in international meetings on combatting international terrorism. Meanwhile, SPLM/A had both military progress in the battlefields of South Sudan and political and diplomatic progress internationally. John Garang and SPLM/A were demonstrating to both the holders of power in Khartoum and to the world at large that there was only one way to stop the war. The conflict had to be resolved politically at the negotiation table.

Outside Africa, important political initiatives were being taken to support the idea of peace negotiations. In the middle of the 1990s Nederland and Norway formed a group called the "Friends of Sudan" with the Dutch Minister of Development Cooperation, Jan Pronk, as the leader. A new group evolved out of this group, "IGAD's Partners Forum", again with Pronk as leader.

The Peace negotiations, Norway, Hilde Frafjord Johnson and the Utstein Group

The Norwegian Labour Party lost the parliamentary elections in the fall of 1997. A new minority coalition government with the three parties in the center of politics, The Christian Democrats, the Liberals and the Center Party formed a new government. Kjell Magne Bondevik became the new Prime Minister, and he appointed his close aid Hilde Frafjord Johnson as Minister of International Development. She was born and had had her childhood in Tanzania and had a deep interest for African politics and development. She wanted to do something about the conflict in Sudan, and she was appointed as the Norwegian Representative to "IGAD's Partners Forum" and succeeded Jan Pronk as its leader in 1998.

That same year she went to see her British colleague, the Minister for International Development, Clare Short, from the British Labour Party, both very knowledgeable, committed and ambitious. During their first meeting in London, they agreed to make the peace negotiations for Sudan their common cause and give it high priority.

At the time, many countries in Western Europe had appointed female ministers in charge of development cooperation.

In Nederland, the social-democrat, Eveline Herfkens, replaced Jan Pronk, while Heidemarie Wieczorek-Zeul from the German Green Party became minister of development in Germany.

Hilde Frafjord Johnson made in cooperation with Clare Short a strategic move. She invited the three other European female ministers for development to a meeting at the old Utstein Monastery, now refurbished a modern hotel, in her own constituency Rogaland.

During the meeting, the four ministers agreed to make their utmost to contribute to a peaceful resolution of the war in Sudan. They made their commitment and priority known while being at Utstein, and they quickly became known as the Utstein group with Hilde Frafjord Johnson in charge. They at the meeting at Utstein further agreed to make a joint working trip to Sudan to see everyday life for people, living close to the battlefields. They were overwhelmed by what they experienced during their journey, the complexity of the conflict, with all the death and destruction it represented. About the same time, as a British Minister, Clare Short requested a study that concluded that the war could continue indefinitely unless a powerful international political intervention put an end to it. After their field visit, the four European female ministers felt more committed than ever to contribute to a peaceful resolution of the conflict.

As Secretary General of NPA, I had frequent meetings with SOLIDAR in Brussels, a European network of NGO's linked to the Labour Movement in Europe and working to advance social justice in Europe, and with EUROSTEP, another network of European NGOs working in the field of development cooperation. I was often in the European Parliament and talked with both members of the European Parliament and EU bureaucrats about the conflict in Sudan. I became during these meetings convinced that the Utstein group had considerable influence on change of the policies of EU towards Sudan, and the conflict ravaging the country.

Before the Utstein group started lobbying their own governments and the EU institutions in Brussels on a peaceful conflict resolution in Sudan, the attitude towards the conflict in Sudan among most of EU member countries was either one of indifference or in support of Khartoum, but from 1999-2000 all this changed in Europe. Increasingly more critique was leveraged at the Khartoum regime, and more politicians began to listen to what the SPLM leaders said.

During the spring of 2002, Garang with a delegation was touring Europe, to explain the SPLM view of the conflict. During his visit in Oslo, I had a private breakfast with him, and he told me that when he was in London he dreaded the meeting with Foreign Minister Jack Straw of the "old Colonial Power in Sudan". He expected to have to repeat his view on the conflict and why they were fighting to a minister being politically deaf and de facto in favour of Khartoum.

Garang arrived at the meeting with Straw and began his exposure. Then Jack Straw smiled, interrupted Garang, lifted his hand and said: "*Mr. Garang, keep in mind that you are speaking to a convert.*" After that, the conversation became very amicable and open.

In 2003 the Utstein group was awarded the American prize "2003 Commitment to Development Award", by the Center for Global Development and the journal *Foreign Affairs*.

Both Hilde Frafjord Johnson and Clare Short were active in persuading the American government to take a leading role among non-African countries being involved in the peace process in Sudan.

Hilde Frafjord Johnson was worked very hard both nationally and internationally, to mobilize support for the peaceful resolution of the Sudan conflict. In Norway, she had the fortune of being very close to Prime Minister Kjell Magne Bondevik and key members of Parliament, (Stortinget) who strongly supported her in this endeavour.

In the Ministry of Foreign Affairs, experienced top diplomats were assigned to assist in the peace process, including Tom Vraalsen, Vegard Ellefsen, Fridtjof Thorkildsen and Hans Jacob Frydenlund. Hilde Frafjord Johnson also employed Kjell Hødnebø, an assistant professor with a doctorate in history based on fieldwork in South Sudan, and the NCA's Sudan veteran, Halvor Aschjem, as her special advisors on Sudan. Endre Stiansen, a researcher of the Peace Research Institute in Oslo (PRIO), also with a doctorate in history based on fieldwork in Sudan, joined the Norwegian advisory group to assist during the negotiations for the CPA.

The Norwegian advisors had permanent and close contact with their Minister during the negotiating process, and whenever special funds were required to pay for expenses necessary to move the negotiations forward, they called on her. If necessary, Hilde Frafjord Johnson then had to talk with her Prime Minister and her colleague, the Minister of Finance to have the necessary amount granted.

In addition, the Minister and her group of advisors had close contact with the leadership of NPA and NCA, making use of the goodwill they throughout the years of the struggle had developed with SPLM/A and the people of South Sudan.

In a meeting I had with Hilde Frafjord Johnson while writing the Norwegian edition of the book, she said the following about the role played by NPA and NCA:

"*The good reputation NPA and NCA had among the people and the leaders in South Sudan, as well as the respect and trust both organizations had earned, was very important for us. The networks they built, were used actively in getting the peace process started. Their reputation and assistance was also a great asset to us during the peace negotiations.*"

A Glimpse into the Environment of the Negotiations

During the spring and the summer of 2002, the town of Machakos in the land of the Kamba people and some 50 km outside Nairobi was the site for the opening rounds of the peace negotiations which took place in the main hotel in town. There was nothing luxurious about it, but adequate and friendly service by a staff who was excited about being in the midst of a very important event. I had the fortune at the time, to pay a few visits to the site in Machakos. Halvor Aschjem, a senior Norwegian advisor at the negotiations and an old friend, was my host and guide. He briefed me about how the negotiations were being conducted.

In the beginning the political distance between the two parties was so big that they could not meet in the same room. For this reason, the Kenyan General Lazaro Sumbeiywo who was in charge of the negotiations, with the assistance of his African and international advisors, discussed the matters at stake. Thereafter, they drafted proposals on how difficult issues could be approached and resolved. Then the drafts were presented to one party and then the other. When both parts had commented, the leaders and advisors of the negotiations would meet again and discuss the outcome of their findings and how to proceed.

Aschjem also told me that the South African Government had an advisor at the negotiations who was no less than one of Nelson Mandela's personal advisors during the negotiations between ANC and the Apartheid government about the future of South Africa. The experience from these negotiations was obviously relevant for the ongoing process between the Khartoum regime and the SPLM.

At my first visit to Machakos, Aschjem invited me to lunch at the hotel. The dining room was full of people taking part in the negotiations. The tension between the two delegations could easily be seen and felt in the dining room. In one corner sat the SPLM delegation. As soon as they saw me, they came over and greeted and embraced me and praised NPA's efforts during the struggle. In the other corner sat the delegation from Khartoum. They saw how I was greeted by SPLM delegation, and they sat their eyes on me, and certainly had their comments on NPA and our role in the struggle.

In the latter part of 2002, the negotiations for some months were held in different towns in Kenya. This proved to be counterproductive and hindered progress. Therefore, Naivasha Lake Simba Lodge in the Rift Valley Kenya was chosen as the permanent site for the negotiations until there was a comprehensive agreement on all major issues in June 2004.

I was on a working visit in Nairobi in the fall of 2003, and one day my old colleague from NPA, NPA's great security officer and my longtime friend, Chaat Paul, called me from Naivasha. He was now part of Garang's inner circle, and he invited me to come on visit. As I arrived, Garang was in closed chamber with Ali Osman Taha, the 1st Vice-President of Sudan and their chief negotiator. I waited for a while, having a nice chat with Chaat Paul and other old SPLM friends who were around.

Then Garang turned up and invited me to a table in a quiet corner of the garden, and he gave me an overview of the current state for the negotiations. We had a very friendly talk that lasted for about 30 minutes before he returned for a new meeting with Taha.

A few days later, John Duku turned up at my hotel in Nairobi and invited me for another trip to Naivasha. John used to be the SPLM Representative to the Nordic countries, but had been called back to assist during the negotiations.

We left for Naivasha in the afternoon in the company of Roger Winter and John Gachie who was the driver. Upon arrival, we met with quite a few of the SPLM negotiators, and Garang came by to greet us and give us a brief update on the state of affairs.

John Duku then invited us for dinner at the dining room, and we suddenly were in the midst of a crowd of people, who all had an interest in the process. Ali Osman Taha was still at the hotel, bet he never dined together with the others, but had his meals served in his room. However, all the other important people were having dinner. We had placed ourselves in a corner with a good overview. The Khartoum delegates, the SPLM delegates and dozens of international advisors were there. There was quite an atmosphere in the room.

We had a table in one corner of the room from which we had a good overview regarding who was dining with whom. I remember John Duku suddenly pointed to a table and said: See who is over there. We looked and saw the British Chief advisor at the negotiations, Mr. Guilty dining with the Head of the Sudan's Intelligence Services, Nafi al Nafi, the latter known to be one of the cruelest men of the Khartoum regime, having been in charge of an intelligence organization that arrested, tortured and killed Sudanese suspected of being in opposition to the regime.

Hilde Frafjord Johnson and her personal Role during the Time of the Peace Negotiations

During the negotiation process, Hilde Frafjord Johnson gained a remarkable personal working relationship with the two main personalities in the peace negotiations, the Chair of SPLM, John Garang, and Sudan's 1st Vice-President, Ali Osman Taha. Both were equipped with encrypted satellite telephones from the Norwegian Ministry of Foreign Affairs, so that they could call Frafjord Johnson at any time for confidential discussions. For example, it might be a political initiative one of them wanted to take, but he was unsure about how the other side would react. Could she sound out the reaction from the other side?

Hilde Frafjord Johnson showed from the time she was appointed in 1997, both great patience and persistence in trying to make the peace negotiations succeed. Her decision to collaborate with Clare Short, her counterpart in Great Britain, and the establishment of the Utstein group was strategically important. The four ministers of the Utstein Group played an important role in convincing USA's President and his government to believe that negotiating peace was possible. One lasting outcome of this was the later establishment of the Troika; USA, Great Britain and Norway as three International watch dogs for the CPA.

NORWAY'S OFFICIAL ASSISTANCE TO SOUTH SUDAN – 2005-2016

It was both logical and reasonable that Norway became one of the troika-countries with a special political responsibility for support and surveillance regarding the implementation of the peace agreement.

To understand more of Norway's relation to South Sudan since the CPA in 2005, it might be useful to look at a few facts.

In terms of the UN's peace keeping forces in South Sudan, (UNMIS) there was at any one time until the end of 2013, 10-12 Norwegian officers seconded for six months at a time. All together there have been about 240 Norwegian officers. Most men, but also a substantial number of women have served in South Sudan during this period.

Many Norwegian ministers had between 2005 and 2013 been on working visits to South Sudan, and I mention the ministers of finance, development cooperation, petroleum, justice and defence. The Norwegian Central Bureau of Statistics had advisors at work in the country to prepare for the census that took place in 2010. Other Norwegian senior advisors assisted until the end of 2013 in several South Sudanese ministries, in their efforts to develop a central government administration and furthermore in preparing important legislation, for instance for the transparent public management of the oil industry and the establishing of a national police force. There is no complete list of how many Norwegian professionals who have been on official assignment in South Sudan until the end of 2013, but probably around 50 civilian professionals for the entire period.

That means that Norway seconded approximately 400 military and civilian experts for work in South Sudan between 2005 and 2013.

Norwegian business was just about to get started in assisting South Sudan in its development efforts when the civil war broke out in December 2013. The hydro power plant that was planned to be built on the Nile near Nimule, was partially to be financed by NORFUND, but was halted by the war. The same goes for the planned involvement of the Norwegian Forestry Group.

However, all these Norwegian contributions to assist in the development of South Sudan were put on hold because of the civil war that exploded in December 2013. How much knowledge that has been transferred from Norwegian advisors to their South Sudanese counterparts that is remaining, is hard to assess. Most likely is most of it lost for the peoples of South Sudan. The institutions that received Norwegian assistance have, to a large extent, been destroyed, and the staff that once gained access to that new knowledge, have either been displaced, fled or been killed.

In 2014 Norway's bilateral assistance to South Sudan was 606.6 million NOK, in 2015 472,5 million NOK and in 2016 561 million NOK. Most of this assistance continue to be used for emergency aid for victims of the civil war that is still ravaging the land and the people of South Sudan although at a lower intensity than in previous years, but some 40 percent is used for longterm development.

Many Norwegian NGOs still have a strong presence in South Sudan, but now they are mainly involved in emergency aid while long-term development cooperation for the most has been reduced.

Between 2005 and to 2013 NPA had an annual budget of about 200 million NOK, a total for the whole period of about 1.7 billion NOK. Until December 2016 NPA, except for UN and the Government, was one of the largest employers with about 900 employees. The number of employees is now reduced.

Norwegian Church Aid has an annual budget of 150 million NOK, and the Norwegian Refugee Council also has a large emergency aid programme. In addition, Doctors Without Borders, ADRA and other Norwegian NGOs are still working in South Sudan.

The official Norwegian bilateral assistance to all of Sudan, was during the period between 2005 and 2010 about 4 billion

NOK. Most of this went to South Sudan. From 2005 to 2016, South Sudan alone has received approximately 8 billion NOK, or approximately 1 billion USD, in emergency aid, all of it have channeled through UN and Norwegian NGOs.

However, since the beginning of 2014, Norway like all other donors, has lost all confidence in the Government of South Sudan. For this reason there i s no development assistance going to government institutions.

As narrated in this chapter, since the middle of the 1950s, an intricate web, spun over time, is linking Norway and South Sudan. The web shines with a rich spectrum of colors, but because of the destructive war that has ravaged the country since December 2013, the web is in danger of collapsing.

The Norwegian Ambassador to South Sudan, Hanne Marie Kaarstad, at a happy moment in 2012 when the relations between the two countries still were amical.

20
DECAY, BREAKDOWN AND DESTRUCTION

October 2013, a Visit to Juba, and what happened in South Sudan until July 2017

I shall in this chapter give some attention to the political forces that since 2005/6 have dominated the state and the society of South Sudan. But I shall put most emphasis on the developments from the summer of 2013 when it became increasingly clear that the political forces of destruction had taken command.

In October 2013, President Salva Kiir Mayardit invited me to South Sudan. The declared reason for the visit was to see if I could meaningfully contribute to finding a solution to the escalating conflict within the SPLM. On my way to South Sudan I spent a couple of days in Nairobi, talking with knowledgeable people in Kenya and from South Sudan about the situation.

Many of my East African friends have solid knowledge of South Sudan and the political forces at work in the country, and one of them said:

"Halle, Salva wants more power, and he is going for full political control. He has clandestinely trained more than 3000 young Dinka men from his home areas of Warrap and Bahr el Ghazal. They are now part of the Presidential Guard. He wants to get rid of Riek Machar, and he is going for a final showdown with the Nuer people. He will also be ordering for the arrest of the communist."

I asked, "The communist?"

"Yes, Pa'gan Amum. They are now calling him the communist because he has a leftist political orientation."

I gave myself the benefit of doubt as to whether Salva Kiir whom I had used to know quite well, and whom I had perceived to be an even handed and open-minded person, could have changed so much and come to harbour such hard-line ideas and dictatorial tendencies. But my friend kept on. We agreed to give the matter some time.

Unfortunately, what I learnt during my visit to Juba in October 2013 and from events that took place in the aftermath, first peaking with the disastrous meeting of the NLC on 13th and 14th December 2013 and the following onslaught on the internal opposition, the massacres of Nuers and the ongoing civil war, has proved that my friend was right.

What has happened in South Sudan in the period since the summer of 2013 has been catastrophic for the people and the society. The biggest loss is for the innocent people of South Sudan who had suffered so much during the long liberation struggle and had such high hopes for what independence and freedom would mean to their everyday life.

But it is also a very big loss for those at the forefront of the liberation war, the leadership of the SPLM and the SPLA who failed in their responsibility to lead the country to peace, freedom and development with social justice. It is furthermore a big loss for all of Africa that saw its youngest state destroying itself without being able to stop it. This loss and the disappointment stretch further to include the international community and close friends of South Sudan like Norway and USA.

Friends of South Sudan trying to save the State and SPLM from collapsing, but in vain.

In the previous chapter, I wrote about the many different threads in the web of relations between Norway and Sudan, that has been woven for over 60 years. Many organizations in the Norwegian civil society led by Norwegian Church Aid and Norwegian People's Aid have invested heavily in South Sudan. Hilde Frafjord Johnson was a driving force in the peace negotiations. No other country in Europe, in terms of its population size, has contributed more than Norway for peace, freedom, development and a better everyday life for the people of South Sudan. No one should be surprised or wonder when I say that the disappointment by concerned people in Norway about the destruction of South Sudan is deep and bitter.

But too many in the national political leadership in Norway and in other countries friendly to South Sudan, were too naïve in their consideration and analysis of the political developments that were taking place in the years from 2005 and until 2011, the period when South Sudan was emerging as a nation and a state. The naivety was particularly big when it came to the President, Salva Kiir. His way of receiving foreigners, wearing his black hat while leaving the impression that he was openminded and listening, has deceived many. I was deceived for quite long, and many others, both Norwegians and others, together with me.

However, there were a few in the wider world who had a foresight that many more should have had. Four renowned Americans, John Prendergast, Eric Reeves, Roger Winter and Ted Dagne who were strong supporters of SPLM/A during the liberation struggle and who were friends and knew the political leadership of South Sudan very well, wrote in June 2013 an open letter to

President Salva Kiir conveying their strong concerns and worry. They warned against a collapse of democracy, given the increasingly authoritarian leadership of Salva Kiir, and they warned against the large scale corruption and the many documented serious violations of human rights that had been and were taking place (see attachment no. 4). The Ethiopian Government sent its foreign minister to discuss similar issues. The Government of South Africa, probably the best friend of the people of South Sudan on the continent, became increasingly worried about the situation. It sent in August 2013 after Kiir's sacking of his own government and the Secretary General of SPLM, Pa'gan Amum, its Vice-President, Cyril Ramaphosa, to Juba to talk with the President and the SPLM leadership.

Ramaphosa used all his political experience, insight and authority when he addressed a meeting of over 300 participants from the political elite, SPLM/A and others, in South Sudan on how dangerous and destructive an internal conflict in the SPLM could be. All the important leaders were present except Salva Kiir and Pa'gan Amum. I have met with some of those participating in the meeting with Ramaphosa, and they were all full of praise.

Salva Kiir was absent because his advisors thought it was unworthy for the President to be lectured to by a leader from South Africa. Pa'gan Amum was banned by the President from speaking in public and attending public meetings. However, I am told that Salva Kiir at the end of the day invited Cyril Ramaphosa to see him in private.

The Liberation Struggle and then Moral Decay

The leadership of the SPLM and SPLA during the liberation struggle was comprised of people with very different backgrounds. Some like John Garang had extensive academic and military education. Garang himself was an educated man with a PhD in Economics who moved with ease internationally. Some like Salva Kiir, had little formal education and no experience from civilian public life. Others were illiterate, but still able guerrilla commanders. The same applied to the soldiers in the liberation army, most of them were illiterate. They came from all ethnic groups, but the Dinka had most leaders, officers and soldiers. Regarding the latter, the numbers of soldiers from different ethnic groups in SPLA changed throughout the years 2008, 2009, 2010 with Salva Kiir's policy of inviting the many different militia groups that with the support of Khartoum had fought against SPLA, to join the national liberation army SPLA. In 2012 and 2013 the Nuer soldiers for this reason came to outnumber the Dinka soldiers.

Those who fought during the liberation struggle, had some important experience in common. They shouldered the painful historic legacy of an oppressed and humiliated people. They had stood up in rebellion, raised the freedom call and fought for long, many for more than 15-20 years. Many had and still have scars both mentally and physically from all the toil and brutality that they had been through. What almost all of them had in common at the end of the war, was that they like all others in South Sudan, were very poor.

Large Scale Corruption

On 30th of July 2005, just three weeks after the beginning of the implementation of the CPA, the country's great hope, the visionary leader John Garang, was killed in a helicopter accident, and Salva Kiir took over as Chairman of SPLM and President of South Sudan. I believe that Salva Kiir at the time never had harboured the idea of being the top-leader of SPLM and the Head of State. He nevertheless became the President and the Head of a new and inexperienced government with the responsibility among other things, to control and use sensibly for the benefit of the people a huge oil income.

Every month, from shortly after July 2005 and until 2016, about a hundred million USD and more in payment for oil was in accordance with CPA transferred from the Khartoum government and into The National Bank of South Sudan. But the bank was nothing more than a kind of a state chest without any form of professional and experienced management. How the International Community could allow for this to happen, remains a mystery. Having received the money, the Bank in the beginning placed large amounts into the accounts of the members of government who in practice could use the money any way they wanted. What a temptation!

South Sudan is very rich in natural resources, and oil is not the most important wealth even though its leaders and many others tend to think so. It's most important wealth is its people whose potential remains totally untapped. Furthermore, its rich soil, cattle and wildlife, lots of water rich with fish, forest and minerals on land and in the mountains, are for the most also vast, untapped wealth.

But the vast majority of the people in South Sudan has since 2005 remained very poor and now in 2017 are totally destitute. The SPLM when it was still one liberation movement, failed as we have seen, to develop responsible policies for the sustainable management of the nation's vast wealth and for the development of the society of South Sudan that could improve everyday life with increasing security and freedom with social justice for its citizens.

The combination of first a long-life experience of war with hardship and suffering, and then when peace came; political power with easy access to money and with the freedom to act without any political guidelines, legal framework and proper administrative procedures, became a very dangerous mix. When all this was being encouraged by foreign wheeler-dealers who were out for a quick buck, it became an even more dangerous mix.

The first signs of corruption were visible to keen observers shortly after the beginning of the transition period in 2005, but it accelerated after independence in July 2011.

A Norwegian Report on Corruption

The Norwegian government sent in 2009 one of its most senior diplomats together with a senior researcher from the CMI of UoB to investigate unconfirmed reports and rumours about corruption in South Sudan. What they found was shocking. They wrote their report and handed it in 2010 to the Minister of Foreign Affairs who was equally shocked by the findings.

Norway, both different governments and NGOs like NPA and NCA, had played a strong supporting role during the liberation struggle. In the aftermath of the CPA in 2005, Norway had demonstrated so much confidence and so much will to support and help in the state and nation building of South Sudan, and now we were being let down by the same people whom we had trusted.

The report was kept away from the Norwegian public for a while and then made public. The many Norwegians who were friends of the people of South Sudan, and more than any, the many of us, former and still present staff of NPA who in solidarity with the people had taken a stand and supported the liberation struggle, we were dismayed and like the people of South Sudan, felt betrayed.

Promised land given away

All South Sudanese are closely connected to land and soil. During the liberation struggle the SPLM promised that land will be owned by the communities according to the old African tradition, and this earned the SPLM many supporters. It was the opposite of the policies that had been implemented by the regime in Khartoum; that the land was owned by the state.

But as soon as SPLM got political power, the promise from the time of the liberation struggle, was forgotten and replaced by an increasing greed for money by some of the new people in power, mostly former freedom fighters. A policy and a practise of selling out "the National Silver" took root.

In 2012, David Deng and Jamus Joseph, two South Sudanese researchers, on assignment for the NPA, carried out an interesting study which has been referred to in international publications like The Economist of London, as very reliable and revealing. The study showed that between 2007 and 2010, about

25 million acres of land in South Sudan had either been sold or leased out on long term contracts to foreign companies. When taken together with what the regime in Khartoum had sold or leased out on long term contracts before CPA in 2005, the total land area contracted out to foreigners amounted to 58 million acres, which is about nine per cent of the land mass of South Sudan.

No matter how one wants to twist and turn around this figure of 58 million acres, it is very big, and a sell-out of national resources. The local population who depended on the land sold or leased, had never been consulted. The contracts were agreed to by leading politicians and top officials of South Sudan on one hand and foreign companies on the other. The contents of these contracts were always confidential.

But some cases have been known, and I have the documentation in one case that tells the story about how these dirty deals were done. In March 2008, the American Company, Nile Trading and Development Inc. in Dallas, USA, entered a contract with a local company in the Central Equatorial State for the lease of six million acres of land. The land which in part is forest and in part agricultural land, was leased for a period of 49 years for about USD 25 000, or less than one US cent per acre per year. The South Sudanese signatories to the contract further agreed that the US leasers of the land could expand the leased land area without further compensation.

The American company did not only secure for itself the right to cultivate plants from which it could produce biodiesel, but also the right to use any other natural resources that could be found in the soil and the mountains of the leased area. On top of that, the company also secured for itself the right to sell carbon credits against green-house gas emissions in the international market.

The people in the area where the land was leased out, was kept in the dark about what had happened to the land SPLM had promised to be their community land when peace and independence came. But according to the contract they were to be driven out of a land that they had cultivated for generations and considered their own, and there was never a question of them being economically compensated for their loss of livelihood. The local South Sudanese company was a company just on paper and established by the SPLM Government Commissioner of the area and his family. He was by the way at the time of the liberation struggle, one of Khartoum most infamous lackeys and militia leaders. What the American company paid under the table to secure such a dirty contract, is not known.

The elected Governor of the Central Equatorial State, Clement Wani Konga, was informed in a letter from the American Director about the contract and the plans the company had for the exploitation of the leased land area. The Governor who at the time still was a confidant of President Salva Kiir Mayardit, accepted the letter without any comment. However, political life in South Sudan is an unpredictable affair. President Salva Kiir in one of his innumerable decrees, in August 2015 sacked Clement Wani Konga and three other governors. They no longer served his interests. Clement Wani Konga was during the time of the liberation struggle a commander of the Equatorial Defence Forces (EDF), a militia supported by Khartoum and fighting SPLA.

The deal of the American company, mentioned above, is one which I know, but there are tens and tens of similar contracts which content we do not know, but which for sure are even more exploiting and rotten in their content. Arab, Chinese Lebanese, Thai, Turkish and companies from other African countries with the tacit agreement of the Government in Juba are leading in the plunder of the natural resources of South Sudan.

Since 2005 there has been increasing competition and clashes over land plots in towns in South Sudan, especially in Juba. People in position of power, being politicians, officers and business people, first and foremost Dinkas from the states of Bahr el Ghazal and Warrap, have been using bribes and murder as means to secure themselves key plots. The process of getting official papers for such stolen plots is always easy. A plot of one quarter of an acre that had been acquired in 2005, and which at the time could be leased out for 8000 USD a year, had a value increase that by the middle of 2013, five months before the civil war, that in the local market stood at 25000 USD or more.

The Dura Saga

The Dura Saga is the name of the first reported big corruption scandal in South Sudan, and it took place in 2008. It is reported that the government initially paid about one billion USD into the project which was aimed at buying and storing the local cereal sorghum or dura to help people manage the predicted drought and famine. Key people in Kiir's own political circle were involved, first and foremost the close relative of Kiir, Benjamin Bol Mel, the Chairman of the South Sudan Chamber of Commerce and the Director of ABMC Company. He wrote to his President and relative, and he insisted on government payment for bogus contracts.

The World Bank auditors found in February 2013 that 290 companies were paid for deliveries without signing a contract while 151 other companies were overpaid for deliveries. Sudan Tribune in a report in February 2012 described the Dura Saga as the largest and most costly corruption scandal in South Sudan since the birth of the nation in 2005, and it held the view that not only one billion USD, but several billion USD had been allocated for a project that in the main was not only a failure but turned into a bogus project to facilitate the stealing of money that belonged to the people. The people of course got no food aid from the project, but starved and died when the famine struck.

Edward Lino's Verdict

Edward Lino is one of South Sudan's most prominent poets and writers and an intellectual. During the liberation struggle, he played an important role as a commander in the Intelligence Service of SPLA achieving the rank of a Major-General. After

2005 he served briefly as a Minister in the President's Office before he resigned from politics. Edward Lino is a very friendly person whom I have met many times. He is an old friend of NPA and has many times praised NPA for its contribution during the time of the liberation struggle.

In January 2014, he wrote three open letters to the South Sudanese people where he strongly blamed Salva Kiir for letting the internal conflict in the SPLM turn into a civil war. He ridiculed the accusation about the attempted coup and the treason charges against people like Pa'gan Amum.

In May 2015, Edward Lino delivered a lecture in Addis Ababa about the moral decay that had poisoned politics and society during Salva Kiir's tenure. He accused the President, his family and business companies they owned, of having stolen 1.6 billion dollars from the people.

Today we have a lot of documented and reliable documentation on the large-scale corruption that have taken place in South Sudan during Salva Kiir's tenure, and it proves that Edward Lino's accusation had a solid foundation.

Some Key Facts from the following Sentry reports;
- South Sudan. War Crimes Shouldn't pay
- Making a Fortune while Making a Famine.
  The illustrative case of a South Sudanese General
- South Sudan. Direct Perpetrators of Violence, and those acting on their Behalf, have benefited from the Plunder of South Sudan's public Wealth,
- South Sudan. The Nexus of Corruption and Conflict in South Sudan, and other Sources on the Corruption in South Sudan.

But first, a small reminder.

On 4th of June 2012 President Salva Kiir surprised both his own people and South Sudan's friends abroad with a very courageous letter to 75 ministers, officers and high-level officials accusing them of having stolen an estimated 4 billion USD of public money which he demanded to be paid back. If they did so, those guilty would be offered an amnesty.

The letter was seen as a proof of the fact that the President himself was a clean man fighting a politically difficult and corrupt environment. I believed so, and I think that for instance members of the Norwegian government believed it as well.

The Sentry reports

In September 2016, four years and 3 months after President Kiir's letter, the Sentry, an American NGO in partnership with the Enough Project, Not On Our Watch and C4ADS in USA, published the first of four reports on corruption in South Sudan, named: **War Crimes Shouldn't Pay. Stopping the looting and destruction in South Sudan**

Two key people who are very good friends indeed of the people of South Sudan, are the Co-Founders of The Sentry, and they have written the foreword of the first report, George Clooney and John Prendergast.

George Clooney is a renowned American actor and film director who has spent a lot of time and work in support of peace for the people of South Sudan and Darfur and other humanitarian causes. In 2007, 2008 and 2009 TIME named him one of the 100 most influential people in the world.

John Prendergast is a human right activist who worked in president Clinton's administration as the Director for African Affairs in the National Security Council. He has for most of his adult life had a strong engagement with Africa and has repeatedly been active in support for South Sudan. John Prendergast is well acquainted with the work of NPA during the time of the liberation struggle.

Those who made the Sentry reports spent more than two years on research and facts findings. They have visited South Sudan,

Australia, Ethiopia, Egypt, Kenya and Uganda to collect documents, and interviewed over 100 individuals currently and formerly in the Government of South Sudan, from the opposition, business and civil society. They have had access to information on social media. They have used publicly available satellite imagery from Google Earth Pro, and they have reviewed thousands of pages of corporate findings, legal records and financial data and correspondence related to trade, money transfer and banking.

All individuals and entities discussed in the Sentry reports were informed in advance about the findings and given the right to comment, but most of them did not respond.

The four reports mentioned above, state that since the signing of the CPA in 2005, politics in South Sudan has been marked by competitive corruption between networks led by President Salva Kiir and Vice-President Riek Machar.

According to the first report, President Salva Kiir and his family, including teenagers, are the big winners in the Kleptocracy Race in South Sudan. President Kiir officially has an income of about USD 60 000 a year, but he and his family have gathered wealth that far exceeds what he could have earned as the President and the Chairman of SPLM. The President has become av very, very rich man.

The Salva Kiir Family

The first Sentry Report has 15 pages which give a detailed account of how much the President and his family have amassed of money and property. The report shows pictures of the infamous Luri camp complex outside Juba which is not only a military camp. Salva Kiir has attached to the same complex a big ranch.

The report states the following regarding Luri:

"The developments at and around President Kiir's ranch in Luri provide a snapshot of how he has governed; by cultivating relationships with private companies and foreign investors; spending tens

of millions of dollars of state money on lethal military hardware, including attack helicopters, that have been used against South Sudanese Civilians; recruiting and training, and unleashing a private military militia on civilians and rival factions within the military; and simultaneously amassing a fortune."

A little later in the report it adds:

"President Kiir's ranch and adjacent properties in Luri is a microcosm of the violent kleptocratic government that President Kiir has cultivated in South Sudan."

ABMC, the biggest of several Corruption Machines

Both the Sentry Report and other sources I have, document some of the other business interests of President Kiir and his family. A very important part of the whole deals with the company called ABMC Thai-South Sudan Construction Company Limited. Many staff members are from Thailand, but the Director is Benjamin Bol Mel. He is a close relative of Salva Kiir and a South Sudanese businessman with investments in construction, banking, energy, hotels and restaurants and aviation. Benjamin Bol Mel also used to be the chairman of the South Sudan Chamber of Commerce. During the peak of the war in the Winter of 2014 he frequently made statements in support of the government, and he also held the view that the SPLM leaders held in detention accused for high treason, deserved the ultimate punishment.

Insiders of the government who have helped with the leakages, have told the Sentry researchers that President Kiir has used his power as Head of Government to secure big construction contracts for this company without any public bidding thus making it possible for the company to operate with profits rates that are far beyond any reasonable seize.

Between 2006 and 2012 the government spent approx. 1, 7 billion USD on road construction with contracts mainly awarded to ABMC, but only 75 km of road were built. One example. On 5th September 2011, according to Wikipedia, President Kiir demanded that 244 million USD should be awarded to ABMC for road construction. The money was transferred, but no road was constructed.

President Kiir's Nairobi Home and Kiir Inc

The Sentry Report that was published first, also provides detailed, information about and pictures of President Kiir's luxurious villa in Lavington, one of Nairobi's most expensive, upper class, residential areas. The villa with several balconies is said to be about 5000 square feet, and it is surrounded by a big and beautiful garden. Members of the Kiir family stay more or less permanently in the villa, far away from the poverty, stricken and ravaged capital Juba in South Sudan. According to the report, four of Kiir's younger children attend a private school in the neigbourhood of the villa, each paying USD 10 000 a year.

How does the family get money to pay for all these expenses? The report provides for more information.

The Kiir Family owns a lot of Business

One more company in addition to ABMC is Combined Holding Limited (CHL), a holding company that owns business and industrial enterprises, and which is owned by the Kiir family. At least seven of Kiir's children are or have been shareholders in the company, the youngest being a boy, 13 years old. One of the elder brothers, Thiik Kiir, 29 years old, used to own 35 percent of the shares of Nile Link Petroleum and 50 percent of the shares in Oil Line & Hydrocarbons Limited while Kenyan businessmen held the rest. Mayar Kiir, another son and 30 years old, is reported to have held 50 percent of the shares in "Specialist Services Co. Ltd", a company servicing the oil industry and supplying petroleum to South Sudan. Other documents which the authors of the Sentry Report have seen, indicates that the daughters of Salva Kiir, Adut Salva Kiir has had shares in Rocky Mining Industries Limited, Anok Kiir has had 45 percent of the shares in CPA Petroleum and Winnie Salva Kiir, 20 years old, had a 11 percent stake in Fortune Minerals & Construction while the major shareholders of the company, are Chinese. The Sentry Report has other records indicating that some of Kiir's children also may have shares in aviation and insurance as well as in investment and trading companies.

This Sentry report also shows that the first lady of South Sudan, Mary Ayen Mayardit, President Salva Kiir's first wife and the mother of some of Kiir's children, is a very active businesswoman with stakes in many South Sudanese companies, Other documents indicate that she has held 50 percent of the shares in a company called Ayang for Roads and Bridges Co. Ltd and that she was involved in the controversial takeover of Gemtel, a telecom company previously owned by LAP Green Networks, the investment arm of the government of the ousted Libyan dictator Moammar Gadhafi.

The General and Brother in Law

The brother of the first lady, and the brother in law of the President, General Gregory Vasili Dimitry, as a Major-General, has an income of approx. USD 20 000 a year.

But he is a very rich man. The first Sentry report and other sources tell that his wealth comes from being one of the biggest actors in business of different shades in South Sudan. He has big farms, and he has held a 20 percent stake in the South Sudan Commercial Bank. As late as in August 2015 he owned 31 percent of Viva Nile Casino Co. Ltd while the rest of the shares are owned by Chinese businessmen. He furthermore held a 20 percent stake in Car Parking Management and Automatic Systems Limited and a big stake in a firm named Petroleum Products Delivery Co. Ltd.

Another company linked to the Vasili family is T-ALFA Investments Ltd. He used to be a big shareholder together with other family members. The company was at the time in 2007/8/9 heavily involved in the Dura Saga. It was not able to fulfil its contractual obligations, and the close relative of Salva Kiir, the infamous businessman and Director of the South Sudan Chamber of Commerce Benjamin Bol Mel requested the government to write off 90 percent of what the company owned. T-ALFA has also been a supplier of fuel to SPLA which must have made it a profit-making machine of a very big size. The company has had business running with Petronas, a Malaysian state-owned oil company that is a major actor in the oil industries of South Sudan.

The Biggest Kleptocrat, the General and the former Chief of Staff of SPLA with his big Family

"The President, Salva Kiir, and the narrow circle of senior individuals in the military and security services, including the Sudan People's Army (SPLA) Chief of Staff, Paul Malong... are waging an aggressive war involving the targeting of civilians and extensive destruction of communities"

(The quote above is from the report by the UN Panel of Experts on South Sudan, January/16)

The official salary of the Chief of Staff is according to the Sentry Report approx. USD 45 000 a year.

But Paul Malong and his family are very wealthy. The first Sentry Report provides information on the question; how did they become so rich.

During the liberation war, Paul Malong was an SPLA commander in his home areas of Bahr el Ghazal, and as a military man he was a shrewd strategist. But he was also a wheeler-dealer in different murky businesses and became rich while fighting. He was at the same time known as a maverick with a penchant for amassing women and cattle. Exactly how many wives Paul

Malong has, is an uncertainty, but he has at least around 50 wives. This has been a way of establishing traditional linkages to most clans in Bahr el Ghazal. Many who see themselves as his friends and beneficiaries, only call him King Paul while those who have fallen out of favour and see him as unfriendly, are afraid to say anything about him. The cost may be too high.

He and his very big family are involved in a lot of profitable businesses and have or have had shares in companies like "Concrete Builders Construction Co." Petroliin Services Co. Ltd. His son Garang Paul Malong has had shares in for instance, "East African Mokuano Contractor Company Ltd.", "Dex Rich Investment Holding" and "Link Telecom Services Ltd."

The report shows further that the Kiir family and the Malong family as partners have been involved in the same businesses, like "Nile Link Petroleum Co. Ltd" which again had up to 50 percent of the shares in "Nile Link Group", a joint venture with several Chinese and Zimbabwean businessmen.

Paul Malong like Salva Kiir has a big and flashy villa in Nairobi with garden, guesthouse, swimming pool and more, and with a security system that beeps whenever anyone gets within six feet distance from the property. In Uganda, he and the family have two big villas, both larger than President Kiir's in Nairobi.

Lawrence Lual Malong is a stepson of Paul Malong. He names himself The Young Tycoon. He has in ways, only he knows, acquired a lot of wealth and lives in South Africa. He is frequently using social media in his communication, and in this way, he conveys a message of a life in extreme luxury. When travelling, he hires private jets or travels 1st class, drives the most expensive cars, stays in the most expensive hotels and dines in the most expensive restaurants.

The first Sentry report has found that he together with foreign companies has big interests and investments in companies holding oil, diamond and gold concessions in South Sudan. This Sentry report carries a quote from Mr. Lual where he says:

"When I do mining, we register a local company and my dad and the president will be involved."

I should add that Paul Malong in May 2017 fell out of grace with his long-time friend, President Salva Kiir, and was sacked as Chief of Staff. But it does not mean that he has lost the wealth he has stolen. His new situation should give him more time to enjoy the benefits of his looting.

Another General, Malek Reuben Riak, also a close associate of the President, who has amazed a lot of Wealth at the Cost of the People of South Sudan

The Sentry Group provided recently a special report on the conflict in Unity State where some 100 000 people were at immediate risk of starvation caused by the parties in the war. The authors of the report at the same time pin-pointed the Government forces for being the main responsible for massive cattle raids and displacement of people. The mass starvation was man made.

The military actions in Unity State were planned and executed by senior military officials who were close the President, Salva Kiir. One of them were Lt. General Malek Reuben Riak who in 2013 was promoted to Deputy Chief of Staff, and in May 2017 President Kiir decided to promote him further, making him the Inspector General of the Army.

Lt. General Reuben Riak has according to the budget of 2016 a salary that amounts to approximately 40 000 USD a year, but he commands millions of USD made available to him at his bank account with Kenya Commercial Bank (KCB) through the kleptocratic networks at work in South Sudan.

In this Sentry's report, the authors state that they have documents showing that between January 2012 and early 2016 some 3 million USD, including cash payments of some 700 0000 USD from several international construction companies operating in South Sudan and backed by Chinese, Lebanese and Turkish investors, moved through the bank accounts of the general. In the same period over 1,6 million USD was withdrawn from the account in the name of the General as cash.

General Reuben Riak and members of his family have many links with international corporations, banks and politicians. The General controls private businesses of his own, one of them called Mak International Services that sells explosives for whatever use to private companies in South Sudan. Not only that, Reuben Riak and his family have other joint businesses with members of the political elite in neighbouring Kenya, Ethiopia and Uganda.

This case of General Reuben Riak illustrates how a relatively small group of politicians, high ranking officers and officials are in full control of a violent kleptocratic system of government. They are plundering the country and amazing wealth, and their families are enjoying "Dolce Vita" in neighbouring and far way countries. At home in South Sudan, the innocent and vast majority of poor and destitute people continue to suffer from, war, man-made famines and death.

Four major Vectors along which the Country's Wealth and Revenues are diverted towards the personal and institutional Interests of Elites:

This is the focal point in a Sentry report from the spring of 2017 that covers the following topics; The Extractives Sector. The Military State, State Spending, and the Money Laundering Hub.

South Sudan has as we know, since sometime in 2014 been facing an increasing squeeze on its economy and finances because of the civil war. It has caused the destruction of increasing parts of the oil industries. The combination of continuing conflict and an ever-increasing corruption on large scale has in addition minimized the effectiveness of foreign investments and humanitarian aid. International donors have for obvious reasons cut long term development assistance. One does not aid a government that does it utmost to destroy its own people and society.

However, as the economic situation has worsened, key elites and institutions have been able to expand the illicit economy to make more profit, and they have been concentrating on four areas:

1. The Extractive Industries

Oil is the government's primary source of income in hard currency. The government has also been using oil as a collateral for foreign loans it has taken to keep the economy running. Oil in 2011 accounted for some 98 % of the government's revenues while it because of the war has shrank to some 70 %.

It is known that the government has obtained a credit line with the foreign oil companies operating in South Sudan, and indications are that most of it is with Chinese companies. A big part of this credit has been used to buy arms to keep the war going. Another part of the credit, some 158 million USD was for the construction of the new airports facilities. But nothing has happened to the project while the money apparently went into corruption networks.

Because of the agreement with Khartoum on repayment of old debt and the cost of using the Khartoum pipeline, the government pays Khartoum some 26 USD per barrel of oil while it receives some 10 USD in net payments. No other government in the world has messed up its economy to the extent that the net income for oil is so little.

There is yet no documentation, but many indications to the fact that illicit mining of gold and other minerals of great value is taking place in far way places in South Sudan hidden away from the public eye.

2. The Military State

South Sudan with a population of some 10 – 11 million people, spends more on the military, security and intelligence that any other country in the region. The formal budget from 2015 for the Military and the related institutions takes up more than 40 % of the whole while some 5 % of the whole was allocated for education in a society where most people still are illiterate. In addition, it is now an established tradition to overspend the budgets allocated. The Office of the President had in 2015 an overspending of 349 %, the Ministry of Defence 150 % and the Veterans' Affairs department had 113%. How is this overspending covered? For a part, money is taken from the other parts of state budget like education, health, agriculture and for instance the institution; Widows and Orphans Commission. The latter received in 2015 five percent of what was allocated.

The armed forces, SPLA, according to the Sentry report, provides no information about the way they are spending the money allocated in the budget. In the audit of the 2008 budget for SPLA, only 7 out of 40 divisions reported their payroll figures as required by the law.

"The Military" in South Sudan is a complex and many headed organization that binds together conventional forces, paramilitaries, militias and security organs. It needs big funding to keep all this going. "The Military" is growing all the time. In 2004, it was estimated that SPLA had some 40 000 soldiers. In 2011, it had grown to 240 000 men. In addition, the number of generals has steadily been growing. In 2011 there was some 750 generals (Ethiopia with some 100 million people is said to have some 8 generals). It goes without saying that there is corruption on a large scale within "The Military".

3. State Spending

This Sentry report states that nearly every facet of state spending is rife with fraud, waste and mismanagement.

Purchases and contracts are awarded to well-connected companies without any proper bidding procedures. Prices agreed in contracts are heavily inflated and do not in any way reflect the real cost. There is both in the public and private sector an almost complete disregard when it comes to reporting standards, or providing documentation of who are benefitting.

Three examples:

The 2012-2013 budget for the Ministry of Roads and Bridges for the reasons mentioned, overspent with 1513 %.

Whenever imports of vehicles take place, it is done at inflated prices, and somebody takes the difference.

The Juba Airport expansion project has since 2005 "eaten" hundreds of millions of USD, but hardly any construction has taken place, and the chaos at the ill functioning airport is in 2017 worse than ever.

In addition, elites in South Sudan, including politicians, have, as we have seen, established a practise of holding undocumented shares in companies and receive payments in exchange for facilitating business transactions. This is of course in violation of the laws of the land.

Money Laundering Hub

While the state of South Sudan in recent years has continued its slide down towards economic collapse and complete failure, South Sudan's illicit actors have shown an impressive ability to find new ways of making money. Some has developed the ability of speculation in the parallel currency market. They find ways and means to have the local currency depreciated and that again causes inflation which again increases the pressure of the Central Bank's foreign exchange reserves. When these reserves have been near depletion, the Central Bank has been borrowing and printing money which of course causes more inflation.

Those in the elite who understand how to manipulate a currency market like the one in South Sudan, while at the same time completely disregarding whatever there are of laws and regulations, can illegally make a lot of money. This Sentry report mentions that some have made up to 400 % in profit in one single transfer.

Private FOREX bureaus have in South Sudan become a very lucrative business. They are very useful whenever money laundering is taking place, and they may service all kind of illicit money transactions. Many members of the corrupted elite in South Sudan have stakes in this business.

Some comments on my use of the reports
I have in my references to the reports dealing with corruption frequently used the words; "have held, have owned aso" on ownership of shares and businesses. I do that because in kleptocratic races like the one I have narrated, the owners concerned in such murky businesses frequently sell shares to others when times of hardship are expected. In this way, they export future losses to new owners. I suspect that this may have frequently been the case in the Kleptocratic Race of South Sudan. I should add one more observation. Not all those who have stolen money in different ways are from the Dinka people, but most seem to be.

Riek Machar, Kiir's neighbour in Nairobi

Riek Machar who is the most well-known leader from the Nuer people, sought in the aftermath of the SPLM/A split in Nasir in August 1991 support from and cooperation with the regime in Khartoum, and as I have written about in other chapters of this book, he got a lot of both. He has from that time had a reputation of being a wheeler-dealer who easily could enter murky business.

He and his family have for long been known to have access to lots of money and wealth. They frequently post messages on social media showing that they enjoy a luxurious life, travelling

Benjamin Bol Mel the director of ABMC and South Sudan Chamber of Commerce in his heydays. Picture: Gurtong

around in the world, spending money on sweet life activities, far away from the sufferings and the pains the common people in South Sudan has been and still is exposed to.

The Machar family has rented or owned lavish villas with gardens in different parts of Nairobi, one of them being very close to the Nairobi residence of Salva Kiir and family in Lavington. They also have had access to similar luxurious housing in Addis Ababa. Whether this is still the case as if it looks like Riek Machar has fallen out of favour with the government in Kenya and possibly also Ethiopia, I do not know. Riek Machar while I write this, is as I have written about in Chapter 19, a de facto political detainee in South Africa.

GURTONG is a netsite for South Sudanese that can print stories in accordance with freedom of expression. The reason is that it is being edited outside South Sudan. IN South Sudan the oppression of freedom is complete.

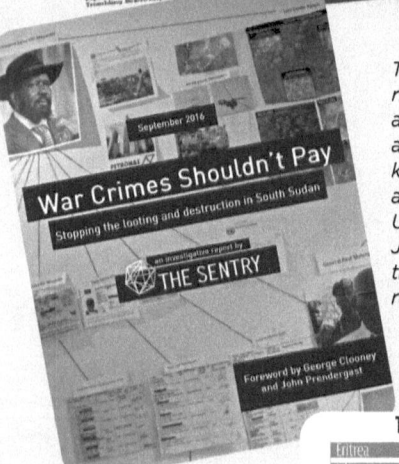

The Sentry reports on corruption in South Sudan are being produced by a cluster of very well-known and well repudiated NGO institutions in USA. George Cloony and John Prendergast wrote the foreword to this report.

TEN MOST CORRUPT COUNTRIES

- Eritrea
- Libya
- Uzbekistan
- Turkmenistan
- Iraq
- South Sudan
- Afghanistan
- Sudan
- Korea (North)
- Somalia

CPI SCORE (LOWER IS WORSE)

In spite of continuing and heavy oppression, people in South Sudan from time to time dear protest against the destruction of their own country. Picture: Gurtong

Lawrence Lual Deng, the stepson of General Paul Malong, is one of the very rich sons and daughters who are enjoying "La Dolce Vita". Picture: The Sentry

The Crisis Management Committee

President Salva Kiir appointed on 11th January 2014, a Crisis Management Committee (CMC) with 27 members, headed by the Vice-President James Wani Igga who is a Eqvatorian. Key advisors of Kiir were among the members. Its mission was to assess the political, social, economic, security and diplomatic aspects of the new civil war that had broken out on 15th December 2013. The committee was given wide administrative powers.

When one looks at the composition of the committee, it is as if the President at the time set up a new parallel government for the country.

The work of this committee is discussed by Hilde Frafjord Johnson under the title; "Crisis is an opportunity-to steal" on pages 220 and 221 in her very important book; South Sudan; "The Untold Story" from 2016. It deals with how the committee came to be a corruption machine. I have taken the following quote from these pages:

"The amount of money allegedly stashed away was shocking, even for South Sudan. A government insider with knowledge of the committee's operation warned the President of a "new dura scandal." The figure reported from confidential sources went beyond most of the corruption scandals of the interim period. This information has been corroborated. Transfers were made directly to the foreign accounts of at least two senior government officials on the committee.

The sums involved were in the hundreds of millions of South Sudanese pounds. People started to call it the CMC, the Corruption Management Committee. Indeed, it presided over a slush fund used for all sorts of things from mobilization of new recruits to the customary servicing of patronage networks. While the latter was probably during a period of conflict, to ensure the loyalty of officers and men, the figures appeared to go far beyond that. Ironically, members of the CMC appeared to be grabbing so much for themselves that a likely result of its work could be a deepening of the security impact of the crisis it was supposed to 'manage'. If, for example, the delays in salary payments to the SPLA could be attributed to this malfea-

sance, with the inevitable increase in disaffection, the CMC made an already tenuous security situation worse.

Whatever the case may be, the leadership hardly seemed to care. By this time South Sudan had received a total of USD 19 billion in oil revenue between 2006 and 2014. Now they were using crisis money to cater for themselves."

After a lot of criticism, the President finally dissolved the Crisis Management Committee in May 2014. The government spokesman at the time told the press that an internal audit of the work of the committee would take place. No one has ever heard of the report from this audit and its findings.

What I have shortly summarized and written about above, I have in the main drawn from solid sources, and not only The Sentry Reports. The plague of corruption is a very important part of the whole in all reports. I mention the following; Final Report of the Africa Union Commission of Inquiry on South Sudan, several UN reports dealing with corruption and other problems in the period since 2013, The Report to the NMFA from 2010, Wikipedia and many others.

President Kiir in his letter of 4th June 2012 to 75 members of government, generals and high-level officials, accused them of having embezzled USD 4 billion. Hilde Frafjord Johnson in her book from 2016; *The Untold Story*, points to the fact that in the period between 2006 and 2014 the government received USD 19 billion from income from oil alone. Development assistance and other sources of income come in addition. My assessment is that much more than USD 4 billion has been stolen or squandered away, probably as much as USD 8 to 10 billion while a similar sum has been used for the military and the security and internal war.

This vast scale corruption is a major cause of the destruction of South Sudan, and those responsible for most of it, have been members of Kiir's government since 2013, and some of them from long before, or they have been generals or had other leading military positions within SPLA.

The President himself and his family in the lead, have had set up and have made use of business instruments for corruption and embezzlement that made them all very wealthy while the people were robbed of what should have been used for their development and well-being.

The Collapse of SPLM

After the eruption of the civil war in December 2013, the proposed SPLM Convention has been postponed many times. It has emerged that during the preparatory process in 2013, only the delegates who would commit themselves to support the re-election of Salva Kiir as party Chairman would be allowed to take part in the Convention. Whether or when the third SPLM Convention ever will take place, is an open question. The SPLM that called the second Convention in May 2008, does not exist anymore, but as I narrate in the following, has been destroyed by its own chairman and his supporters, primarily the Jieng Council of Elders. Nevertheless, Salva Kiir has strongly indicated that he is going to run for re-elections in 2018.

An African journalist friend of mine interviewed Salva Kiir once in the Autumn of 2012, and he asked him if he would seek re-election as Chairman of SLPM and then run for a second time for the presidency at the elections planned for 2015. According to my friend, Kiir replied that he had fought all his life for South Sudan's freedom and independence and that that goal had been achieved. He had been president since 2005, and he was tired and not in good health. He would therefore not seek re-election. The journalist who interviewed Kiir, has shared this with me, and I have no doubt that it is true. But the interview was never published.

The contents of the interview nevertheless became known, and it sparked an extensive discussion in the top layers of the SPLM. Later that same autumn, Salva Kiir invited Deng Alor for a meeting. He was at the time the Minister of Cabinet Affairs, a kind of a prime minister in the presidential system of South Sudan. In that meeting, Salva Kiir confirmed that he was not going to seek re-election as party chairman and therefore neither seek re-election as president. Deng Alor got a confidential assignment to carry the message to the others in the leadership of SPLM.

One day in March 2013, a closed meeting of leading members of SPLM was convened in the Office of the President. Kiir sat on a chair a little away from the others listening, but not taking part in the discussions. The meeting was chaired by Deng Alor and in attendance were among others Riek Machar, Pa'gan Amum and Rebecca Garang. There was one item for discussion: Who would be the SPLM candidate as new chairman of SPLM and then the flag bearer in the presidential elections that were expected to be held latest in 2015?

The current second Vice-President, James Wani Igga who told me this, during a meeting in Juba in October 2013, was not around when the meeting started, but came in an hour later. He wanted to know why Salva Kiir was sitting away from the others and not participating in the meeting. Deng Alor answered that Salva had informed him that he was not going to stand for re-election as Chairman of SPLM, and he was therefore not a presidential candidate either. He, Deng was chairing the meeting because he was from Abyei and could not be a candidate. In the discussion, Riek Machar declared that he would stand. Pa'gan Amum, and Rebecca Garang did the same.

James Wani Igga then said that he as well was going to run, and he asked the others what they thought about the votes after the first round, before he answered himself:

"I as the candidate for the three states of Equatoria will get most votes, but not 50 per cent. You, Riek, will be number two, you Rebecca will be number three and you Pa'gan will be the last with less than ten per cent of the votes. Is that what you wish?"

James Wani Igga continued his considerations and said that he in a second round would get more than 50 percent and become the next president. None of the others around the table thought it would be a good idea. The discussion went on for a while without any agreement being made.

The news from the meeting spread to Kiir's larger family and clan system in his home state of Warrap and sparked an intense discussion. The same discussion took place in the Jieng Council of Elders. The conclusion was clear. It was unacceptable for the Dinka people for Salva to step down. This was communicated to Salva Kiir. He after a while, went on a tour to his home state where he delivered several speeches against his enemies in the SPLM who were trying to take power from him. In some of the speeches the President used a very derogatory language about his colleagues in the leadership group of SPLM.

It might be true what Salva Kiir told in that unpublished interview from the fall of 2012, that he really wanted to resign and leave politics in 2015. Whatever was the truth, the news or rumours about his intention, sparked a strong reaction from his Dinka community, and that may have made him change his stand.

Perhaps it was a planned plot, directed by Salva Kiir's closest Dinka advisors to smoke out Kiir's competitors who were to be seen as his enemies. I do not know.

At the same time, most of the business people and the political class in South Sudan still having the favour of the President, were accumulating wealth from different murky businesses and getting very rich. They could send their children to expensive private schools abroad, buying expensive housing in places like Nairobi and Kampala and letting their families enjoy dolce vita while holidaying abroad.

However, the common people of South Sudan had a very different everyday life going from bad to worse. They hardly saw any dividends for them coming from the CPA, only their leaders getting very rich. It is however true that some basic health and educational services improved for a while after 2005. It was mainly due to services delivered by UN and international NGOs, only to stagnate and degenerate a few years later when the government took it over. The development of infrastructure was minimal. In short, peace and independence did not provide for development and a better life for the people. For this reason, political resentment started to grow, and it affected the political atmosphere inside SPLM. Criticism of the Chairman and the President increased. He was seen by an increasing number within the SPLM leadership and with people at large to be a poor chairman, poor head of state and an equally poor head of government.

In April 2013, Riek Machar declared that he would stand in the coming presidential elections. Salva Kiir's reaction was to withdraw from Machar some of executive powers delegated to him.

The Catastrophic Summer and Fall of 2013

The Summer of 2013 turned out to be politically very dramatic. In early July, Salva Kiir accused Deng Alor, Minister of Cabinet Affairs, and Kosti Manibe, Minister of Finance, without informing them in advance, of corruption, and he dismissed them. Kosti Manibe got the news in the evening newscast sitting with his wife in their living room.

On 23rd July the President dismissed the Vice-President and all other members of his government, accusing them of incapability and corruption. He at the same time without consulting the members of the Politburo of SPLM, suspended Pa'gan Amum as the Secretary General of SPLM, and thus he violated the SPLM bylaws. He further accused Pa'gan Amum of inciting opposition to the president, to be condescending to the President and having stolen money from the SPLM coffers.

Early in August, the President appointed a new government with weak representation from the SPLM. Many of the new cabinet ministers could only trace their political and administrative experience to the administration in Khartoum, or they had been abroad during the liberation struggle.

For the SPLM leaders who had just been dismissed and pushed into the cold, the make-up of the new government was a provocation. Throughout the autumn of 2013, the internal conflict gathered pace. The dismissed members of government and others from the opposition within SPLM were now operating as one group and had with them Rebecca Garang as a powerful partner. On 6th December, they held a press conference where they strongly criticized Salva Kiir for his increasingly authoritarian leadership style and his failing as head of state and government. They at the same time, called for a meeting of the Politburo and the National Liberation Council to resolve the conflict in the SPLM.

When Kiir, who was on a visit in France, heard about the press conference, he was infuriated. Upon return to Juba, he was urged by his close Dinka advisors to take a final action against the opposition and finish off with it.

In South Sudan and most in the Capital Juba, people began to fear that the conflict could get out of control and turn violent. Church leaders and other religious leaders appealed strongly to both the President and the opposition for dialogue and reconciliation. The opposition agreed.

On 14th and 15th December 2013, the National Liberation Council convened. Only a little more than half of the members including those in the opposition, were in attendance.

However, the President and the Chairman of SPLM, Salva Kiir, was on arrival in a belligerent mood and opened the meeting with a thunderous attack on those who were opposing him that swept away all hopes of dialogue and reconciliation. The opposition now in despair left the meeting.

The members remaining in the meeting of Liberation Council, resolved that Salva Kiir should be the only candidate to stand for the position as the chairman of SPLM, and its presidential candidate. It was further resolved that as soon as Salva Kiir was appointed as Chairman he will have the powers to appoint more members to the Political Bureau and to the National Liberation Council. It was in other words, as one witness said, the beginning of the making of a dictator. There are many stories running in South Sudan about the amount of money each member of the

National Liberation Council got to vote the way Salva Kiir and his confidants wanted.

The resolutions adopted at the meeting of NLC on 14th and 15th December 2013 was the beginning of the end of SPLM as the big, proud and unifying liberation movement for the whole of South Sudan.

The Arusha Process and the Agreement on the Reunification of SPLM became its Death Blow

This was an initiative taken in the Fall of 2014 by the ANC in South Africa, and CCM in Tanzania with the support of the Martti Arthisaari Peace Foundation in Finland. The hosting parties invited the three factions of SPLM, SPLM inG, led by Salva Kiir, SPLM inO led by Riek Machar and the group of the former Detainees this time led by Deng Alor. They met in the town of Arusha in Tanzania to try and negotiate an agreement for the peaceful settlement of the internal conflict in SPLM that had caused the new war. The initiative was considered an addition to the peace negotiations going on in Addis Ababa under the auspices of IGAD. There were many meetings in Arusha, and finally to the surprise of the world, the three parties agreed, and on January 21st, 2015 they made public the document named: **Agreement on the Reunification of the SPLM.** It has 12 pages and is signed by Salva Kiir on behalf of SPLM in G, Riek Machar on behalf of SPLM in O and Deng Alor on behalf of the former Detainees. Jakaya Kikwete, the President of Tanzania signed as a guarantor.

I have read the document. It is detailed and concrete regarding the steps that need to be taken. I hold the opinion that it could have served as a good enough base for the peaceful resolution of the internal SPLM conflict, made the war stop, and restored SPLM as a political party and made it start working again, and thereby provided the government of South Sudan with the necessary political and constitutional context for its future work.

Many had high hopes. In June 2015 Pa'gan Amum and a few others from the group of former Detainees returned to Juba, and on 23rd June Pa'gan Amum was reinstated as the Secretary General of SPLM, but as I have already written in chapter 17 in this book, Pa'gan Amum and his colleagues former detainees, after a few days back in Juba, suddenly discovered that there was a plot to assassinate them, planned by people in SPLM inG. Pa'gan Amum and the others had to flee for their lives and escaped to Addis Ababa.

The Death of SPLM and the Meetings in Kampala

What happened in Juba in early July 2015, was the end of the story about the Arusha process and the Agreement on the Reunification of SPLM. Not only that, it was also the death nail to SPLM as a democratic and people based liberation movement and a political party for the people of South Sudan. Whether it is possible to awaken the dead and bring it back to life, I do not know. But South Sudanese friends of mine still hope for a miracle to happen.

As I in the last days of July 2017 am writing the last sentences of this English edition, I am following the meetings being held in Kampala under the chairmanship of President Museveni on what is called another attempt to reunite SPLM. President Museveni is the protector of President Salva Kiir, and Uganda continues to hold military troops in South Sudan. Uganda also benefits in a big way economically from the ongoing crisis in South Sudan.

The meetings in Kampala have come after a plea from President Kiir to President Museveni to make another try. President Kiir wants to stay in power, and he is now using all kind of means to make it happen, including trying to create a kind of reunification of whatever fragments that is left of SPLM.

This is very important to President Salva Kiir and his court in Juba. He cannot fail in this endeavour without having to pay a very high price. Should he peacefully or otherwise be removed from his position as President South Sudan, the verdict is waiting for a man who more than any other individual in South Sudan, is responsible for the destruction of the country.

They who take part in the meetings in Kampala, may sign their documents. President Museveni may bless them and hold a press conference saying that by reuniting SPLM peace, will fall on South Sudan. It will in my view not happen. So many of South Sudan's leaders are absent from Kampala. I mention Riek Machar, but his is no longer the most important one. Young leaders like Thomas Cirillo, Pa'gan Amum and many others will decide the future of South Sudan, neither Kiir nor Museveni.

The final Destruction of South Sudan

In the evening of 14th December, tension and unrest within SPLA and the presidential guard that were stationed in Juba, turned into an armed and bloody confrontation. Throughout the night of 15th December, forces loyal to President Salva Kiir began the massacre of Nuers in Juba that all observers in the aftermath have come to conclude, was planned well in advance.

The next day the President appeared on TV in a general's uniform and accused the opposition of attempting a coup. Special units from the police and the military were already in action, arresting the opposition. A special military unit encircled and attacked Riek Machar's residence, but Riek and his wife escaped miraculously through a backdoor of the house and were rushed away in a waiting car. Most of the body guards, servants and relatives who were in the house or in the garden, were killed, and the house, being state property, finally completely bombed into pieces. The intended purpose was of course to kill Riek Machar and his wife.

It was obvious from the very beginning that the allegation of a coup attempt was baseless. Those then holding power in Juba nevertheless kept repeating the allegations in all types of fora. One of the latest was when Salva Kiir addressed the United Nations General Assembly in the Autumn of 2014.

Pa'gan Amum and others in the leadership group of SPLM were arrested at the same time and accused of treason which was another baseless lie.

In the days following the first armed confrontation of December 15th, perhaps as many as 20 000 people in Juba, the majority being Nuers, were massacred and their bodies thrown into mass graves that had been prepared in advance.

The violence and killings in Juba exploded into a bloody civil war that first was fought in the states of Jonglei, Unity and Upper Nile. Later the conflict that has now de-escalated into a low intensity war, has spread to the whole country with heavy destruction and killings also in the three states of Equatoria.

This war has a tragedy attached to it. It started with political overtones, but it has developed into an ethnic war with the now so-called SPLA dominated by Dinka officers and soldiers. They have let lose the most brutal and raw forms of warfare against the other ethnic groups in South Sudan. This has of course happened without the consent and support of most of the Dinka people, but those innocent Dinkas, will in the future pay a very high price for what Salva Kiir, Paul Malong, Bona Malwal and other Dinka leaders have dragged them into. It has poisoned the relationship between the Dinkas and the other peoples of South Sudan for generations to come. The rebuilding of these relationships shall be very hard indeed.

South Sudan has a population of about 10 to 11 million people. At the time of finalizing the English edition of this book, the situation for the people of South Sudan was the following:

No one knows for sure, but indications are that more than two hundred thousand people have died in the 2013-2017 war or died from illness and starvation caused by the war. The sexual violence committed against women and children has been described as among the worst of its kind ever seen, and the government forces are reported to be mainly responsible for these atrocities. About two million are internally displaced, about 200 000 of them are under protection in UN camps in South Sudan, about two million are refugees mainly in the neighbouring countries and about 5,5 million are food insecure. About 100 000 in the state of Unity are facing starvation and death. They are all totally dependent on international humanitarian aid through UN and international NGOs.

The Kiir government has not at any time since January 2014 done anything to assist the suffering masses in their own country. The total indifference to these sufferings of the innocent people demonstrated by both the President himself and his court has been shocking both to their own people and the world at large *(See interview with Salva Kiir on Deutsche Welle 24th August 2017. The indifference of the President to the suffering of his own people, is chocking).*

South Sudan represents today the biggest refugee tragedy on the African continent, and the tragedy may still grow to become a much bigger starvation catastrophe.

The material destruction is extensive. The states of Jonglei, Unity and Upper Nile were in the beginning of the war hardest hit, but now the destruction of war has hit most states. The oil production is down to approx. 40 percent of what it was in 2010. The government has borrowed billions of USD, mainly from China and Arab states against future oil production and access to other natural resources. But the government now seems to have lost all trust in the market of lenders. The Central Bank has for a long time been printing South Sudanese pound notes that are worth less and less. Inflation is creeping towards 1000 percent.

To put it aptly, the state of South Sudan is technically bankrupt.

Politically, the system has become very repressive, and any resemblance of democracy is gone long ago. South Sudan today is a dictatorship.

Provided peace with security, respect for human rights and freedom once can be restored, it may take a generation or more to bring the country back to the material level the country had in the summer of 2013.

The civil war has destroyed more for the people and the society in South Sudan than the long period of the liberation war from 1983 to 2005.

When the peace agreement was signed in 2005, South Sudan entered a transition period of six years while the government in Khartoum still had some power in the South. In South Sudan and for a while, many both within and outside SPLM, held the view that the new South Sudan to emerge either as a fully independent state or as part of a confederation, should be very different from Khartoum and the slogan was: "One Country, two Systems."

The understanding was that although Sudan formally still was one, the new state to emerge should be the democratic state and society of South Sudan that showed respect for human rights and human dignity.

Today people say the opposite, "Now we have two states, but one political system". The two states are systematically violating human rights and human dignity, and they are equally repressive and destructive to the people who live there. But there might be a difference; the dictatorship of South Sudan might even be worse than the one in Khartoum.

Some say that all the leaders in the old SPLM must shoulder collective responsibility for what has happened since 2012/13. I have a different opinion. The Head of State and the SPLM Chairman, Salva Kiir and his court in Juba, the Jieng Council of Elders included, carry obviously a much greater responsibility than any other actors in the destruction process, because the President and his court all the time had the possibility to make a different choice. President Salva Kiir didn't do that. Strongly influenced by the Jieng Council of Elders and other advisors, many of them have neither been members of SPLM nor fought in the liberation struggle, the President chose confrontation, violence and war instead of dialogue, reconciliation and peace.

The Government's Propaganda Machine and the Witch Hunt

There is an important part of the destruction of South Sudan that is constantly overlooked. The Government in Juba has de facto increasingly taken control of all media institutions. The oppression of freedom of expression is massive. The privately-owned media they intimidate and harass. The state-owned ones, South Sudan Radio and TV, have every day since 13th December 2013 been used as a propaganda machine slanging dirt on most of the leading freedom fighters and commanders from the time of struggle who have fallen in disgrace with the President.

Most South Sudanese do not read and write, but they listen to radio broadcasts from Juba, and the message they hear is one of praise for the President and his court and another one of dirt slanging and ridicule of people like Pa'gan Amum, Kosti Manibe, Edward Lino, Oyai Deng Ajak, Majak D'Agoot, Cirino Hiteng, Thomas Cirillo, Peter Adwok Nyaba, Rebecca Garang, Ann Itto and many, many others. The very poor, illiterate, ignorant and innocent people of South Sudan, they are led to believe that their destroyers, are the good guys while the able leaders now in forced exile, who could have ruled the country in peace and in a decent way, are told to be the bad ones.

Moreover, President Kiir and his government members have a little Goebbels of their own, named Moses Lomayat. He must continuously have access to a lot of money because he travels all over the world making videos and still photos of government members travelling and living the good life, then pictures of South Sudan's ambassadors who of course live the good life in apparently beautiful and costly mansions. All this he distributes via internet, and in this way, provides a totally faked image of South Sudan. Mr. Lomayat has until date never published a picture of a poor and suffering South Sudanese.

This is the way dictators always do when they want to get away from the real issues and the real situation in their own countries.

Omar Bashir and his Confidants in Khartoum are laughing

I have since 2005 been following reactions in Khartoum to what has happened in South Sudan since 2005, and there have been many surprises. In an interview with Washington Post in 2010 President Bashir was asked about the CPA, and why unity did not work. He answered that his government had been very genuine and constructive and had done its utmost to make unity attractive while SPLM and the Southerners unfortunately did not appreciate the efforts and worked against it. This is of course a statement that is very subjective and untrue.

When SPLA attacked the oil installations at Heglig in April 2012, Bashir named the attackers, insects that his forces would exterminate.

I was in Juba on 21st October 2013 when Bashir came on an official visit. He had a big entourage of some 40 people with him, and the protocol people in Juba had a most demanding time entertaining so many guests. On arrival, Kiir was there to welcome Bashir, and he gave a speech that had a content I found very peculiar. He named Bashir the big father who had come to South Sudan to see his children. It was a kind of unreal flower language that I could not understand.

One of the remarks I picked up after the outbreak of the civil war in December 2013, was one by Bashir in the winter of 2014 saying that many foreign diplomats in Khartoum had come to him to share their disgust with the developments in the South and that it showed that he was right. They should never have gotten independence.

Another time he said something to the fact that those people in the South were not mature enough to govern themselves.

In short, it is common knowledge that the ones in Khartoum who with great disapproval in 2011 saw the South getting its independence, they have ever since the summer of 2013 had all reasons to ridicule, to laugh and say: "What did we say? They cannot rule themselves."

No Peace in Sight

When the Norwegian edition of this book was completed in June 2015, I shared with many the hope that an end to war was in sight, and peace was to come.

IGAD and the parties at the peace negotiations in Addis Ababa were in the Summer of 2015 working hard to hammer out a compromise that could serve as the base for a ceasefire and for peace to follow. The initiative taken by Tanzania's President Kikwete and ANC's Deputy President Ramaphosa with financial support from the Ahtisaari Foundation in Finland to invite the conflicting parties of SPLM to Arusha to negotiate to reunite SPLM, had been successful and reinforced the hope that peace might come.

Now in July 2017, we know that the Arusha Agreement signed by both President Salva Kiir and Vice-President Riek Machar was not worth the ink on the paper. As soon as the implementation process started in Juba at the end of June 2015, the Agreement was sabotaged by Kiir and his henchmen.

When the IGAD negotiators in August 2015 insisted that three parties should sign the proposed agreement, Riek Machar signed for the SPLM inO and Pagan Amum signed for the former Detainees while Salva Kiir refused and returned to Juba. However, forced by international pressure, Kiir gave in and signed two weeks later, but only with several reservations attached. It was clear to most people following the negotiations and the fight for signatures, that ARCISS was a very fragile agreement indeed.

A lot of bickering from the SPLM inG towards the other two groups, SPLM in O, the former detainees, IGAD, AU and UN about how to implement the agreement, followed.

Then the Joint Monitoring and Evaluation Commission (JMEC) headed by Botswana's former President, Festus Mogae, which was a very important part of the Agreement on the resolution of the Conflict in South Sudan (ARCISS), came to Juba and started working.

President Salva Kiir then surprised the parties to the Agreement by reorganizing the state structure, abolishing the ten states and creating 28 states, an act which was a stark violation of the peace agreement.

Riek Machar with his key people and a small security force, despite this, finally and only after heavy international pressure returned to Juba 26th April 2016.

A transitional government of national unity with participants from the three factions of SPLM was appointed two days later, eight months after the signing of the ARCISS.

Then the time until 8th July 2016 passed. During that period, there were very few indications indeed to the fact that the transitional government was working at all, but they in one meeting discussed the dress code for ministers attending government meetings.

The President, in the way he acted, did not contribute to reciprocal trust at all. On the contrary, he treated members of the other factions with contempt. One example. Mabior Garang de Mabior, the son of the deceased SPLM/A's iconic leader, John Garang and his wife Rebecca Garang, and a member of the Riek Machar's leadership group, was appointed Minister of Water and Irrigation in the transitional government. When he came to the government meeting on the 6th May, he turned up in a very fitting black suit, but with a bow tie. The President looked at him and told him to leave the meeting as he was not properly dressed. Mabior de Garang's crime was that he wore a bow tie. There was some noise and embarrassment in the meeting, but Riek Machar advised his man to change the tie and come back. Mabior Garang did and came back, only to be chased away by Salva Kiir's body guards with a charged message that his presence was not wanted. When the President did this, it was not only to humiliate Mabior Garang, but also to smear dirt on the reputation of his father and mother, Rebecca and John Garang.

On 8th July, the Vice-President Riek Machar was invited to a meeting with the President at the Palace of the State House. Shortly after his arrival, a shoot-out between his and Kiir's body guards broke out. Many were killed. Riek Machar stayed until he was escorted back to his residence. He later claimed that there had been a plot to assassinate him while he was with the President.

In the days following, there were increased unrest and fighting in Juba. Military units loyal to President Kiir and under the command of Paul Malang, began hunting for Riek Machar who together with his closest aides fled the town. Some of the military units under the Command of the President, Salva Kiir and the Chief of Staff, Paul Malong, at the same time went on rampage and invaded the Crown Hotel, killed some of the guests and raped many of the international female guests staying there. UN has reported that 120 women were raped in Juba during the ravaging of the town by the Kiir forces.

Then a massive hunt for Riek Machar and his immediate military units began, and there are many claims by people in Juba and in the states of Equatoria, and in African and international media to the fact that Kiir and Malong hired mercenaries for the hunt, both gunship helicopters and soldiers, most likely from the Frontier Service Group (FSG) which is headed by Eric Prince.

In August, news arrived that Riek Machar had escaped the man hunt and was safe with UN in the Republic of Congo. He then travelled to Khartoum for medical hospital care, and he is now detained in South Africa, trying to direct SPLM in O from there.

President Kiir in the style of a dictator in mid-July 2016 ordered Riek Machar to return to his post as Vice-President within days. If not, he would be replaced. Machar could of course not return under the prevailing circumstances, and Kiir kept his word. He replaced him with one of Machar's former close political colleagues, Taban Deng Gai.

To most people, whether they are part of the SPLM in opposition or citizens of other countries, this appointment is a violation of ARCISS both in letter and spirit, but it has been accepted by both IGAD and the Troika countries as an established fact.

And to make the story worse, Riek Machar has for reasons that are impossible to understand, if one has making peace on his mind, ended up as a de facto political detainee in South Africa. I cannot understand how this is possible. It must be one more of the dirty political deals that Kiir and his government are getting away with.

They continue to enjoy impunity regardless of what breach of promise, agreement, national and international law and international conventions they commit. It is a very demoralising message to send to the world.

TO SUM IT ALL UP

I am ending my editing and writing of this English edition of the book in the last days of August 2017. While I in June 2015 had a vague hope for peace, I now hardly see any hope. The freedom movement SPLM is torn apart. The freedom army SPLA is not only torn apart, but has been turned into a bunch of ethnically based criminal killers of their own countrymen.

All cease fire agreements between January 2014 and now have been broken, and all peace agreements have suffered the same fate. So many innocent people have been killed, so many maimed for life, so many women and children have been raped and maimed for life.

The state of South Sudan is bankrupt. The ones holding power, have robbed state and society for at least 7 to 10 billion USD. South Sudan is second to the first and worst country in the world in 2016 with corruption, Somalia. The one behind South Sudan is North Korea.

Whatever were of state institutions, have been destroyed. Basic human rights are daily being grossly violated. Human dignity is an unknown concept for those in power.

The most reputable leaders and commanders from the time of the liberation struggle are in forced political exile and refugees in foreign countries. The present government in Juba is in the main composed of members who served the dictatorship in Khartoum during the time of the liberation struggle or drank beer in Edinburgh.

Chaat Paul and other former South Sudanese staff members of NPA in Nairobi and in the field from the time of the liberation struggle have been rotting in the prison cells of Salva Kiir convicted for crimes they never were part of. The good news on this point is that four of the convicted, my friend, Chaat Paul included, have recently been pardoned and released.

While all this is happening, impunity seems to be the guiding principle also for the International Community to protect those most responsible for the destruction of South Sudan, and whenever some member of the UN Security Council takes an initiative that might stop and may reverse the process of continuing destruction, Russia and China being veto powers, always take the lead to make sure that it does not happen. What USA's new President Donald Trump will do with the problem of South Sudan, I do not know, but my guess is that he will allow for the present situation to continue.

They all by their present acts contribute to keeping Salva Kiir and his henchmen in power, the men and women of the present Government of South Sudan who with massacre and war as means have butchered their own people, caused mass starvation and death and destroyed the economy and the democratic institutions of the state.

Salva Kiir and his court are doing all kinds of manoeuvres to stay in power, not because they can bring back respect for human rights and dignity, peace, freedom and development to their people. They only insist because that is the only way they can continue to ride the horse of impunity and save themselves from the justice that one day nevertheless will catch them. There are two sayings that are global that one day will apply to the those who destroyed South Sudan:

"Every journey has an end. There will always be a day of reckoning."

Thabo Mbeki, the former President of South Africa and at present a leading negotiator of AU in search of conflict resolution in Sudan and elsewhere in Africa, was visiting Oslo in the fall of 2016. He had the following comment when asked about the state of affairs in South Sudan: *"Those ruling in Juba at present are nothing but a bunch of kleptocratic tribalists."*

The poor and totally innocent people of South Sudan are paying the highest prize for all this. They have had their future destroyed. Because of them, we all, despite our disappointment, have a moral obligation to try for peace again.

President Salva Kiir on TV 16th December 2013 as he lies about an attempted coup d'etat and declares war against his own countrymen. As Head of State and Government and as Chairman of SPLM and Commander in Chief, he carries the overriding responsibility for the destruction of the country. But now he is tired, old and sick, and in his court there is now a heavy power struggle about his succession.

21
SOME REFLECTIONS

To do or not to do is the Question

For some time after 2005 there was a period of hope and trust that South Sudan would have development with peace, freedom and increasing security for its people, and a state and a government in search for democracy and development, all the time showing increasing respect for human rights and human dignity.

But South Sudan in 2017 is a catastrophe and a tragedy.

We need a discussion in South Sudan, in Africa, in the world and in little Norway about how and why everything went so wrong. What could have been done differently and what could have been avoided of mistakes done?

I am a Norwegian who together with my NPA staff at the time, sometimes with lives at stake, put a lot of effort and risk into supporting the liberation struggle. I have obvious limitations when I now try to discuss why and how all these failures happened in a society and in a context that I still know and understand too little of. But let me nevertheless try.

Many are now asking the obvious question. Was it not very naïve to believe that South Sudan could be a viable state. Its people had suffered a lot from colonial oppression and indifference. Then, the land was destroyed, first by many years of liberation war. After the CPA in 2005, a difficult rivalry and conflict between the two largest ethnic groups, the Dinka and the Nuer developed further, and finally in December 2013, plunged the country into the present ongoing war.

So Sudan in 2015 had no infrastructure, hardly any institution of governance. The vast majority of the people was illiterate. Their new leaders had little or no experience in governing, administrating and developing a country.

We who were part of a developing an increasing Norwegian engagement for the wellbeing of the people of South Sudan, should we have made a stance at some point in time and reflected somewhat more on what we were into? Should we have been more critical and more reserved? With hindsight and having witnessed the tragic events of contemporary South Sudanese history, it is easy to think so.

However, I hold the view that the question rather should be: What did we do right, and what could we have been done differently given the resources, the knowledge and the information we had at the time. What could we have predicted would happen, and what was it impossible for us to foresee?

Norway, with civil society organizations always taking the lead, and with different Norwegian governments following, has since the late 1960ies both in political and economic terms supported the liberation struggle in different parts of Africa. It was done out of a moral and political conviction that it was right and for the good of everyone that Africans got the responsibility to rule their own countries. We had at the time little imagination of the types of difficulties the Africans would face when the liberation struggle had ended, and state building should start. If we had known all the difficulties and challenges that were to come, Norwegian politicians might have taken a more cautious approach and held back support instead of providing it; hence, we would not have played the rather important role we did in countries like Mozambique, Namibia, South Africa, Zambia and Zimbabwe.

Tanzania is another and interesting case. It got its independence and freedom without calling for an armed struggle. It had a peaceful transfer of power. Norway began providing substantive development assistance to Tanzania in the late 1960ies, and it has continued ever since. Only at a few times did that cooperation between the two countries hit the news, simply because it took place in a society that had no big internal conflicts, only tension at times, while having a successful and peaceful and increasingly democratic development process compared with many others.

When Norwegian People's Aid started its work in Sudan in 1986, the regime in Khartoum was very brutal and oppressive. The racist attitudes of the Arabs towards Black Africa were even more intrusive than today. That was why people in the South had raised in rebellion and taken to arms to liberate themselves.

In South Sudan, we could not predict the unpredictable. The country emerged from the liberation struggle in 2005 with John Garang as the iconic leader. He was a strong personality, he was well-educated, had a high moral integrity, was visionary and had the ability to find a compromise and unite different interests and groups. Suddenly he was gone.

He died in a helicopter accident on 30th July 2005, three weeks after he became President of South Sudan and only a few days after he took his oath as 1st Vice-President of Sudan. The official report on the accident concluded that the accident was caused by human failure. I like an increasing number of South Sudanese and other Africans with an interest, now tend to believe that it was rather a very well-planned assassination.

His deputy, Salva Kiir, was elected his successor. He had a lot of experience from the battlefields, but little formal education and hardly any civic experience. As it has been demonstrated in full in recent years, he lacked a lot to succeed as a leader and head of state. He neither had the moral core nor the political experience. After having entangled himself in a power struggle and civil war, he has now become a dictator and the symbol of a failed state and a humanitarian catastrophe.

In August 2005, it was hard for anyone to know that South Sudan with Salva Kiir in charge could fail so miserably. However, it was possible to see both in 2011, 2012 and later that South Sudan with increasing speed was failing, but most foreign leaders looked the other way.

In today's world of conflicts and sometimes chaos, world institutions like the United Nations and national ones like the Norwegian Ministry of Foreign Affairs, NORAD and voluntary organizations find themselves, time and time again in situations where they have a moral obligation to try and find solutions and assist instead of allowing themselves to be overwhelmed by the problems. This means taking risks. It may be a situation in a country like Congo or Niger, Iraq or Syria.

Roles and Risks

The will to take risks is interrelated with what roles one has and the kind of individuals who are in action. The Norwegian People's Aid with solidarity at the centre of its core values and being part of the Labour Movement, plays a different role from the one of for instance the Norwegian Ministry of Foreign Affairs. Civil servants have a different role from politicians. NPA, taking a stand in support of the freedom rebellion in Sudan, caused political controversy. Both leading civil servants in the NMFA and leading people in NCA worked in 1987 against NPA getting a grant. The foreign minister at the time, Thorvald Stoltenberg, saw it differently and decided in favour of NPA. Without that decision, NPA would not in 1987 have been able to continue its work in Sudan. The politician Stoltenberg was the right person at the right place at the right time.

Egil Hagen was the driving force with a lot of vigour but without NPA's decision in 1987 to support the freedom struggle and establish a permanent humanitarian programme in South Sudan, he most likely would not have able to do what he did.

Without a big, dedicated and committed staff with mostly Africans, willing to take risks, NPA could not have done what they did in South Sudan. NPA would neither have been able to carry out its work without the understanding and support from The Norwegian Ministry of Foreign Affairs and from 1993, US State Department and USAID. To them and other likeminded donors NPA because of its political stand, became a necessary partner for them to achieve their own goals.

NPA was a guest in two East African countries, Kenya and Uganda. Without the understanding and support of their governments, NPA would not have been able to do what it did behind the frontlines in South Sudan.

Governments and development agencies like the Norwegian Government and Norad are in many instances dependent on identifying partners willing to take risks. Then, they have to develop good channels of cooperation with the same, if they want to carry out the policies they want. This presupposes trust and a constructive collaboration between the ministries and agencies concerned, and civil society organizations willing to take risks.

In my experience, when anyone, being an individual or an institution, is confronted with a catastrophic situation caused by war, famine or a big earthquake and one has to act, one can only succeed when one is non-bureaucratic, action oriented and willing to take risks. Confronted with the difficult dramas that sometimes life and reality provide for, one has to be able to analyse and decide fast in order to act fast, but by doing that, one runs the risk of criticism in the aftermath.

Media, Catastrophes and faked News

I believe that media's increasingly one-sided focus globally on crisis and scandals, are making international as well as government institutions, NGOs and individuals too afraid of exposure. Consequently it makes them also too afraid to stand up and take responsibility when the situation demands for it. This is certainly so if acting in a prevailing situation may be of a controversial nature, and one runs the risk of criticism.

At present another feature of media behaviour creates new and challenging problems, the production of faked news. We saw the phenomena at work in the US elections in November 2016. But faked news comes in the most surprising situations. While I in January 2017 was writing on the script of this English edition of the book, I one evening first picked a news article said to have originated in the weekly, the East African Standard. It in length reported that Great Britain and Norway had left USA and thereby the Troika on Sudan and South Sudan and were inviting the parties in South Sudan and Horn of Africa for a peace conference i Doha in Qatar. It was a complete lie, but caused political and diplomatic uncertainty. The day after, another and even bigger surprise. The spokesman of the Government of South Sudan accused Norway of plotting to assassinate the Chief of Staff of SPLA, Paul Malong. Really, a very unbelievable piece of faked news, brought to the attention by the spokesman of GOSS. There was no other source.

I suspect that the two pieces of faked news mentioned above was the work of the rumour mongering unit attached to the Government of South Sudan. The aim was to create uncertainty and discredit one of South Sudan's oldest friends in the Northern hemisphere, Norway, its government and Norwegian NGOs working in South Sudan, NGOs like NRC, NCA and NPA.

While I was with NPA, I was again and again taken by how little interest both politicians concerned with international issues and media people in Norway had for the activities of NPA in South Sudan. Between the beginning in 1986 and 1999 there was no Norwegian politician neither from government nor Parliament who wanted to go to South Sudan to see the activities of NPA in the field.

On the other hand, and during the same period, NPA organized visits for many American Congressmen, some dozens of American diplomats and NGO representatives and two-three American undersecretaries of state, one of them being Susan

Rice. The Dutch Minister of Development Cooperation, Jan Pronk, came on his own initiative and asked NPA to take him into the field. After the field visit, he confirmed his recognition of NPA's work with an extra grant of USD five million. NPA also arranged a visit for the Foreign Relations Committee of the Parliament of Kenya.

We in NPA took more than 50 international reporters with us to the field, but only a very few were Norwegians.

The NPA did a lot behind the frontlines. We provided food for between 500,000 to 1 million people yearly when drought and hunger were at their worst. We treated between 60,000 to 80,000 people a year in NPA's five hospitals. While UN and other international NGOs pulled out in periods, NPA never did that. After 1996, NPA on a permanent basis only had African and mainly South Sudanese staff in the field, numbering between 1200 and 1300, and they did wonderful work, so dedicated and so committed.

However, what caused interest in Norwegian media and the public at large was whenever rumours about NPA being gun runners, were spread. That NPA saved hundreds of thousands of human beings from hunger and death, was of little interest.

Limitations

NPA has been widely regarded as an effective channel for humanitarian aid into South Sudan. But there was little understanding of how demanding it was administratively to execute it all in a land at war and without any infrastructure. We had big grants from donors, ear-marked for projects while there was little understanding for how costly it was to administrate the same projects and programmes. We should have had a stronger Norwegian management capacity in the field, and in general, more staff in Norway, Kenya and in the field for a programme that was so complex and demanding when it came to politics, security and professional issues related to aid, administration and personell management.

In view of the complex character of the conflict, the ethnic plurality of Sudan and South Sudan and the role of culture and religion, we, the non-Africans, had too little knowledge and understanding of the society we worked in.

We, from the early 1990ies, should have developed a closer political and development dialogue and cooperation with our key partners, the SSRA and the SPLM, and later linked this to UN and likeminded INGOs. We rightly strengthened the political dialogue with the SPLM between 1998 and 2000, but after 2001 there was a period of uncertainty caused by statements by the NPA President and Secretary General at the time, indicating their intention to cancel the programme.

With the hindsight available today, we had a very simplified view of SPLM/A. We should have asked for and spent more resources and time trying to understand how SPLM and SPLA really functioned. We should have tried to identify some of their weaknesses, and we would maybe then have been able to assist in avoiding some of the catastrophes that have hit SPLM/A in recent years.

Democracy Development

The period between 2001 and 2005 was very demanding for the leadership of SPLM/A. Peace negotiations were on in Kenya, and they took a lot of resources and attention. At the same time, people in the whole of Sudan developed great expectations towards SPLM which was an organization with many weaknesses. SPLM needed to develop a more democratic and participatory organization to be able to take responsibility for the development of the new democratic society primarily in South Sudan, but in the whole of Sudan. John Garang's vision was all the time: **A new, secular and democratic Sudan**.

It is well known that the leadership of SPLM at the political level was missing NPA as a strong and supportive partner in all these endeavours in the critical years between 2001 and 2006.

John Garang was in our conversations from the late 1990ies more convinced than ever that SPLM/A would be so victorious both militarily and politically that peace negotiations would have to come and be successful.

He at the same time got more and more directed towards the future challenges that lay ahead regarding the building of institutions for a democratic society, and he as early as in 1998 conveyed his strong wish for cooperation with Norway to build such institutions. But those wishes were unfortunately rejected by the Norwegian government. Norway and the world at large at the time were more concerned with the famine catastrophe that was ravaging Sudan, and relief aid was prioritized.

In retrospect, this was a misjudgement from the Norwegian side. Something similar happened when the party building project with NPA and the Norwegian Labour Party as partners should have its second grant in 2009. Bureaucrats lacking understanding for its importance, delayed payments for many months.

In retrospect, I now see that not only NPA, but UN and other partners should have started the work to build democracy institutions for the new state to come much earlier, and that these efforts should have been much more forceful.

Nevertheless, NPA and the Labour Party achieved quite a lot when it came to the two projects: The project on Freedom of Expression was successful, the work ending with a proposed legislation that would have rendered South Sudan one of the best and most liberal media laws in Africa, but the President and his court in the Office of the President, had the legislation destroyed sometime in 2014.

The party building project came a long way, but when the project in 2010 entered its second phase with democratisation of the SPLM organisation and members at all levels gaining real influence and with the development of a political programme that had a left leaning social democratic tendency, the antidemocracy groups within and outside SPLM mobilised to stop the project, and they were successful. The project came to an end in the summer of 2013 as the President started to show his real face, the face of the dictator. I should add that these antidemocracy forces inside SPLM had full support from Khartoum for their evil actions. It was the same forces that half a year later let lose the cycle of violence that today has destroyed South Sudan.

I saw while on missions to South Sudan in the years 2006 – 2012, these evil forces of destruction arise and get to work, but I did not have the imagination to see how strong and destructive they would be.

In retrospect, it is easy to see that we were all too optimistic. Most us never understood how a traditional and ethnically plural society, like the one in South Sudan, operates and manages its conflicts.

We did not understand how destructive the 20 years long and extremely violent war had been for the people and the communities. Few if any of us had thought through how the SPLM leaders who had lived as poor guerrilla soldiers during the liberation struggle, would behave themselves once they got the responsibility to manage oil revenues in a situation where there were no management institutions. Many became corrupt and forgot their responsibility to the people and the society. We did not have sufficient insight into how devastating ethnic based power politics can be in an under-developed society like South Sudan.

The death of John Garang on 30th July 2005 has become the ultimate tragedy for the peoples of South Sudan. I am convinced that if he had been allowed to live and stay at the helm in the political and societal development of both Sudan and South Sudan, the lives of the people would have been fundamentally different and good with people seeing their future improve for the better.

John Garang was a rare personality, a strong leader, very gifted with a strong moral commitment and a great vision for the future. He would not have allowed what has happened, to happen.

The Kenyan artist GAdo har his own ways of communicating the destruction of South Sudan.

2012

2015

2015

2016

2016

2017

ATTACHMENT 1:

The author, Halle Jøern Hanssen (HJH) interviewing Thorvald Stoltenberg (TS) on International issues that were important during his time as a Norwegian diplomat and Minister of Foreign Affairs.

Thorvald Stoltenberg (born 1931) began his diplomatic carrier in 1965, was Norwegian Minister of Defence from 1986 to 1989 and Minister of Foreign Affairs from 1987 to 1989 and from 1990 to 1993. He was also the UN High Commissioner for Refugees from 1989 to 1990. Mr. Stoltenberg is together with his friend and predecessor as Minister of Foreign Affairs, Knut Frydenlund, seen as the architects of the Labour Party Foreign Policy programmes in the period 1976 – 1994.

Thorvald Stoltenberg was particular concerned with North-South policy issues and support to liberation movements struggling for independence and freedom in the colonies of Africa. As Mr. Stoltenberg writes in his foreword to this book, he as Minister of Foreign Affairs in 1987 granted the first allocation of 20 Mill.NOK. for NPA's humanitarian work in South Sudan.

The author has in what follows below, a longer interview with Mr. Stoltenberg on international policy issues of particular importance during his time as diplomat and member of Government.

HJH: You were Minister of Foreign Affairs in 1987 when you decided to meet a request from NPA and granted an amount of 20 Mill. NOK for their humanitarian work in South-Sudan. The decision turned out to be controversial.

TS: Yes, some considered the decision to be a kind of meddling into a civil war in an African country by providing support to a Norwegian NGO that had taken a stand in support of the liberation struggle in Sudan. I saw it very differently. I considered my decision to be in line with a long time tradition of Norwegian support to liberation movements in Africa. I consider myself one of the founding fathers from the early 1960ies of that tradition. The regime in Khartoum was responsible for a systematic discrimination and oppression of the African peoples in Sudan and in particular, the African peoples of South-Sudan, which was a continuation of the oppressive policies of the former colonial powers.

HJH: But Norwegian support to liberation movements in Africa was controversial at home in Norway.

TS: You are right. Political parties and interest groups on the right were against support to liberation movements. However, it was not only the Labour Movement that wanted to support the liberation movements. Many church leaders, the student movement and civil society with a few exceptions were in support. This attitude of support had to do with our own historical experience. Norway was colonized for almost 500 years, first by Denmark, then Sweden, and we only had our independence and freedom in 1905. In addition, many young people had a lot of knowledge about the horrible conditions that existed in the colonies in Africa.

I had my first years as a young diplomat in the late 1960ies working in the political secretariat of Foreign Minister Jon Lyng who was a leading member of the Conservative Party.

HJH: Did you work in Mr. Lyng's secretariat, was that possible, you were a young Labourite?

TS: This is an interesting story. I was in 1965 as a young Labourite called by the Labour Foreign Minister Halvard Lange temporarily to join his secretariat. However, Labour lost in the same year of 1965 the elections for the first time since 1945. Halvard Lange then asked me to stay on for a few weeks to assist in the transition period for the new minister. I did so, and when the transition was completed, I told the new minister that I was leaving. He looked at me for a little while, and then he said: "I do not think so. I am asking you to stay". "I lost my tongue for a few seconds, and then I said: But is that possible. You know very well that I am an active member of the Labour Party". Lyng answered: This is the reason why I want to keep you. It might be politically very helpful both for me and the Labour Party if you will stay on"! So I stayed on and became a diplomat.

HJH: And you worked well with Mr. Lyng?

TS: Yes, I had a very good cooperation with Foreign Minister John Lyng. It was marked by mutual confidence. He was very much concerned with how to improve on the East-West relations at the time, and he had a strong interest in developments in Africa, and in particular related to the liberation struggle in the colonies in Africa still held by European powers.

HJH: So you were discussing the liberation struggle with the Foreign Minister.

TS: Yes, of course, and we did more than that. We had in 1967 the Biafra Crises that exploded into a full-scale civil war. A Swiss Public Relations Agency called Mark Press was commissioned by the rebel leaders in Biafra to inform the world about why there was an uprising and a war in Biafra. The agency started a worldwide campaign showing starving and dying children and other war atrocities. The campaign became very successful and strongly influenced public opinion in Europe to favour the rebellion. The impact of the campaign was particular successful in Norway, and within the four political parties that made up the government coalition at the time, there was strong pressure developing in support of recognizing Biafra. Even some members of the government voiced their support for recognition. Foreign Minister Lyng who himself was very skeptical to the demand for recognition of Biafra, became very worried about this development, and he decided to send me to the conflict area. Not only that, as I was about to leave for Africa, he told in person that I was instructed to report directly to him and not to use the conventional channels for diplomatic reporting.

HJH: It was hardly an easy journey.

TS: Not at all. Everything was more complicated when it came to traveling at the time. I had a flight to the capital of Lagos. From there I had to improvise my journey into Biafra. It was at times almost like a fairytale, and at other times so risky that I do not want to remember. But I found my way into Biafra and established my contacts. However, it turned to be impossible to transmit my reports to Oslo. The Chief Command of the Rebellion and Mark Press had established complete control of all communication.

Fortunately, many Norwegian ships were waiting to load and unload outside the coastal town of Port Hartcourt. I met some Norwegian sailors in town who invited me onboard, and I got the permission to use the ship-radio to transmit my reports to my Minister. In my reports, I strongly advised against any recognition of Biafra.

HJH: You gained some valuable experience from that journey.

TS: Yes, definitely. My journey to Nigeria and Biafra provided for important insight into how complicated conflict lines might be in a multiethnic and multi-religious state like Nigeria. I have in my political life benefitted a lot from that experience.

HJH: The popular uprisings that one saw in the African Colonies in the 1960ies were in Norway as in many other Western countries met skepticism and rejection.

TS: That is true. When we had these popular uprisings in Africa, it was about independence and freedom. However, in many Western countries this was misinterpreted and seen as a Communist revolution. For this reason, the West turned its back on what was happening, and the leaders of the freedom struggle had no other option than seeking support from China, the Soviet Union and other Communist countries.

HJH: That was understandable, wasn't it?

TS: Yes, it was. However, we in the Labour movement, churches, civil society, students and human rights groups in Western countries saw it differently. We wanted to support the liberation struggle by expressing political solidarity and providing for humanitarian assistance while we said no to arms. We had to make sure that their liberation struggle did not get dependent on support from China and the Soviet Union only. We saw it as popular uprisings against oppression and discrimination and for National independence and freedom.

HJH: On the other hand, some of the leaders of the rebellion had other agendas.

TS: I have met many liberation leaders. They were concerned with the fact that they and their people were fighting for independence and freedom. They made it very clear that if they did not receive any support from countries in the West, they will then seek whatever assistance they could get from the Communist countries, and they did. Arms for liberation came from these countries.

HJH: Was it a kind of political blackmail?

TS: I will not use that expression. The leaders were mostly strong personalities with high integrity. I met Eduardo Mondlane, the leader of FRELIMO in Mozambique and his wife Janet during their visit to Norway in the summer of 1964. Mondlane made a very strong impression on me. He was a visionary. He had strong values, and he was very knowledgeable. He was a strong personality and a leader with clear goals and visions for the struggle. Unfortunately, he was not allowed to live long. He was assassinated in Dar es Salaam in 1969. Some secret agents sent him a bomb wrapped up in a package like a book, and he died when he tried to open the package. His death was a great loss for Mozambique and for Africa. I have during all the time since maintained contact with his wife Janet, and I did meet her last time not long ago in Mozambique.

HJH: Not all leaders were like Mondlane.

TS: No, another liberation leader who made a strong impression during my first meeting was Robert Mugabe. He impressed me a lot during our first conversations while he still was the leader of ZANU and the liberation struggle in Zimbabwe.

However, as prime Minister and later President of Zimbabwe he has taken the country in a direction that is very destructive and tragic.

I did unfortunately not meet John Garang, the liberation leader in Sudan. It is my understanding that his death in the summer of 2005 was a very big loss indeed for the peoples of Sudan and South Sudan.

HJH: You have not only been politically engaged in support for the liberation struggle in countries in Africa, but also involved in the work for a New World Economic Order aiming at changing the power structures between North and South so that the South could be a more equal partner.

TS: The Norwegian policies for support for the liberation struggle in Africa developed almost at the same time as the proposal for a New International Economic Oder (NIEO) was launched at the UN. I became a strong supporter of this new initiative, and I put a lot of political work into it. The issue of NIEC had in its own way a lot to do with independence, equality and liberation because there is a tight connection between political and economic freedom. If we at the time had succeeded in getting the key points of the proposals for NIEO adopted and put into practice, it would have been an important contribution to fighting poverty in developing countries. We today would have had a more just economic and social world.

HJH: Not much came out of the struggle for NIEO.

TS: No, as we all know, we failed in the effort. Strong forces in our part of the world were mobilized in opposition to the idea of NIEO, and these forces were victorious. Ronald Reagan became president in USA and Margaret Thatcher Prime Minister in Great Britain. They were strongly in favour of a very different world order, the Neo-Liberal one with the market forces being let lose at the cost of the of the political power of International Intergovernmental Institutions like UN and EU, and the National state.

HJH: Back to the issue of support for liberation movements, Sudan and South Sudan and the Norwegian support. There was criticism in Norwegian media regarding insufficient reporting and auditing.

TS: Yes, we faced some problems with reporting on and auditing of the Norwegian grants to liberation movements. The accounting departments in the Foreign Ministry and NORAD had very clear instructions to make sure that proper reporting and auditing of every grant were done. It had to be made sure that the money granted was used for the agreed purpose. However, these demands were sometimes difficult to meet in everyday life in the field. We, who negotiated with the leaders of the liberation movements, told them again and again about the necessity of proper reporting.

Then, they frequently looked at us and said: "Yes, we understand your problem, but we are at war, and we cannot guarantee that every package with food, every pair of shoes or every car we receive money for, are being used in the place agreed upon in the document. We are fighting a liberation war. The frontlines sometimes shift rapidly, and we may be forced by the prevailing circumstances to use the grants allocated in other places than stated in the documents. We who dealt with the liberation movements, had no problems in understanding that. However, the reporting and accounting rules in the Ministry and NORAD were made for peaceful times, not for liberation wars.

HJH: Such criticism was labeled against Norwegian Peoples Aid (NPA) in Sudan.

TS: Let me first of all state that NPA since the mid-1980ies made a tremendous effort in order to provide humanitarian and emergency assistance for peoples of South Sudan. I take it for granted that reporting and auditing under such extreme logistic conditions as were the case in the field of South Sudan, sometimes were more than difficult. The challenges related to transport and logistics were enormous, and inside South Sudan infrastructure was totally lacking.

Keep in mind that in the aftermath of the liberation war, NPA has received a lot of praise for what they did during the time of the struggle. Many of us took note of the words of President Salva Kiir when he in his key note speech at the Independence Celebrations in Juba on 9th July 2011 only stated words of gratitude to two organizations, UN and NPA. It gave me a lot of joy.

Original interview given in in Norwegian Oslo in April 2015 and translated in January 2016

(HJH: Many question marks rested for a long time with regard to who were the assassins of Eduardo Modnlane on 3rd February 1969. However, in the early 1990ies the truth finally surfaced. It was agents of Aginter, the Portuguese Branch of the Western Intelligence Network Stay Behind, who murdered Eduardo Mondlane.)

ATTACHMENT 2:
NPA POLICY DOCUMENT ON SUDAN

Statement by the National Board approved on 13 September 1998 and reconfirmed in an updated and extended version by the NPA Congress on 19 August 1999.

Background:
Geographical data, population, and resources

Sudan covers approximately 2.5 million square kilometres and is consequently the largest country in Africa. Historically there is a demarcation line between North and South Sudan with a border which may be said to stretch roughly from the town of Maban close to the Ethiopian border in the east to the town of Boro on the border of the Central African Republic. On this assumption, South Sudan covers an area of approximately 700-800 000 square kilometres.

Sudan has a total population of some 30 million people, about two thirds of whom live in the North. More than half of the population in the North has an African ethnic background, the most important groups being the Fur and the Nuba in the west and the Beja in the east. The remainder are of Arab origin. It must be added that over the centuries there have been many marriages across ethnic lines. These population groups in the North are largely Muslim and sometimes a product of enforced conversion to Islam of non-Muslims. What makes the plurality of ethnic groups, a clear majority of whom are of African origin, particularly interesting and, in human and political terms, complex and problematic, is that Islam in Sudan is associated with Arabism. As a concept Arabism is a composite of race, ethnicity and culture, the peoples constituting this group regarding themselves as superior to African non-Muslims.

In the South live an estimated 10 - 12 million people. However, the exact figure is uncertain as 40 years of war and instability have hitherto precluded a credible census. The population in the South consists of many different tribes, the Dinka constituting the largest single group. A common denominator of all the population groups in South Sudan is that ethnically, they belong to a group which may be termed "African". Approximately 30-40% of them may be regarded as Christian and the rest identified as adherents of traditional African religions. A small minority is Muslim.

In the Sudanese historical context, the designations "Arab" and "Arabism", and "African" and "Africanism", have distinct cultural connotations. Those of Arab origin or having been assimilated with Arab culture and converted to Islam, tend to claim for themselves a superior Arabic-Islamic identity, and strongly oppose any attempt to identify them with black Africa. The terms "African" and "Africanism" mean different things to different groups. In general terms, they encompasses the racial factor "black" or "Negroid" from which Northerners -Arabs or assimilated or integrated Africans - disassociate themselves. This is also reflected linguistically as when they disparagingly refer to the southern Sudanese as "abeed", meaning "slave".

To the Africans in the South, the terms "African" and "Africanism" is, however, a matter of pride, providing them with a feeling of identity and belonging.

Ironically, most Sudanese Arab in the North has visible evidence of her/his African origin due in part to skin colour, and most have some genetic heritage stemming from slave origins. This basic fact is disregarded by northern perceptions and is a major contributing factor to the historical conflict between North and South.

The majority of the Sudanese people both in the North and South are very poor. However, owing to the protracted war, poverty is undoubtedley more prominent in the South.

There is also a considerable disparity between the North and South in terms of resources. The North consists mainly of enormous dry savannahs and arid or semi-arid areas. The world's largest river, the Nile, flowing from South to North, divides the country in two and represents a huge potential for water supply and irrigation. However, due to topographical and climatic conditions as well as the numerous tributaries of the Nile, accessibility to water is easiest in the low lands of the South. This factor in addition to annual floods have through the centuries contributed to the development of large areas with rich black cotton soil in the South. However, most of the tribes are either pastoralist or agro-pastoralist. There are extensive forested areas in the South which, in common with the savannahs, used to provide a habitat for large concentrations of wildlife which, however, have been tragically decimated by the present war. There are large quantities of fish in the Nile, its tributaries and lakes. South Sudan therefore has a great potential for as yet unutilised food production. In the border areas between the North and the South occur substantial quantities of oil and gas which have so far been commercially exploited only to a very limited extent, and then by the Khartoum regime in collaboration with domestic and international capitalist interests.

Conflict between North and South. A glimpse of the historical background.

The conflict between North and South reaches back many centuries, indeed even further back in time. The African population groups currently living in both North and South Sudan have in ancient times largely resided in the northern parts of Sudan and in Egypt, but have subsequently been pressed southwards by invading Arabic population groups. The religious dimension of the conflict arises as a result of contact with the Arabic groups who for more than a thousand years have been Muslim with a religious call to convert the African population groups in Sudan to the teachings of Islam.

During the 18th and early 19th century, Egypt was a dominant actor in the area today called Sudan. The Ottoman Empire, which in periods stretched all the way down to Port Sudan on the Red

Sea, also had interests in the South. One of several characteristics of these periods was inhuman aggression against the peoples of the South and the Nuba Mountains (the latter group being a custodian of a long Christian tradition). Raids into the Southern regions with the objective of capturing especially women for sale in Arab slave markets, were common and frequent and practised with great brutality. During the last half of the 19th century, the British colonial power also invaded Sudan and established the Anglo-Egyptian dominion. The oppression of the colonial era was experienced by the people of South Sudan as different in form and content from previous occupations. However, the characteristic oppressive relationship between master and servant remained. The British gradually introduced separate administrations for the North and South. It also remains as an indisputable historical fact that the British with their dual colonial administration had a preference for Arab culture and the religion of Islam. Northern Sudan was for this reason more developed than the South. This dual administrative model served to reinforce Arabism and Islam in the North while in the South it encouraged only limited development along indigenous African lines while introducing Christian missionary education and rudiments of Western civilisation as modernising influences. Interaction between North and South was strongly discouraged during most of the colonial period. The divided administration lasted several decades almost until independence in 1956.

Independence and open conflict

Sudan was regarded by the British as a predominantly Arabic nation, and was therefore accorded independence before other countries in Africa (this was in 1956), the intention being the establishment and development of a democratic state. However, the conflicts were so many and the internal distribution of resources and opportunities between the North and the South so unequal that this turned out to be impossible. Strong tensions had developed between the North and the South and a civil war broke out in August 1955, shortly before independence in January 1956. This war continued for 17 years, resulting in great suffering on the part of the civilian population, approximately half a million being killed, hundreds of thousands wounded, and with enormous material destruction. The war effectively prevented any development.

In 1972 a Norwegian TV team broadcast footage from the war zones that shocked viewers in Norway and other European countries. Strong international political efforts, with Norwegian Church Aid as main actor and enjoying the support of the Norwegian Government, were initiated. This led to a cease-fire and a peace agreement the following year. The objective was to introduce internal autonomy and substantial development programmes in the South which would gradually provide education for the populace and reduce the disparity between North and South with regard to human resources and development. For a variety of reasons few of these objectives were realised. With the exception of Norway (through Norwegian Church Aid), few countries were prepared to provide development assistance to the South. Instead of facilitating education and other opportunities for the young people of the South, some 15 000 - 20 000 professionals from the North, bringing with them their superior Arab and Muslim attitudes, were injected into the new civil service and administration of the South. The Khartoum regime broke many of its other promises and the vision of a better future faded. Tensions and conflicts again flared up, and in 1983 the Khartoum regime, giving in to demands from orthodox Muslims, imposed the Islamic Sharia throughout the Sudan. This exacerbated the conflict and civil war again broke out. For the people of South Sudan this now became a war of liberation with the SPLA army as spearhead and the SPLM movement as central organisation.

The Past 15 years - The Experience of Genocide

During the first few years of the war, the battle raged back and forth with great loss of life and widespread destruction. SPLM initially sought the support and cooperation of the communist regime in Ethiopia and the Sudan conflict was therefore seen by the West as part of the global East/West conflict. In 1988/89 there appeared to be a possibility of achieving a cease-fire and peaceful solution. However, military leaders in Khartoum led by the National Islamic Front (NIF), carried out a coup d'etat and established a fundamentalist Muslim military dictatorship. Extensive resources were mobilised for an increased war effort, and an Islamic policy based on the Sharia was introduced throughout the country.

The war was intensified by the Khartoum regime and the use of violence and terror intensified. The NIF regime seemed intent upon a military solution to the conflict. The establishment of the military dictatorship took place at a time when all of Sudan was being drubbed by drought and famine. Especially in the South, many people (approximately 300.000) starved to death as a result of the Khartoum regime's policy of actively preventing relief assistance. During the early 1990s it seemed that the Khartoum regime would win the war. One of the methods used by the regime was systematically to sow discord among the various ethnic groups in the South by, amongst other things, buying loyalty with money and weapons. This very destructive policy was successful to a certain extent. Traditional differences blossomed into full-blown conflicts and temporarily split SPLM in two, SPLM Mainstream and SPLM United, the latter being the break-away group which later has been "bought" by Khartoum and used for different subversive actions in the South. The winds of war shifted to SPLM Mainstream's advantage (at this time - and up to the present - it was under the continuous leadership of John Garang). The liberation war simultaneously intensified in another arena of conflict in the country, the Nuba mountains.

SPLM, being maybe the most poor liberation movement ever in the African continent, currently controls 60-80% of the territory in South Sudan. SPLA's weapons and military equipment have mostly been captured from government forces from the North. SPLM was militarily on the offensive in 1996/97 and also retained an impressive political profile. The SPLM has in recent years entered into a political alliance with opposition parties and groups in the North under the title of «The National Democratic Alliance». This Alliance has launched a military offensive against the dictatorship along new frontlines in the east. Simultaneously, the rebellion continues in the Nuba Mountains north of the dividing line between North and South.

Human suffering over the past 15 years has been enormous. The U.S Committee for Refugees contended in 1995 that at least 1.5 million people had been killed or have died as a consequence of hostilities and the destruction it has brought. More recent estimates place the number of fatalities close to two million. Approximately 4 million people have been rendered homeless and have been internally displaced.

More than 1 million are living in camps in the North, which are basically no more than prison camps. More than 3 million people are dispersed in camps and villages in the South. In 1998, approximately 2.5 million people were threatened by famine and disease, and tens of thousands died in spite of international efforts to provide humanitarian assistance. The problems of famine and disease continue to threaten the lives of the many, also in 1999 and for as long as the war continues. Tens of thousands of orphans without proper education or homes are exposed to extreme living conditions and struggling for daily survival. Material destruction has been extensive. The people and their communities have been denied all forms of development and the possibility of living normal lives. Forty five years after independence, South Sudan is a society which has been comprehensively smashed, its peoples destitute and deprived of every amenity, including educated professionals essential to a modern African society. Compared with other conflicts and wars such as those which have afflicted Vietnam, Afghanistan, Southern Africa and

Central America, Sudan is today much worse off. In hardly any other country with a comparable population, have so many died and are so many suffering extreme deprivation. In summary, this conflict in the largest country in Africa with a population of over 30 million people, is a war which, with an interruption of ten years between 1973 - 83, is the longest ever fought on the African continent. No other war since 1945 has anywhere else in the world caused more death, produced a larger number of wounded, or resulted in greater material destruction. It is a genocidal war for which various regimes in Khartoum must be held solely responsible, having been turned into the most brutal and violent of wars by the present fundamentalist extremist military dictatorship. It is a war that has stolen the present and robbed all the peoples of Sudan of their future, and is the very antithesis of civilisation and development. Conflict and hostilities covering a period of nearly 45 years would shatter any society. Respect for the law, for norms and values and human beings, has been eroded and destroyed. Unscrupulous and strongly authoritarian and egocentric guerrilla leaders encouraged and supported by the Khartoum regime opportunistically switch sides between North and South and let loose their propensity to violence on an innocent civilian population. Arabic militia groups or holy warriors are by the Khartoum regime equipped with weapons and means of transport - and no other reward than what they themselves can plunder from an impoverished civilian population in the South. Abducting (preferably young) women who are then sold as slaves in the markets in the North, is a daily occurrence. The violation of human rights and human dignity has therefore become commonplace. Human rights and democracy are unknown concepts.

The complexity of the conflict

The main line of conflict is between the North and the South with links to areas of hostilities also in the North, first and foremost in the Nuba mountains. It has ethnic dimensions in addition to cultural and religious ones. The conflict is also about resources; water, land, oil and gas. However, there are also internal conflicts both in the North and the South. The dictatorial and fundamentalist nature of the Khartoum regime has resulted in conflicts between Sudan and neighbouring countries such as Egypt, Eritrea, Ethiopia, Kenya and Uganda.

IGAD, attempts at negotiations, a cease-fire, and peace

In 1986 a regional platform was established for addressing the issues of drought and development, the Inter Governmental Authority on Drought and Development (IGAD). The mandate for IGAD has since been expanded to include regional peace negotiations. The two parties in the Sudan conflict, SPLM and the Khartoum Government, are currently represented on this platform. IGAD also includes Kenya (as convenor), Uganda, Ethiopia and Eritrea. In addition there is a group, «Partners of IGAD», with the USA, Great Britain, Netherlands, Italy, Canada, Egypt, Sweden and Norway and others as members. This group is currently striving to acquire a more active political and diplomatic role within the IGAD frame. At present Norway, jointly with Italy, serves as convenor of this group.

OLS - Operation Lifeline Sudan

Following the humanitarian disasters in Sudan towards the end of the 1980s, the United Nations took the initiative to establish a group of relief organisations that would have a permanent presence in South Sudan. The United Nation's own organisations, the World Food Programme and UNICEF, became lead agencies while around forty other organisations (mainly NGOs) have also joined the group. Operation Lifeline Sudan (OLS) has an agreement with both SPLM and the Khartoum regime. However, it is the latter which has the final say with regard to

OLS' freedom of action. It is the Khartoum regime that in reality decides when, where and what sort relief may be provided, and when and what type of relief personnel may be deployed in the field. At the same time, the Khartoum airforce has full control of South Sudan's airspace. OLS has existed since 1989 and has become a bureaucratic and somewhat tardy institution; it has therefore at times been characterised by inefficiency, and in early 1998, it came under fire for its lack of willingness to act. NPA and many others warned of the coming disaster in Bahr el Gazaal in February 1998, but the United Nations' response in May 1998 was that we were exaggerating. NPA is not a member of OLS as we reject the political ties between OLS and the Khartoum regime and the kind of dependency it creates. This political tie and the dependence on the Khartoum regime are the most important reasons why the international relief effort in 1998 got started too late. At the same time, NPA wants practical cooperation with OLS and its network members in the field whenever this is possible. It must also be stated very clearly that the presence and the work of OLS is, despite its limitations, of utmost importance.

SPLM - The Sudan People's Liberation Movement

SPLM is the only representative political organisation for the peoples of South Sudan even though it has many shortcomings and weaknesses. SPLM is also the biggest and strongest group within the Sudanese National Democratic Alliance (NDA) which includes the largest - and for the last years banned - democratic groups in the North. In comparison with other liberation movements in other countries, SPLM has a mixed record. At the same time it is active among population groups which, after 45 years of conflict and war, hardly know what peace is. They have been denied all possibility of development and are living in extreme poverty. SPLM has had in the past - and still has - its moments of glory. However, it also has to share the responsibility for causing ethnic tensions and conflicts in the South, for violations of human rights, the looting of relief supplies, and the protection of warlords who should have been taken to court and punished. In recent years, however, the SPLM leadership has emphasised the development of the organisation with increasing popular participation and influence within the movement. SPLM should also increase its influence on the behaviour and actions of the liberation army, SPLA. The basic limiting factor is SPLM's lack of resources. It has virtually no funds at its disposal for organisational development and the training in democracy of its leaders.

SRRA - The Sudanese humanitarian assistance organisation

SRRA is the humanitarian assistance wing of SPLM and as such the most important of NPA's partners in South Sudan. However, SPLM's lack of resources has made the SRRA an extremely weak organisation. Unfortunately some of the reason for this in the past can probably be ascribed to SPLM's lack of political will to give priority to the development of SRRA. Moreover, many of the few South Sudanese who have received education have as a result of the war fled the region and moved to other countries in Africa, Europe, Canada and the USA. For these reasons, SRRA is, as the humanitarian arm of SPLM, a much weaker organisation than comparable organisational structures involved in the liberation wars in Eritrea and Ethiopia. It is therefore a very important political and development objective for NPA to contribute towards an improvement in this situation. It must be a primary objective to provide financial support for the fostering of the organisational development and the strengthening of SRRA. At the same time, political awareness of the importance of such reinforcement must be taken up with SPLM's leadership. A democratic, strong, reliable and functional SRRA, both administratively and in the field, would in itself constitute an important contribution to the development of civil society and democracy in South Sudan. At the same time, we welcome the cooperation with other local Sudanese voluntary organisations on issues like health, women's situation, human rights and democracy. A multitude of local, voluntary organisations in Sudan working for the improvement of everyday life, is of great value in the development of a democratic society.

NPA as a humanitarian and political actor in the sphere of international development and solidarity

The development assistance efforts in which NPA participates on four continents and 34 countries are predominantly humanitarian. In disaster and conflict situations it is a principle objective to assist the victims, the sick and wounded, the homeless, refugees and prisoners of war. However, this activity also has important political dimensions for NPA. As the humanitarian relief organisation of the labour movement in Norway, we are rooted in the ideals and values characterising Norwegian and international social democracy. This is basically expressed in the political concepts of «unity, solidarity, human dignity, peace and freedom». The leadership of the trade unions and the labour movement that founded the NPA during the 1930s, constantly emphasise these aspects. This tradition has been reinforced through the current General Assembly adoption of the political programme for the period 1999 - 2003 and the political strategy document governing NPA's international solidarity work, «Solidarity Across Borders» (adopted by the Central Board in 1993). NPA therefore takes a stand in political conflicts based on its charter and political programme. Circumstances and historical contexts may vary, as illustrated by our efforts on the side of democratic forces in the Spanish civil war from 1936-39, our support for the ANC and the liberation struggle in Southern Africa, and our involvement at the time with the liberation movements in Central America, Eritrea and Ethiopia. NPA's fundamental stance remains unaltered. It is to struggle against those who are guilty of violations of human dignity and in opposing oppressors depriving people of freedom and solidarity. It also gives continuous support to those who are oppressed and victimised by terror and assists them in their struggle for human rights and the achievement of dignity and freedom.

We have continuously condemned the military dictatorial, fundamentalist and extremist regime in Khartoum for the brutal and unilateral oppression it inflicts and which severely impacts on all the peoples of Sudan, in particular the poorest and weakest. We have continuously criticised and condemned the Khartoum regime for the extremely brutal and ruthless war for which it is principally responsible. We continue to criticise the regime for its severe and systematic violations of international humanitarian law, for its conduct of war with repeated bombing raids on civilian and humanitarian projects such as hospitals in the liberated areas. In 1998 and 1999, more than 50 people were killed and over 100 wounded, all of them civilians, in our project areas with hospitals as key targets.

However, we have at the same time wished for contact, dialogue and cooperation with all the political groups -also in the North - in support of peace and democracy for all of Sudan. Should a cease-fire and a peace agreement become reality, we are also prepared to start development activities in the North. We have continuously criticised the fundamentalist nature of the Khartoum regime as we believe religious fundamentalism and fanaticism are injurious and dangerous to both the individual and society as a whole. We desire freedom of religion and religious diversity for all societies, fundamentalism and extremism being its very opposite. NPA is a secular organisation and therefore has a neutral attitude towards the various religions. We have therefore supported liberation movements and democracy also in Muslim societies such as Palestine, Kurdistan in Northern Iraq, Bosnia and Kosovo. We still have substantial programme activities in these three areas and co-operate with several Muslim organisations which reject fundamentalism and extremism as guidelines for political and development work in the society.

We have therefore since 1986/87 taken a stand on the Sudan conflict both through specific activities, and political statements. We have taken sides for the oppressed and the persecuted, first and foremost the peoples of South Sudan, but also for all the peoples in the North who suffer as a result of war and dictatorship, and we have taken a stand against the oppressors in Khartoum currently represented by a most brutal military dictatorship. Our main partner is SRRA, SPLM's humanitarian assistance organisation. We also maintain continuous contact and open dialogue with the leadership of both SPLM and SPLA, based on trust and mutual confidence which is essential to our practical field work in the liberated areas. It is indispensable also for the role of NPA in contributing to the fostering of conditions for lasting peace and the establishment of a democratic and diversified development of civil society, not only in South Sudan but throughout the whole of the Sudan. This is also a precondition for the creation of a state-wide constitutional structure which respects and enhances human rights and democracy.

NPA in Sudan

NPA commenced its assistance programme to South Sudan as a result of the strong influence of our first Resident Representative in Nairobi, Egil Hagen. During the period 1986-91, assistance channelled to the area was limited, with an average annual budget of approximately NOK1 10 million. It consisted mostly of the supply of medicines and food. In 1992 Helge Rohn took over the management in Nairobi of the NPA Sudan programme, the programme increasing to an annual amount of NOK 20 million. During 1993 the programme was increased further to NOK

---

[1] Exchange rate per 21.09.99 1 USD = NOK 7,87

30 million, and in each of the years 1994 and 1995 it totalled NOK 80 million. During 1996 the budget almost reached NOK 70 million and in 1997 it was approximately NOK 55 million. The 1998 programme, including food and medical assistance, increased substantially and amounted to approximately NOK 100 million. The 1999 programme has a similar size. By the end of 1999, NPA will have channelled assistance to South Sudan amounting to approximately NOK 600 million, and provided the means of survival and development for several millions of people. By way of comparison, total Norwegian assistance to both North and South Sudan over a slightly longer period totalled approximately NOK 1000 million. NPA's large budget figures reflect the circumstance that since 1993/94 we have been a very important conduit for assistance by the USA to the liberated areas of South Sudan, in addition to support received from Norway, Netherlands, Germany, Sweden and EU.

During the most recent couple of years, 850-900 people have been employed in our field operation, our logistics bases in northern Uganda and Kenya, and at our main office in Nairobi. Most of these are South Sudanese and others from East African countries. The international, non-African staff constitutes less than 2 % of the total number of employees.

Since 1994 we have transported an estimated 60.000 tons of food to South Sudan and in 1999 we expect to transport approximately 10.000 tons of food which translates into 20 million daily rations of food. Through our medical programme which encompasses 4 hospitals we intend to provide medical treatment for up to 100.000 people. This represents nearly 80% of the total health services in the liberated areas, which include the only referral hospitals for the treatment of diseases in all of South Sudan. We have transported roughly 60% of all the seeds and 80% of all tools supplied to the liberated areas. In cooperation with British NGOs, we have through the years distributed substantial quantities of food and medicines to the people of the Nuba Mountain region. To the primary disaster area in Bahr el Gazaal, NPA in

1998 brought in substantial amounts of seeds, tools and considerable quantities of medicines and relief food rich in proteins and vitamins. These figures indicate that NPA is the largest assistance organisation in the liberated areas, and that in other periods than the current disaster period, we play the dominant role as SRRA's partner. It must be emphasised that since 1989, NPA has purposely insisted on retaining its independence from OLS in order to ensure adequate political and practical freedom of movement for our work in the field. Experience since 1989 shows this to have been the correct approach. In the coming years we shall continue with a high level of assistance for humanitarian projects and long-term sustainable development in all the mentioned areas. In 1998 and 1999 we have emphasized the importance of visits from Norway and other countries into the field. We have also increased our international lobby work in support of the peoples of South Sudan, and all the peoples of Sudan who suffer from war and the tyranny of the dictators. These activities will be continued.

The National Board emphasises the following:

1. The National Board acknowledges the presentation contained in this document of the history, analysis of, and briefing concerning, the current situation in Sudan.

2. The National Board confirms that NPA will continue to stand by the peoples of South Sudan in their just struggle against terror and oppression and on behalf of human dignity and freedom. At the same time we lend political support to the similar struggle for human dignity and freedom in the rest of Sudan.

3. The National Board confirms that SRRA will continue to be our principal partner in providing humanitarian assistance and funding development programmes in South Sudan.

SRRA will therefore be an especially important instrument for NPA in the development of civil society in South Sudan.

4. The National Board further confirms that the contact between NPA and the leadership of SPLM and dialogue based on trust will continue. However, the National Board wishes in this regard to emphasise that future contact and dialogue will in particular promote the following objectives:

- NPA will cooperate with SRRA and SPLM in order to create increased respect and understanding for human rights and democracy both within the organisation SPLM and in daily life in the villages of South Sudan.

- The development of a civilian administration and other activities such as civil institutions for law and order enforcement at the village and regional levels in South Sudan.

- Support for measures which improve the situation and development potential of women and children. The situation of orphans, women and men who have been caught and forced into slavery shall have special attention.

- In general, special support for measures promoting democracy and thereby political and cultural diversity and a sustainable development of civil society in South Sudan in a state based on a constitution which at the same time recognises the need for national unity and solidarity.

All these measures are deemed essential to the establishment of a new era of accountable democratic rule for alle the peoples of Sudan, based on mutual trust and cooperation between the various population groups. Moreover, these measures are crucial to conditions conducive to a cease-fire and peace agreement for South Sudan and to lasting peace for all the peoples of the present Sudan.

Concerning the hostilities in Sudan

The National Board states that the fundamentalist extremist military dictatorship in Khartoum is employing steadily more brutal and dangerous weapons of mass destruction in its war against the peoples of South Sudan. The National Board has in this connection received with consternation information about the use of chemical and possibly also biological weapons and that these weapons have been used in recent bombing raids against project areas in South Sudan in which NPA is operating. At the same time in 1998 and 1999 more than 50 innocent people have been killed and over 100 wounded, most of them women and children, as a result of some 20 attacks with fragmentation bombs against other NPA project areas in South Sudan. The National Board maintains that this represents the most serious violations and breach of all international conventions on war, and most strongly condemns these cowardly and inhuman acts. The National Board requests the NPA leadership to do its utmost to alert the Norwegian government, the UN and international opinion against this grotesque form of warfare.

The National Board has moreover registered that the regime in Khartoum is contributing towards the maintenance of an ancient and inhuman tradition in the Sudan where Arabic militia brutally capture in particular girls and young women in the south for sale in the slave markets in the north where women are partly used as work-slaves and partly as concubines and sex slaves while their human dignity is constantly violated in the gravest manner. The National Board condemns also these actions in the strongest terms and requests NPA to cooperate with relevant international partners in putting an end to these unhuman practices.

Regarding peace and freedom

The National Board states that NPA, in cooperation with SPLM and other relevant institutions and organisations, will promote the process of achieving a political solution to the conflict in Sudan. However, a process with a cease-fire and lasting and just peace as objectives presupposes several preconditions. Among the most important are:

1. All the peoples of Sudan must be guaranteed the right to live in a future civil and democratic society which respects human rights.

2. The peoples of South Sudan must have the right to decide for themselves through free elections the form to be taken by their future state which may be either a federal solution with equality between North and South, a confederation with a large degree of autonomy and freedom for South Sudan, or an independent secular and democratic state for South Sudan.

3. IGAD, chaired by Kenya, is the forum for peace negotiations. However, IGAD must be strengthened in several ways and as a negotiating forum, it will constantly need both financial, political and professional support for its work. It is a matter of concern that the Organisation of African Unity (OAU) has thus far rejected an open, self-critical debate on the conflict in Sudan, its causes and OAU's possible role in conflict-resolution. OAU's leadership must assume responsibility for initiating such a debate in the various fora within the Organisation as such a debate is a precondition for a constructive role for OAU in the resolution of this conflict and in securing the conditions for lasting peace. The legitimate interests of Egypt may be taken care of both within the context of OAU and by cooperating with IGAD's partners. These partners, among them Norway, should seek to establish a conduit for their influence on and assistance to the peace negotiations that strengthen OAU's and IGAD's responsibility for the establishment of a cease-fire and a peace

agreement ensuring the political conditions for a just and lasting peace for all the peoples of the Sudan.

4. A cease-fire and a peace agreement must be guaranteed by the world community through the protracted presence of peacekeeping forces of the United Nations.

5. The world community must place considerable development resources at the disposal for the new and democratic societies in Sudan.

6. With the political conditions and perspectives underlined by the National Board in the above paragraphs regarding the conflict in Sudan, Norwegian People's Aid supports the efforts at present being undertaken with the active involvement of Norway and other concerned states to establish the condition for a cease-fire, a peace agreement and thereby lasting and just peace for the peoples of Sudan.

NPA General Assembly 19 - 22 August 1999

The 15th General Assembly of Norwegian People's Aid that took place in Oslo 19 – 22 August 1999, also discussed the situation in Sudan and made the following statement:

1. The delegates to the General Assembly, having listened to the appeal for support to the liberation struggle in Sudan stated by the leader of the SPLM, Dr. John Garang, when he addressed the General Assembly on 19 August 1999

2. The delegates, having listened to the statement made by the Executive Director of the U.S. Committee for Refugees, Mr. Roger Winter, on the situation in Sudan and the political and humanitarian catastrophy imposed on the peoples by the continuing war

3. The delegates, in addition, taking note of the contents of the policy document on the conflict in Sudan adopted by the National Board in its meeting 19 August 1999, and endorsing the contents of that statement

further underlined the following points:

– the General Assembly in the strongest possible terms condemns the fact that the regime in Khartoum systematically bombs civilian, humanitarian targets like hospitals and schools and most likely is using chemical weapons in the war.

– the Assembly requests the leadership of Norwegian People's Aid and the Norwegian Government to take adequate action in order to secure laboratory testing of samples from the fields hit by chemical bombs.

– the Assembly further requests Norwegian People's Aid and the Norwegian Government to give priority to humanitarian and development assistance for Sudan. Educational programs for children and youth and polytechnic training programs for adults who will have the responsability for the development of a civilian and democratic administration in the liberated areas are of particular importance.

– the Assembly recommends for Norwegian People's Aid to assist in the establishment of such training centers in the neighbouring countries of Sudan as well as in the liberated areas of Southern Sudan. In this context one should study the experience of NPA with regards to its support to ANC and the liberation struggle in South Africa as well as the experience gained with the Namibia Institute in Zambia that during the liberation struggle provided education to thousands of Namibians for the same purpose while waiting to return home to a free Namibia.

- the Assembly, in particular, requests for action to be taken to stop the slave trade with children and young women from South Sudan. Both in view of this and in general terms, there is a great need for increased support to projects that can improve the living situation for women.

- the Assembly gives its approval to the idea that Norwegian People's Aid, in cooperation with other members of the Norwegian and International Labour Movement, can participate in the development of SPLM (Sudan Peoples' Liberation Movement) as a democratic, progressive and secular organisation.

Mr. Roger Winter
Mr. Eric Reeves
Mr. John Prendergast
Mr. Ted Dagne

Washington, D.C.
USA

July 2013

His Excellency Salva Kiir Mayardit,
President of the Republic of South Sudan
Office of the President
Juba, South Sudan

Dear President Kiir:

We write to you, individually and collectively, as friends of South Sudan—longstanding friends who have committed more than two decades of our lives to the great cause of a just peace for the people of South Sudan. We have lobbied government officials, student organizations, media and nongovernmental groups to build a strong constituency for South Sudan in the United States. We have done our best to highlight the suffering of the people of South Sudan during the long civil war, and to offer our perspectives on the difficult road to completing a true peace.

Some of us have communicated our concerns with you individually and confidentially in the past, always as friends. At this moment, our friendship dictates that we express our concerns about the increasingly perilous fate of South Sudan. From our various vantages, we have all come to conclude that without significant changes and reform, your country may slide toward instability, conflict and a protracted governance crisis. As friends, it is our responsibility to express our serious concerns directly and to offer constructive suggestions for the way forward.

We must first state that over the past several years—but the last six months in particular—South Sudan government security forces have engaged in a campaign of violence against civilians simply because they belonged to a different ethnic group or they are viewed as opponents of the current government.

This violence is shocking and has included rape, murder, theft, and destruction of property. We are particularly concerned about the evidence emerging of abuses by government forces in Jonglei. These terrible crimes occur because government forces believe they have the power to act with impunity.

We joined you in your fight against these very abuses by the Khartoum regime for many years. We cannot turn a blind eye when yesterday's victims become today's perpetrators. We were deeply encouraged by the statement by President Kiir on May 17, 2013:

> It is a sad day for South Sudan to see and receive reports about abuses carried out by ill-disciplined elements of our own armed forces. Many of our comrades fought and died to achieve freedom and justice for our people. It is important that we honor that sacrifice.

At the same time, these atrocities are not isolated incidents but among many deliberate measures taken by soldiers on the instruction of senior commanders and government officials. Some may argue that the failure here lies in the chain of command, but the evidence makes clear that these orders are indeed coming from senior commanders. We urge you to take swift and decisive action against not only those who carried out these heinous acts, but those who gave the orders.

And there must be justice. Crimes by government officials often go unpunished. Many attacks against civilians, including the killing of foreign businessmen, a teacher from Kenya, South Sudanese journalists, and many others, have gone unpunished. We have authoritative reports that government security forces have abused those who allow themselves and their cars to be searched. Many people, including government officials, have faced harassment and have been beaten up by security forces. Again, no one has been held accountable. This inevitably creates a climate of impunity.

There are also many South Sudanese and some foreign nationals languishing in prison, a large number of them facing death sentences. Many of these did not receive a fair trial because the justice system is riddled with incompetence. We strongly urge that the government immediately issue a moratorium on all executions until these cases are reviewed and those convicted given a fair and transparent trial. We further urge you to abolish the death penalty in South Sudan, as more and more countries are doing.

None of this will happen unless the Government of the Republic of South Sudan engages in profound reform. After almost nine years of self-rule, the government is still failing to meet the basic needs of its people. Despite claims that vast sums have been expended on investment in infrastructure, there is very little to show in the way of roads, medical services, and education for millions of South Sudanese who greeted the prospect of independence with eagerness and hope.

Those who have benefitted—who have become wealthy by misappropriating government funds—have often sent their families outside South Sudan, their children to private schools abroad, and have obtained the best medical services available in the world. This occurs while ordinary citizens who remain in South Sudan cannot afford even basic health services or modest educations for their children.

Corruption is at the heart of the many problems facing South Sudan. In a remarkably short period of time, the name of your country has become synonymous with corruption. As President Kiir declared in a letter to his ministers and senior officials:

> The people of South Sudan and the international community are alarmed at the level of corruption in South Sudan. Many people in South Sudan are suffering, yet government officials seem to care only about themselves.

And yet to date, not a single government official has been tried on corruption charges. Again, the absence of justice encourages a climate of impunity, and makes halting corruption all the more difficult. This is the light in which we have examined the findings of the World Bank, which after a long investigation presented to the Ministry of Justice—almost a year ago—presents clear evidence of massive corruption. And yet the Ministry of Justice has not yet prosecuted a single individual.

The Office of the President in the past several months has ordered two important investigations and has suspended senior officials, including two Federal Ministers, from office pending the completion of the investigation. Widespread outrage at the extraordinary levels of corruption and at those who are benefitting from that corruption is very high and continues to grow. This is the source of potentially serious civil unrest, just as it was in the Middle East and North Africa over the past few years.

OUR RECOMMENDATIONS

These problems cannot be resolved overnight, but an immediate commitment can be made to re-shape what now seems a dangerous and crisis-filled future for South Sudan.

- The Ministry of Justice must be revamped and key personnel who have enabled corruption and crimes against civilians to go unpunished must be removed.

- All senior army officials should be put on notice that attacks on civilians are completely unacceptable and will be severely punished up the entire chain of command.

- Existing alleged human rights abuses should be fully investigated and prosecuted.

- Clear oil infrastructure priorities should be set, especially now in light of a financial picture that is extremely grim. The fact that there are no refineries in the South, no oil storage facilities, and nothing in the way of progress towards a southern oil export route reflects an absence of planning and has left oil revenues at the mercy of the National Congress Party regime. As evidence from the past two years has made clear, the regime in Khartoum is perfectly willing to engage in duplicitous negotiations, commit to agreements in bad faith, and simply renege on agreements whenever it wishes, even if it punishes its own failing economy. All this could have been predicted from past behavior, and must certainly guide thinking going forward.

- Schools, medical services, clean water, and roads must top the list of priorities of internal spending. Until the people of South Sudan have ready access to education and health services—services that will need a transport infrastructure—they will be exceedingly vulnerable to disease, and will have little chance to contribute to a modern economy. And without a functional agricultural sector, South Sudan will always be dependent on others.

- South Sudan confronts serious external security threats, and will almost certainly do so as long as the current regime controls Sudan. Nevertheless, the army must begin to make plans to be trimmed substantially, made more efficient, and receive training in international human rights law. Security is paramount, but that security will be squandered if the army does not become more responsive to the needs of its people and to its broader obligations to protect the rights of civilians.

The demands here are great, we well understand. But unless you begin to address them now, the tasks will only grow greater. Again, as friends of South Sudan, we urge you to confront these challenges on an urgent basis, and with all possible resolve.

Sincerely,

Roger Winter, Eric Reeves, John Prendergast, and *Ted Dagne*
Friends of South Sudan

CC: The Honorable Riek Machar Teny, Vice President
 The Honorable James Wani Igga, Speaker

BIBLIOGRAPHY
Books and other sources used while writing the book

1. SOUTH SUDAN, FROM REVOLUTION TO INDEPENDENCE, av Matthew LeRiche and Matthew Arnold, Hurst & Company, London 20123.
2. How Humanitarianism Affected the Conduct and Outcome of War in South Sudan, submitted in Completion of PhD War Studies, Department of War Studies, King's College, University of London, Submitted by Matthew LeRiche. 2008
3. Waging Peace in Sudan. The Inside Story of the Negotiations That Ended Africa's Longest Civil War. Hilde Frafjord Johnson. Sussex Academic Press/CMI, Bergen 2011
4. South Sudan. The Untold Story. From Independence to Civil War. Hilde Frafjord Johnson. I. B. Tauris 2016,
5. DEN VANSKELIGE FREDEN. Når fred ender i ny krig. Hilde Frafjord Johnson, Cappelen Damm 2016
6. Nilen, historiens elv av Terje Tvedt, Aschehoug 2013
7. SUDAN, Ancient Kingdoms of the Nile, Editorial Direction by Dietrich Wildung, Flammarion, Paris – New York 1997,
8. De fattiges leiesoldat. Hjelpearbeideren Egil Hagen. Arild Aspøy, Cappelen, Oslo 1992
9. The Southern Sudan Struggle for Liberty. Elijah Malok, Kenway Publications 2009
10. SUDAN RACE RELIGION AND VIOLENCE. Jok Madut Jok, ONEWORLD Publications, Oxford 2008
11. John Garang Speaks. Edited and introduced by Mansour Khalid, KPI Limited, London 1987
12. James Bandi Shimanyula. John Garang and the SPLA. African History Makers Series, Nairobi 2005,
13. The Root Causes of Sudan's Civil Wars. Douglas H. Johnsen, The International Africa Institute in Association with James Curry, Oxford 2003

14. The Mediator, General Lazaro Sumbeiywo and the Southern Sudan Peace Process av Waithaka Waihenya, Kenway Publications, Nairobi 2006
15. SUDAN DIVIDED. Continuing Conflict in a Contested State. Edited by Gunnar M. Sørbø & Abdel Ghaffar M. Ahmed. Palgrave MacMillan. 2013
16. SUDAN. Race, Religion and Violence. Jok Madut Jok. ONEWORLD, Oxford. 2007
17. I have an electronic copy of   The Black Book, a book made around 2002/3 in secrecy by a group of intellectuals in opposition to the current regime in Khartoum. The book is a documented and harsh criticism of the corruption, the inequality and the abuse of power by the holders of power in Khartoum
18. Short History of Sudan, av Dr. LL.M Mohamed H. Fadlalla, iUniverse, New York 2004
19. Peter Adwok Nyaba: The Politics of Liberation in South Sudan. An Insider's View (1997)
20. Peter Adwok Nyaba: South Sudan. The State We Aspire To. The Centre for Advanced Studies of African Society, Cape Town, Sør Afrika, trykket I 2011, men holdt tilbake av politiske grunner til 2013.
21. Peter Adwok Nyaba: South Sudan, The Crisis of Infancy. The Centre of Advanced Studies of African Society, Cape Town, Sør Afrika 2014.
22. Guerilla Government. Political Changes in Southern Sudan during the 1990ies. Øystein Rolandsen. Nordiska Afrikainstitutet 2005
23. A HISTORY OF SOUTH SUDAN. From Slavery to Independence. Øystein Rolandsen and M. W. Daly. Cambridge University Press. 2016.
24. Bibiana Piene. Norge I Sudan. På bunnen av Sola. Aschehoug 2014
25. Yossef Bodansky. BIN LADEN The Man who Declared War on America. Prima Publishing, Roseville, California, 1999/2001

26. Bengt G. Nilsson: Sveriges afrikanska krig, Timbro 2008,
27. Bengt G. Nilsson, OLJANS PRIS, ETHNO PRESS FØRLAG
28. What's left of the Left? The View from Sudan, Special Issue, Editor Rogaia Mustafa Abusharaf, The South Atlantic Quarterly, Duke University Press 2009,
29. Tomm Kristiansen: Presidentens mann. Oppdrag i Sør Sudan, Cappelen Dam, 2009
30. John Young, The Fate of Sudan, The Origins and Consequences of a flawed Peace Process, Zed Books, London 2012,
31. Phillip Caputo, Acts of Faith, Vintage Books, New York 2006,
31. Dave Eggers. What is The What, Penguin Books, London 2006,
32. Stein Erik Horjen, Lang vei til fred, Verbum, 2009,
33. Deborah Scroggins Emma's War, Harper Perennial, London 2003,
34. Abdel Salam Sidahmed, Politics and Islam in Contemporary Sudan, Curzon Press, 1997,
35. Abel Alier, Southern Sudan, Too Many Agreements Dishonoured, Ithac Press, UK, 1990,
36. Jay Spaulding & Stephanie Beswick editors, White Nile, Black Blood, War, Leadership and Ethnicity from Khartoum to Kampala, Red Sea Press INC, Asmara 2000,
37. Anthony Sylvester, Sudan under Nimeiri, The Boadley Head, London 1977,
38. Hassan Dafalla, The Nubian Exodus, C. Hurst & Company in Association with Scandinavian Institute of African Studies, Uppsala, 1975,
39. Jacob J. Akol, Burden of Nationality, Memoirs of an African Aidworker/Journalist 1970ies-1990ies, Paulines Publications Africa, Nairobi 2006,
40. Jacob J. Akol, I WILL GO THE DISTANCE (Aka Long Way to Tipperary) with foreword by Francis Mading Deng, Paulines, Nairobi 2005,

41. Gabriel Achoth Deng, WARS and a new vision for SUDAN. A Political Lesson. The book was published by the writer himself around 2005/6,
42. Mohamed Omer Beshir, The Southern Sudan. From Conflict to Peace. The Khartoum Bookshop 1975,
43. Edvard Nordrum, Biskop Paride Taban, Fredskjempe I krig, Andresen & Butenschøn Forlag I samarbeid med Kirkens Nødhjelp, Oslo 2002,
44. Chris Alden, China in Africa, African Arguments, Zed Books, London 2007,
45. Raymond w. Copson. The United States in Africa. African Arguments, Zed Books, London 2007,
46. Tom Porteous. Britain in Africa. African Arguments, Zed Books, London 2008,
47. Deborah Brautigam. THE DRAGONS GIFT. The real Story of China in Africa, Oxford University Press 2011,
48. Gabriel Warburg, ISLAM, SECTERIANISM AND POLITICS IN SUDAN SINCE THE MAHDIYYA, Hurst & Company, London 2003,
49. The Sudan Handbook, edited by John Ryle, Justin Willis, Suliman Baldo, Jok Madut Jok. The Rift Valley Institute and James Curry, London 2011,
50. Bjørn Abelsen, a logbook with the lists for all flights to the Nuba Mountains between 1993 and 1997
51. Anders Breidlid, Avelino Androga og Astrid Kristine Breidlid, A Concise History of South Sudan, Fountain Publishers, Kampala, second edition 2014,
52. The Voice of the Voiceless. The Role of the Church in the Sudanese Civil War 1983 – 2005. John Ashworth. Paulines 2014.
53. My own notes from missions and meetings in Nairobi and in South Sudan, particularly for the period 2001 -2013.
54. The archives of the Norwegian Labour Movement and NPA. Fra Arbeiderbevegelsens/Norsk Folkehjelps arkiv.

55. Report from a mission on behalf of NPA into Southern Sudan in April/May 1987. We were a group composed of Mr. Erik Eriksen, social anthropologist at the University of Bergen, Phillip Parry, engineer and part of the NPA staff, Jane MacAskill, nutrition expert from Great Britain and myself as head of mission.
56. My own report from October 2013 on the internal Conflict within SPLM and its implications.
57. Notes from meetings with South Sudanese refugees in Nairobi 13th- 16th January 2014,
58. Meetings, interviews, mails, letters, skype meetings and more with former staff of NPA, SRRA, SPLM/A and many other resource people in Kenya, Sudan, South Sudan and other countries in the Horn of Africa.

I list below those who have had particularly important positions in the NPA Sudan Programme:

Resident Representatives of NPA: Egil Hagen 1986-1991, Egil Wisløff Nilsen 1991, Helge Rohn 1992-1996, Lars Johan Johnsen 1997-1999, Sten Rino Bonsaksen 1999-2003, Elias Mitslale Girma 2006-2009, Jan Ledang 2009-2012 og 2013, Henrik Stabell 2014,

Other NPA staff who have worked in the programme either in Nairobi or in the field; Marit Hernæs, Ling Merete Kituyi, Halima Mutonga Schwarz, Linda Thu, Nina Pedersen, Charles Aloo, Chaat Paul, Dan Eiffe, Ken Miller, Aage Vatnedalen, Audun Herning, Eskild Johansen, Jacob Atem, Jamus Joseph, Diress Mengistu and Jacob Atem.

Former and present staff at the NPA HQ in Oslo who have had or still may have a responsibility for the NPA Sudan Programme: Arne Ørum, Vegard Bye, Svein Olsen, Claudio Fee, Øystein Rolandsen, Øystein Botillen, Mads Almaas, Trude Falck, Liv Bremer, Ivar Christiansen, Magnus Flacké.

Former and present staff in the Ministry of Foreign of Foreign Affairs: Endre Stiansen, Kjell Hødnebø, Tom Vraalsen,

Kjell Harald Dalen, Hans Jacob Frydenlund, Jens-Petter Kjemprud, Hanne Marie Kaarstad, Tone Tinnes, Erling Skjønsberg.

Former Norwegian ministers, state secretaries and members of Parliament with an interest in Sudan and South Sudan: Thorvald Stoltenberg, Hilde Frafjord Johnson, Erik Solheim, Kjell Magne Bondevik, Raymond Johansen, Kjell Engebretsen, Anniken Huitfeldt, Sverre Myrli,

Other international and Norwegian communication partners: Roger Winter, Eric Reeves, Jan P. Eriksen, Tore Torstad, Odd Evjen, Stig Holmqvist, John Gachie, Peter Natana, Stephen Tut, David Kwol Deng, Marina Peter.

SPLM/Juba faction/2013-2015: Salva Kiir, James Wani Igga, Ann Itto, Rebecca Okwachi, John Duku,

SPLM leaders, former Detainees 2013: Pa'gan Amum Okiech, Peter Adwok Nyaba, Kosti Manibe.

SPLM-N: Yasir Arman

59. International media. I have while writing both the Norwegian and English edition of the book almost daily followed events in Sudan, South Sudan and the Horn of Africa, extensively used many different International media outlets and I mention: Sudan Trubune, Radio Tumazaj og Daily Nation, Nairobi, BBC/Africa, Al Jazeera/Africa, the Guardien, The New York Times, The Washington Post, International Crisis Group, Human Rights Watch, Amnesty International.

60. I have had access to and read all reports from UN on developments in South Sudan since 2013 until present. I have read the AU Commission Report with the former President of Nigeria Olusegun Obasanjo as head of Mission on South Sudan after 2013, the reports from Human Watch International, some from IMF and the World Bank and many others.

About the Author

I was born in 1937 in a little, local community about 20 km away from the coastal town of Brønnøysund which is situated about 900 km to the North of my present home on the outskirts of the Norwegian capital Oslo.

I and my five siblings grew up among farmers and fishermen, my father, a farmer's and farmer women's son, my mother, a fisherman's and fisherwomen's daughter. It was a good life, but also a life marked by material scarcity and sometimes poverty. I had at a very early age in life to learn basic skills like tilling the soil, milking a cow, slaughtering a sheep, rowing the boat and putting baits on the fishing lines so that I could catch fish.

I am old enough to remember the Second World War and everyday life in my community in a country under occupation and oppression with both my father and mother in the Resistence. We, the children, did not understand how close we sometimes were to lose them.

I was the third ever youngster from my community who was given the opportunity to go to secondary school and later to study at the University of Oslo.

I am one of some hundred thousand Norwegians still alive who have experienced Norway develop in peace from once being a very poor country on the outskirts of Northern Europe to be the most affluent society with least inequality in the Continent. It is an experience worth studying.

Marit and I married in 1964. We are still together, and we have two great daughters with families.

Working Experience:

While I was young I had to do all kinds of work to make ends meet while I got my education.

When I graduated with a Master in Political Science and International Politics from the College of Europe in Belgium in the summer of 1966, I was fortunate and immediately got a

job as a researcher with the Norwegian Institute of International Affairs.

Three years later, I got employed as a reporter on International affairs with Norwegian Broadcasting Corporation (NRK), and I had the fortune of holding the position as NRK's first Africa Correspondent, residing in Nairobi, from 1978 to 1982.

Then I was the Communication Director of NORAD and the Ministry of Development Cooperation for 10 years before I in the spring of 1992 joined NPA as International Director and later Secretary General.

All this led to an ever-increasing involvement with African society and African politics. I have since 1972 spent some nine years in the continent on working missions to some 40 countries. In this African experience, Sudan and South Sudan have taken a lot of my interest.

I am a political man and have been an active member of the Norwegian Labour Party for more than 40 years.

I am now retired, but keep it still going, writing, lecturing and doing some physical work.

THE TIME OF THE PIONEERS

During the first years, NPA in cooperation with SRRA carried out a lot of heavy construction work, roads, bridges and airstrips had to be built.

Small planes were indispensable means of transport in a country without roads. The people in the picture are refugees being picked up.

◂ Aage Vatnedalen was one of the pioneers. The picture shows him with a killed black Mamba snake, very dangerous and frequently found in our areas of work.

LIVES AT STAKE   I

CHALLENGES RELATED TO TRANSPORT AND COMMUNICATION

South Sudan at the time (and like now) was almost without roads. During the rainy season, it could take weeks to drive a stretch of 100 km.

The roads from Mombasa were from time to time in a very poor state, and the trucks transporting cereals and other food from Mombasa through Kenya and Uganda, had frequent break downs.

This river barge was constructed by the Norwegian Red Cross in Norway around 1990, flown to Nairobi and transported on trucks to the shores of the Nile. It was still in 2013 in operation on the Nile.

Whenever it rained, the airstrips were turned into seas of mud. This plane managed to land, but could not take off again for days until the airstrip had dried up.

CATTLE AND AGRICULTURE

Cattle is the most important property to many ethnic groups in South Sudan, the two largest being the Dinka and the Nuer.

The oxen are held in very high esteem by the cattle people in South Sudan. According to the tradition, it was a degrading act to use the oxen to pull the plough.

This is a modernised version of the traditional Maresha plough from Ethiopia. It has to be pulled by oxen. NPA introduced the plough to South Sudan and saw a doubling of food production taking place in areas where it was being used.

Training of educators in agriculture was a very important part of the activities at NPA's polytechnic educational centres. The picture shows a field with vegetables at one of the centres.

HEALTH

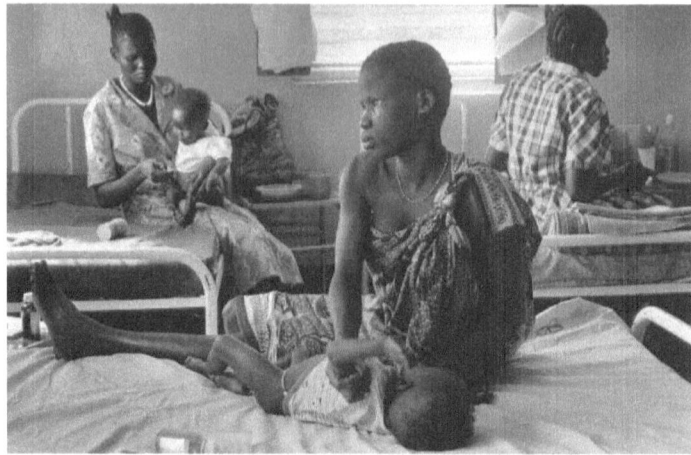

The need for basic health services was endless. The picture, taken by Sebastiao Salgado, is from one of the first NPA hospitals that was put into operation in the early 1990ies. (Photo: Sebastiao Salgado)

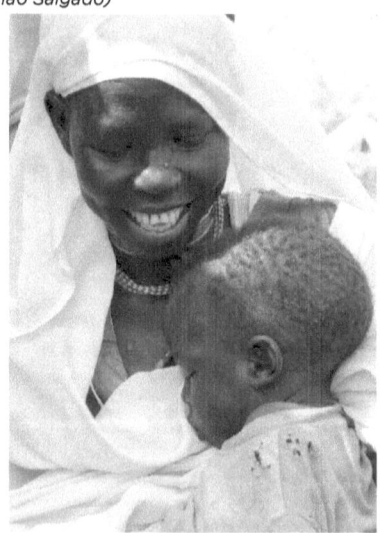

A mother's joy, as her child recovered and survived.

POLYTECHNIC TRAINING

Brick laying and the construction of houses were part of the training which also women benefitted from.

And men learnt tailoring and the production of clothing.

MOBILISATION OF WOMEN

The "Women Can" courses were very popular. Participants at one course convey their joy.

Approximately, some 150 000 women participated at different levels in "Women Can" courses.

FREEDOM DAY, 9TH OF JULY 2011

The woman is in jubilation over her freedom as she is cursing the President of Sudan, Omar Bashir, while he is addressing the celebrating crowd.

This fighter has paid a heavy price for his freedom, but his joy at finally being free in his own country is without limit as he greets the guests of honour.

JOY OF FREEDOM

In the months succeeding the CPA in Nairobi on 9th January 2011, the Liberator, John Garang, travelled tirelessly in all parts of South Sudan and the Nuba Mountains to share with his people that the liberation war had come to an end and that their future would be one of peace and development. His wife, Rebecca is seated to his left.

The joy of peace, freedom and clean water.

WHAT KIND OF FUTURE?

A day in 1993. She has together with her little child fled from war and horror and arrived in the Kakuma Refugee Camp in Turkana, Kenya. But what then? Picture by Sebastiao Salgado.

A young girl with her little brother, hoping for peace and education.

IMPORTANT PERSONALITIES

A day in the field in 1993. John Garang, a strong leader, a farsighted strategist and a visionary. Picture by Sebastiao Salgado.

Marit Hernæs from NPA in discussion with one member of the SPLM Secretariat about the "Women Can" courses.

Roger Winter, the Director of the American Refugee Committee, was a very important partner for NPA. The picture shows him visiting the Nuba Mountains together with a NPA mission.

Some key leaders with NPA during the time of the liberation struggle, from left Elias Mitslale Girma from Ethiopia and Kaneri Gribani from South Sudan, both medical doctors, Ken Miller from Great Britain, logistics and food supply, Margareth Lugor from South Sudan who in 2006 established NPA's first office in Juba.

In 1998, the Tax Authority of Kenya in a surprise move demanded 30 million NOK in back payment for taxes said, not paid. NPA disputed the demand as not justified and won at the end in court. In the process, we had to seek a meeting with President Daniel arap Moi of Kenya who gave the NPA delegation a very friendly reception. In the picture, President, Daniel arap Moi, his advisor Charles Njonjo and other aids. Then, the NPA delegation, from the right, Lars Johan Johnsen, Halle Jørn Hanssen, Vidar Anzjøen and Jens Kristian Thune.

THE SUDD OF THE NILE

The Nile passes through a large area of South Sudan where the river only falls one meter during a length of 25 km. The area has been named the Sudd. During the rainy seasons, the river floods and may flow some hundred km into the hinterland on both sides.

As early as when the British were the colonial masters of Sudan, the first plans were launched to drain the Sudd. In 1978 the regime in Khartoum decided to start the digging of a 360-km long channel. A German company constructed the monster excavator named Sarah. When SPLA destroyed the machine in 1983, it had completed 240 km. of the planned channel.

The rivers and lakes of South Sudan are still rich in fish, and young boys have their ways of catching it.

OIL INDUSTRIES AND POLLUTION

The pollution from the oil industries of South Sudan is on a very large scale, poisonous and a threat to the health of human beings as well as the soil, cattle and other animals. The picture above shows unprotected barrels with poisonous chemicals. The picture below shows a reporter while there still was some degree of freedom of expression, reporting on how vast and dangerous the pollution is.

THE HORROR OF WAR AND ETHNIC HATRED

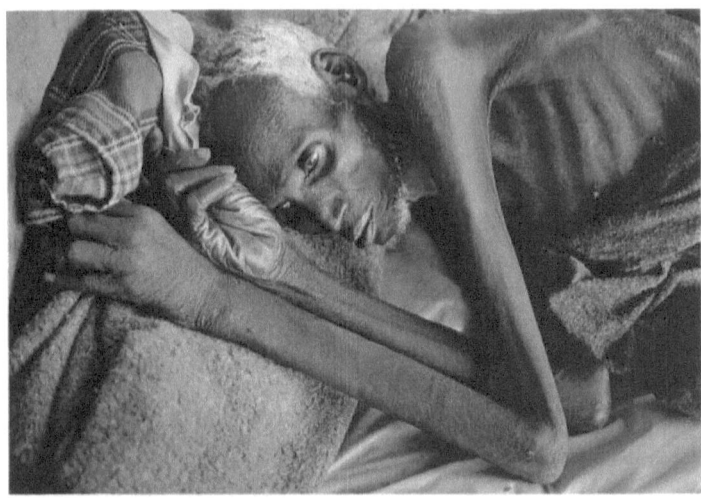

An old man hit by the effects of war, starvation and illness under treatment at a NPA hospital in 1993. Picture by Sebastiao Salgado.

This picture is from the massacres of the nuers in Juba just before Christmas in 2013. The crime was committed by special units from SPLA.

Africa World Books
ISBN 978-0-6482422-2-2
Copyright 2017 Halle Jørn Hanssen

All rights reserved except for brief quotations in reviews and similar.
Every attempt has been made to gain permission for the use of
images in this book. Any omissions will be rectified in future editions.
References to websites were correct at the time of writing.

Design: Amund Nitter Layout: Ellen Renberg

www.ingramcontent.com/pod-product-compliance
Lightning Source LLC
Chambersburg PA
CBHW032020290426
44110CB00012B/614